TO EVERY PEOPLE FROM EVERY PEOPLE

Dr. Larry D. Pate

ISBN 978-1-63814-946-0 (Paperback)
ISBN 978-1-63814-947-7 (Hardcover)
ISBN 978-1-63814-948-4 (Digital)

First Edition

Covenant Books
11661 Hwy 707
Murrells Inlet, SC 29576
www.covenantbooks.com

"*To Every People from Every People* is a shining example of the phrase "greater than the sum of its parts." It is not simply a book to read and enjoy—it serves as a tool and manual for Christians worldwide to carry Christianity out to the places where it is needed most. This is no small feat considering the complexities of the various cultures and ways of life around the globe, but Dr. Larry D. Pate tackles this problem with stride and real-world experience. He points out that just reaching people is not enough. You must be able to transmit the Gospel well so that the message is received loud and clear, free of being muddied by the crossing of language barriers and cultures. Anyone who wishes to successfully plant the seeds of Christianity so that it can grow and prosper in any environment will be well-equipped with *To Every People from Every People!*"

Denice Hunter
President
Covenant Books, Inc.

CONTENTS

PREFACE AND INTRODUCTION

October 2020

We are living in a new age of worldwide Christianity. As of the middle of 2020, there are 2.53 billion Christians in the world. Approximately 1.186 billion people are evangelical Christians. They are growing faster than the world population. Evangelical Christianity around the world has grown 981 percent since the year 1900.[1] During the last 200 years, evangelical Christianity has grown from being a relatively small movement of approximately 118 million believers to the fastest-growing segment of Christianity. This does not include the growing population of Roman Catholics (especially Charismatics) who consider themselves evangelical believers. Today, the majority of the population of Africa consider themselves Christians. By any measure, evangelical Christianity has shown itself to be the fastest-growing segment of the world's population. If you are one of these people, this book is written for you.

This book clearly demonstrates the what, why, and how the Church of Jesus Christ can fulfill its biblical mandate to win the lost around the world to Christ. It is designed to be inspirational, instructional, and practical. It is more than adequate to serve as a textbook in Christian universities while remaining a practical manual for everyday Christians to fulfill the Great Commission in this generation.

---

1 https://www.gordonconwell.edu/wp-content/uploads/sites/13/2019/04/StatusofGlobalChristianity20191.pdf.

The first chapter lays a biblical foundation for the necessity of doing evangelism across cultural boundaries. The focus is on unreached peoples as a priority of the Church's cross-cultural ministry mandate. Chapter two clearly outlines the scope and task that remains in order to fulfill that mandate before Jesus returns (Matt. 24:14). Chapters three, four, and six present a framework of principles and insights useful for effective cross-cultural evangelism anywhere in the world. Chapter five introduces a system for learning any foreign language efficiently without incurring significant expense. Chapters seven, eight, and nine provide a practical system for planning and using effective cross-cultural evangelism strategies. The final chapter presents principles, tools, and methods for organizing and multiplying the churches started through cross-cultural evangelism.

This book is written to present a clear, easily understood system to help members of any culture know how to take the Gospel to the unreached peoples of the world. It gives them the tools to do so effectively. Working in another culture requires much greater commitment and understanding than doing evangelism in one's own culture. A rice farmer who wants to grow wheat must learn to use different tools and methods if he wants a fruitful harvest. Likewise, an evangelist who wants to be fruitful in another culture needs to learn how to use the tools and methods of effective cross-cultural evangelism. This book is an attempt to present those tools and methods in a way which will increase the faith, vision, and determination of every believer—especially those who take up their cross and carry the Gospel to another culture.

It should be noted that the traditional terms "missions" and "missionary" are not used in this book. "Cross-cultural evangelism," "cross-cultural ministry," and related terms are used instead. There are two main reasons: (1) "missionary" is a term that is often held in derision within too many countries of the world; (2) governments in many countries restrict people and materials from entering into their country when associated with those terms.

This book was originally written for believers in Latin America. It is available in an earlier form in the Spanish and Portuguese languages. For many years, it has been the best-selling book of its kind in those languages. Unlike most books available in Latin America, it was written specifically for that part of the world. It has helped thousands of Latin American believers carry the precious message of the Gospel to other cultures in Latin America and around the world. This updated and completely rewritten version is designed for an international audience.

It is offered with the sincere desire that English-speaking cultures around the world will elevate their commitment to world evangelism. It is also offered with the hope that it will be translated into other languages as well.[2] It is written with the firm conviction that the Church that Jesus came to build on earth (Matt. 16:18) will not be finished with its work until "every people and language, tribe and nation" (Rev. 5:9) have an adequate chance to know Jesus as their personal Savior. That can only happen when the Gospel is carried **TO EVERY PEOPLE FROM EVERY PEOPLE**! All scripture quotations are taken from the Holy Bible, New International Version, copyright 1978 by New York International Bible Society; published by Zondervan Bible Publishers, Grand Rapids, Michigan.

---

[2] If it is your desire to make this available in another language, please contact the author at www.peoplesmissioninternational.com. This book is under copyright. Do not reproduce it or any part of it, except short quotations, without the permission of the author.

CHAPTER ONE

God Has A Mission

IMPORTANT POINTS IN THIS CHAPTER

1. Cross-cultural ministry has its source in the nature of God.
2. God chose Israel for partnership in His mission to redeem all of mankind.
3. Cross-cultural ministry is central to the nature and purpose of the Church's existence.
4. Full-hearted obedience by man is the key to his participation with God in His mission. It is also the key to God's promises and blessing.
5. God does not look at any culture of people as superior to any other, and He does not want His Church to do so either.

God has a single overriding passion in His present dealings with mankind. The victory of the cross is history. Satan's doom is sealed. But God still has an active mission! He still seeks to find men and bring them to repentance through Christ's finished work (Luke 19:10, 2 Pet. 3:9). Throughout history, God has expected those who serve Him to participate in God's mission to redeem mankind. Noah built the ark, which became God's instrument of renewal and salvation at the flood. As we shall see, God chose Israel to be His witness to the nations. Today, Christ's Church is God's divine agency for participating with God in His mission.

God's love is not confined to any race, nation, or cultural group of people. He loves all peoples. He loves African pygmies as much as He loves Asian businessmen. He wants to redeem Iranian soldiers as much as he wants Argentine farmers to find Christ. God's love crosses all cultural, racial, linguistic, and ideological boundaries. He wants everyone to have an adequate chance to follow Christ. That is what this book is all about—learning how to be effective in crossing boundaries of every kind in order to give everyone on earth a truly adequate opportunity to accept Christ and serve Him effectively in the mainstream of his or her own culture.

The true people of God have always wanted to participate in God's mission. God has always encouraged them to do so. God wants a church made up of people from every "tribe and language and people and nation" (Rev. 5:9).

THE BIBLICAL BASIS OF CROSS-CULTURAL MINISTRY

The character and nature of God is the foundation for learning the importance of cross-cultural ministry. The Bible reveals God's character from Genesis to Revelation. Above all, God is the eternal and sovereign ruler of the universe. There is nothing in time or place which is outside His knowledge and ultimate control (Ps. 10:16, 103:19). Down through the history of mankind, God's sovereignty, foreknowledge and ultimate control have never been diminished. He is the greatest source of good, and His love is constantly demonstrated and impacting human history.

THE LOVE OF GOD IS THE BASIS OF REDEMPTIVE HISTORY

The one characteristic of God's nature upon which mankind is totally dependent is God's love. His grace toward mankind is based on that love. God views all His creation as important, but He has especially selected mankind to be the recipient of his unmerited favor and grace. From the outset, God was faced with a dilemma concerning mankind.

God delegates authority. This is true of the Kingdom of God in heaven as well as on earth. He organized angels as a hierarchy, giving degrees of responsibility and authority. God gave one specific archangel great beauty, wisdom, and power (Ezek. 28:12–17, Jude 9). His name was Lucifer. God gave him a throne and authority to rule as a prime minister of God. Lucifer had great power, beauty, and splendor, all given to him by God. He also had freedom of choice. The true test of that gift is constant allegiance to the will of God. As some point, Lucifer became so dazzled by his own beauty and greatness that he overstepped his position and tried to become "like the Most High" (Isa. 14:14). He led a rebellion in heaven in which one-third of the angels joined him in trying to establish a counterfeit heavenly kingdom (Rev. 12:4–7).

The rebellion earned God's judgment and banishment from heaven for Lucifer, now called Satan (adversary). Though under the condemnation of ultimate defeat, Satan still acts in rebellion against God and His purposes. Originally an angel of light, he presides now over a Kingdom of Darkness. His kingdom is a constant source of evil focused on an effort to lead mankind to join him in rebellion against God.

Sometime after Satan was banished from heaven, God made another creation who was also given freedom of choice: mankind. This freedom to choose is essential for men and women to be created in the image (likeness) of God (Gen. 1:26 [NIV])—to possess traits of personality enabling people to love, be trustworthy, and pursue spiritual holiness. This moral freedom gives mankind the power to please God most by returning His love. Fellowship with God and love toward God requires moral freedom of choice.

The bond of love is much more powerful than the force of might. God established a relationship of communion with Adam and Eve based upon love, not force. He even made them partners in His rule on earth. In order to continue in this relationship with God, they only had to pass the test of complete obedience to the will of God. They were told not to eat of the "Tree of the knowledge of good and evil" (Gen. 2:6). Had they not succumbed to the enticement of Satan, they might have eaten off the "Tree of Life" and been given eternal status as creatures of righteousness. Their disobedience brought the fall of the human race. They failed the test. This disaster identified mankind with Satan's Kingdom of Darkness. Mankind had failed the test of God's trust.

This left God with two problems. By creating moral creatures, God risked their disobedience, which was a direct affront to God's love. First, Lucifer defected, fell into a state of sin and steady moral decline. God's kingdom was divided and partly usurped. The crucial question at the time of mankind's sin was what would God do about it? Would He destroy mankind and the earth in one sweep of His judgment? The answer to those questions we now know due to the Word of God and history. The cause of God's mercy and actions on behalf of mankind lies in the nature of God's character.

Redemptive History Is Written by God's Love

God would have been justified in destroying all or part of the rebels in His creation. He foresaw the possibility of sin and devised a plan to rescue mankind. The plan was to accomplish two objectives: (1) reclaim the usurped portion of God's kingdom and (2) redeem mankind from the penalty of sin. God did not treat His desire to defeat Satan and rescue mankind as two separate problems. Satan had used man in his attempt to overthrow God's Kingdom. God was determined to redeem mankind and give him power to overcome sin. Man would defeat Satan using God's power!

In his fallen, sinful condition, man was powerless to receive God's restoring power. He needed help from beyond himself. God's sovereign solution to this problem was the incarnation of Christ into the world as a human being—one who was fully God, yet divorced Himself from using His divine power to overcome sin. He defeated sin as a human being, suffering death for that purpose (Phil. 2:1–11). That is what allowed God to substitute His death for our sin (Isa. 53:5–6). Even before mankind had fallen into sin, God had foreseen that possibility. In His great love for mankind, God had already determined to make the supreme sacrifice—He would personally pay the penalty for sin through His Son, Jesus Christ (Eph. 1:4, 1 Pet. 1:20).

This act of God's grace in history illustrates the depth and overcoming power of God's love (Rom. 8:38). Though God holds the sovereign power of immediate or ultimate judgment, He has withheld that judgment in order that believing mankind can be redeemed. No greater revelation of God's loving character has ever been seen in human history than when God sent Jesus to redeem those who believe in Him. In this one mighty act of love, God snatched mankind back from Satan's kingdom and authority.

Christ's victory was the very apex of redemptive history. But it was really the climax of a strategy which God had started when man fell into sin. When God announced His judgment upon Satan for his role in man's fall, He said, "I will put enmity between you and the woman, and between your seed and her seed; He shall bruise you on the head, and you shall bruise Him on the heel" (Gen. 3:14–15). This passage is often called the protevangelium. This is the first reference in the Bible to Christ. Christ was man's seed who would crush Satan's head by his sacrifice on the cross. Satan would bruise mankind's heel, constantly enticing him to sin. It is important that Christ is first mentioned in reference to defeating Satan. That is the essence of the evangel—the good news of history.

This prophetic passage outlines God's twofold program in human history. The crushing of Satan's head does refer to Christ's death on the cross by which Satan's power over mankind was defeated. The crushing of the head portrays total defeat. God's primary activity in history has been to prepare man and the world for the coming of Christ. God's ultimate victory over Satan is in covering man with Christ's righteousness to overcome the sin initiated by Satan.

Mankind was not destined to have instant deliverance from his guilt. His heel would be bruised by Satan, repeatedly attacked to induce rebellion against God. Man failed by disobedience. God intended to build the foundation for redemption by teaching mankind the importance of obedience to His will. The history of God's dealings with the people of Israel was a continual challenge to obedience. God called Israel to obey his law. The apostle Paul wrote that the law was a "schoolmaster" to prepare Israel for faith and righteousness through Christ (Gal. 3:24–25 [KJ]). The history of Israel is one of recurring failure in obeying the law of God. Israel was to know firsthand Satan's bruising. Her repeated disobedience caused Israel to fail in her mission for God and brought God's judgment repeatedly upon the whole nation.

The most direct sense in which Genesis 3:14–15 was fulfilled was in Christ's crucifixion. Satan was the driving force behind the extreme suffering of Christ just prior to His death. The heel-crushing by Satan during the crucifixion was only temporary compared to the eternal value of the head-crushing of Satan by Christ's finished work on the cross. Christ's death was real but temporary. The ultimate doom of Satan and his kingdom was sealed at the death and resurrection of Christ. Satan's daily defeat in the lives of believers is empowered and superintended by the Holy Spirit (John 16:12).

It is not just Christ who plays a role in the defeat of Satan. It is all mankind. God's program since the fall of man has changed in method, but not in purpose. God is always seeking to lift, redeem, and empower mankind to be victor over Satan's kingdom. God wants Satan defeated daily, as well as in his final judgment. History is the account of a loving God constantly intervening in human affairs to elevate mankind above his fallen nature and enable him to withstand and conquer the influence of Satan. God has never been passive insofar as mankind is concerned. He has never been inclined to simply leave man to follow his own path. He has always stood with a watchful eye ready to seek and save every lost sheep, to chastise and encourage all who follow Him.

THE REDEMPTIVE MISSION OF GOD'S CHOSEN PEOPLE

Many people have wondered why God chose the people of Israel to be His special people in history. Did God love them more? Did He want to bless them and forget about the other people of the world? Why did God choose the Jews? They were a stubborn people, slow to follow God's laws. Why did God get so involved with one group of people?

God favored the Jewish people partly because of the faith of their founding patriarch, Abraham. God responds to real faith in anyone's life. God also chose the Israelites to be special participants in His plan to provide redemption for mankind.

The Cross-Cultural Promise in the Abrahamic Covenant

Four thousand years ago, a man named Abram left the land of his fathers in the Euphrates River valley to go to Palestine. He traveled because of simple faith in the promises of God. Before Abram began his journey, God had covenanted to bless Abram by making him a great nation. Furthermore, God said, "I will bless those who bless you and whoever curses you I will curse; and all peoples on earth will be blessed through you" (Gen. 12:1–3).

With His promises to Abraham, God started a new chapter in human history. God's plan to redeem mankind, both individuals and nations, had not changed. But He had started a new method. He would especially identify Himself with a specific nation of people. He would nurture their growth, determine their social and political system, and protect and deliver them from their enemies. He would become known as the God of Israel. All this was part of God's promise to Abram, later known as Abraham. Israel became a great nation not because Abraham was its father, but because the one true God chose to be personally identified with the Jewish people. It was on the basis of God's personal identification with Israel that Moses was successful in pleading with God not to destroy the whole nation when they sinned at Mount Sinai (Exod. 32:11–14). God had identified Himself with Israel in order to reveal Himself to the world.

The promise to Abraham, "and all peoples on earth will be blessed through you," is a direct reference to the coming of Christ, the messiah. Jesus Christ, son of David, son of Abraham, is the only one through whom all the peoples on earth can be blessed. So even in choosing the nation of Israel, God was determined to reach, lift, elevate, and redeem all peoples on earth. Jesus is the fulfillment of God's promise to Abraham.

While Jesus was the ultimate direct fulfillment of God's promise, God intended to use His special relationship with Israel to reveal His nature to the world. God's dealings with Israel was a learning laboratory whereby mankind could glimpse the glory of God's love and power. It provided an opportunity also to witness His patience, judgment, and righteousness. It was an opportunity for mankind to receive guidelines and principles for right living. The laws God gave to Israel have become the basis for the laws of many nations on earth today. Their principles have guided men toward a right relationship with God and man for centuries. The political systems based most closely upon those principles have been the most lasting. The societies which kept the moral values depicted in God's laws have been the most productive, civilized, and enduring.

It was not just Israel which was the object of God's desire. He chose Israel to prepare the whole world for a right relationship with Himself.

Let's examine the promise more closely. In Galatians 3:8, Paul wrote, "The Scripture foresaw that God would justify the Gentiles by faith, and announced the gospel in advance to Abraham: All nations will be blessed through you."

God gave to Abraham three specific personal promises (verse 2):

1. "I will make you into a great nation."
2. "I will bless you."
3. "I will make your name great."

Then God pauses to give a purpose clause: "and (so that) you will be a blessing" (parenthesis added here). Nobody is ever allowed to simply consume for himself God's blessings or promises. Great blessing demands great responsibility. God blessed Abraham in order to bless others!

Then God gives Abraham two power promises (verse 3):

1. "I will bless those who bless you."
2. "Whoever curses you I will curse."

God promises Abraham power to fulfill his mission for God.

Those who aided Abraham would be aiding God's purposes, and would therefore receive God's blessing. Those who opposed Abraham would oppose God's purpose and therefore bear His judgment. Abraham was promised God's protecting power as he fulfilled God's mission.

God concludes with another purpose clause: "and (so that) all peoples on earth will be blessed through you" (parenthesis added here). This is a further statement of the same thing God was saying in the first purpose clause of verse 2. In verse 2, God promised to make Abraham a blessing. In verse 3, God prophesies the scope of that blessing. He would become a blessing to "all peoples on earth." What a promise!

Notice the verbs in these two verses. Three times God says "I will." Then He says "you will." After this follows two more "I will." But then "you will" does not follow. It is now "through you," referring to Abraham's seed. It is a future time God is predicting. All the peoples of the earth would be blessed, but not by Abraham personally. It would be through Christ, his direct descendant.

This "I will, you will" pattern in God's communication with Abraham is typical of how God has approached man ever since. It is the opposite of how man tries to approach God. Man says to God, "If you will…I will." Man usually tries to coerce God to do man's will, which is rebellion against God! But God says, "I will bless you so that you will be a blessing to others." God acts in human history, declaring and demonstrating His purposes and will. Then He challenges man to align his will with God's will. God blessed Abraham so he could in turn bless others. God delivered Israel from slavery so they could bless the nations around them. God has blessed the church with the power and presence of the Holy Spirit so the church can bless "all peoples on earth." The key variable is man's "will." It is man's response to God's "I will." God's decrees and purposes have been made plain. Man must align his will with God's will. He must align his reason for being with God.

God reveals both His promises and His purposes progressively. In Genesis 12:1–3, He revealed the broad scope of His promises to

Abraham. After leaving Haran and arriving in Canaan, Abraham heard God promise, "To your offspring, I will give this land" (verse 7). Abraham obeyed God's command to leave Haran. After he did, God further revealed the meaning of His promise to bless Abraham. He promised him a land. Later, as recorded in Genesis 17, God further defined His promise to give Abraham a land. In the process, He gave Abram a new name. Abram (honored father) was changed to Abraham (father of many). God not only changed his name, but also, He promised the childless patriarch an heir! So down through Abraham's life, we see a gradual revelation of God's promises.

We also see a gradual revelation of God's purposes. It was after Abraham received his new name that he was invited to join in a covenant relationship with God, as symbolized by the rite of circumcision (Gen. 17:9–14). As Abraham continued in following His direction, God continued to bless him and reveal to him His divine purposes (Gen. 18:17–19).

Abraham's grandson Jacob was a deceitful man. He obtained his brother's inheritance through trickery (Gen. 25:29–34, 27). He destroyed the Shechemites through deception (Gen. 34). But he was still a son of the Abrahamic Covenant! When he was in danger of being revenged by his brother, Esau, he sought the face of God, and humbled himself (Gen. 32:9–12). As he was fleeing from Esau, Jacob wrestled all night with an angel of God. He persevered in his struggle until he obtained a blessing. Before blessing him, the angel declared, "Your name will no longer be Jacob, but Israel, because you have struggled with God and with men and have overcome" (Gen. 32:28). Jacob means "deceitful one." Israel means "he struggles with God."[3]

As Jacob grew spiritually stronger, God gave him greater revelation of His promises and His purposes. When Jacob sought God at Bethel the second time, God confirmed Jacob's call to become Israel. God reconfirmed the Abrahamic Covenant with Jacob (Gen 35:9–15). As before, God promised Israel the land of Canaan for him and his descendants (verse 12). But God also was proclaiming His purpose to make the lineage of Abraham, Isaac, and Jacob the

---

[3] https://www.myjewishlearning.com/article/israel-means-to-struggle-with-god/.

lineage through which God would bless "all peoples on earth" (Gen. 12:3).

By establishing His covenant with Abraham and his descendants, God was informing the world about Himself. He was showing Himself to be loving and merciful, as well as just and righteous. By intervening in human affairs through the lineage of Abraham, God was showing that He was unwilling to idly watch mankind degenerate continually. He would not allow man to destroy himself without hope or knowledge or His Maker. God called Abraham and the nation of Israel in order to rescue all of mankind, not just one nation. As men and nations respond to God's revelation, God reveals Himself still more.

ISRAEL'S CALL TO GOD'S MISSION

Mount Sinai was a landmark in the history of God's revelation to His chosen people. It was at the base of Sinai that Israel camped three months after escaping Egypt. It was at Sinai that Israel rebelled against God in their worship of the golden calf. It was at Sinai that God gave the law to Moses. But it was also at Sinai that God called Israel to be instrumental in His worldwide Mission (Exod. 19:1–2).

As God was preparing to reveal to Moses the special laws which would govern His chosen people, He challenged Israel to a special relationship with Himself. This has come to be called the Mosaic Covenant, and is recorded in Exodus 19:3–6:

> Then Moses went up to God, and the Lord called to him from the mountain and said, "This is what you are to say to the house of Jacob and what you are to tell the people of Israel: You yourselves have seen what I did to Egypt, and how I carried you on eagles' wings and brought you to myself. Now if you obey me fully and keep my covenant, then out of all nations you will be my treasured possession. Although the whole earth is mine, you will be for me a kingdom of priests and a holy nation."

God gave Israel three specific promises. They were to become His treasured possession. They were to become a kingdom of priests, and a holy nation.

Treasured Possession: The word in the Hebrew translated "treasured" carries the sense of "special items which one would protect and keep with himself, like jewels." God was showing what a high value He placed on His people. The keeping of His covenant would make the Israelites like precious jewels of God, to be displayed to all by the God who possessed them" (see Mal. 3:17, Dan. 12:3).

A Kingdom of Priests: Israel, if she kept God's covenant, would also become a nation of priests for God. In order to understand the picture God was painting, we must ask ourselves, "What were priests for in the Old Testament?" Their primary function was to act as mediators between God and man. They represented mankind's need to God, and they represented God's promises to mankind. But how is it that God is declaring that He intended to make a covenant-keeping Israel into an entire nation of priests? If all Israel were to fulfill the role of priests, for whom would they become mediators? To whom would they represent God?

The answer lies in the promise God gave to Abraham: "And through your offspring, all nations on earth will be blessed" (Gen. 22:18, 18:18) God intended for Israel to become priests for the nations!

A Holy Nation: The word *holy* means "separate, especially righteous." It does not mean separate in the sense of "set aside" or "untouchable." It carries the sense of being set apart for a specific purpose. God's new covenant was a call to Israel to be set apart, especially selected, for God's purposes. Israel was to be holy in two respects: (1) She was to be dedicated to worshipping the one true God in singular devotion to Him. Israel was to imitate God's righteousness by pure observance of His laws and decrees. (2) Israel would also become God's agent in dealing with the sinful nations.

By establishing a correct vertical relationship with God, Israel would be a shining (jewellike) example to the nations. At that point in history, the nations around about Israel were engaging in many forms of ungodly activities in the name of religion, such as temple prostitution and child sacrifice. Those ungodly forms of heathen worship would stand in stark contrast to an Israel alight with the glory, righteousness, and presence of Jehovah God! God intended for Israel to stand out among the nations like a precious jewel. He intended that the beauty of Israel's holiness would act like a magnet to draw the rest of the nations unto Himself! The keeping of God's laws and covenant would make Israelite society appear like a utopia in contrast to the sin, greed, and degradation of other societies.

That is how Israel was to become a nation of priests! God intended to so establish a holy relationship with His people that they would become living priestly examples of the power and grace of God to the nations. Those nations would be summoned to the righteousness of God through the mediation of the priestly Israel.

That this was the intent of God's words, there can be no doubt. And the Israelites understood what this call meant. Even Peter referred to this same priestly role, though he taught that Israel's priestly function was transferred to the church since Christ had established a new covenant (1 Pet. 2:9, Eph. 3:10).

God's law made provision for the role to which He had called Israel. Israel was required to treat the foreigner who traveled among them with kindness and love (Lev. 19:33, 31). Jews were to be hospitable to such strangers, remembering that they were also sojourners redeemed by God from a foreign land (Exod. 20:10). There were only two requirements for an alien to join Israeli society. Their males had to be circumcised, and they had to follow the law.[4] But joining Israel, or becoming a proselyte, as it came to be known, accorded the new member full partnership in God's covenant. If a Jew owned a slave, and he became converted, he would be set free. Jews were not allowed to own Jews as slaves. Many other benefits came to aliens who became Jews. There was much in the law of the Israelites which would be attractive to the people of other nations.

God called Israel to display His power, glory, love, and compassion to the nations. Like Abraham, the whole nation was called to a special, holy relationship with God. The effect of the presence

---

[4] https://en.wikipedia.org/wiki/proselyte

of God in Israel was to make Israel holy as a reflection of Gods own holiness. The resulting righteous society, coupled with God's power working on Israel's behalf, would act like a powerful magnet to draw the nations unto God. God's new covenant law encouraged converts to God's law from among the nations. Israel was called to God's mission. She had a priestly call to minister to the nations. When the nations would listen to God's call given through Israel, they would be received into God's people (Exod. 12:42, Ruth 1:16–18). If they rejected God's decrees, God would use Israel to destroy them as He did the Canaanites (see Deut. 6–8). Israel was to be God's primary channel to reach all the peoples of the earth. That was God's plan right up until the finished work of Jesus Christ on the cross!

The Key to Israel's Success

All of God's promises to Israel depended upon one important response from His people. He promised to make them His treasured possession, a kingdom of priests, and a holy nation, if they would obey Him fully and keep His covenant.

Obedience has always been the key factor in seeing God's promises fulfilled. It was Abraham's continuing obedience to God's commands which opened the door for God's continued blessing and revelation. When God tested Abraham, telling him to offer up Isaac as a sacrifice, his obedience greatly pleased God. God spared Isaac, and Abraham's faithful obedience prompted the Lord to reconfirm His covenant.

> "I swear by myself," declares the Lord, "that because you have…not withheld your son, your only son, I will surely bless you and make your descendants as numerous as the stars in the sky and as the sand on the seashore. Your descendants will take possession of the cities of their enemies, and through your offspring all nations on earth will be blessed, because you have obeyed me." (Gen. 22:16–18)

Faith is agreement with God's will. Obedience is the willful response of faith. It is the proof of faith (James 2:20). It is the proof of aligning man's will with the will of God. Obedience is faith in action. Just as it is impossible to please God without faith, so it is impossible to please God without obedience (Heb. 11:6, Deut. 6:24–25). That is why the fulfillment of God's promises require man's faith-filled obedient response.

After God made His covenant promises to Israel at Sinai, Moses delivered the words of the law to the people as commanded by God. The response of the people was "We will do everything the lord has said, we will obey" (Exod. 19:8; 24:7). But within forty-seven days, Israel was caught up in drunken debauchery before the golden calf they were worshipping! This was typical of Israel's response to God's commands and promises throughout the Old Testament. God's chosen people continually disqualified themselves from the promised blessings of God on their nation through their disobedience.

What were the results of their disobedience? Israel spent forty years wandering in the wilderness instead of going directly to the Promised Land before Joshua's conquest of Canaan. Israel spent 250 years under the judges, over 400 years under the reign of Israelite kings, and 70 years in Babylonian captivity. As the centuries rolled by, Israel increasingly defiled herself with the idol worship and heathen practices of the nations around her. Instead of being God's righteous, evangelizing, cross-cultural witnesses to the nations, Israel became disobedient rebels, ensnared by the vices of the nations they were to reach for God. What a sad picture of the fruit of disobedience.

After all those hundreds of years of cyclical rebellion against God's law, Israel finally truly learned one important truth: there is only one true living God. But Israel never learned to listen to Him and obey Him.

Israel had her great moments under godly leaders, such as King David and King Solomon. David gained glimpses of God's desire when he wrote:

> May your ways be known on earth, your salvation among all nations. May the peoples praise

> you, O God; may all the peoples praise you. May the nations be glad and sing for joy. (Ps. 67:2–4)

The prophet Isaiah glimpsed the potential of Israel in the "Servant of the Lord" passages of Isaiah 42 and 49. Israel herself could have been "a light unto the nations" had she only learned obedience. As it was, Israel's failure led God to raise up a new "branch" from among Israel's offspring. He would be the true Servant of the Lord, fulfilling His mission to be a new

> "covenant for the people and a light for the Gentiles, to open eyes that are blind, to free captives from prison and to release from the dungeon those who sit in darkness." (Isa. 42:6–7)

Israel was called to receive God's blessing, demonstrate God's power, and fulfill God's mission to the nations. Through disobedience, Israel failed in their mission. She frustrated God's purposes, but did not change them. God still wants the Gentiles (and Jews as well) brought to the light. Salvation through Christ is God's fulfillment of the Abrahamic promise to bless "all peoples of earth." Israel failed in her cross-cultural ministry. But the mantel of cross-cultural ministry has been transferred from the children of Israel to the children of the New Testament—God's church! It is now the church which is called to participate with God in cross-cultural evangelism. You and I carry the responsibility of the call. Unlike Israel of old, we must not fail!

THE CHURCH IN CROSS-CULTURAL MINISTRY

The church has never seen greater opportunities to minister the Gospel than what exists today. The church is larger than it has ever been by far. The number of evangelical Bible-believing Christians was set to surpass one billion people by the middle of 2020. The church is getting large enough to really have a worldwide impact for the cause of Christ in this generation. But there are also far more people in the world who do not know Christ as Savior than ever before—28.3 percent of the world's people are considered "unevangelized."[5] The Church is growing around the world only about as fast as the population is growing.

There has never been a time when there was a greater need to make Christ known to the nations. Every pastor, evangelist, teacher—indeed, every true believer no matter how young or old—should know how important the church is for fulfilling God's purposes for mankind. Every believer must become an active participant in the cross-cultural ministry of the church. The challenge of this age demands it. The Word of God demands it!

The Mystery Revealed

The disobedience of the Jewish people down through Old Testament history cut them off from fulfilling their cross-cultural mission to the nations. Eventually, it even distorted their view of themselves. Disobedience is a form of selfishness, and the Jews focused more and more upon themselves as they sought the false gods of the nations around them. They spent centuries attempting to obtain God's promises for themselves, but they paid little attention to the responsibility God placed upon them to reach the nations.

Neither a nation nor an individual can continue to consume God's blessings without attending to the responsibilities of those blessings or else it will distort one's thinking. The Jews eventually began to see themselves as very special to God in their own right. They forgot that God had redeemed them out of Egypt and called them to nationhood for His own purposes. They forgot that their very right to exist depended upon God's mercy, and upon their fulfillment of God's call to service.

Eventually they came to believe God loved them simply because they were Jews! In their view, Jewishness was the closest thing to godliness on earth! If anyone wanted to please God, they would have to do so through the Jewish law, according to Jewish forms of worship,

---

5 https://www.gordonconwell.edu/center-for-global-christianity/resources/status-of-global-christianity/.

and in the Jewish language. They did not recognize the selfishness, greed, and ungodly ways of their own culture. They thought they were the only people who knew how to please God!

This distorted thinking led to great prejudice against non-Jewish peoples. They were racially and culturally prejudiced. They distorted the law God gave to Moses. Jews were not allowed to touch non-Jewish people. They were not even allowed in the same room where Gentiles were eating. The Jews came to feel they were in every way superior to the Gentiles.

It was almost impossible for the Jews to conceive that God could receive Gentiles without making them Jewish first. This strong cultural prejudice did not disappear when the church was born in the book of Acts. It remained all too strong, as we shall see below. Even after the churches had been established all over Asia Minor, Paul found it necessary to explain to the Jewish believers in the church in Ephesus about the "mystery of Christ" (Eph. 3:4–6). Paul wrote under the guidance of the Holy Spirit:

> Surely you have heard about the administration of God's grace that was given to me for you, that is, the mystery made known to me by revelation, as I have already written briefly. In reading this, then, you will be able to understand my insight into the mystery of Christ, which was not made known to men in other generations as it has now been revealed by the Spirit to God's holy apostles and prophets. This mystery is that through the gospel the Gentiles are heirs together with Israel, members together of one body and sharers together in the promise in Christ Jesus.

This passage must have been quite a shock to those Jewish believers who still clung to the old attitudes of Jewish superiority. Paul attacks that attitude directly by declaring that Jews and Gentiles are equal partners in receiving God's grace through Christ.

Important: Paul directly links the Abrahamic Covenant, the foundation of Jewish nationality, directly to the Gentiles also. The Gentiles were also "heirs together with Israel...in the promise." This is a direct reference to the covenant promises given to Abraham. Paul was declaring that the epicenter of God's acts had been relocated. It had shifted from Israel to a new people created through Christ from both Jews and Gentiles.

The apostle was describing a great turning point which had taken place in the history of Israel as the people of God. Israel had failed in her call to bless the nations directly, and God had taken control. God reconstituted the people of God in His mission to reach the nations. Jews and Gentiles would unite around the work of Christ on the cross, becoming the Church—the new people of God. And it would be the Church which would also fall heir to God's promise to Abraham to bless "all the peoples on earth."

Paul made the mission of the newly constituted church very plain, when he went on to say

> His [God's] intent was that now, through the church, the manifold wisdom of God should be made known to the rulers and authorities of the heavenly realms, according to his eternal purpose which he accomplished in Christ Jesus our Lord. (Eph. 3:10–11)

The "rulers and authorities of the heavenly realms" refers to the same spiritual forces referred to in Ephesians 6:12. The picture Paul is painting to his readers is figurative. He refers to the earthly rulers, and the evil spiritual forces which support them in maintaining Satan's kingdom of darkness on earth. Paul is using picturesque speech to show that the church has been commissioned to tear down the strongholds of Satan's earthly realm by proclaiming to every ruler and all who live under their domain "the manifold wisdom of God."

This refers to the Gospel, pure and simple. It was the good news that all peoples can join together in the church of Christ, which is God's eternal purpose. The Church has replaced Israel as God's agency for drawing the nations to Himself.

Centripetal-Centrifugal Mission: There is one very important difference between the methods God gave to Israel and those He gave the Church for fulfilling their mission. Israel, as shown in the Mosaic Covenant, was to serve as a spiritual magnet to draw the people of other nations to God. They were to serve as holy priests unto God, revealing God to the nations, and serving as mediators to bring other peoples to God. They were to reveal God to the nations and serve as mediators to bring other peoples to Him.

The nature of their mission was centripetal (figure 1.A). They were to draw the people of other nations into their nation, and teach them obedience to God's laws. Their effectiveness in doing this was directly related to their own obedience as the people of God.

Figure 1.a Centripetal Mission

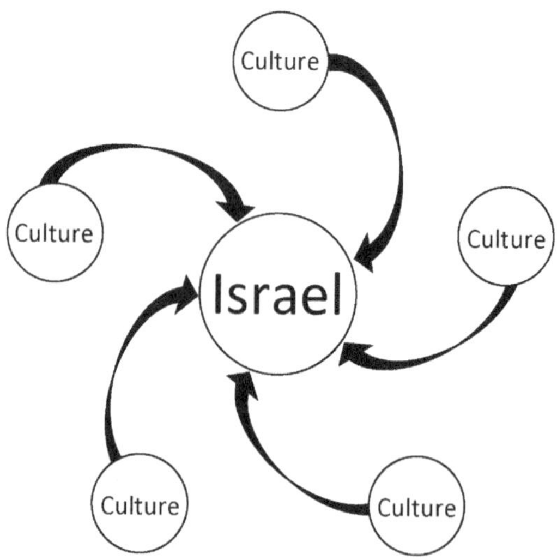

Figure 1.b Centrifugal Mission

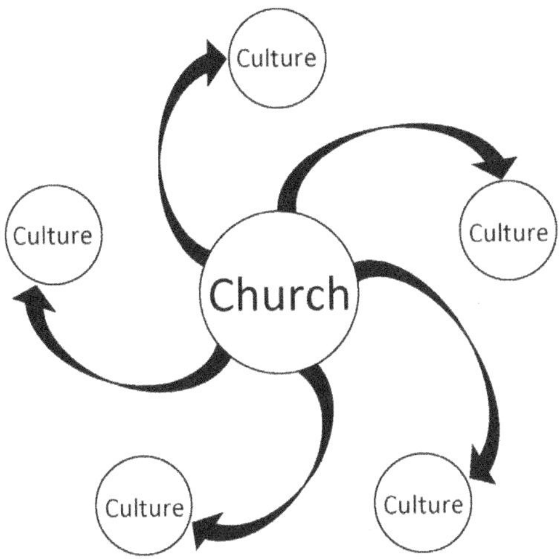

The Church is also called to a priestly ministry (2 Cor. 5:16–19, 2 Pet. 2:9–10). But the nature of its ministry is centrifugal (figure 1.b). Unlike Israel, the Church is challenged not to stand still and draw other peoples into its own culture and nationality. It is challenged to go forth unto the peoples of the earth, winning men to Christ where they are. After men are won to Christ, they are to form branches of the church were they are, among their own people. Then those churches themselves are to carry out centrifugal mission, a going-out mission (Matt. 28:19, Acts 1:8).[6]

Before Jesus ascended into heaven, He told the disciples that they would be witnesses in Jerusalem, Judea, Samaria, and the uttermost parts of the earth. This is a perfect picture of the centrifugal nature of the mission of the church. The church must never wait for

6 Trevin Wax, "The Mission of the Church: Centripetal to Centrifugal, and Why It Matters," August 26, 2019.

the lost to come to her. She must continually be going out to the lost, in ever widening circles of influence.

The Nature of the Church

Jesus told His disciples, "I will build my church, and the gates of Hades will not overcome it" (Matt. 16:18). What did Jesus mean by the "church"? We know He was not talking about a church building. He was referring to the people who would follow Him down through the ages. The New Testament shows that when believers are together as the church, they are more than just a group of believers. Individual members are given spiritual gifts which allows the church to work together for common purposes as the "Body of Christ" (Rom. 12:3–8, 1 Cor. 12). But what are those purposes? What is the nature of the church?

The Bible often speaks of the "Kingdom of God." Generally speaking, we can refer to the Kingdom of God as the totality of God's reign in the universe. Yet, the Bible uses the term in three different ways: (1) Some Scripture refers to the Kingdom of God in its universal sense—God's rule over everything. (2) Some Scripture refers to the Kingdom of God as God's spiritual reign on earth in the lives of believers. (3) Some Scripture refers to the Kingdom of God as a future kingdom where heaven, earth, and mankind will be finally united to experience the fullness of His reign after the return of Christ. The church is directly related to the second definition of the Kingdom of God—God's activities and rule on earth.

The church is not the Kingdom of God, but it is the closest representation of that kingdom on earth. It represents the invasion of God's kingdom into the Kingdom of Satan. The church is God's spearhead into the spiritual darkness of the world. The church is not perfect, and never will be until Christ returns to rule the earth. But the church is the closest equivalent and representation of the Kingdom of God on earth.

That is why Jesus gave much teaching concerning the Kingdom of God. The church is to be God's reflection of the kingdom. It is to mirror the nature of the Kingdom.

Jesus taught us about the nature of the church through "kingdom" parables. The theme of expansion and growth is common to those parables. Jesus likened the kingdom, and therefore the church, to the following:

- a net that is cast into the sea in order to draw in many fish (Matt. 13:47)
- the mustard seed which, when planted, grows large enough to support the birds of the air (Matt. 13:31–32)
- the leaven which is kneaded into a small piece of dough, but leavens the whole loaf when mixed in the same bowl (Matt. 13:33)
- the seed is scattered in order to gather an abundant harvest (Matt. 13:47)

There are a number of principles Jesus was teaching through these parables, but the single theme included in each one was growth, expansion, harvesting. The growth of the church is central to the nature of the church.

Jesus wants a church which is concerned about sending forth laborers—harvesters in a world where the harvest of souls is plentiful (Matt. 9:37–38). Jesus wants a church which is not just interested in the wheat gathered into the barn but also the wheat in whitened harvest fields. He wants a church which is constantly reaching out, expanding in number and quality of commitment. He wants a church which is centrifugal in its mission for God—a church which grows by virtue of what it is. The church is the instrument of God's activities on earth. It is the closest thing to the Kingdom of God on earth. The church Jesus had in mind when He said, "I will build my church," is an ever expanding agent of God's grace which grows by its very nature.

Stewards of the Good News

The church has inherited Israel's exclusive right to be the people of God. The Church has joined Israel as inheritor of God's promises

(Eph. 3:6). God has "destroyed the barrier, the 'dividing wall of hostility' between Jews and Gentiles, and both have been formed into a new body—the church—the Body of Christ" (Eph. 2:14). This Church has inherited the promised blessings of God. But, like the Jews of old, it has also been charged with the responsibilities of those blessings.

The Church has been given a stewardship by God. Paul recognized this responsibility when he wrote, "Let a man so account of us, as of the ministers of Christ, and stewards of the mysteries of God. Moreover, it is required of stewards that a man be found faithful" (1 Cor. 4:1–2). The phrase "mysteries of God" is primarily referring to the Gospel, as we discovered from Ephesians 3:1–6.

The use of the term "stewards" is an important New Testament word. Jesus even told a parable about stewardship (Matt. 25:22–26). A steward was an agent, one to whom valued resources had been entrusted. He was expected to take the resources of his master, use them for the master's purposes, and return with the fruit of the effort and the original resources to bring glory to his master. The key principle behind good stewardship is faithful, productive service for the glory of the master.

No wonder Jesus used the picture of stewardship to describe the responsibility God has given the church! As Paul indicated, the church has been given knowledge of the precious Gospel—free pardon from sin for everyone who will accept Christ as Lord. God has invested this truth in the church, and ordained that the church would be the only earthly institution entrusted to make it known to the world. The church has been given the greatest, most important stewardship the world has ever known. It has been entrusted with what man needs most—salvation.

As Paul said, it is required that a steward be found faithful. Israel made the mistake of confining the knowledge of God to her own nation. Her disobedient spirit caused her to fail in her stewardship of representing God to the nations. Jesus left no doubt concerning the scope of the church's stewardship. It is to pick up the mantle of responsibility which Israel forfeited. The church is to "go, make disciples among all nations, baptizing them in the name of the Father and of the Son and of the Holy Spirit, and teaching them of obey everything I have commanded you" (Matt. 28:19–20). The church has been given a responsibility to be God's stewards, His ambassadors in cross-cultural ministry to "all the peoples on earth" (Gen. 12:3).

Every portion of God's church must be good stewards of Christ's command. No local church can afford to simply consume God's blessings upon themselves, as did Israel. No national church, or group of churches of the same race, can fully be the church Christ came to build, unless they reach out to make disciples beyond their own city, nation, and people. We have all been given the stewardship of cross-cultural ministry. That is the reason for this book. We must help every believer in every church learn to do his part to work in partnership with God to make disciples among every people on earth!

THE AGENDA OF THE HOLY SPIRIT IN THE BOOK OF ACTS

During His earthly ministry, Jesus spent most of His time teaching the disciples. He not only taught them about God's kingdom, but also, He taught them how to minister to the masses of people who followed Jesus wherever they could. Jesus was not preparing them for a present ministry so much as for a future ministry, which would begin after He was to be ascended into heaven.

His three plus years of ministry with His disciples was their apprenticeship. He sent them out penniless to the Judean towns and cities, telling them to accept the hospitality offered them. They were to proclaim the Kingdom of God, heal the sick, cleanse those who had leprosy, drive out demons (Matt. 10:5–20). At the end of Jesus' ministry, He told the disciples:

> I no longer call you servants, because a servant does not know his master's business. Instead, I have called you friends, for everything that I learned from my father I have made known to you. (John 15:15)

Jesus spoke these words just before going to the cross. The disciple's apprenticeship had ended. It was also during that same time of last-minute instructions that Jesus promised the disciples:

> I have much more to say to you, more than you can now bear. But when he, the Spirit of truth, comes, he will guide you into all truth. He will not speak on his own, he will speak only what he hears, and he will tell you what is yet to come. He will bring glory to me by taking from what is mine and making it known to you. (John 16:12–14)

Jesus was telling His disciples about the Holy Spirit's ministry to them after He was gone. He was promising the continuation of His own ministry to them, but in a greater measure. He told them, "It is for your good that I am going away. Unless I go away, the Counselor [Holy Spirit] will not come to you; but if I go, I will send him to you" (John 16:7). Jesus was telling them they were better off for the Spirit to become their teacher. The Spirit would not be confined to a physical body, like Jesus had been. He will not only be "with" them, as Jesus had been, He would also be "in" them! He would be an ever present comforter, a constant guide. He would give them power to carry on the ministry of Jesus on earth.

It is these same kinds of thoughts which Jesus had just before He ascended into heaven. He had been resurrected for forty days. He had spent much time with His disciples. He had enlightened them about the prophecies concerning His death and resurrection. They finally began to truly understand the meaning and importance of the Kingdom of God. He had told them to "go into all the world and preach the gospel" (Mark 16:15). They were ready to go. But as He was about to leave them for the last time, Jesus told them to wait—wait until they receive the necessary power:

> You will receive power when the Holy Spirit comes on you, and you will be my witnesses in

> Jerusalem, and in all Judea and Samaria, and to the ends of the earth. (Acts 1:8)

These were the last words Jesus spoke on earth. We can assume they were among His most important. He even instructed them to wait ten days until the power of the Holy Spirit filled them and enabled them. He was calling His disciples to centrifugal mission. They were to minister the Gospel to ever widening circles of territory and increasingly different kinds of peoples. They were not to stop at any cultural or geographical boundary. They were to continue widening their ministry until they had reached the "ends of the earth."

What happened ten days later is well-known. The day of the Feast of Pentecost had arrived. They were together in one place. The Spirit descended upon them and filled the whole house—and the disciples. They were filled with the Holy Spirit, and began to speak with other tongues, as the Spirit overwhelmed them with His power!

We know this story of the beginning of the church very well. Many people can quote it by heart. But many people miss the true significance of the Day of Pentecost in Acts 2. For many, the most important thing about that day is that believers spoke in tongues as the Spirit enabled them. But it is also important to realize (1) **who was listening?** What kind of people witnessed this divine manifestation? (2) **What did they hear?** What was the significance of this event to the hearers?

Who **was** listening to the disciples on the Day of Pentecost? Primarily, a group of people known as Hellenist Jews. These were Jews who, for two or three centuries, had been scattered all over the Greek and Roman world by job opportunities, military conscription and periodic persecutions. They had scattered and settled in all the major Greek and Roman cities, and most of the minor ones as well. There were approximately 2.5 million Jews living in Judea during the time of Christ. But there were approximately 3.6 million Hellenist Jews living outside Judea and Palestine.[7] These Hellenist Jews had

---

[7] This is an approximation based on the best historical estimates. See Peter C. Wagner, *Our Kind of People* (Atlanta: John Knox Press, 1979).

mostly been scattered during the reign of the Greeks (second and third centuries BC). They had absorbed much of the Greek culture, and that is why they were known as Hellenists to the Jews of Palestine.

The Hellenists were trilingual peoples. They were still Jews. They worshipped in their own synagogues, no matter where they had settled. They learned Hebrew in the Synagogue schools. Most of them learned Koine Greek, the trade language of that era. But they also learned the local languages and dialects of the peoples in the regions where they had settled. So the Hellenists usually spoke at least three languages! They put down roots in those far-flung corners of the Roman and Greek world. A few migrated even as far as India and China! They absorbed the cultures and ways of many lands! The languages of the peoples among whom they lived became their true mother tongues, as they had learned those languages as children growing up.[8]

But the Hellenists never forgot Israel. It was still the Promised Land! If they were successful in their work or business, and they wished for a place to retire, many would move to Jerusalem. Many had relatives living there. To them, it was still the holy city—the Mount Zion of God. The new temple had just been built by Herod. Some forty-six years in the building, it was stupendous in its glory and beauty! There was mounting excitement and expectancy concerning the coming of the expected Messiah foretold in the prophets. Nationalistic identification with Jerusalem and Judaism was rising in the hearts of Hebrews all over the world. If the Hellenists could afford it at all, they wanted to return to live or retire in that high-rent city of Jerusalem!

And to Jerusalem they came—by the thousands! In fact, according to the Talmud (Jewish History), there were 480 synagogues in Jerusalem at the time of the Day of Pentecost in Acts 2! These were called Hellenist synagogues because those who migrated back to Jerusalem wanted to retain their own cultural identities. They worshipped in their own synagogues in the Hebrew language much like any other Jew. But when they fellowshipped together on the steps of the synagogue or in each other's homes, they spoke in their mother

[8] R. P. H. Green, *The Works of Ausonius* (Oxford: Clarendon Press, 1991), 276.

tongues—the languages and dialects of those regions where they had lived in the far-flung corners of the Roman world.

The Jewish law required all Jews to make a pilgrimage to Jerusalem for each of three special feast days in the Jewish calendar.[9] The second of these was the Feast of Pentecost. It was a good time of the year to travel. So Hellenist Jews by the tens of thousands converged on the city of Jerusalem from all over the Roman world. They came to celebrate the Feast of Pentecost to be sure. But many came to also see Grandma and Grandpa who had retired in Jerusalem. Makeshift marketplaces sprang up everywhere—even along the sides of the crowded roads leading into the city. People were everywhere. The streets were full of Hellenist Jews from all over the Roman world. It was primarily these people who were in the streets at nine o'clock in the morning when the Holy Spirit filled the disciples!

They flooded into the city from every direction. Three times the population of Jerusalem poured into the city for the festival. The babble of many languages filled the dusty air. Suddenly, the roar of heavy gusts of wind drowned out everything else. Then the people heard something that amazed them.

The upper room where the 120 believers were meeting was the rooftop of a large house. It had a small wall surrounding it, opening the rooftop to the air. It was clearly visible from the streets. The top of the whole building began to glow with the presence of God.

Then the people in the streets were suddenly shocked to hear the believers' praises and adoration of God in their own mother tongues! The believers were speaking in at least fifteen distinct languages of the far-flung corners of the Roman world (Acts 2:8–11). The people in the streets could see the believers were dressed like Galileans and Judeans. As the wind gusted, the house glowed and the amazing words echoed across the rooftops. The crowd swelled in size. They were bewildered as they listened to the praises of God in their own mother tongues. Parthian and Elamite Jews, Hellenists from Phrygia, Pamphylia, and Egypt, Hellenists from at least fifteen distinct regions of the Roman Empire heard the praises of God in

9 This is recorded in the Jewish Talmud, Maimonides, Isure Biah, 13–14.

their own mother tongues—and so far away from home! Their eyes were riveted toward the upper room where the disciples ecstatically praised God.

If the semiliterate, uneducated Galilean believers had spoken in Greek, most everyone could have understood. But they miraculously spoke in at least fifteen different languages of the wonderful works of God. All the people in the streets, hearing their own mother tongues so far away from home, gaped at one another in wide-eyed wonder. "What does this mean?" they asked one another?

THE TRUE SIGNIFICANCE OF THE DAY OF PENTECOST

God was showing the world something very special at that moment. He was declaring that He would no longer reveal Himself through a chosen people called the Jews. He would now reveal His power, purpose, and love through the Church of Jesus Christ! But not just a new people—it would be a church so empowered by the Holy Spirit that it would be capable of bursting across every racial, cultural, linguistic boundary on earth to penetrate the mainstream of every single people with the Gospel of Christ. It would be a church determined to penetrate the mainstream of every society, presenting the Gospel in the mother tongue, the heart language of every people. God was declaring that the agenda of the Holy Spirit in the Church of Jesus Christ would be to plant churches in the mainstream of every culture among every group of people of earth!

Overcoming Jewish Prejudice

As discussed above, the Jews were very prejudiced against the Gentiles—racially, religiously, and culturally. Any kind of association with the Gentiles was detested by religious Jews. The Romans dominated the Jews politically, but this heightened the sense of spiritual superiority over all Gentiles felt so intensely by the Jews. A regular prayer of thanksgiving by Jewish priests was "God, I thank you that you have not made me a slave, a woman or a Gentile."[10] Jews were not allowed inside a Gentile home (and vice versa), to eat with them, accept food from them, or interact with them in public.[11] And it was upon this prejudiced people that God poured out His Holy Spirit! It was one thing to expect them to evangelize their own people, but quite another to call them to evangelize the Gentiles! The Holy Spirit really had a task ahead, if the Jewish church was to truly fulfill His purpose!

That is really the theme of the Book of Acts—how the Holy Spirit broke through the Jewish prejudice, and spread the Gospel among the Gentiles. It was not easy. On the Day of Pentecost, Peter stood up and preached the Gospel. Three thousand people were saved! Almost all of these were Hellenist Jews in Jerusalem for the special feast. Then the number of believers grew rapidly: five thousand, ten thousand, and then fifteen thousand. In a short time, there were approximately twenty-five thousand believers in the city!

At first, most of the believers were Hellenist Jews. But very quickly the number of believers from Judea overtook the number of Hellenist believers. This led to a division in the early church (Acts 6). The Hellenist (Greek-speaking) believers began to feel some resentment because they were treated as less important in the growing church. Judean Jews considered Hellenists to be cultural half-breeds. They were less than pure Jew, and therefore inferior to Aramaic speaking Jews. This same prejudice was felt in the early church.

The surface problem was the issue of making sure the Hellenist widows were well cared for in the daily distribution (Acts 6:1). But the apostles quickly recognized the problem was really a twofold problem. First, Jews were trained to think Jewishness was next to godliness, which meant it was natural to take care of Judean Jews as a priority. The second reason was a lack of leadership for the Hellenist segment of the church. The Judean believers had the apostles to whom they could go. But the Greek-speaking believers did not feel they had as much access to the leadership. They usually spoke to each

---

10 https://www.myjewishlearning.com/article/who-has-not-made-me-a-woman/.

11 Wagner, *Our Kind of People*.

other in Greek, not the local Aramaic dialect. None of their own number were among the apostles.

Wisely, the apostles told the Hellenist believers, "Choose seven men from among you who are known to be full of the Spirit and wisdom. We will turn this responsibility over to them" (verse 3).

Some people assume these men were simply appointed as deacons, and were expected to administrate the charitable work of the church only. Actually, these men became **apostles** over the Hellenist believers in the church. A quick examination of the names of those who were chosen reveals that each man had a Hellenist (Greek) name. And they had **apostolic ministries** in their own right. After all, Philip did not start a revival in Samaria by waiting on tables (Acts 8:4–8)! Stephen was not stoned to death for caring for widows (Acts 6:8–15)! These men's ministries were parallel to those of the original apostles. They were apostles over the Hellenist segment of the new church!

After the Hellenists gained their own leaders, their zeal and influence increased. Many of the Hellenist Jews in Jerusalem, and even their priests, began to follow Christ (Acts 6:7). This threatened the very existence of the synagogues that were in the city at that time.[12] Many of them consisted of Hellenist Jews who had been conscripted into the Roman army, but retired back in Jerusalem. Others were from many parts of the Roman world and came back to Jerusalem in their old age to be with relatives. Those who were in their Hellenist synagogues worshipped in Hebrew, but rather than speaking Aramaic when they exited the synagogues, they preferred to speak in the languages of the far-flung corners of the Roman world where they had grown up. And their priests spoke those languages also. But if you lose your priest who speaks your language because he converts to Christ, that threatens the very existence of your Hellenist synagogue! The language everyone speaks is what binds the synagogue together. Priests who speak that language are rare! One such

[12] https://books.google.com/books?id=yp1dAOakYK8C&pg=PA49&lpg=PA49&dq=480+Hellenistic+synagogues+in+Jerusalem&source=bl&ots=fMIlBnM8bt&sig=ACfU3U3KMQ5K22c2bkGkJNYXtX5xBAEGZQ&hl=en&sa=X&ved=2ahUKEwjA_-Gdk_3pAhVII6wKHQLAABcQ6AEwAHoECAoQAQ.

synagogue became so incensed after losing its priest, its members produced the false testimony which led to the stoning and death of Stephen (Acts 6:8–15).

After Stephen's death, persecution of the church increased dramatically (Acts 8:1). It was especially intense against the Hellenist believers. Many of them fled Jerusalem for other parts of Judea. But most of the Hellenists began to make their way up the Phoenician coast, or south toward Egypt, and over to North Africa. They started churches in Ptolemais (Acts 21:7), Tyre (Acts 21:3–4), and Sidon (Acts 27:3), and many other places where they went. The Hellenists had roots in the many places where they went. It proved providential that they started churches in most of those places. But they did so among other Hellenists Jews like themselves. But the most important was the church which was planted in Antioch!

Acts 11:19–20 records one of the most significant events in the history of the church. Let us examine this Scripture carefully: "Now those who had been scattered by the persecution in connection with Stephen." This refers to the Hellenist believers in the Jerusalem church "traveled as far as Phoenicia, Cyprus and Antioch, telling the message only to Jews." (They started churches among other Hellenists like themselves.) "Some of them, however, men from Cyprus and Cyrene, went to Antioch, and *began to speak to Greeks also, telling them the good news about the Lord Jesus.*" This marks the first time in the history of the church, as far as we know, when Jewish believers began to systematically and purposefully preach the Gospel to purely Gentile people!

Even though the last words of Jesus on earth was a command to cross-cultural ministry—"to the ends of the earth" (Acts 1:8), Even though the first demonstration of the Holy Spirit's power in starting the church on the Day of Pentecost was a dramatic declaration of God's intention to reach all peoples in cross-cultural ministry, even though ministry outside the Jewish culture was primary to the commands that Christ gave to the apostles (Matt. 28:19–20)—still, it took the church seventeen years after the Day of Pentecost to begin to speak to the Greeks also! It was seventeen years before the church began to fulfill the agenda of the Holy Spirit that was so evident on the Day of Pentecost!

What were the results? "The Lord's hand was with them, and a great number of people believed and turned to the Lord" (verse 21). God began to move mightily among the Greeks in Antioch. They sent Barnabas (Son of Encouragement) from Jerusalem to investigate this Gentile movement toward Christ. It was too early for the Jerusalem church to believe that Gentiles could serve God without following Jewish law (see Acts 15).

Being a man of the Spirit, Barnabas immediately recognized the hand of God in the newly formed Greek church. He gave approval to the ministry among the Greeks (verses 22–24). This encouraged the Greek revival even more!

Then Barnabas thought of Saul, who had been smitten on the road to Damascus eleven years before (Acts 9). He had gone to Damascus to kill and persecute believers, but God met him on the road. He returned to Jerusalem preaching the Gospel he went to destroy! This amazed the Jerusalem church, and they were not too sure they wanted to trust Saul. This was especially true when they heard him declare that God had called him to be an "apostle to the Gentiles" (Rom. 11:13). Paul had been in Tarsus about eight years when Barnabas went to bring him to Antioch.

Barnabas and Saul ministered in Antioch for one year. Saul's ministry to the Gentiles was proven during that time. By the time the Acts story progresses to chapter 13, Barnabas and Saul have come to be called Paul and Barnabas. They were the first cross-cultural evangelism team in the early church to be sent to evangelize the Gentiles. They became a model of cross-cultural evangelism teams in the early church to be sent to evangelize the Gentiles. They became a model of cross-cultural evangelism. They were the first of many teams which would start churches in most of the cities and towns of the Roman Empire (Acts 13:1–3). So effective were these cross-cultural ministers that before they were finished, even their enemies exclaimed that they had "turned the world upside down" (Acts 17:6)! Once the early church began to do cross-cultural evangelism, God blessed their efforts mightily!

It is the agenda of the Holy Spirit to "turn the world upside down" with the Gospel of Jesus in every generation! He wants every church and every group of churches in every country to be continually and vitally involved in doing cross-cultural evangelism and church planting. Too often, national groupings of churches are too much like the early Jewish church. They are too prejudiced, in favor of their own people and against other peoples, to hear the voice of the Spirit tell them to go. If we are listening, we will hear the voice of the Spirit telling us to fulfill His primary agenda for the church—cross-cultural ministry to "all peoples of the earth."

Every church should seek God to discover how to send cross-cultural evangelists. Groups of churches should work together to be certain such evangelists are well trained in cross-cultural ministry. They should be sure they are faithfully supported in their important ministries. Cross-cultural ministry is a central and primary ministry on the agenda of the Holy Spirit for the church. **The degree to which our churches are moving in the mainstream of the Spirit's flow on earth will be the degree to which they are vitally involved in cross-cultural evangelism.** Every people in every generation must hear. Cross-cultural ministry is the agenda of the Holy Spirit!

The people of Israel took their special position as God's people for granted. They consumed God's blessings upon themselves without giving attention to their responsibility for the nations. They correctly understood themselves to be the object of God's desire. But they never fully grasped that they were also to be the instrument of God's love for the nations.

Even though the last thing Jesus said to His followers was "to the ends of the earth"—and even though the first act of the Holy Spirit in giving birth to the Church was to demonstrate its cross-cultural ministry purpose, seventeen years were required before the early Church even began to pursue cross-cultural ministry and "speak the gospel to the Gentiles also."

We must allow God to overcome our self-centeredness. We must all realize we are not only the object of God's desire but also the instrument of His purpose. Every person and every church must demonstrate their commitment to the agenda of the Holy Spirit.

We must do everything necessary to be sure every people and every tongue has an adequate chance to know Christ in every generation!

QUESTIONS FOR UNDERSTANDING

1. What is the one characteristic of God's nature upon which man is totally dependent? Why?
2. According to this chapter, what characteristic do men and angels have in common? Why did God create them that way?
3. What were God's two problems after Adam sinned? How did God solve them?
4. What is the protevangelium? Why is it important? What does it teach us about God?
5. What are the three specific "personal promises" God gave to Abraham? What are the two "power promises" God gave to Abraham?
6. When God made a covenant with Abraham, He promised that Abraham's descendants would have a cross-cultural ministry. Quote that portion of Genesis 12:1–3 where God made this promise.
7. What does the name Abraham mean? What does Israel mean? How was each name related to the mission God gave them?
8. Why did God choose Israel?
9. What three promises did God give Israel in the Mosaic Covenant? What did they have to do with Israel's call to God's mission?
10. What three promises did God give Israel in the Mosaic Covenant? What did they have to do with Israel's call to God's mission?
11. What was the "mystery" revealed to Paul, according to Ephesians 2 and 3?
12. Who inherited the call of Israel to cross-cultural ministry after the resurrection? What is the key to fulfilling that call?
13. What is the closest representation of the Kingdom of God on earth today? What is its basic nature, according to Jesus' parables on the Kingdom of God?

14. After Jesus' resurrection, what did Jesus say, and what did the Holy Spirit do to show the importance of cross-cultural ministry for the church?
15. Where did the New Testament church really begin its cross-cultural ministry? How long after the Day of Pentecost did this occur? Why did it take so long?

QUESTIONS FOR DISCUSSION

1. Analyze God's characteristics of love and mercy, justice and righteousness. How do they relate to God's way of dealing with man today? Why does God allow evil to continue in the world today?
2. Discuss the "I will, you will" character of God's promises to Abraham in Genesis 12:1–3. For you personally, how important is it to learn to obey God? What is the relationship of obedience to learning to hear God's voice in your daily life?
3. Think of five churches you know about which are actively supporting cross-cultural evangelism. What kinds of help do they give? What does your church do? What should it do?
4. If a friend in your church told you that God was not interested in cross-cultural evangelism, how would you answer him? What Scriptures would you use to support your answer?
5. Is there cultural prejudice among your people like there was among the Jews in Jesus' day? List some facts to support your answer. If there is prejudice, how has this affected the cross-cultural ministry vision of your people's churches? What steps can be taken to involve your churches in cross-cultural ministry more effectively?

CHAPTER TWO

Unreached People: The Unfinished Task

IMPORTANT POINTS IN THIS CHAPTER

1. God is the originator of human diversity. His redemptive plan allows for different groups of people to serve Him and still keep their own cultural identity.
2. The unity of the Church is based on spiritual unity, not physical closeness or cultural uniformity.
3. Evangelism which ignores the cultural and social differences between people groups will not reach all kinds of peoples, and will drive many people away from the Gospel.
4. The key factor in defining people groups is to discover which group people feel they belong to.
5. Most people have been trained not to see the world like God does. God is more concerned about the boundaries between people groups than He is about the boundaries between countries.
6. The greater the cultural distance, the greater the difficulty in evangelizing other people groups.
7. Good cross-cultural evangelism strategy considers the needs of each people group separately and seeks to evangelize them with strategies to win one people group at a time.
8. People like to become Christians without crossing racial, linguistic, or class barriers.

9. There is a great need to train and send cross-cultural evangelists from every reached people group to every unreached people group in the world.

Everyone knows there are different kinds of people. But if you ask your friends what makes people different, you will get many different kinds of answers. Some will describe different personality characteristics. Others will point to social or economic status as the main difference between different kinds of people. Still others will point to differences in race or language. And they will all be right. People are different for a multitude of reasons. If we are to be effective cross-cultural ministers, we must learn about the differences between people and how they affect our ministry.

God is the source of human diversity. Many of the conflicts between countries, and between the peoples of one country, are a result of the racial, linguistic, and cultural differences between peoples. Sometimes politicians seek to erase these differences for the sake of national unity and personal power. Sometimes religious leaders seek to overlook these differences in the name of Christian unity. But we must remember that God is the source of human diversity.

After the flood, God specifically commanded Noah and his sons to be fruitful and increase in number and fill the earth (Gen. 9:1). Noah's descendants eventually disobeyed God's command. They found a plain in Babylonia and decided to build a great city there, saying, "We will make a name for ourselves and not be scattered over the face of the earth" (Gen. 11:4). God had told them to populate the whole earth, but they wanted to stay in one place and "make a name" for themselves. At that time, they all spoke the same language. They had the same basic standards of behavior, and they were more unified in their purpose than any of the peoples before the flood. In order to turn them back toward His own purposes, God performed a miracle. He confused their languages so they could not understand one another. God instantly created many different groups of people who were separated by a language barrier. These groups scattered over the face of the earth. They eventually developed their own codes of behavior and systems of values. They did not grow closer to one another. They usually grew further apart. Their languages divided and became even more diverse over time. Today, according to the most authoritative sources, there are more than seven thousand languages spoken in the world.

God could have done many things to force the descendants of Noah to scatter across the earth. But he chose to confuse their languages. He knew this would eventually be the basis of misunderstanding and conflict between human beings. He also knew that cultural barriers would be a large hindrance to the spread of the Gospel. But God does not make mistakes! He also knows that cultural diversity keeps man from unifying the whole race in sinful rebellion against God. It blocks corrupt political leaders from easily controlling the whole human race. He knew it is better for people groups to face conflicts with each other than to be in conflict with God and bring about their own destruction. And as we shall see later, it allows the Gospel to spread very rapidly within homogeneous groups of people.

WHAT IS A PEOPLE GROUP?

People exist in cultural groupings. They always have ever since the Tower of Babel. From Bible times up to the present, people have most often been thought of in terms of the group of people to which they belong—their tribe, caste, language group, etc. In modern history, the rise of nationalism and increasing urbanization have obscured the differences between people groups. But those differences remain. They either form a barrier to the spread of the Gospel or they represent a significant vehicle for the spread of the Gospel.

Here is a list of people groups which are named in the Old and New Testaments of the Bible:

Figure 2.a: People Groups in the Bible

Old Testament		New Testament	
Edomites	Moabites	Parthians	Medes
Canaanites	Philistines	Elamites	Mesopotamians
Amorites	Hivites	Judeans	Cappadocians

Anakites	Rephaites	Pontus People	Asians
Hittites	Perizzites	Illyricumites	Phrygians
Jebusites	Amalekites	Pamphylians	Egyptians
Arameans	Kerethites	Libyans	Romans
Pelethites	Ammonites	Cretans	Arabians
Harodites	Paltites	Pharisees	Saducees
Hushathites	Ahohites	Galileans	Epicureans
Netophathites	Pirathonites	Lystrans	Galatians
Arbathites	Barhumites	Ethiopians	Lydians
Shaalbonites	Hararites	Freedmen	Slaves
Ithrites	Israelites	Priests	Levites

Notice there is no common factor which can be used to identify the people groups in figure 2.a. Some are identified by a common ancestor such as the Amalekites and Ammonites. Others are identified by the geographical location where they live, like the Pamphylians and Galatians. The Pharisees and Saducees were a people group because of their religious beliefs. The Freedmen were Jews who had been used as slaves and soldiers by the Romans. After the Roman wars, they were set free.

Notice also that some of these groups represented large numbers of people, such as the Egyptians and Romans. Other groups represented small numbers of people like the priests. There is no common factor which can be used to identify people groups. There are many factors—such as race, language, religious beliefs, value systems, social class, and many more.

So people groups must be defined in more general terms. The Lausanne Committee for World Evangelism, a global organization that first met in 1972, defines a people group as **"the largest group within which the gospel can spread as a church planting movement without encountering barriers of understanding or acceptance."**[13] It is a very useful definition for doing cross-cultural evangelism.

[13] https://www.google.com/search?q=Laussane+definition+of+people+group&rlz=1C1JZAP_enUS828US828&oq=Laussane+definition+of+people+group&aqs=chrome..69i57.13927j0j7&sourceid=chrome&ie=UTF-8.

This definition emphasizes the things which people share in common—whether it be their ethnicity, language, religion, class, caste, residence, social or legal situation, or any combination of these. The key factor is how the people in the group see themselves! They share a common bond not because outside observers can identify them as part of a certain ethnic, racial, religious, or class group. Regardless of how it came about, they share that bond primarily because they see themselves as members of that group. Members of a people group share a common set of problems, needs, and opportunities. They think of themselves as "we" and others outside their group as "they."

While it is true that people belong to many groups they choose to associate with for specific reasons, we are defining people groups as collections of people to which members feel their strongest allegiance. For instance, one person may belong to a soccer (football) club because of his interest in sports and the local education committee because of his interest in his children's education, but still belong to a specific people group beyond his personal interest, such as the city-dwelling Cantonese speakers of Hong Kong. He feels his primary allegiance is to that Cantonese speaking group. Here are two more examples of people groups:

1. The Bengali-speaking Muslim tenant farmers of Bangladesh and East India (sharing common language, ethnicity, occupation, and economic status)
2. The Spanish-speaking upper-middle-class business and professional people in the urban areas of Mexico (sharing common economic status, language, residence, and nationality)

For our purposes, a people group must be large enough to target for evangelism as a distinct people group. They must neither be too small, such as a sports club, or too large, like a country. A large single family, consisting of extended relatives, fits our definition of a people group. They share many common bonds which are important to them, but they are too small to merit a separate evangelism strategy. On the other hand, choosing to evangelize a whole country like India with a single strategy would be choosing too large and diverse a number of people for a single strategy. India has 2,585 people groups (Joshua Project)! This represents too many people groups for one strategy to be effective. This chapter will show the importance of learning to evangelize people within their own people group!

THE GREAT COMMISSION: A PEOPLE-CENTERED APPROACH

In chapter one, we discovered that cross-cultural evangelism is a fundamental part of the nature of the Church. This truth is clearly demonstrated in the words of Jesus in Matthew 28:19–20, often referred to as the Great Commission. Our ability to comprehend Jesus' command depends upon how we see the world.

We have been trained to see the world much like what appears in figure 2.b. Most of us see the world as a series of nations, states, or territories. According to the Joshua Project, there are some 238 countries in the world representing a population approaching 8 billion people. Countries are made of political boundaries dividing the land masses of the earth. But that is not how God chooses to see the world.

Jesus' disciples understood this reality. After all, there was only the Roman political power in those days, not a lot of countries. That is also why Matthew quoted Jesus as saying, *"Poreuthentes matheteosate panta ta ta ethne"* (in Greek). *"Poreuthentes"* means "You [plural] must go [imperative]." *"Matheteosate"* means "make learners, followers, disciples." *"Panta ta"* means "among every." So the passage means "Go! Make disciples among every *"ethne."*"

"Ethne" has been translated "nations" in many Western languages since the sixteenth and seventeenth centuries. But the word derives from *"ethnos,"* a Greek term meaning "peoples," so a more accurate translation of the meaning of Jesus' words is "Go, make disciples among every people." Down through most of history, the world was divided more by ethnic and tribal boundaries than political ones. With the rapid rise of nationalism in recent centuries, the world has come to be viewed in political terms as represented in Figure 2.b. That is the continent of Africa divided by the "ethne" or "people groups" that live there, each one speaking its own local lan-

guage. It does not show the fifty countries that are in Africa, but just the major tribal divisions that live on that continent. Figure 2.c does not represent just Africa. It represents the whole world! Every country is populated by many people groups, sometimes thousands of them!

Figure 2.b: Africa as Countries

That is how God sees the world. He is the one who divided the people of the world at the Tower of Babel into different people groups, and that is how He has always viewed them ever since (Gen. 11:1–9). Some of these groups could even be further divided into subgroups of more than one people group. These thousands of people groups are separate from one another by their individual cultures—by their different languages, classes, behavior patterns, value systems, religions, and often even by whom they will marry and associate with, and even by the foods they will and will not eat. These people are often more separate from one another than peoples of different countries.

God views the world much closer to what is pictured in figure 2.c than in figure 2.b. That is why the apostle used the word "ethnos"—people group—instead of country. Jesus commanded us to "make disciples among every people." If we are to be faithful and effective cross-cultural evangelists, we must send evangelists to every people, not just every country. Churches must be planted in the mainstream of every people group's society, so every family and individual can have an adequate chance to receive the Gospel of Christ. This book is about the best principles and methods to do exactly that.

JESUS' PLAN TO REACH EVERY PEOPLE

Figure 2.c: Africa as People Groups

Jesus was raised in a relatively remote part of Northern Israel (Galilee) and ministered for only 3.5 years. Yet His goal was to bring the Gospel of the Kingdom to the whole world. He needed to train leaders to carry on His ministry after he ascended into heaven. He did not choose the leaders you and I might have chosen. We would probably want some of them from the area around Jerusalem—perhaps a Pharisee or two, a scribe, and a couple of members of the Sanhedrin. We probably would choose representatives from both Northern and Southern Judea, and maybe an expert in the Greek version of the Scriptures from Alexandria in Egypt. We might also want a well-known Greek philosopher and a politician associated with Roman leaders. If we had chosen the first disciples, we might have wanted a powerful team something like that one!

But that is not how Jesus chose his disciples. He chose His disciples on the basis of their willingness to follow Him and learn from Him. They were all from His own ethnic group, and they were not distinguished from those in their group in any special way. They differed only in their occupations and their positions within their community. What they had in common was the fact that they were willing to follow Jesus full-time, and they were all *Aramaic-speaking Galilean Jews*. They all spoke the same Galilean dialect (Mark 14:70). They all understood one another's behavior patterns. They all shared a mutual way of life. They were culturally from the same ethnos or people group.

It is interesting to note that there was one of Jesus' disciples who was not part of that same ethnos. Judas Iscariot was from the Judean city of Cariot, not Galilee. He was the betrayer of Jesus. After Jesus' resurrection, the disciples asked God to help them choose a disciple to replace Judas. The choice was between Joseph, a Judean, and Matthias, a Galilean. The lot fell on Matthias (Acts 1:23–26). All twelve apostles were Aramaic-speaking Galilean Jews. They were all from the same people group. They were bonded together both spiritually and culturally in their commitment to spread the Gospel. The Lord knew that their cultural bonding would be a good foundation for reaching their own people group, and the peoples of "Jerusalem, Judea, Samaria, and the uttermost parts of the earth" (Acts 1:8).

Jesus was not only people-centered in selecting His disciples, but He was also primarily monocultural in His ministry. He purposely directed His ministry to Galilean Jews. He spent most of His time in ministry in Galilee. When He went to Judea (Jerusalem area), it was in order to fulfill the Jewish law by attending the feasts in Jerusalem. Though much attention is given to His ministry in Judea in the Gospels, the amount of time spent there was small compared to the time spent in the region around the Sea of Galilee.

When Jesus sent out His disciples to learn how to minister, He directed them not to go to the Gentiles or the Samaritans, but only to the "lost sheep of the house of Israel" (Matt. 10:5–6). When Jesus was seeking a rest on the coast of Tyre and Sidon (where the weather is better), He was approached by a local woman seeking deliverance for her demonized daughter (Matt. 15:21–28). Jesus ignored her plea, saying, "I was sent only to the lost sheep of Israel" (verse 24). Even after she knelt in front of Him pleading, Jesus said, "It is not right to take the children's bread and toss it to their dogs." The woman responded humbly, and Jesus answered her, saying, "Woman, you have great faith. Your request is granted." And the daughter was healed at the same time.

This is an amazing account which has troubled many Bible scholars. Was Jesus in the habit of sending away the needy? Was he prejudiced against Gentiles like the other Jews of His day? Some would say that Jesus was simply needing a rest, and to bring healing to the woman's daughter would only invite greater needs to come His way. Others have said Jesus was simply testing her faith. Both are probably true. But the main reason Jesus was reluctant to minister to the woman's need is the reason He gave. He was sent to minister to Israel first, knowing that would be the catalyst to change the world. Even though Jesus was to die for the sins of the whole world, the Father had given Him orders to spend his time in ministry to the Jews.

The only time Jesus purposefully ministered to Gentiles was during the two days He spent in Samaria (John 4:1–43). Even his ministry there was an object lesson against the strong Jewish prejudice toward the Samaritans, as described clearly in chapter one of this book. At other times, when Jesus had the opportunity to minister to Gentiles, He sought to avoid doing so. When the Gentile "God-fearers" (John 12:20) sought an opportunity to meet with Him, Jesus ignored their request. After Jesus healed the Gadarean Demoniac in the Decapolis area bordering the Sea of Galilee (Mark 5:1–20), the man wanted to follow Jesus like others were doing. If Jesus had wanted a great testimony and loyal Gentile follower, this was a perfect opportunity. But He forbade the man to follow him. He told him to go tell his family how much the Lord had done for him.

So we may conclude, by Jesus' words and actions, that Jesus' ministry was primarily directed toward the Jews in general, and the Galileans in particular. Though His works of compassion and healing included many Gentiles, His preaching and teaching ministries were directed primarily toward the "the lost sheep of the house of Israel."

But Jesus did intend to reach the whole world! He knew his time of ministry on earth was limited. He knew he could most effectively do this by building a strong, cohesive group of followers among one people group. Jesus was not an anthropologist, sociologist, or missiologist, but He understood the principles of such fields much better than we do. He built a strong, committed, cohesive group of disciples out of one people group. He taught them how to minister by sending them to their own ethnos. Then He commanded them to "make disciples among every ethnos" (Matt. 28:19). He told them to expand their ministry to the "the uttermost parts of the earth" (Acts 1:8).

In the book of Acts, Luke records the developing stages of the success of the disciples' ever-expanding ministry. First, their ministry to Jerusalem (chapters 1:1 through 6:7), then throughout Palestine and Samaria (6:8 through 9:32), then its extension to Antioch and other Hellenist centers (9:32 through 12:24), then Asia Minor (12:25 through 16:5), Europe (16:6 through 19:20), and finally Rome (19:21 through 28:31).

The disciples were successful in their cross-cultural evangelism because of cohesion and commitment. Their ability to travel freely throughout the Roman Empire was also a factor. Most importantly was the power of the Gospel to change lives when demonstrated in their ministries. They were successful because they followed the pattern that Jesus Himself had established. They established the Church among their own people first, but they were also compelled to reach other peoples with the Gospel. They sent teams of evangelists across cultural, racial, and linguistic boundaries, establishing churches among other groups of peoples. And they taught those churches to help send missionary teams to other peoples. We don't even know the names of most of these cross-cultural evangelists. But we do know that they were very effective because "all the Jews and Greeks who lived in the Province of Asia heard the word of the Lord" (Acts 19:10). Even their enemies proclaimed they had "turned the world upside down" with the Gospel (Acts 17:6).

A TYPOLOGY OF EVANGELISM

Our world is much more complex than the world of the believers in the early Church. There are more countries, more languages, and more people groups today than when the early Church was so effective in cross-cultural evangelism. They required no passports or visas, and Greek was a common language acceptable to many peoples. But that was only in the Roman world. Today we know there are more people groups than there were in that part of the world at that time. There are also far greater distances between peoples—politically, geographically, and culturally. If we are to be effective cross-cultural evangelists, we must learn all we can about those differences, and how to overcome the barriers they represent to the effective communication of the Gospel.

It is very important to understand the concept of cultural distance—how much one culture is different from another. We know it is much more difficult for a Malayalam-speaking Christian from Southern India to evangelize a Hindi-speaking countryman in Northern India than it is to evangelize people in his own culture. But it would be even more difficult for that evangelist to effectively reach the farmers of Japan. *The greater the cultural distance, the greater is the difficulty in evangelizing other peoples.* We need to classify evangelism according to cultural distance.

E-O Evangelism is evangelistic ministry without any cultural barriers—no cultural distance at all between the evangelist and those who receive his message. This is real born-again Christians winning nominal Christians—those who are Christian in name only. E-O evangelism is winning other church members who have not yet accepted Christ as Lord and Savior.

E-1 Evangelism is winning other members of the evangelist's own culture who do not profess to be believers. It may be secular humanists, atheists, or members of a religious sect that do not preach Jesus Christ as Lord and Savior of the world. The culture and language are the same, but the religious beliefs do not conform to biblical truth.

E-2 Evangelism is winning people to Christ who are in another but similar culture. Their culture is not the same as the evangelist's culture, but it may be close. The culture being targeted may or may not speak the same language as the evangelist, but there is a significant difference between their cultures. An example in the Bible is the Samaritans. Like the Jews, they spoke Aramaic, but there were great historical and cultural prejudices between the two groups of people (John 4:9). They did not want to associate with each other. So when Phillip began a revival among the Samaritans, he was doing E-2 evangelism (Acts 8:4–8). Another example of E-2 evangelism in the Bible is when the Hellenist Jews began to start churches among the Greeks (Acts 11:20) as we discussed in chapter one. They crossed a barrier of great religious and racial prejudice to win the Greeks, and they did so in a language other than their historical mother tongue. E-2 evangelism is cross-cultural evangelism. When the language and/or cultural barriers are great enough to require a separate church among the evangelized people, it is cross-cultural evangelism. Most of the specific instances of cross-cultural evangelism recorded in the Bible are E-2 evangelism.

E-3 Evangelism is winning people in another far different culture. This distance is not necessarily geographical, but it is definitely cultural. There is no cultural similarity between the evangelist and the people he/she is trying to evangelize. The language and culture are much different, and the evangelist must take the time to learn it. When a Korean goes to win Batak Indonesians to Christ, it is E-3 cross-cultural evangelism. When a Singaporean goes to Africa to evangelize Turkana tribesmen, he is doing E-3 evangelism. But so is a Brazilian who plants a church among recent immigrants to Brazil from Japan! The key factor is cultural distance, not geographical distance.

E-3 evangelism is considered unnecessary by some people, but it is actually very important. Some people think that evangelizing a certain people group or region of the world is solely the responsibility of the Christians in that part of the world. They reason that since they are culturally and geographically closer to those peoples, and may even be able to learn their languages easier, they are the ones who should evangelize the people there. There is some validity to that way of thinking because historically, that is the way the Gospel has spread most. Most cross-cultural evangelism has resulted from the spread of the Gospel to nearby cultures. Language and cultural barriers to the Gospel may be less difficult to cross than they would be if the evangelists go to distant language groups.

On the other hand, there are three important reasons for us all to feel personal responsibility for other parts of the world: (1) Jesus commanded us to carry the Gospel to "the uttermost parts of the earth" (Acts 1:8). Since this was the last instruction He gave us while He was on the earth, it is safe to say that it is very important. (2) E-2 evangelism may be less effective than E-3 evangelism among some groups of people. Local Christians can face great cultural and racial prejudices in trying to reach other peoples of their own region. For example, the Christians who live in the Middle East right next door to Muslims may be the least likely to reach them due to centuries of animosity and fighting between their cultures. A North American might more effectively evangelize the Indian tribes of Paraguay than a Spanish-speaking Paraguayan believer because of the animosity which has built up between the Indian tribes and the Spanish-speaking majority there. (3) Some regions of the world have very few real Christians compared to the number of unreached groups there. It is only fair that Christians from other parts of the world share the responsibility for spreading the Gospel to such regions. The Middle East, North Africa, and Northern India are examples of regions of the world where an effort from Christians around the world should be harnessed to help evangelize the many people groups there.

E-2 and E-3 evangelism are both cross-cultural evangelism. Their importance becomes clearer when we realize that 30 to 40 percent of the non-Christian world lives at E-2 or E-3 cultural distances from existing Christians. We will discuss this further later in this chapter. The important fact to realize is that the greatest single need in training Christian workers is the need to train and send many, many thousands of cross-cultural evangelists to plant the Church of Jesus Christ in E-2 and E-3 cultures.

ONE PEOPLE AT A TIME

Since it is necessary for the Church to engage in cross-cultural ministry in order to reach as much as 40 percent of the non-Christian world, and the task seems so large, one may be tempted to ask, "How can this be done?" The answer sounds deceptively simple—*one people at a time*! But it also calls attention to the fact that cross-cultural evangelism is very complex. It recognizes that every people group is unique. It admits that trying to evangelize all groups of people with the same strategy, methods, and forms of communication is like trying to catch butterflies with a fishing hook. Reaching one people group at a time helps the cross-cultural evangelist avoid some common mistakes, and helps to make his work fruitful.

Standard Strategy Approach: This approach assumes that the same strategy which is used in one place successfully will work in another. For example, one North American group launched a "Scripture distribution" program in Pakistan. In some of the cities or areas of the country, every home listed in the telephone directory was to receive a copy of the New Testament in the Urdu language. By the time the packages arrived in the post office, some of the addresses had changed. Others refused to accept the gifts they had not asked to receive. When word went around that it was Christian propaganda, tons of Scriptures were being stacked up in post offices and eventually auctioned off as "wastepaper." In Muslim countries, great respect is attached to the Koran, their Scriptures, and even to other scriptures like the Bible. The Muslims were horrified to see the pages of the Bible glued together and being used as paper bags for selling merchandise in the markets! While some people no doubt appreciated the gift, the impact on society as a whole was very negative. The Muslims could not understand how the Christians could allow the mass desecration of their Holy Book. It caused more disrespect for Christians and Christianity. And it turned many away from the Christian message.

Since there are some strategies which are very effective among more than one group of people, this sometimes causes believers to make those strategies standard or even almost sacred. This is dangerous because it makes the unbelievers responsible to decipher the Gospel message across many boundaries and impediments. Instead, it should be the responsibility of those who proclaim the Gospel to present it in such a way that it is understandable and positive in the minds of the ones who hear it. It should not be allowed to be an injection into the souls of unbelievers that creates a negative reaction to the Gospel like the Bible distribution in Pakistan.

As another example, mass media has spread around the world in many forms. Television, radio, and print media are being replaced by the Internet, cell phones, YouTube, Facebook, and on-demand content. In many countries of the world, telephone landlines have traditionally been too difficult and costly to install and maintain. Only the rich could afford them. Even if they could, copper wires were often stolen, or bribes had to be paid to keep your line. Now, in most countries of the world, cell phones are available even in villages without electricity and are solar powered. Major cities around the world often have almost as many cell phones as people! Increasingly, those and similar devices are capable of downloading person-to-person content, news, TV shows, movies, and advertising in remote parts of the world. And they are increasingly affordable. As mass communication proliferates around the world and more people use English, it is tempting to assume that the Gospel can be spread using English and these tools so that the whole world will be reached with the Gospel. *Nothing could be further from the truth!* As valuable as those tools can be in spreading the Gospel, the barriers of language and culture will enable such tools to reach only a small percentage of the unreached people groups in the world! As this book will explain clearly, the Gospel only lives and spreads effectively when it resides in the mainstream of each culture and language. That cannot happen simply through the use of mass media.

While there is no standard strategy for reaching all people, ***we are convinced there can be a standard approach for devising specific strategies to evangelize each people group***. The strategies will be very different, but the principles and methods for finding those strategies can be the same. That will be the subject of most of this book.

Standard Forms Approach: Evangelizing one people at a time also helps us to avoid many common errors in communication. Each group of people develops a code of symbols, both spoken and unspoken, by which they communicate what they mean to be understood. They do this with language and nonverbal forms of communication. A wink of the eye, shrug of the shoulders, the way a word is spoken—all are indicators of meaning. They are the kinds of forms which make up the communication codes and symbols of a people.

In cross-cultural evangelism, there are two levels where the Standard Forms Approach can cause problems. The first level is commonly understood. People going to another culture quickly learn that there are certain gestures which they may make in their own cultures which must be avoided because they mean something entirely different in their target culture. Their own forms of gestures, body language, and facial expressions cannot be standardized. Even the translation of one word from their own language into the target language may not carry the same positive meaning it did in their own language. They must adapt to the forms (language and otherwise) of the host culture if they hope to be correctly understood.

There is a deeper level where the Standard Forms Approach is a great hindrance to effective cross-cultural evangelism. It is at the level of *standardized methods* of communication. Different peoples not only learn to accept differing methods for conveying their symbols of communication, but they also learn to *value* some methods more than others. Anthropologists know it is not just words and gestures that become accepted forms of communication. Cultural values cause a people group to place more importance on different forms and symbols more than they do on other ones. Some methods become an accepted and highly valued form of communication in and of themselves. Singing, folk dancing, poetry, chanting, and art are examples. They can be highly complex and highly valued means for communicating heartfelt meanings for a people group. For instance, many Muslim cultures highly value poetry, but think of singing as worldly. Yet, as we shall see later, the Motilone tribe of Colombia highly values singing, using it as a means of communicating their most important messages.

The danger to the cross-cultural evangelist lies in confusing the forms with the meanings they communicate. This is discussed in depth in chapter four. The key is to realize that forms of communicating do not equal meanings. They only are symbols of meaning. For instance, there is nothing closer to the heart of a people group than the forms they use to worship God. One people may emphasize collective group worship in which the people shout praises to God all together and sometimes *loudly*. They cannot understand one another, but they are very intense in expressing their innermost feelings toward God. In another culture, the people may believe the same doctrines and go to the same kind of church, but they might worship with everyone remaining silent while one person at a time expresses praise to God on behalf of the whole group. Everyone understands and joins their hearts with the worship of the one speaking. This is an example of two different cultures which use two different forms of worship to express the same meaning—their true heartfelt adoration of God. Each form is equally valid and pleases God because the worship in both cases comes from the people's hearts. No form is superior to the other.

Each culture has accepted forms for spiritual worship, teaching, singing (or not), and many other ways of conveying spiritual meaning. The successful cross-cultural evangelist will be careful not to force the people of another culture to use the forms for communicating spiritual meaning which are acceptable in his own culture. The target people must be free to use or develop their own forms.

Nationalistic Worldview: The twentieth century was one of nationalism. The people of each country which has become independent experienced a movement toward national unity among its peoples which helped bring that independence. Independence is the proper right of every country. But nationalism is also a mixed blessing. After independence, many governments realized they must keep their country unified for the common good of the nation. This is done by continually fanning the flames of nationalistic zeal. The things that all the people share in common are emphasized. The differences between the country's peoples are downplayed by the government, the schools, and even the religious institutions. A national language is adopted. The needs of the nation are to be pursued more than the needs of one's own people group and language group. There is always a dominant culture, and the needs and rights of minority peoples in the country are minimized and given less attention. After a generation or so, the members of the dominant culture begin to put pressure on members of minority cultures to become assimilated into the majority's way of life. This is often resented by minority cultures, and may cause them to withdraw into their own cultures even further. These "nativistic movements" (movements back toward their historic language and culture) only increase tensions, and the dominant culture may even pass laws that discriminate heavily against minority cultures.

Our purpose here is not to speak against nationalism. It is a necessary part of each country's special identity and is not going away anytime soon. But nationalism blurs the lines of distinctions between people groups. Cross-cultural evangelists who are trained and educated in strongly nationalistic countries will have to work hard to cast off any cultural prejudices and assumptions about people groups other than their own. They will have to work hard on how to see the people to whom God calls them as valuable before God, culture, and all! They will have to learn to value their target culture and its people as much as God does without a desire to change the culture themselves. They will have to trust God to change the culture to be more biblical, not necessarily to be more like the national culture or their own culture. They must learn to gain the trust and respect of the peoples God sends them to evangelize by being respectful of the culture of those peoples. The cross-cultural evangelist can never allow nationalistic pride or feelings of cultural superiority to rob him or her of being an effective witness. The effective cross-cultural evangelist will learn to clearly identify target people groups, make special strategies to reach those groups, and target one people group at a time. The degree to which they are able to genuinely love and respect the people group to which they are called will determine how successful their efforts will be.

THE HOMOGENEOUS UNIT PRINCIPLE

It is obvious that all people share a common humanity. Beyond obvious external differences like language, clothing, and customs, people share a lot of things in common the world over. Human needs such as the struggle for security and happiness are priorities in every culture. But human emotions such as anger, pride, and self-righteousness are also common problems among every people. Because of this commonness, and sometimes because of other forces such as nationalism, the differences which exist between peoples around the world are considered small and unimportant.

It is a great mistake to minimize cultural differences. Basic human needs and emotions are universal, but which ones are most important at any given time, and how they will be dealt with varies from culture to culture to culture. The thousands of cultures making up humanity have each established their own systems for dealing with life and ways of looking at the world in which they live. This system of values and behavior that results—this lifeway of each people—is what makes their culture unique and special.

Peoples of different cultures will interact with each other very willingly in some areas, such as business, politics, and sports. But religion touches the very deepest parts of their lives. It deals with the basic way they see the world. *People like to become Christians without crossing racial, linguistic, or class barriers*. This important truth is called the **Homogeneous Unit Principle**.[14] It is the basic reason why it is important to reach the whole world *one people at a time*! People do not like to cross cultural barriers to accept Christ. What does this mean in practice?

The Homogeneous Unit Principle recognizes that people do not exist simply as individuals, but as interconnected members of groups of people. These groups of people give allegiance to one another, and form patterns of mutually acceptable behavior. Some of these homogeneous units (HUs) of people come together on the basis of biological factors, such as race, sex, age, and kinship. Other groups are based more on locality, cultural, economic, or socio-personal factors as shown in figure 2.d.

Figure 2.d Classification of Homogeneous Units

BIOLOGICAL	CULTURAL	LOCALITY	ECONOMIC	SOCIOCULTURAL
RACE	LANGUAGE	ORIGIN	PROFESSION	HOBBIES
AGE	CLASS	RESIDENCE	EARNINGS	SPORTS
SEX	NATIONALITY	PLACE OF WORK	TRADE	CLUBS
KINSHIP	ETHNIC NORMS	PLACE OF STUDY	FAMILY STATUS	SERVICE GROUPS

Those factors which are to the left of the chart in figure 2.d are generally more important than those factors toward the right. Race

14 https://www.lausanne.org/content/lop/lop-1.

and ethnicity are more important than profession and hobbies in determining the homogeneous groups to which people give their loyalties. People groups are homogeneous units which are large enough to require a specific strategy for evangelization.

Picture a tent "crusade" in a typical Latin American city. The city has several million people making up a number of people groups. There is a Spanish-speaking business and professional class group. There is a lower-middle-class Spanish-speaking group of factory workers and day laborers. There are groups of local indigenous tribes called Indians in Latin America who are struggling to survive in the city. Most of the people of the city understand Spanish, except the Indians use it as a second language to get around and buy things. They do not speak it at home, and they do not speak it well.

The meetings in the stadium last three weeks. Many people are saved, and those responsible for the meetings rejoice as they are continued in local churches where attendance is swelling. Sixty-seven percent of those saved in the crusade were from the lower-middle-class factory workers and day laborers. Twenty percent of those saved were from the lower-class Spanish-speaking group, most of whom had recently arrived in the city from the farms and ranches. They were still trying to find jobs, and survived in shanty towns growing in the steep hills surrounding the city. Ten percent of those saved were middle-class Spanish-speaking small business people. Three percent of those saved were from three different indigenous Indian tribes. Spanish was their second language, and they were the few among the large Indian population who reached out to embrace the hope of the Gospel. During and after the crusade, all the converts were given instruction—both at the stadium and in the churches. But it was all in Spanish.

One year after the meetings in the stadium, only thirty-two percent of the converts were still in church and serving God. More amazingly, almost every single one of those who remained were from the lower-middle-class factory workers and day laborers group of people. Only a handful of middle-class businessmen, and one or two from the lower class remained in the church. No business- and professional-class people and no tribal people remained in any of the churches. Why was this?

The problem was not spiritual. It was the sociological realities of the Homogeneous Unit Principle. The churches were almost entirely made up of the same Spanish-speaking lower-middle-class people group as the converts who remained in the churches a year later! Those who remained could relate well to that group, and they felt like they were accepted among their own kind of people.

The lower class, the professional class, and the Indian people groups all stopped attending the churches shortly after the crusade meetings were over. Even though they were the most eager from their groups to try to live for God, and even though they were ready for change as city dwellers, they could not relate well enough to stay in the churches.

Let's analyze what happened a little more closely by taking the example of the converts from the three Indian tribe people groups. One tribe was rather large, and made up 12 percent of the population of the city. Another made up 7 percent, and another 2 percent. Twenty-one percent of the population of the entire city was made up of people from the three Indian people groups. Yet, even though the crusade was very well-accepted in the culture and there were many converts, only 3 percent of them were willing to try to cross the racial, linguistic, and cultural barriers to accept Christ. But even those 3 percent were unable to cope with the demands of trying to fit in with the people of the churches who were almost completely in the lower-middle-class Spanish-speaking part of the society. Those problems were even greater because the Indians felt like the Spanish-speaking majority had a history of not treating their people well. This demonstrates how the Homogeneous Unit Principle is true. It is not about spirituality so much as it is about culture!

What should have been done to reach those people groups who were not like the people in the churches? Jesus said, "Go, make disciples among every 'ethnos' [people group]." Disciples are not made until people accept Christ AND they also decide to serve Him in the fellowship of a church body! There should have been plans made to start churches among those other people groups. There should have been a new church or churches for each of the three Indian tribes. A new fellowship of believers should have been started for each people group in the city! If the converts in the evangelistic outreach wanted to join the older existing churches, they should have been allowed to do so. But they should have first been given an opportunity to worship and learn to serve God in a church among their own kind of people. They would have felt comfortable there, and most of them would still be in churches serving God!

As important as starting churches for each people group in the meetings is, it is even more important to realize that it would allow the new converts to reach out freely to others in their own groups and win them to the Lord much more quickly and effectively. This illustrates the need to plant churches in the mainstream of every people group. It is the only effective way to win the world for Christ. To do anything less will mean that there will be many millions of people who will never have an adequate opportunity to know and serve Christ as Savior and Lord.

There are some who would say this kind of teaching is against the unity of the Church. They would argue that God wants all kinds of people in His Church, not just a lot of different kinds of churches. We would agree that God does want all kinds of people in His Church. But the basis for Christian unity is spiritual, not physical closeness. God wants every church to open its doors to peoples of all races and classes. That should be the attitude of every maturing church. But God especially wants all people to be saved (2 Pet. 3:9). People will be saved in far greater numbers when the Gospel is proclaimed in a way and in a language that is designed specifically for their own people group. More importantly, such a strategy will include starting new churches in the mainstream of their own people group so converts can effectively evangelize the rest of their own people. As different churches are planted among many people groups, they will eventually mature and desire to work together in true spiritual unity. The Church as a whole expands much more rapidly this way, and is much more on fire with faith and service for the Lord.

Advantages of a People-Centered Approach: The people-centered approach to evangelism is a new idea to many people.

But it is a much more effective way to obey the Great Commission (Matt. 28:19–20). Here are some of the benefits of people-centered cross-cultural ministry:

1. It best fulfills Christ's command to make disciples among every *ethnos*.
2. It places the responsibility for effectively communicating the Gospel message onto the evangelist. His success is measured not in how many hear the message or how many times he proclaims the Gospel. It is measured by how many actually become disciples and serve God!
3. It gives respect and validity to each group of people and their culture.
4. It wins many more people to Christ, and establishes many more churches in a shorter period of time.
5. It does not pressure people to forsake their own family, tribe, or people group in order to serve God.
6. It emphasizes God's way of seeing the world. Figure 2.c becomes the model for seeing the world, not figure 2.b. Cultural boundaries become more important than political boundaries.
7. It makes strategies for cross-cultural evangelism much more clear and specific, and therefore much more effective. It defines the overall task as cross-cultural ministry.
8. It changes the emphasis of the Church's responsibility to a much more biblical pattern. The Church is not just in the business of sending evangelists. It is to be in the business of making disciples among all peoples. So churches must make sure those evangelists are well trained and that they are making disciples and starting new churches among unreached people groups.
9. Reaching specific groups of people is a good example to other churches, both among our own people and among other peoples. The people-centered approach, when practiced by one group of churches, should be successful

enough to encourage other groups of churches to follow the same approach.

10. It aids the Church in prayer for world evangelization. Prayer for specific people groups is inspiring and effective. It is also in prayer where God calls people to reach specific people groups.

TO EVERY PEOPLE: THE OPPORTUNITY AND THE CHALLENGE

Rupal is a bright young boy from a middle-class family in Central India. He lives in the state of Madhya Pradesh in the district of Shivapuri. We won't mention the exact location. He is more fortunate than most people in his area because his father works in a Bata shoe factory and makes a steady income. Rupal has two sisters and one brother. He is the oldest at fourteen years and studying very hard to gain an opportunity to go to the university. As the oldest child, he is duty bound to become successful, help his family, and help take care of his parents when they are old.

But Rupal has such a good mind, and he is curious about many things. He loves to learn. He still has nightmares about the time his oldest sister died when they were in the village six years ago. Her name was Chumki. Her fever had risen higher and higher every day. Ama (his mother) became increasingly fearful day by day. Finally, it was determined that a homeopathic doctor should come to help Chumki. The doctor insisted that he had a powerful potion that Chumki should drink, but that it must be diluted because it was so strong. So he went through a process of pouring a very dark liquid into one container after another full of nothing but water. Then he told Chumki to drink as much of it as she could drink. She did. She was soon bent over in extreme pain while the doctor said it was normal. Late into the night she moaned in agony and she died early the next morning. That was the beginning of Rupal's nightmares.

Rupal's father worked long hours, and Rupal became restless in the evenings. When he could no longer stand studying, he would sometimes visit a tea shop near their home. Sometimes he would meet friends, but sometimes he would go to have tea and simply think to himself. One day there was a group in a nearby street greenbelt playing a tawbla (drum) and other instruments while they sang some melodious, rhythmic, and appealing music. Rupal moved closer to listen. They were singing some interesting and happy music about "Jishu." Rupal was familiar with many kinds of religious music because he had been in many *pujas* extolling the importance of worshipping various gods with accompanying Hindu religious ceremonies. But this music was different. It had more beautiful and popular sounds than religious ritual. It had some interesting words and a catchy tune. It drew Rupal closer to listen.

They were not singing about rituals to perform, but about freedom to be found in *Jishu* (Jesus). The appealing music was more like a ballad, and it told an extraordinary story. All Hindus know they are sinful, but there is little hope to assuage their guilt using all their rituals. This song proclaimed freedom from guilt because of the God Jishu who rid people of guilt. The song said He was the only perfect guiltless person to ever live, and was therefore a sacrifice for the sins of everyone. It only took one time, and that is why He died on the cross. It was a final payment for sin before the creator God Isshor, the One who made the universe. It was a beautiful song with a taunting melody and beat.

They were singing in Rupal's language with common words, and it prompted Rupal to draw close and listen. After a few songs, a man stood up to talk to everyone. He told how he was born and raised in the Kolkata area of Bengal, and grew up speaking Bengali, not Rupal's language. Yet he spoke Rupal's language fluently just like everyone else. That interested Rupal a lot, so he stayed to listen to what he was saying about his own life. He talked about being born to a prostitute in Kolkata, living in horrible conditions in the city for years before being rescued by someone who told him about *Jishu.* He testified to the changes it had brought to his life. Rupal immediately started to leave because this man was so low caste. But he decided to stay a little while because his words were powerful and his voice was very appealing. It sounded wonderful! Rupal was even more amazed that this man testified that it was Jishu who had told him to move to his area and live there so he could tell others about *this new life he had found*. He told how he had worked hard to survive and learn the new language. He also told how God had helped him so many times that a deep-settled peace had invaded his soul and given him courage to sing and tell others what he had learned.

Peace, thought Rupal! Is it really possible to have peace? He remembered the many times he had participated in religious *pujas* and how everyone was doing everything they could to bring peace and prosperity to themselves and their loved ones. But all it had ever produced inside Rupal's heart was an incessant fear that he could never get the peace he wanted. Could *Jishu* really provide that? Rupal decided to stay longer.

Timidly, Rupal even stayed after the meeting was over to ask these singers and the speaker more questions. They invited him to a meeting they were going to have in a home that Saturday. Rupal found a way to be there, and he kept going. Eventually, he accepted *Jishu* as his only Lord and Savior of his soul.

Rupal's family saw the difference in his life. He obtained a New Testament in his own language and began to study it. The family at first thought he was simply preparing for exams. But eventually they saw it was a religious manual, and they questioned him about it. Rupal's father recognized that it was the Scripture of Christians, and he became furious. But when he cooled down, the change in Rupal was so appealing that he began to ask him questions. Over time, the father, the immediate family, and the extended relatives—almost all of them became believers and worshipped together with others in their own home. They also learned some of the songs from the other believers. They sang songs like:

Such sadness filled my darkened heart
I found no peace living in fear
But Jishu's love has filled my heart
Praise Isshor! He's my savior forever!

There are now about forty-five house meetings of believers in Rupal's town and the surrounding villages. Most of the people there regularly are believers in *Jishu*. Their friends and relatives are joining these meetings in ever-increasing numbers. Once every three months, they rent a building in the town and have a celebration of their faith. Hindu priests and dignitaries are not happy, but they tolerate it because they have become so well-liked in the community that nobody can speak against them. They do so much to help others and seem so happy that a lot of people envy them, including the community leaders, though they cannot let many people know it!

As more and more people turned to following the teachings of *Jishu*, the cross-cultural evangelist who came from the Kolkata region spoke less and let Rupal take the lead in speaking to the group, especially in the larger meetings. The evangelist simply led the joyous and delightful music and singing.

Every people group is our challenge! The real name of the man from Kolkata is not named here on purpose. Neither is the exact place all this took place. So we will call him Rupom. He was a cross-cultural evangelist who did his job for the Lord very effectively and had much fruit in what could have been a hostile environment. God helped him greatly.

There are literally thousands of people groups without churches existing within their culture enough that they can have an adequate chance to hear the Gospel in their own language in a manner they can receive and in the mainstream of their own culture! According to the Joshua Project, there are 17,072 people groups in the world who require their own churches in their own language. They list 7,142 such groups as Unreached Groups. Of the total of 2,585 people groups in India, it is estimated that 2,290 people groups with a population over 1.2 billion are still listed as Unreached.[15]

15 https://www.southasiapeoples.org/listing?data_type=rog3&data_value=IN

That means over one billion people like those in Rupal's village will never have an adequate chance to know Christ unless someone like Rupom leaves his own culture and goes to those locations, learns another language, and exhibits the love of Christ while proclaiming the Gospel. That means each one of us has a responsibility to do something to see this need to spread the Gospel to every people group succeed. And it needs to happen in our lifetime! It can be done! It is not fair that the Gospel be proclaimed among the people and cultures of our own nation however successfully, unless we are all active in some manner to be sure it is also proclaimed among unreached peoples. Jesus said that would happen before He returns to earth (Matt. 24:14). That means it is a priority to Him and it must be to us also. So we must understand this task in its global terms first.

So first, we should talk about what it means to be a "reached" people group. By our definition above, reached peoples are those which have enough Christian believers who live in the mainstream (not the fringes) of their own societies that they can reasonably be expected to tell others about Christ in their own language and in the heart of their own cultures. Almost 10,000 such reached people groups exist, representing some 58.5 percent of the world's 7.6 billion people (2019).[16] That means 3.187 billion people live in countries and cultures where very few, if any people, identify themselves as evangelical Christians—people who believe and follow the Bible as the authoritative Word of God. These unreached groups are often called Frontier Peoples, or people groups who will never have a chance to know Christ without significant cross-cultural ministry carried out by believers from other cultures.

Among the 7,110 unreached people groups around the world, approximately 5,044 groups having 1.941 billion people have fewer than 0.1 percent who are Christians. The focus of this book will concentrate on the needs of the 25.0 percent of the world population who truly require pioneer cross-cultural ministry and are the least reached people groups of all.[17]

---

16 https://joshuaproject.net/

17 https://joshuaproject.net/frontier

Figure 2.e[18]

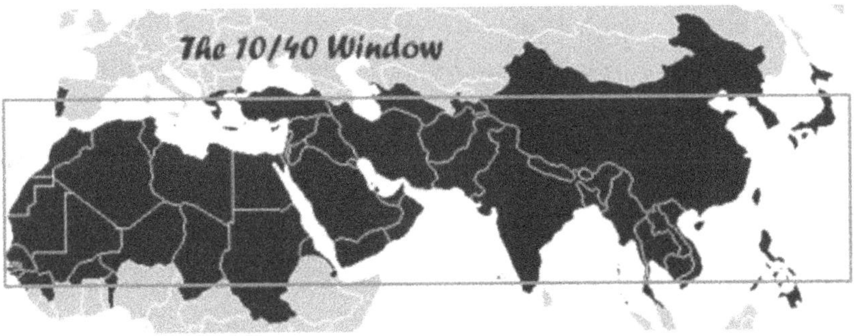

These are the countries in the world that are the least reached and almost entirely need pioneer cross-cultural ministers to plant churches in the mainstream of their cultures. Most of the unreached people groups of the world live in these countries. They are listed below, together with two numbers each. The first number represents the number of unreached people groups in that country according to the Joshua Project. The second number after each "/" is the total number of people groups in that country:[19]

Afghanistan, 67/72; Albania, 3/16; Algeria, 36/40; Azerbaijan, 24/38; Bahrain, 7/16; Bangladesh, 291/323; Benin, 13/63; Bhutan, 71/74; Brunei, 8/24; Burkina Faso, 27/81; Cambodia, 31/43; Chad, 77/141; China, 445/545; China: Hong Kong, 10/24; China: Macau, 5/12; Djibouti, 7/11; East Timor, 0/23; Egypt, 25/42; Eritrea, 10/18; Ethiopia, 34/123; Gambia, 16/30; Guinea, 30/48; Guinea-Bissau, 19/35; India, 2,311/2,585; Indonesia, 234/785; Iran, 85/95; Iraq, 25/35; Israel, 23/105; Japan, 23/36; Jordan, 13/20; Kazakhstan, 31/66; Korea (North), 2/5; Korea (South), 11/23; Kuwait, 13/28; Kyrgyzstan, 26/41; Laos, 109/128; Lebanon, 8/26; Libya, 30/43; Malaysia, 79/183; Maldives, 4/4; Mali, 45/74; Mauritania, 15/19; Mongolia, 23/29; Morocco, 27/31; Myanmar (Burma), 50/145; Nepal, 267/275; Niger, 29/37; Nigeria, 89/541; Oman, 26/34;

[18] http://Joshuaproject.net/resources/articles/10_40_window

[19] https://joshuaproject.net/filter.

Pakistan, 414/422; Qatar, 13/24; Saudi Arabia, 28/44; Senegal, 26/56; Somalia, 20/22; Sri Lanka, 78/173; Sudan, 130/162; Syria, 17/36; Taiwan, 9/36; Tajikistan, 24/41; Thailand, 79/114; Tunisia, 12/14; Turkey, 45/68; Turkmenistan, 21/38; United Arab Emirates, 27/32; Uzbekistan, 34/61; Vietnam, 67/118; West Bank-Gaza, 8/20; Western Sahara, 10/10; Yemen, 20/29.

In listing these countries, there are some things we must remember:

1. These are the seventy countries of the "10–40 Window." They lie mostly within the ten degrees to forty degrees north latitude of the eastern section of the globe. The majority of the people on earth live in these countries. It is also the location of the vast majority of unreached peoples, most of whom are Muslim, Hindu, Buddhist, or materialist in their faith. (Materialism is a faith.)
2. These are countries, consisting of people groups, which are our target for cross-cultural ministry. Each country may have hundreds or thousands (like India) of people groups. Sending people to evangelize people groups is not the same and is more effective than sending them to evangelize countries.
3. Not all the people groups in these countries are unreached. There are a total of 8,678 people groups in all the countries of the 10–40 Window. Of those, a total of 2,742 (31.6 percent) are considered reached, and we should praise the Lord for that. But there are still 5,936 people groups (68.4 percent) that are considered unreached. That should be our primary focus—those 5,936 unreached peoples representing more than 2.2 billion people.
4. There are still 1,165 unreached people groups who live outside the 10-40 Window representing approximately 580 million people who also need an adequate opportunity to know Christ. They should not be neglected as laborers are sent into the harvest fields of the world.

So let's get personal for a moment. What if you were the Holy Spirit who functions on earth right now as "the Lord of the Harvest?" If You were directing those who belong to You (Christ followers) to evangelize those who do not know You, to which cultures would you send them? To cultures who have already heard the Gospel many times, or to those cultures which still have never had an adequate chance to know Christ? Exactly! You would send them to the unreached! So if we are really listening to the Holy Spirit to direct our lives, is it not reasonable to assume that He would send many more of us to the unreached than have gone already? That is where there is the greatest need!

If evangelizing these cultures were easy to do, most of it would be done already! It is not always easy, and it takes a long-term commitment and sacrifice. And a lot of faith! The Holy Spirit will never make you personally responsible for reaching all those unreached people groups. But He might make you responsible to evangelize one of them! If enough of us obey that call when He gives it, the world can have an adequate chance to know Jesus personally during most of our lifetimes! This book is written for those who have enough faith to actually commit themselves to that purpose. It is written not as an academic exercise, but as a practical manual for learning how to do it—and do it well!

When are unreached people reached? There have been a number of international meetings around the world where evangelical Christian leaders came together to answer that question and make plans to reach the unreached. The first in modern history was sponsored by the Billy Graham Association and was held in Lausanne, Switzerland, in 1974. The second was in Manila, Philippines, in 1989. Those two came to be known as the Lausanne Congress I and II. There have been a number of similar congresses regionally and internationally around the world since that time, but those two congresses did a good job of defining the principles surrounding the remaining tasks of world evangelism. The seminal documents and declarations surrounding the surge in world evangelism that has occurred in the decades since that time are available online under those names. Representatives from almost every country attended the meetings. The reader is invited to investigate their results if a deeper or academic perspective is desired.

Before moving on to practical instruction concerning this task, it is important to encourage you with an important sociological principle that makes our task less daunting. It is a simple but important principle from the *diffusion of innovation theory*.[20] Figure 2.f illustrates this theory which was first developed by E. M. Rogers.

Figure 2.f: Diffusion of Innovation

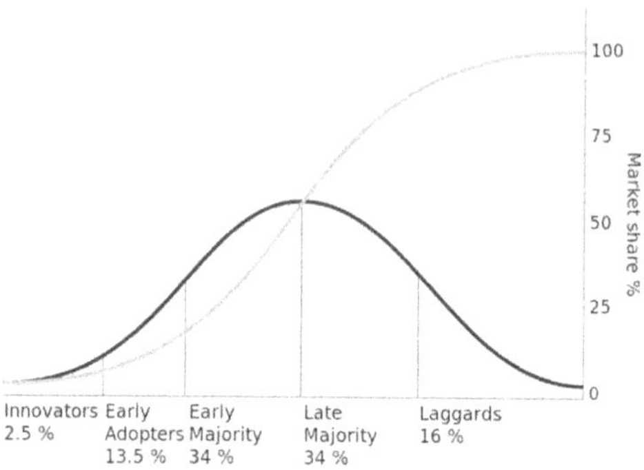

Rogers's theory has been proven to be correct in terms of adopting changes in business markets and a host of other innovations. Anytime there is an innovative product or way of doing something in a society, there are innovators, early adopters, majority adopters, and so on until the change grows rapidly toward full acceptance by the population. These studies were concerned with the amount of time and input required to bring change to a whole society. It does not matter if the efforts are focused on introducing new farming methods, new types of medical care, or a new religion into a society, the pattern of accepting that change by the population is the same. Acceptance follows an S-curve pattern (see figure 2.g).

The blue (darker) line represents the people who bring the change to the population. The gold (lighter) line represents the members of the population who adopt the change introduced into their society. In order to introduce a new kind of health care—birth control, for example—a lot of health-care workers, clinics, and equipment would be needed at first in order to show the benefits of the medical innovation. At first, people would resist the change due to tradition, religion, fear, and other factors. But if the health-care workers are successful, they will eventually convince some brave people to try the new system. These are the innovators.

If the results of their efforts to adopt the change cause no harm and show benefit to the adopters, then more and more people will

[20] https://en.m.wikipedia.org/wiki/Diffusion_of_innovations.

also try the change themselves. These are the early adopters. After a short time period, the majority of the population quickly adopts the birth control innovations. At that point, the inputs (dark line) can dramatically decline, and the innovation will still be rapidly adopted by all or most of the population.

This is also true when analyzing the people who come to Christ within a people group. There are innovators, who initiate the movement toward Christ, and early adopters, who follow their lead until the majority of the population begins to see the benefits, and the population adopts the Gospel message rapidly and in large numbers.

There is an important point in evangelizing a people group to which we must pay attention. When 15 to 20 percent of a population willingly accept Christ as Savior, then much of the rest of the population will rapidly follow them and do the same. This will continue rapidly until 80 to 90 percent, or in some cases almost 100 percent of the population will accept Christ also. Usually, it will require less time to evangelize the 20 to 80 percent portion of the population than it took to get to the first 20 percent (see figure 2.g). That is rapid growth, and it follows the principles of the theory of innovation.

Figure 2.g: Growth in Accepting Christ

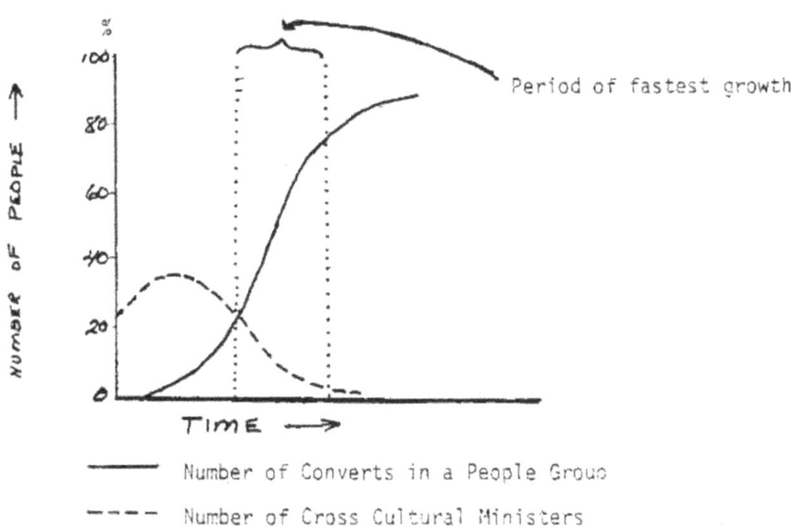

This is important in practical terms for those committed to cross-cultural ministry. As the illustration shows, once 20 percent of the population accepts Christ, those who brought the Gospel to them can go on to evangelize another unreached people group! The rest of the population will get an adequate chance to know Christ as Savior even if they go away! It has been proven that this is a sociological and communication principle that applies in every culture! That is why when 10 percent of a people group's population have accepted Christ, the Joshua Project labels them as minimally reached. It is also why they are labeled reached when 20 percent of the population accept Christ. From that point forward, they will be capable of reaching the rest of their own people by themselves.

So the goal of all our efforts to evangelize unreached peoples should focus on the first 20 percent coming to Christ! That diminishes our task by 80 percent!

To add emphasis to our discussion, you should know that the above discussion is a result of work accomplished by the leaders of the Lausanne Committee for World Evangelism and their Strategy Working Group. This is the root of the classifications adopted by the Joshua Project. They recommend that the unreached peoples be classified as shown in figure 2.h. This is similar, though not the same as the later classifications of the Joshua Project. Hidden Peoples are classified as less than 1 percent Christian, Initially Reached Peoples are classified as between 1 to 10 percent Christian, 10 to 20% are classified as Minimally Reached, and 20 percent and above are classified as Possibly Reached.[21]

[21] https://joshuaproject.net/global/progress.

Figure 2.h: Lausanne Unreached Peoples Profile

Unreached Peoples:

Hidden People:	No known Christians within the group.
Initially Reached:	Less than one percent, but some Christians.
Minimally Reached:	1 to 10 percent Christian.
Possibly Reached:	10 to 20 percent Christian.
Reached:	20 percent or more practicing Christians.

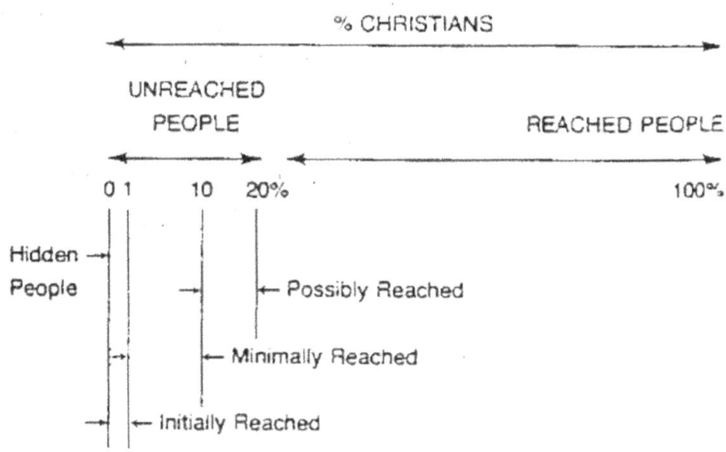

So it is safe to say that the evangelical leaders of the entire world have agreed to analyze the unreached people groups according to the percentage of people in each group who have accepted Christ. They know that the goal of attempting to see 20 percent of each population become Christians is the focus of cross-cultural evangelism. It must be ours as well.

The focus of this book is on the evangelization of what Lausanne calls Hidden Peoples—those people groups in the world who have less than 1 percent of their population who are Christians of any kind. Most have few, if any, evangelical Christians and are in need of a concentrated effort to bring the Gospel to them in their own language and in the mainstream of their culture.

The population of the world in 2020 is approximately 7.8 billion people. Of that number, approximately 1 billion are evangelical Christians—people who believe the Bible is true and follow Scripture as the authoritative Word of God. Evangelical Christianity is growing faster than the population of the world! In the year 1900, less than 1 percent of the global population was evangelical Christian. Now, more than 1 out of 8 people on the planet are evangelical Christians. The World Christian Encyclopedia calculates that evangelical Christianity is the fastest-growing global movement in history.[22]

That means we evangelicals are growing and becoming large enough to truly evangelize the world within our generation! But in order to do so, we need a 'Lord of the Harvest' perspective on the task that remains. It is an important harvest principle to "pick the fruit that is ripe," meaning we should go first to cultures that are receptive to the Gospel and gain all the followers of Christ possible. Then we should join with them to evangelize the less "ripe cultures."

But I am afraid we have abused that principle. We have sent most of our cross-cultural evangelists to the more reached people groups of the world. Evangelical Christians have been thinking about and focusing on unreached peoples for over forty years at this point. We should by now have sent more cross-cultural workers into unreached peoples than we have sent to reached or semi-reached people groups. But we have not done so. We do not have accurate statistics on this subject, but it is clear that more cross-cultural ministers are still going to reached or semi-reached cultures than are going to "hidden" people groups. This fact means some of us are not sufficiently attentive to the direction of the Lord of the Harvest! We are still too focused on the one who goes with the Gospel than we are the one who hears the Gospel! It also means we must become more innovative in creating new ways to reach the unreached as the world becomes increasingly hostile toward Christianity.

---

22 Refer to Wikipedia and all three editions of the *World Christian Encyclopedia* (Oxford University Press; varying editors; 1982, 2002, 2020) for comparison and tracking of these numbers.

This means that every Bible school, Christian university, every group of evangelical churches, and every individual should focus wholeheartedly on evangelizing unreached peoples. We should define exactly what that means from a biblical, sociological, cultural, and historical perspective, as this book attempts to do. We should also send a lot more cross-cultural evangelists! Church leaders should work together to establish principles, methods, and organizations to establish Christ's Church among unreached peoples. The task is within our reach! We do not need to win every one of the three billion unreached peoples. But, we must establish strong churches in the mainstream of every people group so they can win the rest of their own people to the Lord!

If every people among whom the Church has been planted firmly will work to train and send workers to plant the Church in the mainstream of other societies, we will succeed in reaching every people. The task cannot and will not depend upon one part of the world, race, or language grouping. Jesus commanded every Christian to "go, make disciples of every people." We must all join in this important task. The Gospel must GO TO EVERY PEOPLE FROM EVERY PEOPLE!

QUESTIONS FOR UNDERSTANDING

1. Why are there different kinds of people groups in the world? Give at least two disadvantages and two advantages in having so many diverse groups of people on earth.
2. Define a people group. Give three examples of people groups from your own experience.
3. What does "*poreuthentes matheteusate panta ta ethne*" mean? Who said it? Why is it important?
4. Why was Jesus mostly monocultural in his ministry, even though He commanded His disciples to go to "every people...unto the uttermost parts of the earth" (Matt. 28:19, Acts 1:8)?
5. A Cebuano-speaking Philippine evangelist going to evangelize the Muslim Fulani tribesmen of Upper Volta, West Africa, is doing what type of evangelism?

6. A Malayalam-speaking Christian from South India who goes to evangelize Hindu-speaking Hindus in North India is doing what type of evangelism?
7. Which of the following are cross-cultural evangelists? A. E-O, B. E-1, C. E-2, D. E-3.
8. What is the "Standard Strategy" approach to evangelization? Why is it dangerous, and sometimes harmful?
9. Define the *Homogeneous Unit Principle*. How does it support the idea that every people should have churches in the mainstream of their own people group's society?
10. Study until you can list from memory at least five advantages to a people-centered approach to cross-cultural evangelism.
11. Why were there no professional class, lower class, and Indians in church serving God one year after the evangelical crusade took place in a major Latin American city? Who were in the churches? What percentage of crusade converts were in church one year later? What should have been done as a follow-up to the crusade meetings?
12. What does "Hidden Peoples" mean? How many unreached people groups are there in the world? In what parts of the world are the most unreached people groups and population?
13. When is the work of cross-cultural ministry ordinarily finished among a particular people group? Why?
14. What is the greatest need in evangelizing the peoples of the world? How can this need best be met?

QUESTIONS FOR DISCUSSION

1. As far as God is concerned, is any one culture better than another? Are the people of your culture better than people in another culture you know about? Why? Why would it be dangerous to have only one culture on earth? Will there ever be a time where there will be only one culture? Will it be on earth or in heaven? If so, will it be dangerous then?
2. Can you name some unreached people groups in your own country? What about outside your own country? For each

group, what kind of evangelism would be necessary for you to reach them?

3. To what degree are your own people blind to the differences between people groups? What has caused the blindness? What part has cultural prejudice played in that blindness? What about nationalism? What is the dominant culture or people group in your country or region? What feelings do other people groups have toward them? Why?
4. What is the difference between forms and meanings? Should true heartfelt worship have the same forms among every people group? What should be the same for all societies—biblical principles or biblical forms, or both? Why?
5. If you were planning a strategy to evangelize an unreached people group, what questions would you ask yourself? Are there evangelism methods you would use? What principles would guide your planning?

CHAPTER THREE

Starting Autochthonous Churches

IMPORTANT POINTS IN THIS CHAPTER

1. Cross-cultural evangelism which ignores the cultural differences between different people groups is poor evangelism. It drives more people away from the Gospel message than receive it.
2. Starting churches using autochthonous principles is the best way to give the greatest number of people an adequate chance to hear the Gospel and accept Christ.
3. When starting autochthonous churches, biblical principles are more important than biblical methods.
4. Worship forms may differ from culture to culture while the meaning and effect on the believers can be the same.
5. It is important to start churches which are culturally compatible with the societies in which they are planted.
6. New Testament patterns of leadership varied from culture to culture. While there are biblical principles for church leadership which apply to every culture, patterns of biblical leadership in the churches vary from culture to culture.
7. It is desirable to measure the degree to which churches follow autochthonous principles. This provides good goals for starting new churches, and helps existing churches improve their ministries.

8. Jesus gave us important instructions about the two primary ministry functions of the church. It is important that every church be balanced between these two important areas of ministry.
9. In order to be effective, cross-cultural ministers must practice principles of indirect leadership.
10. It is important to use autochthonous principles from the very beginning in starting new churches. It is far easier to start a church correctly than to change it into an autochthonous church after it has already been established.

Figure 3.a

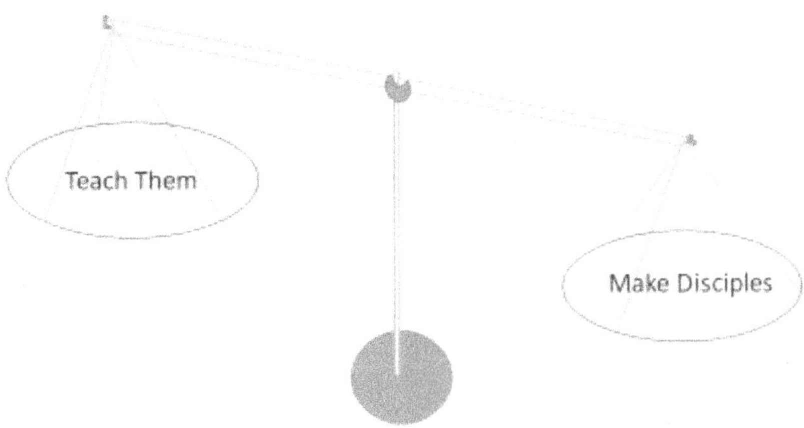

Before we begin to explore the important dynamics of cross-cultural ministry, it is important to further define our goal. *Our primary ministry purpose is to participate in the plan of the Holy Spirit to see a strong, vital, effectively witnessing group of believers in the mainstream of every people group on earth.* It is only the existence of such a church in every people group that will allow every person on earth to have an adequate chance to know Christ as Savior and Lord. So we must focus on the goal of starting just the right kind of churches among those people groups which do not have such an effective witness. We must start autochthonous churches!

THE CHURCHES JESUS CAME TO BUILD

Jesus said, "I will build my church, and the gates of Hades will not overcome it" (Matt. 16:18). We need to know the primary ways the Church Jesus came to build should function. Jesus gave us clear instructions concerning the ministry of the church in Matthew 28:19–20. He told us to "make disciples among all peoples." That "making disciples" process is complete when they testify to their new birth in Christ through the public witness of baptism. Second, Jesus told us to be "teach them to obey everything I have commanded you." In this Scripture, Jesus set forth the **twofold ministry function** of the Church. He was telling us the two primary ministries in which the Church must be engaged: (1) making disciples and (2) teaching them (see figures 3.a and 3.b).

Making disciples includes all the activities necessary to bring a person from an incomplete knowledge of Christ to accepting Christ as Savior, and joining a group of believers in a local church of some kind. Most people do not understand the "making disciples" ministry function enough to be effective in doing what Jesus told us to do. Making a disciple is not an event, it is almost always a process (figure 3.d). The key to being good at making disciples is making the effort to learn what the unbelievers we witness to know about Christ and how they feel about Christianity. Figure 3.d shows that there are at least seven possible steps a person may progress through before they are able to make an informed and sincere commitment to Christ.

Notice there are some people who know nothing about Christ at all. That is true of some unreached people groups. Others know something about Christ and Christians, but their view about them is negative because of what they have heard from others. They never knew a real Christian. Others know the basic idea of salvation through Christ, but do not know who Christ really is or how salvation is possible. Still others think there must be some kind of catch because nothing is free and their religion teaches them God or the gods can only be placated by doing many things to appease them or earn status with the supernatural.

An effective cross-cultural evangelist will be very careful to know what people know and what they feel about the Gospel before presenting it to them. He must also judge how far along the continuum toward a real decision the people he is witnessing to have come. It is not uncommon, for instance, to require a week of constant teaching for some animistic or Hindu people groups to adequately understand salvation through Christ by grace and nothing else. Remember that, as we stated in chapter one, it is our responsibility to do whatever is necessary, be patient as long as required and loving enough in our witness to guide unbelievers along each step in the path toward the point where they have an adequate chance to accept Christ as Savior and Lord of their lives.

Evangelism is not finished when a person accepts Christ. It is only complete in a person's life when he also is baptized and joins a group of believers. After a person begins to serve God in a local church fellowship, the process of "teaching them" really begins. This obviously does not mean that he received no teaching before. It simply means that from that point forward, the church's primary ministry to that person will be in "teaching" him—the second of the twofold ministry functions of the Church given by Christ Himself. The church will nurture him in his faith to help him become a mature, responsible member of the Body of Christ.

It is important that churches remain balanced in their primary ministries. This cannot be overemphasized. A church which only emphasizes evangelism (making disciples) will not be strong. They may see many people make "decisions" for Christ, but if they do not do well in teaching them, those people will often backslide or go to another church to get the teaching they need. Such a local church will not grow very much for very long, and the Christians will be weak (figure 3.c).

A church which does not emphasize "making disciples" (evangelism) very much will be imbalanced in the direction of "teaching them." An imbalance of the church's ministry in this direction occurs most often, especially in the English-speaking world. Though the people may be taught **<u>about</u>** evangelism, they are not taught to actually **<u>do</u>** evangelism enough. So the church does not spread the Gospel effectively, few new people are becoming believers, and the church does not grow. This is the danger of emphasizing the teaching function of the church's ministry above the "<u>make disciples</u>" function.

Figure 3.b

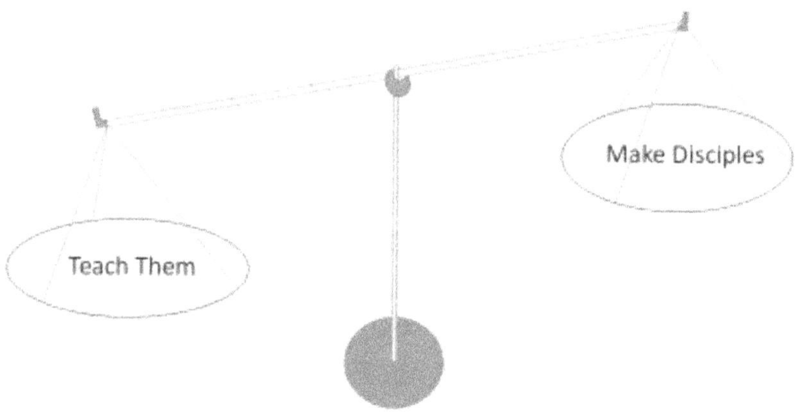

Each local church, in whatever culture and in whatever form it takes, must be balanced as Christ commanded in order to be truly autochthonous. In starting churches among other people groups, the cross-cultural minister must constantly work to help new churches maintain a balance between the twofold ministry functions. This needs to be kept in mind by leaders of churches and cross-cultural evangelists around the world.

Missionary and evangelism efforts and programs must constantly be evaluated in terms of their balance between those two ministry functions. This can be done by measuring the ministry of each new group of believers (local church) using the Scale of Autochthonous Reproducibility.

Reproducibility is an important principle for increasing autochthoneity. It is based on Paul's instructions to Timothy in 2 Timothy 2:2: "And the things you have heard me say in the presence of many witnesses entrust to reliable men who will also be qualitied to teach others." Paul (1) taught Timothy (2) who was to teach others (3) who, in turn, would teach even more people (4). Notice that this represents FOUR GENERATIONS of Christian reproducibility! It also illustrates the **Principle of Reproducibility**.

If it had been me choosing the twelve men I intended to use to change the world, I would probably have chosen a couple of people who were willing to believe in Christ from the Jewish leadership, a couple of senators in Rome, a Greek-speaking apologist, and several Old Testament scholars from Alexandria in Egypt. I would have appointed a real team of leaders!

Jesus did not do that! He chose a few men from his own area and culture of Galilee—fisherman types—practical, normal people! Why? Because He knew that there was an inherent power in the Gospel message capable of reproducing itself through the lives of ordinary people! People like you and me! The Gospel is powerful in its message! So it is important for us to learn the best ways to make the Gospel as reproducible as possible in the mainstream of any culture!

If one person is taught to do evangelism, he should be taught in a way that will enable him or her to teach others how to do what he has done and reproduce it in the lives of those they reach! Each believer must not only feel responsible for doing ministry, but he should also feel responsible to train at least one other person to do what he himself is doing. With this rule as a basic rule for believers in a new church, and if the church maintains a balanced autochthonous ministry, it should grow steadily over a long period of time.

Whether you are starting a new church in another culture or you want to analyze the autochthoneity of one which already exists, the scale below will help you. The first section will help you analyze four ways the church should carry out its "teaching" ministry function. The second section helps you measure how effectively the church carries out its "make disciples" ministry function.

WHAT IS AUTOCHTHONOUS CHURCH PLANTING?

Local churches are the primary building block of the Kingdom of God on earth. When Jesus said, "I will build my church" (Matt.

16:18), he was referring to the church as a whole—all the people who would believe and follow Christ down through the ages. But by using the word "build," He was also referring to the single units of His Church, the local churches which would become the cells of the Body of Christ.

It is in local churches that the dynamic of spiritual power moves so effectively. It is in local churches that the Spirit imparts gifts to believers so the whole unit can function as a witnessing representative of God's love and power in one place. Local churches are the building blocks of the Kingdom. Like in real building construction, the building blocks of each local church must be constructed carefully. Also, consider that local churches are like the tiny cells of the human body. If human cells do not act like they are supposed to, then the whole body is sick. We must establish the right kind of local churches among every people, or they will be unable to grow and multiply.

In this chapter, we will describe the kind of healthy, growing churches which we should establish in other cultures. We call these autochthonous churches. But we also want to set forth some important guidelines to help you establish autochthonous churches. In fact, that is the primary purpose of this whole book. If we are to be effective cross-cultural ministers of the Gospel, we must always be learning more about how to be effective in starting autochthonous churches.

Autochthonous means "native to a particular place, aboriginal, indigenous" (*American Heritage Collegiate Dictionary*). It's meaning can be taken in two senses. It can refer to something which actually originated in a particular place. For instance, Christianity is autochthonous to the Middle Eastern region of Palestine. In a second sense, autochthonous refers to something which is well compatible to or thrives in a particular place or area. For instance, it is believed that the banana plant originated in India. Yet when introduced into Central America and parts of South America, Africa, and Asia, it thrived as if it had always been there. So the banana plant is autochthonous to many tropical and semitropical parts of the world, even though it is believed to have started first in India. And though at least one hundred varieties of banana plants have developed over the centuries around the world, they still look and grow like bananas.

When we talk about autochthonous churches, we are using the second sense of the meaning of the word. Though Christianity originated in Palestine, Jesus intended that it grow and flourish within every people group in the world. The Gospel is simple and powerful enough to appeal to and flourish among every people group in the world. Much of the material in this book will help cross-cultural evangelists spread the Gospel well. We won't use the traditional term "missionary" because it carries a negative connotation in many parts of the world. When the Gospel is communicated well in any culture, it has the capacity to take root in the hearts of people who can live its truth within the mainstream of their own cultures.

When the Gospel is established within the cultural mainstream, it changes the way people see God, themselves, and other people in their world. Such changes have a profound effect upon their society and becomes highly valued by the people of that culture. When this happens, the Gospel can spread very rapidly, and many people from the mainstream of that society will be interested to hear the Gospel. Many will accept Christ as Lord and Savior. That is when the Gospel can truly be said to be "autochthonous" to that culture. That is our goal for every cultural grouping of people.

Making the Gospel autochthonous to any culture requires autochthonous churches. Autochthonous churches are churches whose members live out the spiritual, social, and moral truths of biblical Christianity in culturally appropriate patterns within their own society, and who view the transformation of their lives by the Gospel as the answer to their felt needs as provided by God through the guidance of the Holy Spirit and the truth of the Scriptures. Notice the key elements of this definition: (1) Members of autochthonous churches do not just believe the truths of the Gospel, they live them out in their daily lives in a way that has positive meaning within the mainstream of their own culture. (2) The Gospel becomes so much their own, it affects the way they worship, the way they treat their neighbor, and even their personal values and ethics. (3) They are not alienated from their society by adopting foreign cultural patterns. They have valued and internalized the Gospel enough that they understand how to live out its truth meaningfully within the cultural patterns of their people. (4) They truly value their Christian lives because they see the Gospel as the answer to their emotional frustrations and spiritual needs. (5) They recognize the authority of Scripture as the foundation of their faith, and that they can rely on the Holy Spirit to teach them what they still need to know about serving God.

Autochthonous churches are appealing to the general population of their society. The behavior of their members does not appear foreign. The believers' social and moral behavior conforms to the general patterns of the society, but they exhibit higher standards of behavior following principles of Scripture. This is appealing to the general population of their cultures. The most significant barrier to people in their culture becoming believers is whether they will repent of their sins and accept Christ as Lord of their lives.

The established religious authorities who feel threatened by the rapid growth of autochthonous churches may feel threatened and may bring persecution, but this may cause even faster growth because the general population respects the autochthonous church. This certainly happened in Acts 6. When the Hellenist believers gained their own leadership (see chapter one of this book), they became very effective in making new disciples among the Hellenist Jewish synagogues in Jerusalem (Acts 6:4–7). This so threatened the Hellenist synagogues in Jerusalem, it led to the false accusations against Stephen and his death. The ensuing persecution scattered believers from Jerusalem, and the church spread even wider and more rapidly in an autochthonous fashion (Acts 11:19–20). Autochthonous churches may experience persecution in some societies, but they will still have the quiet respect of the general population because they live the truth of the Gospel in a culturally meaningful way.

Autochthonous churches have strong and respected local leadership. The churches are organized according to patterns that fit the cultural, political, and religious needs and realities of the people. The forms of behavior and spiritual goals fit the needs of the culture, yet conform to the biblical principles also. The church is supported by local people in ways that are acceptable to those in the culture. The songs and other forms of worship are in the common language and style of the people in that society. The believers witness and communicate the Gospel in ways which are natural and permissible to the people within the context of their own society. No matter what outward forms the churches take, they appear genuine to the society as a whole. Its members also appear genuine and sincere. They are not despised outcasts, or a fringe group of society. They may suffer persecution for a time, but the people increasingly learn to respect them as genuine and sincere in their faith.

Figure 3.c Split Image Spectrum of Autochthonous Churches

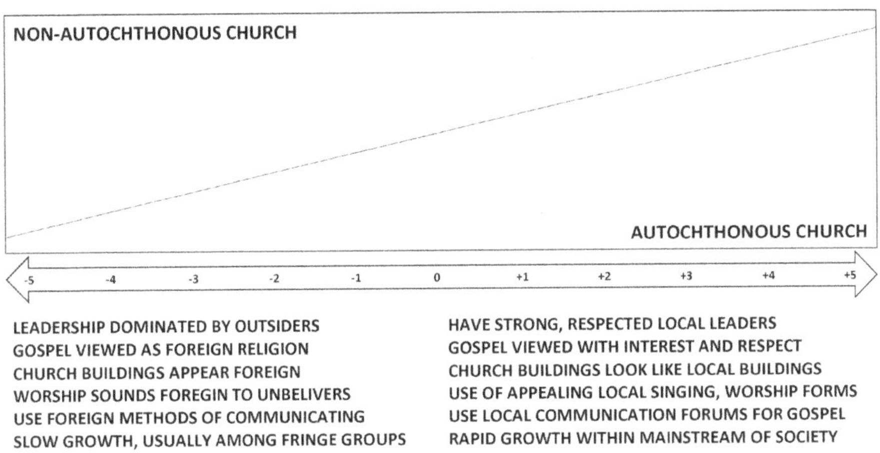

For example, in a certain Muslim country, a government official was complaining to one of the Christian leaders of that country. The official was being paid by the Muslim government to find those who had turned from Islam to Christianity and try to force them back into the Muslim faith. He complained that there were already at least one million Muslims in that country who had illegally converted to Christianity. Of course the Christian leader was not going to help the official to do his job. But that leader knew that there were several times that many people in that country who had converted secretly to Christ. They were meeting privately together, but they did so in many different places and homes. These believers are reporting that the Gospel looks much more appealing than Islam to many people in that country, while Islam looks more and more corrupt and evil in the eyes of a large percentage of the population. This is made possible by the power of the Spirit of God, but it is also a result of the fact that the Gospel is a living, vibrant witness in the mainstream of that Muslim culture. We need to discuss the principles for accomplishing the same thing in any culture!

The Goal of Cross-Cultural Evangelism

The primary purpose of cross-cultural evangelism is to start autochthonous churches. They are the basic building blocks for seeing the Church grow and thrive among unreached groups of people. It is very important that the cross-cultural evangelist know the principles for starting autochthonous churches, and for helping to keep them strong and effective building blocks for the Kingdom.

It is helpful to contrast autochthonous churches with those which are weak, ineffective, and non-autochthonous. This is illustrated in figure 3.a. The more autochthonous a church is, the more it will show the characteristics listed on the right side of the chart. The less autochthonous it is, the more it will exhibit the characteristics on the left side of the chart.

Principles vs. Methods

It is important to distinguish between biblical principles and biblical methods. Biblical principles are not temporary. They represent spiritual and practical truth which applies to the church in every generation among every people group. Biblical methods may or may not be temporary. They are culturally relative. They may apply in one culture but not in another. This statement, at first, may sound offensive to some people. Because we all hold the Bible as God's authoritative Word, we sometimes think we must copy everything in the Bible in order to do God's work correctly. But let's consider that idea more closely.

The Bible not only communicates the principles of God's will for man, but it also records the history of how some people tried to follow those principles in their own lives. Sometimes they failed, or succeeded only partially. Consider the Old Testament character of Samson, for instance. Samson demonstrated God's power of being filled with the Holy Spirit. He proved what a mighty force the presence of the Holy Spirit can be. But few people would want to copy the pattern of his tragic life. King Saul was another leader who began his reign anointed and filled with the Holy Spirit, but later he tried to do God's work in man's way. Few would want to copy his methods just because they are recorded in the Bible! The principle in both men's lives is important and for all time—the importance of the indwelling power of the Holy Spirit!

Consider the life of Paul in the New Testament. He was called by God to preach the Gospel to the Gentiles (Acts 13:47). The primary principle which motivated him was to preach that Gospel everywhere he went. But one of Paul's usual method of preaching was to go to the Jewish synagogue first. He would preach the Gospel, and many of the "God-fearing Greeks" and proselytes to Judaism would gladly receive his message. But the strong orthodox Jews would reject the message, and the synagogue would immediately be divided (Acts 14:1–7). The principle which we must follow in Paul's ministry is to preach the Gospel wherever people will be most likely to hear the message. Because he was a Jew of high standing, that happened to be the synagogues. But it would be wrong to make preaching in synagogues first (the form) the only way to begin our cross-cultural ministry! Neither should preaching in Muslim mosques or Catholic cathedrals be the places to begin cross-cultural ministry. Paul used that method because he knew he would get a hearing and people would listen to his message in the synagogues. If Paul were living today, he would use different methods, depending upon the people he was preaching to and the methods available to give them a good chance to hear it. While this principle seems obvious, it is important and has many implications for how we present the Gospel, as we shall see. In starting autochthonous churches, biblical principles will never change, but the methods will differ according to the needs and culture of the people we are trying to reach.

DEVELOPMENT OF AUTOCHTHONOUS PRINCIPLES

Missiology is the science of studying the biblical mission of the church and formulating principles for expansion of the church around the world. Missiology is important to cross-cultural evangelists because it helps to more clearly define their task and the principles by which they can best fulfill their calling. *TO EVERY PEOPLE FROM EVERY PEOPLE* is a missiology book. In addition to careful study of the Bible and its principles, missiologists also use principles from the social sciences. They seek to find the most practical, as well as biblical principles for fulfilling the Church's call to make disciples among every people.

One of the best ways to learn effective cross-cultural ministry is simply by experience. Some very godly and very effective evangelists from different parts of the world have been very successful in starting churches among other peoples. These people were led by the Holy Spirit and learned many things in their lifetimes. Unfortunately, very few have taken the time to study what they were to do and set forth principles by which they could teach others. Some of these men have written down their ideas and have made important contributions to the development of autochthonous principles.

During the mid-nineteenth century, two men—Rufus Anderson and Henry Venn—came to some similar conclusions about cross-cultural ministry. Both men worked as leaders of their group of Protestant cross-cultural ministers. Their hearts were burdened because the churches they had started were weak, ineffective in winning converts, and too dependent on foreign help. They came to realize that it kept the churches from growing and multiplying as they should.

Both men began to study the life of the apostle Paul, seeking to glean important principles from his own cross-cultural ministry in the book of Acts. Though they did not become aware of each other's work until later, both men came up with very similar conclusions about the basic principles by which Paul established new churches. Andersen coined three phrases, later borrowed by Venn, which have come to be widely accepted as the basic goals in starting churches cross-culturally. They and other missiologists of the last century and a half have emphasized that churches started through cross-cultural ministry should be "self-governing, self-supporting, and self-propagating."

Self-governing means that new churches should have their own leaders who control the ministry and finances of the church. Self-supporting means that local churches should be supported by the local congregation entirely, without help from foreign sources. Self-propagating means that the churches which are planted in other cultures should take the responsibility for spreading the Gospel among their own people.

Taken together, these "three-self" principles have become the primary foundation for what is called indigenous church principles. The missiology books which have been written on the subject of the indigenous church became more numerous in the twentieth century as these principles became more widely accepted. One experienced cross-cultural minister and church leader (now deceased), Melvin L. Hodges, wrote an important book on the subject called *The Indigenous Church*, which has been widely used in several languages.

While most of the missiological teaching on indigenous principles is very sound, practical, and biblical, it usually does not go far enough. Most of the teaching so emphasizes the three-self principles, it begins to resemble a set formula for cross-cultural church planting. It fails to distinguish between principles and methods. It seeks to describe the goal of starting indigenous churches in such clear, concrete terms that resulting churches more resemble North American or European churches than churches which can easily multiply in every culture. It too often neglects to describe what the church should be in the community where it is born, except in terms of its responsibility to spread the Gospel. Too often, it is more "what" than "how."

Equally important, indigenous church teaching too often fails to consider adequately the societal implications of planting churches cross-culturally. Too often, evangelicals have wanted to see the planted churches as a spiritual society unto itself. We have too often resisted attempts to apply the knowledge of the categories of the social sciences to the Church. But the Church was instituted by Christ within society, not separate from it (John 17:11, 15–17). The Church is subject to most of the same social laws as the rest of society. That is why Paul, when instructing his fellow workers about church organization, appealed mostly to common sense, based on his knowledge of society, rather than to theological arguments or rigid methods of church planting. Indigenous church principles, while basically sound, have too much neglected to take into consideration the laws of sociology, anthropology, communications, and common sense! The results have sometimes been tragic.

Some churches which conformed to the basic definition of being an indigenous church have been far less than what Jesus had in mind when He said, "I will build my church." It is possible to have churches which support themselves, even paying their own pastor's salary, and still have a stingy, self-centered church which is ineffective in its witness to the community. It is possible to see local leaders govern a church with complete authority and without outside interference, but do so in a manner that is alien and offensive to the local culture and biblical principles. It is possible to see a church with its own evangelists to spread the Gospel, but do so using foreign or inappropriate methods which are ineffective. In fact, some churches have been labeled as indigenous by outsiders when they were obviously unappealing and off the mark in the eyes of local leaders. In such cases, the entire concept of indigenous principles was disdained and abandoned by those leaders.

That is sad because there is much about indigenous principles which is sound. They were hammered out in the crucible of good biblical scholarship and difficult and costly cross-cultural ministry around the world. The principles are basically sound, but they do not go far enough. That is the reason this book teaches the principles for starting **<u>autochthonous churches</u>**.

Autochthonous church planting seeks to give a broader definition to indigenous principles. It seeks to add principles from the social sciences and common sense to our principles for doing good cross-cultural evangelism. It seeks to emphasize principles, not methods. The most effective methods will vary from culture to culture. Churches will look and act very different from culture to culture. For example, crusade evangelism has proven to be very effective in Latin America and parts of Africa, but it is totally ineffective in Saudi Arabia where it would be illegal. Not only do indigenous principles need to be given better and broader definition, but also, there are other autochthonous principles which need to be given equal importance. Studying autochthonous principles given throughout this book should give you a much clearer picture of your goals in starting churches among the peoples of other cultures.

MEASURING AUTOCHTHONEITY

Autochthonous churches do not spring up automatically. In fact, unless sound principles of cross-cultural ministry are followed, churches started by cross-cultural evangelism will likely be very non-autochthonous. The churches started will appear very foreign and will be difficult to grow and multiply. The message they present to their community will likely appear unimportant and irrelevant to the needs of the local people. That does not mean they are poor evangelists or unspiritual people. It simply means they need to clearly understand and apply principles for starting autochthonous churches. It will bring this subject into focus if we develop a way to measure how well churches we start will fit into the mainstream of the cultures where they are planted.

Figure 3.d: THE SCALE OF CULTURAL AUTOCHTHONEITY*

	AUTOCHTHONOUS							FOREIGN & IRRELEVANT		
WORSHIP FORMS	10	9	8	7	6	5	4	3	2	1
WORSHIP SONGS	10	9	8	7	6	5	4	3	2	1
EVANGELISM PATTERNS	10	9	8	7	6	5	4	3	2	1
LEADERSHIP PATTERNS	10	9	8	7	6	5	4	3	2	1
ORGANIZATIONAL PATTERNS	10	9	8	7	6	5	4	3	2	1
CEREMONIAL FORMS	10	9	8	7	6	5	4	3	2	1
FINANCIAL SUPPORT METHODS	10	9	8	7	6	5	4	3	2	1
COMMUNICATION FORMS	10	9	8	7	6	5	4	3	2	1
LANGUAGE FORMS	10	9	8	7	6	5	4	3	2	1
EDUCATIONAL METHODS	10	9	8	7	6	5	4	3	2	1

*INSTRUCTIONS: Select the number for each subject for each church being planted. Add the total numbers from each line. The answer is the Cultural Autochthoneity Quotient (CAQ).

The **Scale of Cultural Autochthoneity** (figure 3.d) sets forth important categories of autochthonous principles. In each category, churches can be analyzed according to how closely they resemble the patters or forms used in the local culture. Again, the basic premise of autochthonous principles is that biblical principles are absolute, and apply to every cultural grouping of people. But the methods, forms, and patterns by which those principles are demonstrated will vary from culture to culture. The closer those patterns, forms, and methods resemble those where the church is planted, the more the church is autochthonous. The more the patterns, forms, and methods of the church are alien and different from those of the local culture, the more ineffective and perceived irrelevant will be its ministry to the local community.

So take a close look at the categories on the Scale of Cultural Autochthoneity. The higher the combined score of all ten categories, the more autochthonous a church is rated, and the higher the Cultural Autochthoneity Quotient.

This system of analysis balances the need to carefully follow biblical principles while using changeable relative cultural forms to convey those principles effectively within a target people group. The dynamics of cultural forms are discussed more completely in chapter four. Guidelines for learning how to discover and define biblical principles are given in chapter six. This rating system assures biblical principles are being followed and focuses on those categories which are crucial in helping a local church or group of churches to effectively give witness to those Gospel truths to their own people.

It is important to define the categories on the Scale of Cultural Autochthoneity. A clear understanding of those subjects helps us to more clearly picture our goal of the autochthonous Church. After defining these categories, we will examine another method of determining autochthoneity, the Scale of Autochthonous Reproducibility. Then we will apply these principles to two local churches so we can see more clearly how to use them.

Defining the Categories

Worship Forms: In your mind's eye, travel with me to bush country of Africa. See a small village center where some men begin to haul some drums and hollow logs into the cleared area. They talk with one another as they gradually begin to beat out the intricate staccato rhythms common to the bush country of that part of Africa. Soon other people begin to arrive. Eventually they begin to form a big circle and start swaying back and forth with the beat. The women are dressed in typical traditional African bush country costume. So are the men, who also have the spears they carry through the bush. The drums begin to beat louder, and a leader begins to shout out the first line of a chant-like song. The whole group, swaying and bouncing with the beat of the drums, echoes back the words of the song leader in well-timed unison. More and more people are still joining the circle.

The chant-like singing continues for an hour and a half. Sometimes it is interrupted when someone breaks into the middle from the circle to speak. But the drumbeats, though quiet now, continue. And he speaks in a chant-like singsong rhythm that matches the drums. The music gets louder again after the speaker rejoins the circle. The people wave their arms with the beat of the music and words they sing.

Another speaker steps into the circle, but this time the drums and the singing stop. The man starts a dialogue with the crowd. His speech is animated. The crowd sometimes answers him or agrees with him with a shout in unison. Sometimes, one person will talk to him. An hour later, the drums start the singing again.

Late that afternoon, as the people begin to make their way back toward their own villages, they talk excitedly about the events of the day. Some carry baskets on their heads, full of food they had traded for or wares that did not sell in the market that day. The main remark on everyone's lips is what a wonderful service they had that day. Didn't the Spirit of the Lord move in a wonderful way in the meeting! We must invite more of our neighboring villages to our Spirit-filled meetings!

Now let's go to a church service in the Eastern European country of Romania. The old church building is packed. Some people have to stand for the service, which they are content to do for three or four hours until the service is over. But the hymns are very slow and sung very unemotionally. As they sing, a few people close their eyes, but no one smiles. The choir sings a slow, beautiful hymn, and a woman on the front row quietly sheds a couple of tears as they sing. Soon after the singing, the preacher stands up to speak. His message is challenging, but he does not speak loudly or emotionally. He speaks a full hour and fifteen minutes. There is another song. Finally, the service is over and the crowded room is empty.

That afternoon around the lunch table, the same kinds of comments are heard in the apartments of many of the church members. "What a wonderful service this morning! Didn't the Spirit of the Lord move in a wonderful way in the meeting! We must be careful to invite more of our neighbors to our Spirit-filled church!"

Which of those two churches is the most pleasing to God? The answer is both of them! Both churches preach, teach, and live the same Gospel. They believe the same doctrine. Their members are on their way to heaven, and God is pleased with them. The only differences were in their worship forms. As will be discussed further in the next chapter, God is very interested in worship that comes from the heart. Human beings use different forms in different cultures to express the same meanings that are in their hearts. Some of those forms might seem offensive or insignificant to people of another culture, but they are full of cherished meaning to the heart of true worshippers. Full expression of worship touches the deepest aesthetic sense of human beings. It is very important that every people be allowed and encouraged to express their heartfelt worship to God using their own culturally appropriate forms of expression. God accepts that kind of worship because it draws the human spirit close to God.

That does not mean a tribal group that once offered food sacrifices to tribal deities should now offer them to God. It means that people groups should be given the opportunity to hear the Word of God, accept it, and then be given the freedom to choose and develop forms of worship that fit their culture. The more they are encouraged to do so, the more the Gospel will be attractive to others of that culture. And the more autochthonous the churches among that people group will be.

Evangelism Patterns: Experienced and effective cross-cultural evangelists know it is important to share the Gospel using methods which fit the patterns of the daily lives of the target people group. This not only includes using the most appropriate communication forms (see below), but it also means sharing the Gospel at the right times in the right places to the right people first. This includes such things as waiting to start a preaching or witnessing effort until the crops are harvested or when there are no national holidays. It may include gaining the permission or confidence of leaders first in a new area. It may even mean being patient enough to convert the men first in a certain culture, knowing the family will follow much more quickly in accepting Christ than if a young person or child of a family becomes the first Christian.

Using autochthonous evangelism patterns requires extensive experience in living with the people and studying their way of life (chapter five discusses this more thoroughly). By doing so, the cross-cultural evangelist will learn the best patterns for individual and group witnessing and preaching. He may learn that it is important to send older believers along with young ones to talk to others about Christ. Or he may learn that witnessing should never be door-to-door due to cultural mores. All these things can be learned by spending time with the people and by being careful to share the Gospel using their patterns of everyday living as much as possible.

Leadership Patterns: Every people group has its own culturally accepted ways of selecting leadership, regulating standards of leadership performance, and patterns of leadership interaction. It is important that the cross-cultural evangelist learn those patterns so he can encourage the right kinds of leadership patterns to emerge with the new churches he starts in a target culture.

Attitudes about leadership is an area where cross-cultural ministers can make serious mistakes. It is too natural for him to dominate the leadership of the new churches he starts, imposing the patterns of leadership he is accustomed to among his own people. It is important to realize specific kinds of leadership did emerge in the New Testament under the guidance of the Holy Spirit. Different kinds of ministries were eventually recognized as ministry gifts to the Church, such as apostles, prophets, evangelists, pastors, and teachers. There were also leadership roles for elders, deacons, and others in the churches. But notice that while the Bible lists qualifications and gives examples of the ministries of such gifted leaders, there is no specific list of behaviors for how each leader should function. This left considerable room for cultural flexibility. That is why Paul the apostle was able to proclaim, "I have become all things to all men that I might win some" (1 Cor. 9:22).

History tells us that the leadership of the churches in Judea followed the patterns of the Jewish culture, with strong authoritarian leadership as the common pattern (Acts 5:1–10). But the leadership patterns of the churches in Asia Minor and Macedonia more closely followed the democratic patterns of Greek culture. The offices and ministries remained the same, but their functions and patterns of leadership varied according to the cultures of the churches.

Though there are biblical offices of leadership given by the Holy Spirit to churches in all cultures, the patterns by which they lead God's people can and should vary according to patterns of the local culture. More will be said below about the proper attitude of the cross-cultural evangelist toward assuming leadership roles.

Organizational Forms: One of the greatest dangers in starting new churches among another people group is the temptation to organize churches according to the forms used back in your own culture. The cross-cultural evangelist carries an image in his mind based upon experience in his own culture as to how a church is to be organized. It is a grave mistake to organize churches cross-culturally according to that image.

It is far better for him to pay careful attention to how local institutions in a target culture are organized and pattern the churches along those lines. As leaders begin to emerge among a new group of believers, it is important to rely on them to decide what kind of organization there should be and how much it is needed. It is best not to tell them about the church organization back home, even if they ask. Assume the role of an adviser, showing them everything about organization in the New Testament churches. Encourage them to discuss different needs for organization among themselves, but do not push them to organize a function or activity until they know they need it. When they do, the results will be much better and follow their cultural patterns much better. If they start to decide something that will obviously bring problems later, you may want to ask them questions about it until they decide on a better leadership pattern. Pleasing you should never be the goal. Meeting the needs of their people and pleasing God should always be the goal.

So never suggest your own way. Trust the Holy Spirit to lead them. They should decide the who, how, and when of collecting offerings and disbursing funds. They should decide whether and when a pastor should be paid by the church to support his family. They should decide if and when a church should have a board of elders, how it should function or if there should be a constitution or governing set of rules. Good cross-cultural evangelists know that the more local leaders and church members form and lead the organizational development of the church, the more it will have a positive image in the community and the more autochthonous it will be.

Ceremonial Forms: Every culture develops special ceremonies for special times in the lives of individuals and groups. Different ceremonies for birth, puberty, marriage, death, death anniversaries, and other special occasions are common for individual members of cultures around the world. Other group-oriented ceremonies include such things as harvest festivals, new year ceremonies, and other less desirable ceremonies such as those dedicated to the worship of false gods or appeasement of spirits.

God respects human need for ceremony. He even used it to help Israel remember God's goodness to them by instituting special ceremonies as a part of Jewish law (Deut. 16). Special events in people's lives should be celebrated as blessings from God (James 1:17). A cross-cultural evangelist must study the special events and ceremonies in a target culture. When the time is right, he should suggest that the leaders in the new church institute new ceremonies for Christians.

There should be the observance of the two ceremonies Jesus gave us, the Lord's Supper and baptism. Remembrance ceremonies for Christmas and Easter are also appropriate. The new believers might also consider the Day of Pentecost when the Church was established as an event significant enough for annual celebration.

Besides the more common ceremonies a Christian may want to celebrate, attention should be given to those ceremonies in the culture which are the most elaborate and consume the most time and expense in the celebration. These may be weddings or puberty celebrations, for instance. The cross-cultural evangelist should make it a priority to discuss with emerging leaders in the new churches the best ways they can substitute Christian symbols into those ceremonies which are traditional and important in the culture. Special emphasis should be given toward making ceremonies rich with Christian meaning. Basic biblical teachings should be clearly symbolized within the ceremonies. The local leaders will likely enjoy developing such ceremonies, becoming creative in their efforts. And the Christians who participate in the ceremonies will find great meaning in them. If done right, so will the community at large. The development of positive Christian ceremonies will greatly enhance the image of the church in the community and therefore have a positive impact on its witness.

Financial Support Methods: As a general rule, the support of a local church's ministry should come from local sources right from the beginning. Outside funding should be totally avoided unless there is an emergency situation of some kind beyond the ability of the local churches to take care of. Outside funds bring direct or indirect control of the local church's ministry by outsiders. A responsible attitude on the part of the local congregation toward the work of God is crucial to the development of the church. As a general rule, the only time outside funds should be used is when the following conditions are present: (1) a very important need for ministry exists and is recognized by the local church; (2) the local church attempts to meet the need with its own resources; and (3) the need is a temporary one of an emergency nature, or if an ongoing need concerns the collective need of a group of churches that they cannot possibly meet by themselves. Examples would be emergencies caused by natural disasters or ministerial training programs like Bible schools.

Equally important, the people should be encouraged to determine from the Word of God how much money and what kind of offerings they should give to God. The cross-cultural church planter must trust the Holy Spirit to teach them to give from their hearts. He should give himself and preach the principles of giving in the Word, but the local people should decide how, when, and why to give under the direction of the Holy Spirit. They should also decide on how much money should be spent. If they feel they should support a full-time evangelist before they support a full-time pastor, they should be encouraged to do so. The system of financial giving and support does not have to resemble the system of the churches "back home" to be autochthonous. In fact, the more autochthonous it is, the less it may be like those in the culture of the cross-cultural evangelist's home church. The giving, spending, and accountability procedures should be left completely to them under the guidance of the scriptural principles and the Holy Spirit. The cross-cultural evangelist should emphasize biblical principles and examples for supporting God's work, but not how and in what order they should be applied in the target culture.

Communication Forms: In New Testament times, the Greek culture had popularized public speaking in open forums. Public debates were common between different philosophers. The apostle Paul debated with the philosophers in the marketplace of Athens, using the opportunity to proclaim Christ. He spoke in their language, quoted their poets, and declared the nature and power of the "unknown God" they worshipped in ignorance (Acts 17:16–34).

But when Paul spoke in the synagogues, he used the expository monologue form of speaking, proving, and illustrating what he was saying with Old Testament Scripture as the Jews were accustomed to doing (like in Acts 13:16–42). Paul used two different communication forms to speak to the people of two different cultures.

The word "preaching" in our Bibles actually is translated from several Greek words, depending upon the way it is used. Those various words in Greek carry different senses of meaning, such as "announcing the Good News" (Acts 8:4); "to proclaim, publish, a proclamation" (1 Cor. 2:4); and "reasoning, discourse, a treatise, a communication" (1 Cor. 1:18). The word "preaching" is used in so many situations and with so many various meanings that the best general definition would be any kind of communication which is intended to convince others of biblical truth.

There are many forms of communication in different cultures which would fall within that definition of preaching. Some peoples commit their most important messages to singing. Some Muslim cultures communicate their most important messages by chanting. Telling stories by dancing is an important form of communication to some peoples. The forms of communication are not as important as the significance they give to the message in the mind of the hearers. In fact, in some cultures, a preacher who speaks loudly with tremendous gestures as is common in some Western cultures might be considered strange, angry, and perhaps mentally deranged!

Language Forms: It is extremely important to use the mother tongue and local dialect of the people where you want to start a church cross-culturally. The Holy Spirit demonstrated the importance of this when He helped the disciples speak in the mother tongues of at least fifteen different people groups on the Day of Pentecost (Acts 2:1–12). Some people think it is adequate to preach to different peoples through interpreters. While a few people from a certain society might respond to an invitation to accept Christ through such preaching, it will seldom touch the mainstream of the people group. There must be somebody willing to live among the people of that society, teach any converts in their own mother tongue, and live the good news before the people. That is the only way the mainstream of most societies will be truly affected by the Gospel. Without this kind of help, local churches will rarely be started among a people group. And even if they are, they will not be very autochthonous. They will be incapable of winning very many of their own society to the Lord.

Starting churches in the local language is also very important in communicating biblical truth. Language is only symbols of meaning, but it is a very important system of symbols for every people group. The person who can define biblical truth using the same phrases, patterns of speaking, and same words as the people use in their every-day language will by far be the most effective cross-cultural representatives of the Gospel among any people.

Educational Methods: Christian education is an important part of "building up" the Body of Christ (Matt. 28:20. Eph. 4:12–13). Teaching believers to become mature members is an important part of any church's ministry. But sometimes cross-cultural ministers, without really knowing it, teach new churches foreign methods for training their members.

Every culture has a formal and an informal way of learning. In most industrial countries, formal education is emphasized far more than informal methods. This is the case not just in rural areas, but many cities as well. Many formal education systems emphasize much memory-oriented learning, especially in non-Western countries. Others emphasize discussion, analysis, and debate. Most informal methods of education depend upon older family members to teach the younger ones. They may teach them reading, writing and arithmetic, but they will also teach them how to do things important to their way of life, such as farming, weaving, sewing, construction and how to treat other people.

The wise cross-cultural minister will notice the dominant methods of teaching among the people where he is starting churches. His objective is teach them deeply so they in turn can teach others the principles of the Word of God (2 Tim. 2:2). But knowing they will likely follow his example, he must be careful to teach as they are accustomed to learning. If the people are not accustomed to formal classrooms and formal methods of learning, it would be wiser to discover the informal methods they use and copy them. They will learn more comfortably and quickly. Even more important, they will be much more effective as they begin to teach their own people. Learning to do rather than simply learning to know should stay at the forefront of their learning. And the who, where, when, and how of Bible learning will feel natural to the people. That goes a long way toward starting autochthonous churches.

By following these ten principles for starting Autochthonous churches, the cross-cultural minister will greatly increase the value of his work. The more autochthonous a church is, the greater respect it will gain in the community and the more effective will be its witness to the truths of the Gospel. Furthermore, it will increase the satisfaction of the church members and the value they place on their service to God through the church. Such attitudes are very important for penetrating the mainstream of any people with the precious good news of Christ!

MEASURING AUTOCHTHONOUS REPRODUCIBILITY

The Scale of Cultural Autochthoneity (see figure 3.d) is a very useful guide for starting autochthonous churches in another culture. It is also useful for measuring the cultural autochthoneity of a church which has already been started in another culture. But it is not complete in itself. The scale measures the degree of cultural fit. That is the degree to which a church is culturally compatible with the society in which is planted. A church which has a low score on the Scale of Cultural Autochthoneity will have great difficulty in growing in number, or having its message accepted in the mainstream of the target people.

In addition to a church's cultural fit, there are other important factors which determine the autochthoneity of a church. How well-balanced the church is in its actual ministry is an important factor. How well the church members apply the Bible to their daily lives and how well they do in personal evangelism are also important factors. These factors are combined below in the Scale of Autochthonous Reproducibility.

Missionary and evangelism efforts and programs must constantly be evaluated in terms of their balance between those two ministry functions. This can be done by measuring the ministry of each new group of believers (local church) using the Scale of Autochthonous Reproducibility.

Reproducibility is an important principle for increasing autochthoneity. It is based on Paul's instructions to Timothy in 2 Timothy 2:2: "And the things you have heard me say in the presence of many witnesses entrust to reliable men who will also be qualitied to teach others." Paul (1) taught Timothy (2) who was to teach others (3) who, in turn, would teach even more people (4). Notice that this represents FOUR GENERATIONS of Christian reproducibility! It also illustrates the **Principle of Reproducibility**.

If it had been me choosing the twelve men I intended to use to change the world, I would probably have chosen a couple of people who were willing to believe in Christ from the Jewish leadership, a couple of senators in Rome, a Greek-speaking apologist, and several Old Testament scholars from Alexandria in Egypt. I would have appointed a real team of leaders!

Jesus did not do that! He chose a few men from his own area and culture of Galilee—fisherman types—practical, normal people! Why? Because He knew that there was an inherent power in the Gospel message capable of reproducing itself through the lives of ordinary people! People like you and me! The Gospel is powerful in its message! So it is important for us to learn the best ways to make the Gospel as reproducible as possible in the mainstream of any culture!

If one person is taught to do evangelism, he should be taught in a way that will enable him or her to teach others how to do what he has done and reproduce it in the lives of those they reach! Each believer must not only feel responsible for doing ministry, but he should also feel responsible to train at least one other person to do what he himself is doing. With this rule as a basic rule for believers in a new church, and if the church maintains a balanced autochthonous ministry, it should grow steadily over a long period of time.

Whether you are starting a new church in another culture or you want to analyze the autochthoneity of one which already exists, the scale below will help you. The first section will help you analyze four ways the church should carry out its "teaching" ministry function. The second section helps you measure how effectively the church carries out its "make disciples" ministry function.

THE SCALE OF AUTOCHTHONOUS REPRODUCIBILITY

Section I: Teaching Ministry

Doctrinal Teaching: This measures the amount of doctrinal teaching given to church members, how well they learn it, and their ability to explain their faith to others (1 Pet. 3:15).

1. Church members know only basic salvation truths, they cannot explain it well to non-Christians, and they receive no regular teaching on basic biblical truth.
2. Church members know only basic salvation truths, they cannot explain them well to unbelievers, but they do receive a small amount of teaching on basic biblical truths.
3. Church members know basic salvation truths well, they can explain them well to non-Christians, and they receive a small amount of teaching on basic biblical truths.
4. Church members know a good range of teaching on biblical doctrine, they can explain most of it well to non-Christians, and they regularly receive training on biblical truths.
5. Church members know a good range of biblical doctrine, they regularly receive training in these truths, and they regularly teach or preach Bible truths to Christians and non-Christians.

Number ___

Growth in the Use of Spiritual Gifts: Since the Church is the Body of Christ, it is important to keep measuring the development of spiritual gifts. Members must be growing in their ability to effectively exercise spiritual gifts both inside and outside the church (1 Cor. 12, Rom. 12:3–8).[23]

1. Church members know very little about spiritual gifts, and they think the pastor, if anyone, is the one who should use them.
2. Church members do not see spiritual gifts as important, and except for a few leaders in the church, they hardly learn about or use their spiritual gifts.
3. A few members understand and use their spiritual gifts, but there is little teaching on them. Other members feel little responsibility to use them.

[23] See Wagner, 1994

4. The church consistently teaches members to understand, discover, and use their spiritual gifts, and a growing number are learning to do so.
5. Most believers know their spiritual gifts, and are regularly using them inside the church and outside the church as well.

Number ___

Applying Bible Truth in Life Situations: Reproducing churches have members who not only learn biblical truth well, but they also learn to be good at applying those principles to their daily lives.

1. Church members think the Bible is a good book, but it is too foreign to their world today and hard to understand.
2. Church members believe what the Bible says is true, but when they face problems or illness, they still depend upon the old ways to solve their problems.
3. Church members believe the Bible is God's Word for all persons, and a few of them have learned that the Bible helps them solve their daily problems.
4. Church members believe the Bible is the only God-given book, and most members rely only on biblical principles to solve their daily problems.
5. Church members see the Bible as God's most important communication to their people. They constantly tell others, both Christians and non-Christians, how the Bible has helped them in their everyday lives.

Number ___

Serving the Community: A very important part of a church's responsibility is the need to be involved in solving the problems of the people in their own community. The more a church is involved in ministries of this kind, the more the community will respect the church, and the Gospel as well. When balanced well with evangelism, this kind of ministry will have a very positive impact on a church's reproducibility.

1. The church does not give any help to those who are suffering or participate in community development projects.
2. The church gives a little help to those who are suffering in the church, but does not participate in projects that help the whole community.
3. The church tries to take care of any of their own members who are suffering, but does not participate in community development projects.
4. The church takes care of any of their members who are suffering, and tries to help others in the community as well. It also tries to join with other groups to do its share in community development projects.
5. The church gives help to any of their own members who are suffering, and helps as many non-Christians as they can. The church also starts its own community development projects and participates in other ones as well.

Number ___

TEACHING MINISTRY QUOTIENT (four sections x 5) _______

Section II: Discipling Ministry

Personal Evangelism: This measures how much individual church members are involved in personal witnessing. (Since "church members" means different things in different cultures, we are defining a member as those individuals who regularly attend worship services at the church, whether they are official members or not.)

1. Church members do not participate in personal witnessing at all.
2. Church members share what happens at the church with unbelievers only if unbelievers ask them to do so.

3. Most church members openly share what happens at church with unbelievers without being asked to do so.
4. Most members openly share what help Jesus Christ has given them in their own lives with their friends.
5. Most church members openly and regularly share the Gospel and personal testimony with non-Christians, and some of them do become believers themselves.

Number ___

Group Evangelism: This measures how much the church members participate together in group evangelism activities (like public witnessing, starting outstation meetings, home meetings, underground churches, or secret witnessing in groups, etc.).

1. The church does not sponsor, encourage, or participiple in any evangelistic efforts outside the church.
2. The church emphasizes evangelism in a few meetings inside the church during the year, but no effort is made to evangelize outside those meetings.
3. The church emphasizes evangelism within church meetings often, and gives a small amount of training in evangelism to its members.
4. The church often conducts evangelism efforts that are appropriate for their own cultural context, both inside and outside the church meetings. A lot of training in evangelism is given to the members.
5. The church regularly sends evangelistic teams or cross-cultural workers to start churches among their own people and among other people groups as well.

Number ___

Meeting Community Needs: This measures how well the new believers are contributing positively to the felt needs of their communities among their people group. It is important because the Gospel will be perceived as positive in the minds of unbelievers within the community according to how much followers of Christ exhibit the love of God by helping to solve the problems that press against the well-being of the whole community.

1. Followers of Christ do not help people outside their group at all, unless they want something from them.
2. Followers of Christ only help people in their own extended families with their problems and they are the only people believers give any attention to at all.
3. Followers of Christ help people in their extended families with their problems, but they also spend a little bit of effort to help people in the broader community.
4. Followers of Christ help people in their extended families and challenge them to join them in helping with the important problems of the broader community.
5. Followers of Christ help people in their extended families and members of the community alike, leading believers and nonbelievers in effort to solve community problems.

Number ___

Reaching the Community Leaders: This measures how well the church is doing in reaching those people in the community who have the greatest influence on community life. It is important not only because these people need salvation like everyone else, but also because they are the ones who help shape the opinions of the majority of the rest of the community. Their influence can be very useful or damaging to the church and its Gospel witness. It is important to have a favorable impact on these people.

1. There are no community leaders in the church, and the members of the church are generally unliked in the community.
2. No community leaders are in the church, and only a few members are liked by the people of the community.

3. No community leaders are in the church, but many church members are liked and respected by the people of the community.
4. There are a few community leaders in the church, and most church members are liked and respected by the people of the community.
5. There are many community leaders in the church, and most church members are liked and highly respected by the people in the community.

Number ___

DISCIPLING MINISTRY QUOTIENT (four sections x 5) _____

How to Use the Scale: For each subject in Section One, decide which statement most closely describes the church you want to analyze. Put the number of that statement where indicated just below that set of statements. Do the same for section II. Total the numbers in each section and write the total in the space called Total Score. Multiply that score by 5. The first score for section I will give you the **Teaching Ministry Quotient**. The score for section II, also multiplied times 5, will give you the **Discipling Ministry Quotient**. Finally, add the two quotients together and divide by 2. The answer is the **Scale of Autochthonous Reproducibility**! Compare your answer with this rating chart (figure 3.e) to see how reproducible the church really is:

Figure 3.e: Autochthonous Reproducibility Chart

RATE	RATING	SUGGESTION
0-40	Not Reproducible	Church members and leaders should work together to raise the scores that are below 3 on each scale.
41-60	Poor Reproducibility	Church members and leaders should work together to raise the scores below 4 on each scale.
61-80	Good Reproducibility	Church members and leaders should work together to raise the scores below 5 on each scale.
81-90	Very Good Reproducibility	Church members and leaders should work together to raise scores below 5 on each scale.
90-100	Excellent Reproducibility	Church leaders should teach other churches and their members how to be reproducible.

Figure 3.f: Nam Nai and Yong Tuk Church Reproducibility

DESCRIPTION	NAM NAI CHURCH		YONG TUK CHURCH	
	SEC 1	SEC 2	SEC 1	SEC 2
AUTOCHTHONOUS	5	5	3	2
REPRODUCIBILITY	4	4	2	2
SCORES	3	5	2	2
	4	5	2	2
TOTALS:	16	19	9	8
MULTIPLY BY 5:	X5	X5	X5	X5
TMQ:	80		45	
DMQ:		95		40
RQ:	**87.5**		**42.5**	
CAQ	92.5 (see Page 3.15)		52.5	
EQUALS:	180		95	
DIVIDED BY 2 EQUALS:				
AUTOCHTHONEITY QUOTIENT	**90**		**47.5**	

Calculating the Autochthoneity Quotient: By combining the scores on the Scale of Autochthonous Reproducibility with the Cultural Autochthoneity Quotient (above), you can determine the **Autochthoneity Quotient**. To do this, add the Autochthonous Reproducibility Quotient and the Cultural Autochthoneity Quotient together, then divide by 2. For instance, figure 3.f shows the scores and the results of analyzing two Asian churches:

The Nam Nai Church was started in an Asian refugee camp. The people were driven from their land, were homeless, and had seen many of their relatives killed. They were very glad to receive the hope and the message of the Gospel. The Church was started by a cross-cultural minister who used autochthonous principles in his work. The people received regular instruction in the Word of God and in witnessing. They absorbed these teachings into their daily lives and told many of their fellow refugees in the camps about Jesus. They came to believe that God allowed them to go through so much so they could find the peace in their souls that comes from knowing Christ. Their spiritual strength came to be known throughout the camp. The people respected them because they were always partnering to relieve the suffering of those in the camp who needed the most help. Everyone knew that they were not being paid to help others like this. This all resulted in rapid growth of the church in the camps. That is why the Autochthoneity Quotient is 90.

The Yong Tuk Church was also started by a cross-cultural evangelist. It was started in the capital city of an Asian country some years ago. But the church was not started using autochthonous principles. The people who joined the church did not always do so for the right reasons. Though they had some teaching on the Bible and evangelism, it was usually done only by the cross-cultural evangelist, instead of local leaders. The people understood basic biblical truth, but had not yet learned to apply that truth to their daily lives. They would still use some of their old animistic rituals when someone was sick, getting married, dying, etc. They have done little witnessing or evangelism, and the people in the city who know about them think they belong to a foreign religion. It is not a very autochthonous church. Those are some of the reasons why the Autochthoneity Quotient is only 47.5.

THE PRINCIPLES OF AUTOCHTHONOUS RESPONSIBILITY

There is another basic principle for starting autochthonous churches which is important. It concerns the attitude of the people in a church toward the work of God. When starting a new church, the cross-cultural evangelist should be sure to encourage the believers to assume all the responsibility they can for the Lord's work. This is an important key to autochthonous church planting. The evangelist must avoid the "hothouse church" strategy and encourage the priesthood of all believers.

Avoid the "Hothouse Syndrome." In some countries, especially where there is cold weather a large part of the year, vegetables and plants are grown in hothouses. These are usually long buildings made of a light framing material and covered on top and the sides with glass or plastic. They are called hothouses because they trap the heat of the sun inside, helping the plants grow even when it is cold outside. Farmers can also control how much water they get in that protected environment. The plants are grown in pots or boxed planters, watered regularly, and cared for well. Many flowers and vegetables are grown this way in many parts of the world. Of course, many of the plants that are grown would die if they were taken outside the hothouses and planted in the soil there. They would not survive the colder weather or poor soil conditions.

Some cross-cultural ministers start churches which are too much like hothouse plants. Like the plants in the hothouse, the churches have everything done for them by others. Foreigners send funds to build church buildings that look like what foreigners like. The cross-cultural minister uses funds he receives to pay the expenses of the church, hoping the people will someday do it themselves. Even the pastor's salary and living expenses might be paid with foreign money!

Just like a hothouse plant would die without the hothouse environment and care of the nurseryman and the protection of the hothouse, so this kind of church would probably die if the cross-cultural minister left and the foreign funds stopped coming. The church would have become much too dependent on foreign influence and money to be able to survive without them. Furthermore, such churches are robbed of the opportunity to develop strong local leadership and assume the responsibility of ministering effectively to the local community. Also, the church would appear very foreign to members of the target people group. The Gospel would not be very appealing to them.

So the basic reason churches with the Hothouse Syndrome do not grow well is that too much foreign influence and money robs them of the opportunity to assume the responsibility for ministry themselves. Feeling a responsibility for ministry before God is different than feeling it before men. Responsibility before men can easily be produced if it is paid for by men. But for churches to grow, there must be room for that sense of responsibility toward God to grow in the life of every believer from the beginning of his Christian walk. The cross-cultural minister must be very careful to do nothing which will hinder the development of that sense of responsibility in the lives of believers in their target culture. He does not have the right to diminish that obligation because that responsibility is given to every believer by God Himself. It has nothing to do with how much money and resources are available within any given people group. It is essential for autochthonous churches to have such believers.

The Priesthood of all Believers: When God called out the nation of Israel to obey Him and follow His laws, He wanted them to serve Him as a nation of priests (Exod. 19:5–6). He intended to use them in a priestly function as a nation and as individuals to draw the other nations unto Himself (see chapter one). Paul wrote that we in the church are "heirs together with Israel, members together of one body, sharers together in the promise in Christ Jesus" (Eph. 3:6). The apostle Peter also recognized that the call and promises of God to Israel are given to believers in the Church. Writing to New Testament believers, he said, "You are a chosen people, a royal priesthood, a holy nation, a people belonging to God, that you may declare the praises of him who called you out of darkness into his wonderful light" (1 Pet. 2:9). From the time he or she accepts Christ as Savior, each believer has a sacred responsibility to minister to others for God.

All people's gifts and calling are not the same (Rom. 12:3–8). But all believers are to be built up in their faith, learn how to develop and use the spiritual gifts God gives them, and assume responsibilities in God's Church. God gives ministers (who have ministry gifts) to the Church in order to help them mature in their faith, and to lead them in service to God (Eph. 4:11–13).

Effective cross-cultural ministers are very careful in choosing leaders over new churches. They try to follow a number of important principles in choosing leaders:

1. Do not choose leaders yourself. Instruct the believers in spiritual ministry gifts (Eph. 4:11–13). Ask them to prayerfully choose from among their own number those who are developing spiritual gifting for leadership.
2. Emphasize the development of gifts for ministry, not offices of authority. In many cultures, authority is derived from family status, age, money, or a number of other things. Avoid such customs with the words and teachings of Jesus,

such as in Matthew 20:26–28, "Whoever wants to become great among you must be your servant, and whoever wants to be first must be your slave." It is absolutely crucial that this principle is followed, even if it appears to be against the customs of the target culture.

3. Ask them to understand New Testament examples and qualifications for leadership (1 Tim. 3, 1 Cor. 3:10–15).
4. The cross-cultural minister should avoid assuming any high office in the church, such as pastor. Instead, he should spend his time training and encouraging leaders chosen by church members. They should assume more and more duties as leaders in the church before they appear fully prepared. Serve them by humble example. Let them grow into their leadership roles with the help of the Holy Spirit by doing ministry, not just hearing about it!
5. Allow the people to devise steps for increasing ministerial authority and clear qualifications for each step. Devise titles for those steps of authority, such as "trainee" or "lay pastor" or some similar title for each position. Be sure the qualifications for rising authority are based upon faithful and effective service and nothing else.
6. Serve the leaders. The cross-cultural minister should be the friend, servant, encourager, and confidant of leaders chosen by the members. Their success is his only success. He is not playing the role of teacher who gives them all the answers. He may describe the issues or where to find examples in the Bible, but they must fully embrace the responsibility to make decisions on every important issue.
7. The cross-cultural minister should spend less and less time teaching and preaching in a new church himself. He should keep encouraging and helping the local leaders learn so they can teach the people. For the cross-cultural minister who has the spiritual gift of teaching, this may be difficult at first. But he or she should focus on the principles of 2 Timothy 2:2, teaching leaders who teach others. He should

take joy when he finds they are teaching the "others" in the target culture.

This type of nondirective cross-cultural ministry leaves room for the sovereign Spirit of God to take control of the leadership training process. That will accomplish five important benefits:

1. It will develop the ministry gifts of local leaders rapidly.
2. It will encourage members of the congregation to develop their own ministry gifts following the example of their own leaders.
3. It will help the people in the target community to accept the new church and view the message of the Gospel more favorably.
4. It will help the church grow and become completely autochthonous much faster.
5. It will help the cross-cultural minister have more time to start other new churches.

The Importance of a Right Beginning: The principles outlined so far point toward the important fact that a right beginning is crucial in starting autochthonous churches. If a church begins using autochthonous principles, it will likely continue to grow and multiply its ministry in an autochthonous way. But if a church is started using non-autochthonous methods, it will be much more difficult to change it into an autochthonous church later. For instance, if the cross-cultural evangelist begins a church by being the first pastor himself, it will be very difficult to convince the people to choose another less trained and less experienced man from among themselves to learn to pastor the church. It is better for the cross-cultural minister to exercise indirect leadership as discussed above. If he assumes too much direct leadership, it will become very difficult for the new church to develop its own leadership. It is very important to study autochthonous principles, and use them from the very beginning to start new churches within other people groups.

DEVELOPING RESPECT FOR OTHER CULTURES

In order to be effective, cross-cultural evangelists must develop understanding and respect for other cultures. The whole foundation for communicating the precious Gospel to other peoples is mutual respect between those telling and those hearing the Gospel. Yet it is typical of people to show disrespect for other cultures when they first enter them. They tend to judge the behavior of the people in the other culture according to the way it looks in their own culture. They have not learned to see things the way the local people in the target culture see them.

Every culture thinks of their own lifeway as normal, or even the best way of life. *Every cultural grouping of people tends to judge other peoples by their own cultural standards.* This is called **ethnocentrism**.

Ethnocentrism is something cross-cultural evangelists cannot afford. Since all people have a significant amount of ethnocentrism in their thinking, it is important to learn about the nature of culture and how to speak into that culture while overcoming ethnocentrism. We must learn to see into the lifeway of other peoples more like God does, and learn to have respect for them. It is important to learn how to live in another culture in such a way that our lives will be good news (Gospel) to the people. That is the starting point for learning how to personally start autochthonous churches. That is also the subject of the next chapter.

QUESTIONS FOR UNDERSTANDING

1. Write the definition of autochthonous churches. Explain what it means in your own words. List some of the benefits of autochthonous churches.
2. Write as many reasons as you can to show why autochthonous churches are appealing to the people of the society where they are planted.
3. Write the letter(s) for each statement which is a characteristic of autochthonous churches: (a) use foreign methods of communicating the Gospel, (2) use of local forms of worship and sing-

ing, (3) use local communication methods in communicating the Gospel, (4) focusing on people who represent groups at the edge of a target culture, and (5) have strong and respected local leadership.

4. Explain this statement: "In starting autochthonous churches, biblical principles will never change, but the methods will differ according to the people we are trying to reach." Do you agree with it? Use the Bible to support your position.
5. What are some of the weaknesses of the traditional teaching on the "indigenous church" concept? List some of the ways autochthonous principles overcome those weaknesses.
6. Two churches, one in Africa and one in Romania, are given as examples of different worship forms. Which one do you think God is most pleased with? Why?
7. Give an example of different leadership patterns in different cultures of the New Testament Church. What does this teach us about leadership forms in different cultures?
8. How is the word "preaching" defined in this chapter? Why is such a broad definition important for doing cross-cultural evangelism?
9. What is the "twofold ministry" function of the Church? Why is it important that these two ministry functions be balanced? Does the Principle of Reproducibility apply to one ministry function only? Why?
10. For each of these three examples, tell which ministry function of the church is primary in these people's lives: (a) Toshib was saved last year, and is very happy that he became a member of a growing church. (b) Amila went home to her flat with a troubled mind, after going to a study of the Christian Bible. She was concerned about how her efforts to live right did not seem good enough to God. (c) Harun was excited by the joy of finding peace in his heart after accepting Christ, but he was unsure of what to do next.
11. Which church is the most autochthonous, Church M with Autochthonous Reproducibility scores of 4, 3, 5, 4 and 5, 4, 4, 5; or Church P with a Cultural Autochthoneity Quotient of 75?

12. Which one of the following three churches is the most autochthonous? (a) Church X has total scores of 19 and 18 on the Scale of Autochthonous Reproducibility. (b) Church Y has an Autochthonous Reproducibility Quotient of 72. (c) Church Z has a Teaching Ministry Quotient of 90 and Discipling Ministry Quotient of 70.
13. Which church is the most autochthonous, the Nam Nai Church or the Yong Tuk Church? For the one which is the least autochthonous, list ways you think it could be changed to make it more autochthonous today.
14. According to this chapter, what is a hothouse church? How do hothouse churches fail to follow the principle of autochthonous responsibility?
15. List as many principles for choosing leadership when starting autochthonous churches in another culture as you can remember without looking at the text. Now check your answers. How many did you get right? How many did you forget?

QUESTIONS FOR DISCUSSION

1. Analyze the different parts of the definition of autochthonous churches given in this chapter. What are the key parts of the definition? Give examples of what each part means.
2. Discuss biblical principles and cultural methods. Can you define the conceptual difference between them and defend it? Under what conditions would biblical methods not be the right methods to use in a particular culture? Can you give an example?
3. Discuss the way this chapter defines "preaching." How do you feel about the definition? According to this definition, what kinds of communication could you classify as preaching which you never thought were preaching before reading this chapter?
4. If you were starting a new church among an unreached people group, list the things you would try to avoid and the things you would try to do in order to train leaders for the new church.
5. Analyze your own church in your own culture according to the Scale of Cultural Autochthoneity and the Scale of Autochthonous

Reproducibility. What is the Autochthoneity Quotient? What could you personally do to help increase the autochthoneity of your church?

CHAPTER FOUR

Communicating Across Cultural Boundaries

IMPORTANT POINTS IN THIS CHAPTER

1. Communication across cultural boundaries introduces an infinitely greater possibility for hindering the transmission of messages.
2. Understanding basic communications theory is very useful for understanding the dynamics of cross-cultural ministry.
3. There are seven categories of cultural differences which should be understood by every cross-cultural evangelist.
4. Communication requires the use of symbols to transmit meanings. Different symbols are required in different cultures to transmit equivalent meanings. Meanings are difficult to transmit from one culture to another by using language symbols. This is because the meanings of word symbols are not exactly equal when translated from one language to another.
5. Cross-cultural evangelists often fail to distinguish between forms and meanings in communicating within another culture. An understanding of forms and meanings is essential for effective evangelism in an unreached people group.

6. Worldview is the generator of culture. It is at the center of the lifeway of a people group, and it is the source of value systems and behavior patterns.
7. Syncretism results from changes within a culture at the level of behavior patterns only. Effective communication of biblical truth should effect change at the worldview level and the value system level also.
8. When an evangelist enters another culture, he should follow the five principles for enculturation. This will lessen the culture shock and enable him to work toward an *emic* position within the culture. This is the best position from which to communicate the Gospel.
9. It is very important to understand the dynamics of cross-cultural communication before trying to evangelize the people of another culture.

UNDERSTANDING THE COMMUNICATION PROCESS

In chapter one, we examined the biblical basis for cross-cultural ministry. In chapter two, we studied the nature and number of the people groups, and we became aware of the many unreached people groups which must be evangelized one people at a time. In chapter three, we learned the basic goal of cross-cultural ministry—the planting of autochthonous churches. In this chapter, and in the following one, we turn to examine the role of the cross-cultural minister himself.

Communicating the Gospel across cultural barriers is far more complex and difficult than preaching the Gospel to one's own people. To be successful, the cross-cultural evangelist will be wise to learn the basic dynamics of cross-cultural communication. By learning to overcome the barriers to communication which are based upon cultural differences, he or she can be many times more fruitful in his work. This chapter emphasizes the nature of those barriers, and provides principles to help the cross-cultural evangelist become effective in communicating the Gospel in another culture.

The Basic Communication Process

Before looking at the process of cross-cultural communication, it is important to understand the basic theory of the communication process. Figure 4.a shows the basic parts of that process.

Figure 4.a

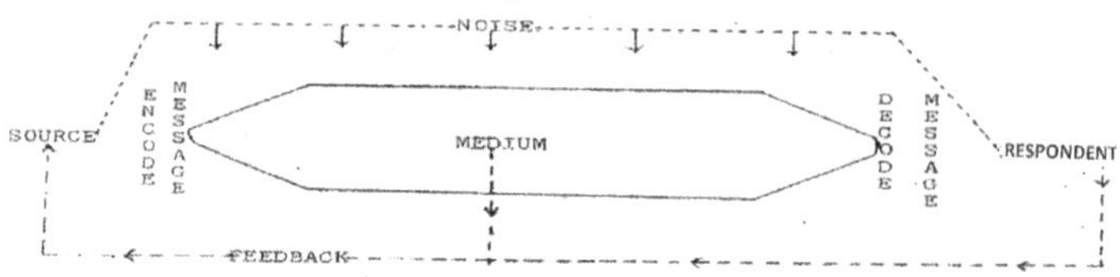

THE BASIC COMMUNICATION PROCESS

The Source: When you want to communicate a message, that message comes to you in the form of thoughts in your mind. Those thoughts are the actual message you want to communicate. Messages do not exist independently of people. Once they are encoded in some form and transmitted to another person, they are no longer the original message. They are changed somewhat by the communication process before they enter the mind of the person who receives the message (respondent). The original message, in its complete and accurate form only exists in the mind of the source person. This will be clearer to you as you read further.[24]

Encoding the Message: Once the source has thought of a message he wants to communicate, he or she must choose a way to convey that message. He must *encode* the message in a way that the respondent(s) will be best able to understand the intent of the message. He can encode the message in many ways. A common way is to use speech. Or he can write the message or speak into a microphone so the message can be coded electronically into radio, television, telephone, or a host of online and wireless mediums of communication. To understand the message, the respondent must have a device

---

[24] David J. Hesselgrave, *Communicating Christ Cross-culturally*, 2nd ed. (Zondervan, 1991), 41, 51.

capable of receiving the message and converting it into an audible, written, or visual form understandable by the one who receives the message. There are many other ways to encode a message besides using language. Gestures, the way a person stands, the expression on one's face, and even art and dancing are all ways to encode messages.

The Medium: This is the means for transporting the message to the respondent. If the respondent is far away from the source, the medium may be a telephone, radio, television, art, sculpture, or online system of communication. If the respondent is located close to the source of the message, the medium may simply be the air between them which carries the sound of the source to the ears of the respondent. The medium is anything which conveys the encoded message to the respondent. The printed page is the medium through which you are receiving the messages of this book.

Decoding the Message: Once the respondent receives the message through one of his five senses (seeing, hearing, touching, tasting, smelling), he must interpret what it means. This process of interpreting the symbols of the message and giving them meaning in the respondent's own mind is called *decoding.*

Noise: Anything that interferes with the communication process so as to detract from communicating the message is called *noise.* It can actually be noise, such as when a machine is running close by, making it difficult to hear someone's words. But in this technical sense, noise can be anything else which in any way keeps the meaning of a message from being completely received by the respondent. For instance, if you are reading this book when you are tired, your weariness will keep you from fully understanding everything you read. So your weariness becomes noise in the communication process between the author and you. Noise can be static in a radio receiver, or it can be a prejudice against educational tools like books. Noise can be a faulty Internet connection leading to your impatience and unwillingness to wait for the messages to be completed. Or it can be an upcoming football game that makes you want to finish this chapter without taking enough time to understand its importance. Noise detracts in some way from the ability of the respondent to receive and understand the message that the source is trying to communicate.

There is noise in the communication process almost every time someone tries to communicate a message. Encoding itself puts a message into some kind of symbol system in order to convey it to the respondent(s). But the very symbols used usually carry some noise effect with them. For instance, consider the use of words as symbols. When we put our thoughts into words, the words we choose carry the full meaning of what we are trying to say as far as we are concerned. But the listener (respondent) may not understand the meaning of those words exactly like we do. His own experience has taught him that those words mean something a little bit different than what we think they mean. So the message may be a little bit or a lot different in his mind from what we think we were communicating. This fact is easy to demonstrate. Sometime, when you are in a room with twenty people or more, whisper to one person about four sentences of a specific message. Ask the person who heard you to whisper the same message to the person next to him and ask him to do the same to the person next to him (or her) and so on, until every person in the room has received the message. Ask the last person to tell the message to everyone. Be sure to write down exactly what you said to the first person. When the message is recited by the last person, it will be changed quite a lot from the message you originally communicated. This demonstrates that people do not always hear what we think we have said. Each time someone in the room transmits the message to the next person, he or she tells it in his own and slightly different words, interpreting the message slightly different each time. This shows that the words themselves can be a part of the noise in the communication process.

Respondent: The person who hears the message also has an effect on the communication process. His attitude toward the source, how he feels about the message which is being communicated, and even how he feels about the medium of communication—all are important parts of the communication process. They help to determine how well the communication is received. Anyone who has done much personal witnessing of the Gospel can remember people who would not receive their message. Many people are trained to be against the Gospel message, but as we learned in chapter one, it is our responsibility to break through such barriers. When we meet people trained to be against the Gospel message, it is automatic that they will also be against the messenger! So the attitude toward the Gospel message in the minds of the respondent can be an important element of noise in the communication process. This becomes especially important in the cross-cultural communication process. If the respondent only sees the cross-cultural evangelist as a foreigner who really does not understand the respondent's people and their way of life, his attitude toward the evangelism and the Gospel will be negative. His attitude will be noise in the communication process.

Even the ideas that are already in the mind of a respondent when he hears a message are factors in his ability to receive a message as intended. As a more famous illustration, consider the words Jesus spoke to His disciples. He told them ahead of time, as recorded fourteen times in the Gospels, that He would be killed and resurrected as the Messiah. But their idea of the Messiah was that He would deliver the Jews from Roman rule and set up His kingdom on earth. That concept had been drilled into their heads from the time they were small children in the Jewish culture. Jesus told his followers, "My Kingdom is not of this world" (John 18:36) and "The Kingdom of God is within you" (Luke 17:21). Yet because of their preconceived ideas of the role of the Messiah, they could not fully receive His messages about the true nature of the Kingdom of God. Those preconceived ideas created noise in the communication process between Jesus and those who heard Him teach. Even after His resurrection, the disciples had trouble believing it had happened, even though He predicted it very specifically many times. That is how the ideas in the minds of people who hear our messages can become noise in the communication process. As we will learn more below, this concept represents a source of great barriers to the Gospel in the minds of those who hear our messages in another culture.

Feedback: When talking with someone, we all look at their facial expressions to see if they are listening and understanding what we say. This "body language" is a form of *feedback* in the communication process. While encoding a message, the source may be constantly receiving messages back to himself about the effect of what he is trying to communicate. A preacher will try to get feedback from his congregation even while he is speaking. Some feedback can come through the medium being used. For instance, a singer in an auditorium will want a small speaker in his ear to assess the quality of his voice and clarity of the message. Feedback is any kind of message received back by the messenger that indicates the apparent clarity of the message in the mind of the respondent. Feedback is a very important part of the communication process, and we depend upon it all the time during and after our communication efforts.

Feedback demonstrates that the communication process is very complex. Even while the source is communicating a message, he is also receiving messages back concerning the effect of his communication. For instance, the way a person stands or sits, the expression on his face, and dozens of other ways of communicating messages will tell the source whether the person is listening, disinterested, impatient, or wanting to know more. Feedback shows that personal communication is almost always two-way communication. This becomes very important for cross-cultural communication of the Gospel.[25]

THE NATURE OF CULTURE

Culture has been defined in various ways by anthropologists. The broadest and still most widely accepted definition is the one which came from anthropologists in early nineteenth-century Germany: Culture is the total nonbiologically transmitted heritage of man.[26] Culture is the total system of learned behavior patterns which are common to the members of a particular society, and which are not the result of the instinctive biological nature of man.

In more specific, modern, and expanded terms, culture can be defined as the total lifeway of a people group. It includes the way a people view cosmic reality, the values they share, and the patterns of

---

25 http://www.eltingo.org/images/Communication%20Theory.pdf.

26 C. H. Kraft, *Christianity in Culture*, 45.

behavior which are accepted as normal among their own people. It includes the way they look at the existence of the world and mankind, the things they work hard to obtain or maintain, and the way they interact with everything and everyone around them.

Every person has a mental mindset—a way of looking at everything and responding to everything—which is mostly shaped by the culture in which they live. Our culture is transmitted to us from the time we are small children until the time we die. Each culture transmits to each of its members the specific behaviors and values which are considered normal for its people. There is a set of rules, some spoken and some unspoken, which determine what kind of behavior is acceptable or desirable in each culture. The culture also defines the boundaries or limits to which a person can stray from these normal behaviors without being punished by the other members of his culture. For instance, each culture defines what kind of behavior is acceptable and desirable between young unmarried men and women, what character traits are admired in men and women, the rules for good hospitality, the ceremonies surrounding special events like weddings and funerals, and the duties of husbands and wives toward each other and their families.

Even those things that human beings do because of their biological nature are controlled by culture. For example, everyone has a biological need to eat and sleep. But when, how, what, where, and with whom we do those things is determined by culture in a major way.

Culture does not stay the same. It is not static. Cultures are in the constant process of change. The changes usually come slowly. Sometimes cultures change because their people come into close contact with people of another culture and begin to adopt some of the ways of the other culture. This is called ***acculturation***. Sometimes cultures change because the people of the culture find that some of the cultural rules that were agreed upon in an earlier generation no longer seem adequate for their own generation. When this happens, key leaders who are called *innovators* begin new kinds of behavior which previously would not have been acceptable, but now are being copied by others in their culture. Eventually, enough people adopt this new behavior which causes it to become the new normal behavior in that culture. As we shall discuss below, it is important to evangelize such innovators in a society because they can bring the message of the Gospel to a people group most rapidly. (See also the discussion on diffusion of innovation theory in chapter two.)

CULTURE AND THE COMMUNICATION PROCESS

Communicating across cultural boundaries introduces an endless possibility for noise in the communication process. Cultures differ from one another in languages, ways of looking at the world, the behaviors they value, and in many other ways. So when a person from one culture tries to communicate a message, even an important one like the Gospel, a myriad of cultural differences causes the message not to be understood and received as it was intended. It is like there is a cultural screen between the source from one culture and the respondent in another culture which is blocking the message (figure 4.b). Worst of all, so little of the real message may be communicated that the respondent will not respect the message or the messenger!

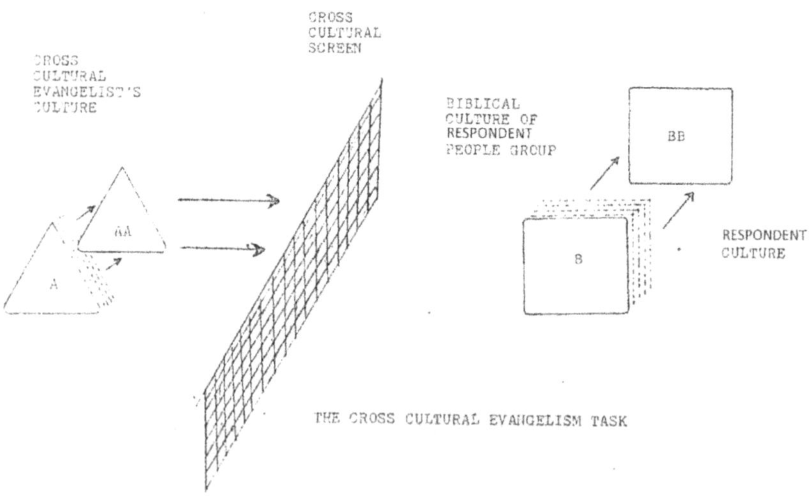

Figure 4.b: The Cross Cultural Screen

Figure 4.b shows how difficult it is to communicate across cultural barriers. It is as if each section and strand of the screen represents a separate point of difference between the two cultures. These differences cause the message to be deflected as the source in Culture A tries to communicate through the screen to the respondent in Culture B. As long as the source tries to communicate through the screen, most of the message is deflected or distorted, and is not received by the respondent correctly as intended.

The cross-cultural evangelist who tries to communicate from the position of Culture A through the screen to Culture B will not be successful in effectively communicating the Gospel. When faced with the barrier of culture, some cross-cultural evangelists have made the mistake of trying to force the respondent to figuratively come through the screen over into his own culture (Culture A). He forces the respondent to learn his own cultural patterns of communication and behavior. Even if he finds a few people willing to move through the screen toward him, and he is successful in evangelizing them, they will no longer be considered a part of Culture B by their own people. They, too, will seem so foreign that there will be another screen between them and their own people. And Culture B will still need to be evangelized.

There is only one effective solution to the problem of culture, as far as the cross-cultural evangelist is concerned. He or she must learn to move through the screen. He must learn the culture of the people he is called to evangelize. He must communicate in their language, using their behavior patterns and symbol systems of meaning. This is called *enculturation*, and it is discussed more thoroughly in the last section of this chapter. The evangelist must learn how to effectively communicate just as a person in Culture B would communicate. Only then will the message he represents have real value in the minds of those who live in the mainstream of the target culture.

Culture of the Kingdom

Notice that figure 4.b shows Culture BB as "Biblical Culture of Respondent People Group." As more people in Culture B become Christians, it will have an impact on the entire culture. Since the goal is to reach the mainstream of every culture, part of the goal of evangelizing people groups is to see their culture change more and more toward a biblical culture as is pictured in 4.b. Good cross-cultural evangelists know that all cultures are in a constant process of change. So one of his objectives in evangelizing a people group is to help the church change their society's way of life to become closer and closer to biblical standards. Since cultures are constantly in the process of change anyway, it is far better from every perspective that they become more and more a biblical culture.

This is where a major problem arises for the cross-cultural evangelist. Notice that Culture BB in the illustration is not the same as Culture B or Culture A, but is closer to Culture B. The fact is that there is *no single biblical culture*! If the people of Culture A and the people of Culture B both adopt correct principles, they will both move toward a biblical culture (Cultures AA and BB). Those biblical cultures will really benefit their peoples. They will incorporate the values of the Kingdom of God into their way of life. Both those biblical cultures will be pleasing to God, but they will be different from each other. Even though both cultures may adopt the same biblical principles, the way they live those principles will differ between their cultures. That is good! It means the Gospel and the principles of living the Gospel adapt to the needs of every people group!

This all points to the fact that it is difficult for the cross-cultural evangelist to know what is biblical behavior in another culture. For example, one experienced cross-cultural evangelist was working among a certain tribal people group in Africa some years ago. God gave him success in his work, and about 60 percent of the people of a particular area accepted Christ in a short period of time. The evangelist was accustomed to the loud intricate rhythms of African drums when the villagers gathered together on market days. The women would dance in a lewd and suggestive manner, and the men would join in with similar dancing moves. It was not a wholesome scene. But in his first encounter after they became Christians, he was a bit dismayed to see the villagers gather together and begin to beat their drums like before. As the tempo of the drums would increase, the Christian women began to dance and the men then joined in the dance also like before. Imagine the evangelist's surprise when he heard the Christians begin singing about their salvation as they danced and clapped to the beat of the drums. The evangelist thought the drums sounded evil like before. He realized this was a celebration of their new life in Christ!

The cross-cultural evangelist talked to one of the drummers after the "service" was over. "Why do you still play the drums like you did before you accepted Christ? Won't that make your sisters and brothers turn back to their old ways?" asked the evangelist.

"Oh, no!" replied the drummer. "Since becoming Christians, we only use good beats when we play the drums. We would never play the drums like we did before."

"You mean there are good drumbeats and bad drumbeats?"

"Yes, of course," said the drummer. "Everyone knows which drumbeats are good and which are bad. We would never play bad drumbeats in the church services."

The evangelist learned a valuable lesson. Because all drumbeats were so foreign to him, they all sounded the same. Whenever he heard drumbeats, he automatically thought of the ungodly behavior he had seen so often when the drums beat before. He made the mistake of assuming the drumbeats themselves were bad, not just the way they were played. When the drums were played the right way, they became a spiritual blessing to the believers! He wisely accepted that, and many more people have come to Christ in that people group since then.

The new Christians were moving the behavior of their people toward a biblical standard (Culture BB). Their culture was becoming more biblical, and it was causing the Gospel to become more appealing in the eyes of the unsaved villagers. Everyone knew which drumbeats were "good" except the evangelist. Some evangelists would have taken charge of the celebration services themselves. They would have probably patterned the service after what they were accustomed to in their own culture. This would have been a mistake with serious consequences. It would be moving the people toward the biblical culture of the evangelist, instead of allowing a biblical culture to arise out of the people's own cultural context. In figure 4.b, it would be moving the people toward Culture AA instead of Culture BB. It is better to trust the Holy Spirit to help the believers make the right decisions in changing their culture. The cross-cultural evangelist was wise to trust the African's judgment concerning the drums.

CATEGORIES OF CULTURAL DIFFERENCES

Since the cross-cultural evangelist must learn to move through the screen into the target culture, it is important to understand what makes up that screen. Before the evangelist can learn to move through the screen, he must learn how cultures differ from one another. We can divide those differences into seven categories: (1) worldview, (2) value system, (3) behavior patterns, (4) linguistic forms, (5) social system, (6) communication forms, (7) cognitive processes. These are explained below. They can be thought of as the major sections of the cross-cultural screen. It is in these seven major areas that cultural differences can best be defined.

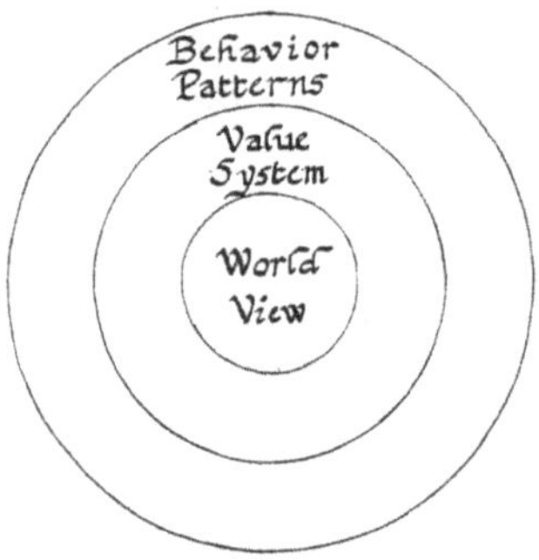

Figure 4.d

Worldview: This is perhaps the most important of the categories because it describes the very heart or center of a culture. Every people group develops a system of concepts or ideas about reality. There is common agreement within their group about the world—how, when, and by whom it was created or came into existence. There is common agreement about mankind's place in the world, about spiritual beings and forces, and about man's relationship to other animals, the spirits, and the universe itself. A people's worldview is their basic perception of the way things are, and how they became that way.

Worldview becomes the mental framework through which everything else is viewed by a people group. For instance, a number of Asian cultures have a worldview which sees spirits capable of inhabiting plants, animals, trees, and even parts of the ground! Some of those cultures have made prohibitions against plowing some or all the soil to raise crops so they will not offend the spirits of the ground. Other cultures will allow the ground to be plowed only a certain way for fear of the spirits. Their worldview generates their values, and their values generate their behavior patterns. Worldview provides a basis for interpreting and understanding events. It determines the things people will value, and the larger primary goals pursued by a people group. That is how worldview becomes a kind of mental framework which controls the other aspects of culture. In that sense, worldview can be considered the main generator of culture. It determines which values and thereby which behaviors are acceptable within a people group.

Value Systems: To value something means to judge it better than something else. So when we talk about value systems, we are referring to those ideas or patterns of thinking which a culture thinks are most important. For instance, cultures in Latin America, Africa, and Asia tend to value the extended family more than the Western cultures of North America and Europe. In the non-Western cultures, life surrounds the needs, opinions, and welfare of the family in a mutually dependent structure of relationships. Also, duty to family in such cultures becomes more important than duty to other institutions of most such societies. The high value placed on the family affects the behavior of every member of the family and the society as a whole. A fuller discussion of value systems can be found in the last part of this chapter.

Behavior Patterns: Every culture establishes broadly accepted ways of doing things. The way people transact business, eat their food, give and receive hospitality, compete for work, dress, and do hundreds of other things are determined by their culture. These are called the behavior patterns of the culture. Some cultures do some things the same way as other cultures, especially when those things depend on environmental and economic conditions. But no culture does everything exactly the same way as another culture.

Cultural behavior patterns emerge from the value systems of their cultures. The values of a culture give rise to patterns of behavior which support those values, and help to define what they are. For instance, Europeans and North Americans place a great value on youthfulness, while most Asians, Africans, and Latin Americans place a higher value on age and maturity. So westernized countries' peoples try to act young, placing a great emphasis on youthful appearance, cosmetics, and physical fitness (even though they tend to be the most overweight in the world). To them, old age is to be dreaded, gray hair is to be colored, and old people are ignored or socially unwanted. But to most non-Western people groups in Latin America, Africa, and Asia, the opposite is true. Old people are highly respected, youthfulness is something which needs to be overcome, and gray hair is called "ripe hair" in some languages. These values have a great effect upon the behavior, language, social structures, and communication forms to be found in each people group. When the elderly are respected, the young still look to them for wisdom, and still try to learn from them. When the elderly are not respected, the old try to act young, and the young have few examples they respect to teach them how to become mature. Behavior patterns are important signs indicating the values of a particular culture.

Linguistic Forms: One of the most obvious barriers to cross-cultural evangelism is the need to communicate the Gospel in the mother tongue of the target people. Perhaps not so obvious to many people is the fact that communicating in another language involves much more than simply learning to speak in that language. Language is a set of encoding symbols used in the communication process as we have studied before. Therefore, it only represents the meaning of a message. It is not the message itself. So even when using one's own language, linguistic symbols (words) are usually unable to carry the full meaning of messages. This is much further complicated when the communicator is using another language.

For instance, the word "salvation" carries great meaning in countries that have been "Christianized" such as those in Latin America and the westernized countries. It is most commonly used to mean eternal life in heaven. But there is no word in many languages which carries the same meaning. For example, "poritran" is used in the Bengali language in the subcontinent of Asia. It is the seventh most spoken language in the world. Probably the best translation for that word in English is "changed soul." To the Hindus of that part of the world, eternal life is something they already have, and not something of particular value. They believe in the "transmigration of souls," the idea that every living thing possesses a soul which never dies, but simply inhabits different bodies successively. This is called reincarnation. To them, life is a constant cycle of being born into one body which eventually dies, then reborn into another body, and so on. To them there is no fundamental difference between the bodies of humans and cows, except that cows are superior to humans! The important thing is that the soul lives on! (Think of the implications when translating the words of Jesus about being "born again"—John 3:3.) To nurture the growth and development of the soul is important to them. The idea that Christ can give us a "changed soul" is a valuable thought to a Hindu mind.

The danger here would be if a cross-cultural evangelist from a westernized country went to start autochthonous churches in India among Hindus, but assumed that the world "salvation" meant the exact same thing to Hindus that it did in his own culture and language. He would likely talk to Hindus about salvation in terms of eternal life. To the average Hindu, eternal life is not something which is appealing, especially to the poor and to those of lower castes. To such people, eternal life can easily be something to be endured, not something that is appealing. The evangelists could be thinking that he is conveying one meaning with the word "poritran," and his Hindu respondents could be hearing a completely different message. If the evangelist truly understands the linguistic forms of the target people who are Hindus, he would emphasize how Christ can change the soul and how the freedom that Christ brings delivers them from reincarnation. He would explain what the Bible says about living with God in heaven with our spirits free from the bondage of the flesh, and with our spirits purified and at peace with God by the sacrifice of Christ.

This is just a glimpse of how linguistic symbols differ between cultures. This can be multiplied times almost every single word in every language. Experts have estimated that there is virtually no word in any language which can be translated into another language and carry exactly the same meaning in every context! Culture defines the meaning! Even simple words like "no" and "yes" carry far different meanings at different times among the different cultures of the world.

At this point, the reader may conclude that it is almost impossible to learn how to effectively communicate in another language. Actually, it is not as difficult as it appears, if the right methods for learning the languages of other peoples are followed. This is such an important subject, it is discussed in more detail in chapter five.

Social Structures: This is a very important category of cultural differences. Social structures refer to the way people interact in groups within a society. It includes such things as the way people act toward their families and relatives, the roles of leadership and how leaders are given status, social groups which emerge in the society, and the hierarchy which determines which people have the greatest influence on other members of society. Social structures are a form of behavior patterns which arise out of the values of the society.

If the family is very important in a society, a great deal of time and energy will be given toward family needs and desires. The hierarchy of authority in the family will be important, and relatives will feel a great loyalty toward one another's welfare. If the religion of a people group is very important to the people, many of the institutions of the society as a whole will surround the religion of the people.

Social class is an important part of the social structure. Each society has an upper, middle, and lower class. Within those three classes, there can be many subclasses. People belong to different classes for different reasons in different cultures. In many societies, class is determined primarily by wealth, education, and vocation. In other societies, class is determined by lineage (ancestry). In some societies, class may simply be determined by physical strength. It may also be ascribed by the amount of spiritual or magical knowledge a person possesses. Class can also be determined by a combination of such things. Each society has its own rules for assigning people to social class.

Some cultures have open classes. This means that somebody from a lower class can find opportunity to move to a higher class by meeting the requirements for membership in that class. If a culture assigns class primarily according to how much money or education a person possesses, it would be an example of an open culture. Open cultures also allow for a free flow of communication between classes, up and down. Though people may spend most of their time with members of their own class, it is acceptable for them to spend time with members of another class.

Some cultures have more closed classes. An example would be India. Traditionally, though less so now, it has been forbidden for members of lower classes (called castes) to interact with high classes in that country, except when performing services for those higher classes. There are many castes at all levels in India. This has created a severely stratified, or layered, society. Members of closed cultures generally forbid marriage outside of caste or class. In recent decades, India has passed laws to make the caste system illegal. Yet, it still exists in practice to a lesser degree than before. The more closed a culture, the less intermarriage between castes and classes is tolerated.

Cross-cultural evangelists must study the social structure of people groups to which God calls them very carefully. As a guest among those people, he should learn to work through those structures as much as possible and not against them. A knowledge of these structures will help him evangelize a people group much faster and more effectively. For instance, in cultures where family and kinship is very important to the people, they build strong webs of interrelationships between families through intermarriage. Experienced cross-cultural evangelists have discovered that the Gospel can spread very rapidly among a people group by means of those webs of relationships. By using that knowledge when planning strategy, some evangelists have been very fruitful among such peoples.

Communication Forms: We have already discussed communication forms in chapter three. Remember, different cultures value different methods of communication over others. One cross-cultural evangelist working among an isolated tribal group in Latin America, the Motilone, finally succeeded in gaining one convert after two years. He earnestly wanted the young man to tell many others about Christ so they would accept Him and churches would be formed. But month after month went by after the young man accepted Christ without the young man saying anything about his new faith to his people group. Finally, the tribe held a special annual meeting for all the people. Each year they would gather together for a singing competition. Different contestants from different villages would climb a tree and sing to everybody, composing words of their song as they sang. Sometimes one person would sing for a long time. While the competition was in progress, the cross-cultural evangelist suddenly noticed that the young man who had accepted Christ was climbing the tree to compete in the competition. To his amazement, the young man began to compose words that told the story of the Gospel from beginning to end! He sang for a very long time with melodic, rhythmic phrases that held the attention of everyone.

Within a few weeks after the competition, many people of those villages had become Christians! The evangelist had been anxious because the young man had not witnessed about his faith. But he purposely had waited for this yearly event and the singing competition. Whenever someone had an important message for the people, he would wait for the singing competition to communicate it. That would make it very important to all the other people of his tribe. The young man waited for the competition because he knew it was the most important message they had ever heard. The evangelist wisely did not push him. He just waited in frustration. He gave him the freedom to choose how, when, and if to communicate. By using the communication forms so highly valued by his people, the young man became a very successful evangelist himself![27]

Cognitive Processes: Every culture builds up a body of knowledge which is commonly accepted as true by its people. This may be "knowledge" which is focused at the worldview level, or it may simply be knowledge about plants, animals, or people at the behavioral level. But behind what a people group knows, it is important to find out how they know what they know! What kind of thinking do they do to know what is true or important?

Christians believe the Bible is the Word of God. The Bible presents truth in a way which can be reasoned logically and rationally. It represents the history of mankind as beginning at one point, leading

[27] Bruce Olson, *Bruchko* (Charisma Media, 2006).

up to the present, and leading toward Christ's reign in the future. Many cultures base their thinking on a different worldview. The Hindus see history as an endless repetition of the same events. Tribal groups in parts of the world see the world as controlled by unseen spirits. Koreans have a very highly educated population, yet when the moon is full, some Koreans still sacrifice chickens at the intersections of major roads. These practices represent different ways of thinking about reality.

People with different worldviews and cultures make decisions different ways. Some people groups may make decisions based mostly on intuition or feeling. This would be true of people groups which are very concerned about spiritual forces which may control their lives. Other people groups may make decisions based on scientific, rational thinking. Western cultures would fit this category. Many Eastern cultures make decisions on the basis of how it would honor or dishonor people. In each of these cultures, people may do some things the same way, but the reasons they decide to do them that way can vary greatly from culture to culture.

When Paul preached to the Athenians (Acts 17:18–34), he used the Greek way of reasoning to communicate his message. It is important for the cross-cultural evangelist to learn the way his target people group thinks. Jesus taught with many parables because the people were accustomed to drawing conclusions from life's experiences. If the cross-cultural evangelist is careful to learn the thinking patterns of the people he is called to reach, he will be more successful in leading them toward a decision to truly follow Christ.

Each of these seven categories of cultural differences should be understood by every cross-cultural evangelist. He should constantly seek to learn more about his target people in each of these categories. As he learns to understand how his target culture differs from his own culture, he will have much of the understanding necessary to be successful in communicating the Gospel to those people. Even in the same country, different people groups can have widely varied assumptions about reality in these categories of cultural differences.

EXPLORING FORMS AND MEANINGS

To Africans, the dance has long been a major tool for transmitting values, ideals, emotions, and history. The African understands it as one of his most important communication forms. Cross-cultural evangelists who have gone to Africa have sometimes made serious errors in judgment concerning the meanings attached to African dance.

Some years ago, an important women's leader from one country went to visit Africa. Her country had sent cross-cultural evangelists to Africa who had successfully started churches among a certain tribe of people. Upon hearing that this well-known leader was coming, the Christian ladies of the African tribe wanted to do something very special to welcome her. They decided to perform a dance drama in which they portrayed the history of the Gospel coming to their people. They wanted to show appreciation for the sacrifice of those who had brought the Gospel to them.

They began the drama by portraying themselves naked. They had a bunch of leaves in front and some more behind as their only clothing. This is similar to the way they often dressed in the fields and in out-of-the-way places where outsiders would not see them. Then they danced an elaborate and detailed story showing how the Gospel had been brought to them. The tempo of the drums increased as the drama unfolded. It ended with everybody going to church together in their brightest and newest clothing. But their foreign visitor, seeing the naked women dancing so enthusiastically, their whole bodies bouncing with every beat of the drums, simply could not contain her shock! In a storm of indignation, she began to berate them for their "heathen" display as unworthy of Christians. The poor African Christians were stunned by this reaction. After all their elaborate preparations, their sincere effort to show their gratitude for those who had brought them the Gospel, they were hurt, crestfallen, and humiliated. Their joyful act of appreciation and very real joy of worship they had been in the process of displaying through their drama story dancing had been cruelly spurned by their honored guest![28]

The Goal: Absolute Meanings and Relative Forms

We have already given a number of examples of ways people groups use symbols to communicate meaning. The whole communications process requires the use of symbols. As we have already seen, different people groups come to value different communication forms and different symbols. The foreign visitor to the African group above was totally unprepared for the communication forms and symbols of the African dance drama. To the Africans, they carried an important and beautiful message of joy and celebration of what Christianity had done for them. To their honored guest, however, they carried an entirely different set of meanings. She did not understand the symbolic meaning of the dance gestures of the African women. She also did not understand the purpose of clothing to the Africans. To her, clothing was used to cover nakedness, and for being modest. To the African, the clothing was used mostly for ornamentation. In many African cultures historically, wearing clothes has been considered to be immodest, attention-grabbing, and disrespectful to elders. To the foreign lady, the drama did not tell a story at all. It only conveyed vulgar and suggestive meanings because she did not understand African symbols and forms. The Africans did not understand her behavior either. They could not conceive that the meanings of their dance drama could be so hard to understand for anyone. Even the smallest child in their villages understood the significance of the message of the dance drama.

The basic problem in this illustration is a failure to distinguish between meanings and forms. The dance drama and all its symbols was a form of communication which carried one kind of meaning to the Africans, and another kind to their lady guest. The lady interpreted the forms the only way she knew how—according to the standards of her own culture. If she had understood exactly what

[28] https://www.asa3.org/ASA/PSCF/1958/JASA6-58Smalley.html.

the Africans were trying to do, and if she understood the principle of absolute meanings and relative forms, she would not have been upset. She would have recognized the great honor being given to her. She would have been much more gracious and kind, as she should have been.

When we speak of something being absolute, we are talking about something that does not change. It is the opposite of relative. When we speak of absolute meanings in cross-cultural ministry, we are talking about the need to follow closely the biblical principles in the Bible. Earlier, we discussed the need to follow biblical principles with cultural methods. The principle of absolute meanings and relative forms refers to the need to communicate the biblical principles, which never change, through the use of culturally meaningful forms, which do change.

In the story above, the lady guest did not understand the meaning of the dance drama form of communication in the African tribe. She also did not understand the meanings behind their forms of dress. The absolute principle which was in question was the scriptural principle of modesty for Christian women. Though the lady did not know it, the Africans would have wholeheartedly agreed with the need for Christians to be modest. But the way they defined modesty was much different. Some African tribes like the Gava people of Nigeria have traditionally thought of people covering their body only if they have something to hide, are untrustworthy, or want to attract immodest attention to themselves! Historically, it was considered dishonorable for a woman to wear clothing, especially above the waist! Perhaps only a prostitute would do such a thing. So the Gava people historically wore little or no clothing in order to prove their sincerity and trustworthiness in public. Other tribal groups, like the Higi people of Nigeria, historically wore clothing on occasion, and mostly for ornamentation. They may change or rearrange clothing in public without feeling immodest, since it only represented decoration to them. It appears that the people to whom the lady guest went to join their celebration were more like the Higi people group.

The lady did not understand the meanings behind the symbols and gestures of the fervent African dancing. To her, the event was a bizarre display of ungodly, offensive, and unchristian behavior. She judged the open nakedness and dancing as "heathen" and lewd behavior, which it would have been in her own culture. But the Africans saw it as a display of excellent talent, full of important Christian meaning. The only meaning the nakedness had to the Africans was that it helped to tell the joyful story they were telling with the dance. To them, the whole event was full of joyful celebration and Christian meaning. Both the lady and the Africans saw the exact same cultural behavior, but each interpreted it according to the meaning of their own culture.

There is a great lesson in this story. It important because too many otherwise good cross-cultural ministers make the mistake of confusing forms and meanings. The results may not be as dramatic as in this story, but the damage to their ministry can be even more long-lasting. There are absolute biblical meanings (principles and truths) which must be communicated effectively to a target people group in order for the Gospel to penetrate their hearts and mainstream of their culture. The problem comes when we realize that each culture has different forms to communicate the same meanings! In figure 4.c, this common mistake is diagrammed. So is the method for preventing the mistake.

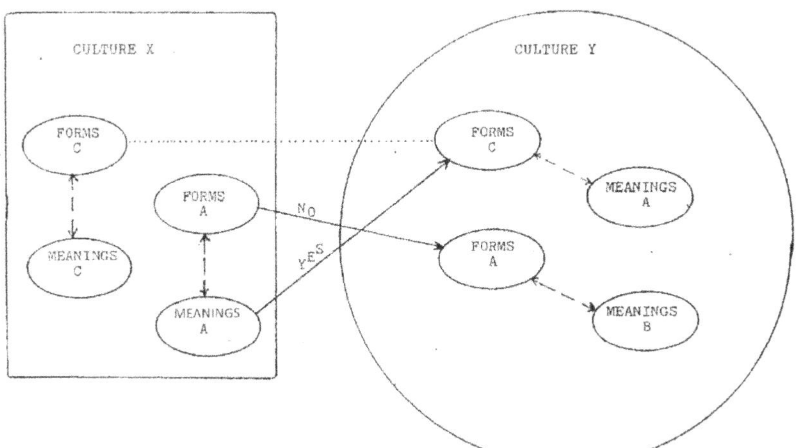

FORMS AND MEANINGS DIFFERENTIAL

Figure 4.c

Let us assume a cross-cultural evangelist from Culture X is working in Culture Y. His goal is to communicate the biblical meanings contained in Meanings A. In his own culture, the way to effectively communicate Meanings A is to use Forms A. Forms A stands for all the language and behavior symbols which effectively represent biblical Meanings A in Culture A. But if the evangelist attempts to use Forms A in Culture Y, the Culture Y people think he is communicating Meanings B. Since those forms in his own culture do not represent Meanings A, the evangelist must work to learn the culture well enough to learn what forms to communicate Meanings A in Culture Y. After learning the target cultural norms, the evangelist realizes that it will require Forms C to communicate the biblical Meanings A in Culture Y. Even though Forms C might even have unbiblical meanings in his own culture, he recognizes they have valid biblical meanings in Culture Y. Therefore, he gladly adopts those Forms C to communicate biblical meanings when working among the target people of Culture Y.

In the story above, the lady guest saw Form C (the naked dancing) only from the perspective of what they would mean in her own Culture A. But Form C conveyed Meaning A to the Africans and was a very positive representation of the value of the Gospel.

The task of the effective cross-cultural evangelist is to find the cultural forms which best communicate the biblical meanings of the Gospel within the mainstream of the target culture. They will seldom be the same forms of his own culture. In a world of mass communication and cell phone usage, there is an international "metaculture" which is emerging, adopting the forms and many of the meanings more common in the Western world by those utilizing such high-tech tools. As we will discuss in more detail below, it is important for the cross-cultural minister not to assume that such a metaculture represents the mainstream of the target culture he is called to reach. He must adopt the forms of the target culture in the mainstream of its population, not a fringe metaculture.

Paul used the debate-dialogue method of communication common to Greek philosophers when preaching on Mars Hill (Acts 17:16–34). The young convert from the Motilone tribe of Colombia used the singing contest form to communicate the Gospel effectively. Converts from Islam in a Southern Asian country utilized a prized poetic and rhythmic public soliloquy to communicate the Gospel in their culture. Even if the valued forms of communication in a target culture are unfamiliar to him, so that it is difficult for him to know how to use them himself, the evangelist should still encourage the use of those forms by converts in the target culture. This will make the true meaning and worth of the Gospel understandable to people he is trying to evangelize.

AN ENCULTURATION STRATEGY

It is important for the cross-cultural evangelist to develop a workable strategy for moving through the "cultural screen" and into a position within a culture. He or she must not only understand how cultures differ from one another, and know principles for effectively communicating biblical truth, but they must also know how to personally become enculturated within a target people group.

Enculturation is the process of learning to be as mentally, emotionally, and linguistically comfortable in another culture as we are in our own culture. It is a lengthy process of language and culture learning as will be discussed in the next chapter of this book. There are important principles to assist the cross-cultural evangelist in achieving this objective.

Before the principles of an enculturation strategy can be set forth, a further discussion of worldview, value systems, and behavior patterns is helpful. Worldview is at the center of every culture. It is the primary generator of culture (see figure 4.d). What a people thinks is true at the worldview level will create a set of values that will conform to that picture of reality. Those values, in turn, will generate a set of behaviors for people in that culture.

Figure 4.d: Worldview, Generator of Culture

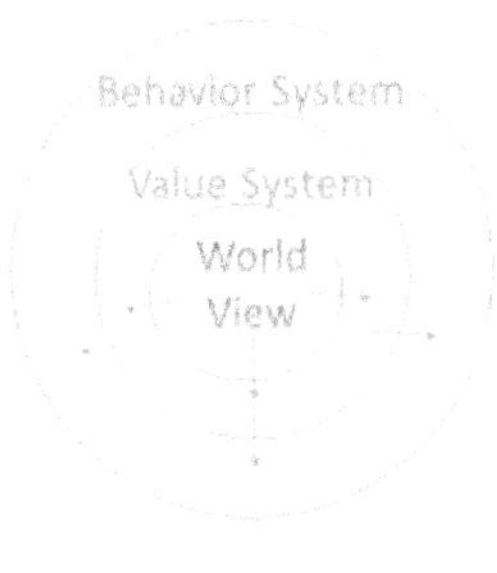

In many Eastern cultures of Asia, for example,

a common worldview is the idea that mankind was created to live in harmony with nature. This has led to a number of cultural values. One of the most common among such cultures is the strong emphasis placed on avoiding conflict between people. Open interpersonal conflict of any kind is to be avoided if at all possible. Specific kinds of behavior which have resulted from this worldview and cultural value system are the following: (1) Becoming angry in public is to be avoided at almost all costs. Angry people are immature and unworthy of positions of trust or authority. (2) Do not confront a person with a mistake or weakness even indirectly. Do not cause another person to lose face, or be ashamed before others. (3) It is more important to tell a person what he or she wants to hear rather than what you really think, if telling him would cause him shame or humiliation.

The behavior of people in a culture with the above values and behaviors can be very frustrating to people from other parts of the world. Westerners, and particularly Americans and Australians, are much more individualistic and direct than the peoples of Eastern cultures. A common problem arises when people of Eastern cultures say "yes" when they really mean "no." For instance, the author was once in an Asian culture where he invited a Christian leader to meet him at a church to discuss an important matter for the work of the Lord. The leader sensed that there may be some disagreement or conflict arise in such a meeting, so he did not want to go to the meeting. So when I asked him if he could meet me at the church, he said, "Yes, I could come." To me, it meant he had promised to be there. But he did not meet me there. To him, he was telling me that he would not be there. "Could come" was not saying he would be there at all, in his mind. To refuse a request openly would have caused me to "lose face," so he was carefully choosing his words to let me know that he would not be there. If he had really intended to come, he would have said, "Yes, I will come." I was fairly new in that culture. So I did not understand that he had politely refused to be at the meeting. I waited for him for about an hour before I realized he would not be there. I did not realize that he had politely told me he was not coming. I left wondering what kind of Christians the leaders of that country are. How could he have "lied to me"? But to him, he had not lied at all.

He had simply refused the invitation to potential conflict in a polite way. This little story is one of many little incidents in the experience of this cross-cultural evangelist author that illustrates how behavior patterns stem from value systems which result from worldview.

Culture Shock

The enculturation process begins the day the cross-cultural evangelist first begins to study the people to whom he has been called. When he actually arrives in that culture, he must begin by learning to understand the behavior patterns of the people (figure 4.d). He will not understand why people do things the way they do. At first, he may even be impatient or irritated with the way they do things. This is a normal reaction to entering another culture, and it is part of what is known as culture shock.

Everyone experiences culture shock when entering another culture. The degree of culture shock depends upon the degree to which the host culture is different from the home culture. It also depends upon the personality and preparation of the person entering the new culture. Everyone will experience some culture shock when they enter another culture. This is especially true of cross-cultural evangelists and their families who know they will be living and working in their new culture for a long time. Below are some of the symptoms of culture shock, presented in increasingly deeper order:

1. **Disorientation around local people:** An uncomfortable feeling and an anxious, nervous feeling are common, especially when the language is not understood.
2. **Desire to withdraw:** Communication with local people is difficult. Unspoken negative feedback is common by locals. The initiate has a strong urge to escape from gatherings of local people, and spend time mostly around people of his own culture if possible.
3. **Comparison of the two cultures:** The initiate constantly is noticing the differences between the behavior patterns (called norms) of his own culture and those of the host

culture. The initiate finds himself voicing those differences to those around him. By doing so, he is unaware that in the minds of locals, he is often insulting their way of life and showing that he thinks his own culture is better than theirs.

4. **Cultural norms rejected:** The initiate does not understand the values and reasons behind the way people do things. He interprets local norms according to what they would mean in his own culture. He may show contempt for local behavior norms, and even vent his frustration through anger, or by making fun of the local people's way of life (local people will be very offended if they hear about or witness this emotion).
5. **Feelings of failure:** There will often be a feeling that progress in language learning or ministry has slowed to almost nothing. Normal plateaus in learning or work progress seem much more important than they are. Discouragement and intense frustration are common. Feelings of self-worth are diminished greatly.
6. **Feelings of imprisonment:** The initiate may begin to feel so much like a failure that he doesn't want to try anymore. He feels trapped, like a prisoner. He cannot leave the culture because of his commitment, yet he fears he cannot learn to live in the culture for the rest of his life and be effective. He often feels like he would like to escape, but he cannot.
7. **Feelings of hostility:** There is secret or open bitterness toward those responsible for the initiate's present situation. It could be those who assigned him to where he is, or in the work he is doing. He may blame the local people, other leaders from his own culture, or even God.
8. **Loss of spiritual vision:** The initiate loses sight of the original purposes for coming to the host culture. His faith in himself and in God is greatly diminished. He can see nothing in his present situation to give him hope.
9. **Rejection of cultural norms:** The initiate finds fault with local forms of behavior. He may label them stupid or prim-

itive or unscriptural. He emotionally begins to reject everything about the local culture, and he wants out of it, or wants to retreat to places where he can be around his own kind of people.

10. **Self-rejection and guilt:** Because he no longer wants to spend time with the local people, he increasingly feels guilty. Inwardly, the frustrations, feelings of failure, loss of vision, and discouragement about language learning cause the initiate to feel like a failure. He may often consider quitting the cross-cultural ministry he committed himself to do, and perhaps the ministry itself.

Though the above symptoms of culture shock are presented in the order of increased intensity, a person can experience one or all of them at any point in the enculturation process. And they can be experienced in varying degrees. It is safe to say that the initiate into another culture will experience at least some of them.

The depth and intensity of culture shock will be dependent upon how well prepared the cross-cultural evangelist and his family are before entering the target culture. Studying the material in this book will greatly diminish the level, length, and intensity of culture shock. The more the principles of this book are absorbed prior to departure for the target culture, the less effect it will have on those who do ministry cross-culturally.

It is important to understand that culture shock is normal when entering a target culture. It is caused by a drastic change in cultural norms of behavior. In the initiate's own culture, he has learned from childhood the behavior patterns commonly accepted by his own people. He knows how to act so that people will give him positive feedback and reinforcement as a person. When he or she enters another culture, however, many or most of the norms in his culture do not fit those of the new culture. Positive behavior among his own people often becomes negative behavior in the new culture. Even before he speaks the language, he may sense a negative reaction to his presence. People in the new culture may not tell him they do not like his "foreign" behavior, but they give him negative feedback through their gestures and facial expressions. This makes the initiate feel uncomfortable, but he is not sure why. This happens in many different ways when one enters another culture. The initiate can increasingly feel out of place because when he tries to act normal (using his own cultural patterns of behavior), people seem to reject him. He may have been a highly respected preacher in his own culture, for instance. But in the new culture, he can hardly communicate anything. Even when he says nothing, his behavior seems unacceptable. He feels like a child starting over again. This is the kind of process that leads to culture shock.

Culture shock can be greatly minimized by following good principles of enculturation. The most important ones are discussed below. Using these principles as guidelines, together with those found in chapter five, the cross-cultural evangelist can experience rapid enculturation, minimal culture shock, and have a very effective rapidly growing ministry among those whom he has been called to serve.

Principles for Enculturation

1. **Copy the behavior patterns of the host culture:** When a cross-cultural minister first enters another culture, he will enter at the level of behavior patterns. His understanding of that culture's value system and worldview will be minimal. He must learn to understand them over a period of time. He is not competent to judge the rightness or value of behaviors from a Christian biblical perspective until he understands them fully. And as we see, he will want to focus on changing a target culture's worldview, then the values and behaviors will gradually conform to biblical principles under the leadership of the new believers. Two to five years is normally required for the enculturation process to be complete. Even after five years, the process will not be complete unless the correct principles are followed. Some cross-cultural ministers never completely become enculturated because they never attempt to fully adopt the general behavior patterns of the host culture.

The evangelist must learn to eat, sleep, travel, entertain guests, and do a host of other things just like the people of the host culture. By doing things their way, he will soon begin to understand why they do things their way. This will also eventually lead to an understanding of the values behind those behavior patterns. He will not only learn to understand, but also he will begin to adopt many of those values himself. They will begin to make sense to him. He will also become competent to judge which of their values and behaviors are in conflict with Scripture and therefore should not be followed by himself. The more the cross-cultural evangelist can adopt the behavior of the local people, the more they will know he respects and values them and the more effective he will become in influencing them to embrace the Gospel.

It is a mistake to enter another culture to evangelize its people, then only spend as little time as possible with those people, as we shall see in chapter five. The most effective cross-cultural evangelists are those who determine from the beginning to adopt the social and behavior patterns of the host culture, instead of trying to maintain the patterns of his own culture. He will spend time with the people whenever and as much as possible. He will learn to relax and have fun with members of the host (target) people. This is important because everyone needs times of relaxation. If he does not learn to relax with the target people in the same manner they do, he will likely turn to people outside the host culture for meeting his and his family's need for relaxation and fellowship. That would cut him off from the deep and meaningful times of communication and the enculturation process. Nonformal times of communication are most often the most effective.

Adopting the behavior patterns of the host culture does not mean the evangelist must adopt behavior which would compromise his own sense of morality. He does not have to "go native" in order to identify with the behavior patterns of the host people. And they will not expect him to be exactly like them. The host people recognize that he is from another culture, and that he will never act exactly like them. And they will notice very much those things in their culture that he does not copy. Hopefully, he will choose the things in their culture to avoid copying because he is basing his decisions on good biblical principles. Hopefully, the things he chooses not to do like them will point to a better way of life that they recognize is needed. The key is to adopt as much of their behavior as possible in order to identify with them and in order to learn their value system and their worldview.

2. **Help the Gospel change their worldview:** It is not enough to preach the Gospel to another people, then settle for changes in their lives only at the level of their behavior patterns (figure 4.d). Until the Gospel affects their worldview and their value system, it is not really affecting their society in a powerful way. An evangelist may be able to persuade some of the people to behave differently according to his own example. They may go to church and participate in Christian activities, yet still resort to witchcraft, Spiritism, or other non-Christian activities when they are sick or afraid. This is ***syncretism***, the mixture of Christianity with other religions or spiritual practices. It includes Christianity in the religious beliefs of the people, but does not follow biblical truth at the deepest and most vital levels.

   Syncretism is overcome by penetrating the worldview and value system of a target people with the implications and spiritual benefits of the Gospel. The people must truly believe the Gospel enough that they adopt a Christian perspective about reality. They must formulate and adopt biblical values as they see the necessity to do so. They must see the power of the Holy Spirit as greater than other spirits or forces—enough so that they learn to rely on the Holy Spirit alone. This will become evident not only when they are acting like Christians in church, but also when they are sick, in danger, or in distress. When their Christian faith becomes their sole source of help and the framework for expressing their greatest joys, then it will have penetrated their culture at the worldview and value system level. It will then be capable of having a very effective impact on the whole target culture.

3. **<u>Make a basic value profile of the target culture:</u>** After learning most of the behavior patterns of the host culture, the evangelist will begin to understand the basic values of the people. It is helpful to study those values very carefully, and to contrast them with the values of his own culture. This will give him a clearer understanding of how to communicate the Gospel to the people, what mistakes to avoid, and what autochthonous churches among those people should be like. Perhaps just as important, it will help him explain some of their behavior which he still does not understand fully. Figure 4.e is a chart for learning and evaluating the basic values of a culture.

Figure 4.e: Basic Values Profile

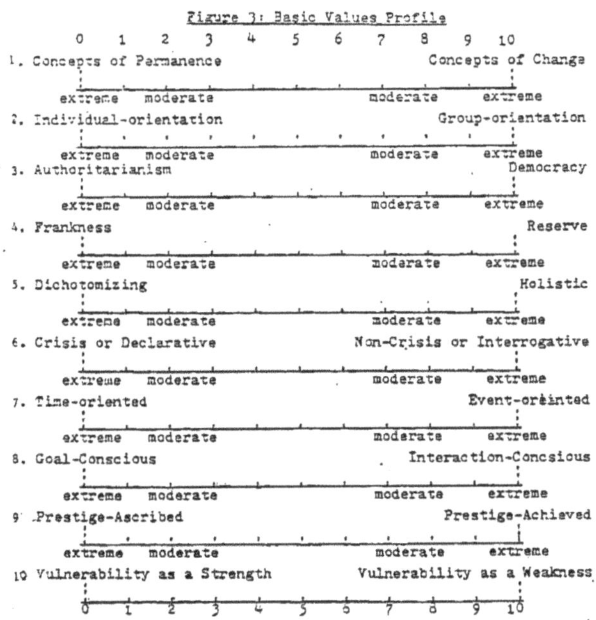

To use the chart, place an X on each line about where you think your own culture would lie. Then put a Y on the same line where you think your host culture would lie. For instance, line one on the chart measures the willingness to accept rapid changes in the society. So if your own society is moderately willing to see rapid changes as desirable and part of progress, you should put an X on the line below 7 or 8 column. Then, let's say the host culture is much more traditional and afraid of rapid changes. They may see change as a threat to their people, its leaders, and their way of life. If that is the case, you should put a Y on the same line in the 1 or 2 column. The greater the distance between the value for your culture (X) and the value for the host culture (Y), the more important it is for you to study, ask questions, and learn about that aspect of their culture. You need to learn what assumptions at the worldview level are responsible for that value in their culture. You also need to discover as many behavior patterns as you can which are a result of that value. Here is a list of other basic values on the profile together with an explanation of their meanings:

A. **Individual / Group Orientation:** If the people feel strong duties toward their families or tribal group which are as important as taking care of their own needs or desires, then they are group-oriented. They might be about an eight or nine on the scale. In such cultures, people often live in joint families, with many relatives living in the same place. In cities, they may even live in the same home or apartment. In individual-oriented cultures, the people spend most of their energy taking care of the needs and desires of their own immediate family or themselves. They feel less obligation toward the whole family or tribe. More than 50 percent of the world's population now live in cities, some of them with tens of millions of people. Out of financial necessity, urbanization tends to break down group orientation. People need to live near where they work in cities. That does not mean group orientation disappears. It simply takes on different forms of behavior. While it does move families closer to individual orientation, the ties to family and rural roots remain strong. Urbanization tends to move families toward the left of the scale.

B. **Authoritarian/Democratic:** If the political, religious, and public institutions of the host culture emphasize authoritarian leadership, and if decision-making involves little discussion or involvement by the people those decisions affect, then the culture is authoritarian. It belongs at nine or ten on the chart. Democratic cultures tend to be the opposite, with many people participating in decision-making. Even in Western-style business meetings and church meetings, Eastern cultures tend to be more authoritarian than it appears. While working in Asia, the author came to realize that real decisions were made informally around dinner the night **before** an important business or leadership meeting. The consensus on what should be done was thoroughly discussed, and decisions were made before the formal meetings the next day. The formal meetings were just that—an important set of formalities designed to confirm the relative authority and status of the individuals at the meeting. The younger people would be allowed to participate in discussion to help pave the way toward the direction the discussions would take. Older leaders would begin to participate as the discussion went forward. Finally, the senior or most respected leader would state his opinion just before the final vote. That would indicate the results of the vote. Yet, everyone knew the decision had already been made the night before, and that the meetings were simply a ritual formality to satisfy the Western participants at the meeting. The author soon learned how to get invited to the meetings the night before the formal meeting. This process made sense to local leaders and was in perfect harmony with the need to "save face" that is so prevalent in Eastern cultures.

C. **Frankness/Reserve:** If the people usually do not say what they actually think openly, and they do not offer their opinions spontaneously and often, they are more reserved cultures. They would be at six or above on the scale. Cultures that value frankness are the opposite. Eastern cultures tend to be much more reserved than Western cultures. The frankness and openness, the "telling it like it is" which is so valued in Western cultures, is abhorrent and unthinkable in many Eastern cultures. For example, Eastern leaders may feel much more comfortable having a Westerner express an opinion that is controversial in meetings such as those discussed above. They may have the same opinion, but would rather the Westerner express it openly, reducing their own risk of being viewed as disruptive of the norm. In their mind, the Westerner can be excused for openly expressing such opinions. He is not one of them. It is an effective way to introduce change without much risk, just in case the change is rejected by other leaders.

D. **Dichotomizing/Holistic:** Peoples which tend to see issues, problems, and opportunities in terms of their opposite extremes, in black-and-white terms, are dichotomizing cultures. Cultures which see things as a part of a whole picture are more holistic. They see something that affects one part of a subject as affecting the whole. Islamic cultures and Western cultures are most often dichotomizing in comparison to Hindu cultures, for example. Hindu cultures are very holistic because they see the universe, its people, its animals, and its spirits inextricably linked together and influenced by all interdependent components. So Islamic and Christian cultures would lie somewhere at six or above on the scale, while Hindu cultures would lie toward the far left, perhaps at three or below on the scale.

E. **Crisis/Non-Crisis:** Crisis-oriented cultures tend to be authoritarian as well. They value special people who lead them when they have problems or a crisis which threatens everyone. Non-crisis peoples are usually group-oriented in their decision-making. They value being able to choose from a number of alternatives. They analyze a problem or situation together much more before making decisions. The characteristics of either side of this behavioral scale can be found among peoples in any part of the world. It is important for the cross-cultural evangelist to learn a culture deeply, before making premature judgments about the dynamics of this behavior pattern.

F. **Time / Event-Oriented:** Time-oriented cultures schedule their day very rigidly, and they do not like to interrupt their schedules. Such peoples are usually individual-oriented and goal-conscious. Event-oriented peoples do not place so much emphasis on time. People and events are more important than time schedules. They will interrupt their time plans, if they have any, in order to entertain guests or to participate in a special occasion. For example, many cultures in the Middle East and Eastern Mediterranean regions are more event-oriented to the point that their culture demands that they entertain guests as a priority. If someone is accepted as a guest in such cultures, he is "honor" ("besa") bound. While in someone's home, that whole family is obligated to protect the guest even at the risk of members of their family, if necessary. The event of having a guest takes precedence over the needs of the family in order to serve, feed, house, and protect the guest. Such cultures would be at nine or ten on the scale (see an example in Genesis 19).

G. **Goal-Conscious / Interaction-Conscious:** Interaction-conscious cultures place great importance on social events, ceremonies, elaborate hospitality patterns, and the importance of interpersonal interaction. They are usually event-oriented and group-oriented. Most Latin cultures, tribal cultures, and rural cultures are interaction-conscious. As urbanization increases, economic and urban realities assault such cultures and require that they become more goal-conscious in order to survive in urban environments. Goal-conscious cultures are usually also more time-oriented. They highly value material success and production goals. They are more common in urban environments. They are less likely to interrupt their schedules to accommodate other people. Even when they do, their obligations to such people are diminished. They are expected to do less for them than they would in a rural setting, yet they still feel bound by traditional values and try to follow them as much as possible.

H. **Prestige-Ascribed / Prestige-Achieved:** In some cultures, a person can gain status and prestige by working hard and accomplishing significant goals in any sphere of activity. Such a person can gain those things which the culture values and admires. It could be wealth, physical strength, or many other things the culture values and he strives to obtain. Those cultures where such a gain in prestige is possible as a result of a person's own efforts are called prestige-achieved cultures. In other cultures, a person can obtain status and prestige mostly by having it given to him by others or as a result of his birth. For instance, if a Hindu is born into the high Brahmin caste (class) in India, he is automatically given much more prestige, privilege, and honor than someone born into a lower caste. The prestige he receives is ascribed to him automatically based on his birthrights.

I. **Vulnerability as a Strength or Weakness:** Vulnerability refers to a person being transparent enough to allow other people to see his weaknesses. Many cultures, such as most oriental cultures which are called shame cultures, do not value character traits which allow other people to see one's personal weaknesses or failures. Their behavior tends to try to keep such weaknesses covered up before other people so as not to shame the person or family involved. This keeps people from becoming vulnerable to those who know their weaknesses. This kind of culture is a "vulnerability as a weakness" culture. Other cultures, particularly Western ones, tend to see this kind of behavior as being phony, deceptive, or even dishonest. Notice how judgmental such words sound. Every culture's people do not want to broadcast individual weakness to some level. But to the Western mindset, Christianity has deeply ingrained the idea that everyone is a sinner in need of a Savior. Therefore, admitting sinfulness, failure, and the errors of human nature are a positive behavior to the Westerner. Trying to cover them up is a mistake which will not succeed. Therefore, Westerners admire people who are the most open, transparent, and not threatened by allowing their weaknesses to be known. To the Westerner, they are the most genuine and believable kind of people. Many African cultures are more like Western cultures in this regard, compared to Asian cultures. Many Asian cultures, devoid of Christian worldviews, think of such vulnerability as dangerous, if not plain stupid!

By charting the position of a target culture on the basic values profile and comparing it to his own culture, the evangelist can gain great insight into the value system of the people he is evangelizing. It will help him to make sense out of the value system of the people group he is evangelizing. It will help him understand their worldview much more quickly as well. Just as importantly, it will accelerate the process of his own enculturation, which is vital to his success.

4. **The effective cross-cultural evangelist will judge his own social, moral, and religious behavior according to the standards of the host culture.** Cross-cultural evangelists must avoid ethnocentrism. Instead of judging the behavior patterns of the host people group by his own cultural standards and definitions, he must do the opposite. He must judge his own behavior according to the meanings given to that behavior in the local culture. Acting like a devout Christian according to his own cultural standards may appear to be very unholy or even offensive behavior to the people in the local culture. For instance, it may be normal behavior for the woman in the evangelist's own culture to wear dresses which are a few inches above the knee. That could be considered modest clothing in the evangelist's own culture. But if the evangelist and his family are to go to another culture (such as India) where the women should not be seen in public unless their clothing is long enough to cover their ankles,

then his family's behavior should conform to the standard of the host culture. To do less would unnecessarily lessen the respect the people have for his family, and also for the Gospel he represents.

The evangelist should follow the norms of the host culture in every possible way. If the people believe it is important to pray early in the morning, as is the case in Korea, then he should learn to do so also. If the culture sets a higher standard for personal honesty than his own culture, then he should also set a higher standard for his own family. If anything, the behavior of the evangelist should signify greater genuine piety and devotion to God than the average person in that culture. He must be careful to avoid any behavior which is considered unworthy of a religious person. The behavioral standard of the host culture is not the goal. It is the starting point. The wise evangelist follows those standards as much as possible so he can gain a hearing for even greater standards—those of the Bible and the life and teachings of Jesus!

5. **The effective cross-cultural evangelist will refrain from introducing important ideas, messages, and innovations until he is sure he has built a platform from which he can be heard in the minds of the respondents.** One of the most common mistakes made by cross-cultural evangelists is to start "preaching" the Gospel as soon as they arrive in a new culture. They preach the same kind of messages and use the same illustrations and communication forms they would use in their own culture. When this is done, the thought processes, communication forms, illustrations, and the attitude of the messenger will all appear very foreign and often undesirable in the minds of the audience. Even if the people understand the message of the evangelist fairly well because of a good interpreter, they will likely not value it very much. This is especially true among a people group which is not acquainted with the Gospel message. To them, such preaching may actually become an inoculation against the Gospel!

The problem does not lie in the Gospel message. It lies in the ability of the messenger to communicate the Gospel effectively. Until the enculturation process is well advanced, the evangelist will not likely possess the ability to communicate the actual Gospel in a way the people can receive it. Too many times, cross-cultural evangelists carry the Gospel to other cultures all wrapped up in their own cultural wrapping. When they offer it to other cultures that way, it only looks appealing to themselves, not their hearers! The people don't see the Gospel so much as they see its cultural wrappings. It looks foreign and unappealing. They do not have the ability to take off the cultural wrappings themselves and should not be required to do so. The evangelist must do that. The only way he will be able to do that is to spend enough time enculturating himself to their lifeway so he will know how to present the important life-changing message of the Gospel in a way they can understand, value, and receive.

One African cross-cultural evangelist asked an African chief if he could bring his family to live in his village. The chief asked why. The evangelists said he had an important message for the chief's people. "What is it?" asked the chief. "I will tell you if you allow my family and I to live in your village for two years," replied the evangelist.

The chief agreed to the plan, wondering what was so important that a foreign family would be willing to do that. Everyone liked the foreign family, so the chief agreed to the plan. During the two years, the evangelist and his family learned the people's language, learned to farm, cook, eat, and behave much like the people of the village. Everyone was curious about them, especially at first. The children even followed them to the bush when they went to the bathroom, just to see if they were "white" everywhere! They watched them pray. They saw how they loved their children. They saw how they became friends with the people. After a full two years had passed, the whole village decided to hold a special celebration and feast so the evangelist could finally tell them his important message. They had learned to love and respect him and his family and had even adopted some of their behaviors because they loved their children too. Everyone was anxious to learn what message was so important that the evangelist's family would leave his own people, an unthinkable sacrifice, and live among them for two years!

After all the feasting and ceremonies, the chief talked to everyone about how they had come to love and respect the evangelist and his family. He also related how he, like everyone else, was anxious to know what message the evangelist had that was so important that he would leave his own people and live like them. When the evangelist stood up to speak in their mother tongue, the whole village was really listening. He began at the beginning, just like the elders did when they would tell stories around the campfires at night. He told them a story about a special man sent by God. An hour and a half later, after the message had been told, the evangelist waited for the chief to speak. He did not give an altar call. The chief asked some questions, especially about Christ's sacrifice for sin and about His power over evil and evil spirits. The evangelist declared what the Bible says in response to each question. The village decided to come back the next night and hear more. They extended the celebration and feasting. The following night, the evangelist repeated the message and gave more biblical illustrations of Gospel truth. He also gave more biblical answers to the chief's questions. There were more questions because the people had had a chance to bring their questions to the chief during that day. This process repeated itself a third and a fourth night. Finally, the chief stood and declared to everyone that he wanted to follow the Christ way. The chief was the first to be baptized, and in a short time, the whole village had genuinely accepted the "Christ way."

The evangelist had painstakingly built a platform in the minds of his hearers from which the Gospel message could truly be heard. This resulted in the whole village becoming genuine Christians. If he had started preaching to the villagers as soon as he arrived, he might have had a small group of converts. But if he had any converts, there would likely have been no leaders in the village among them.

It is not wrong to withhold the important message of the Gospel if by telling it, the people will not be able to receive it as important good news. It is far better to build a platform of respect, mutual understanding, and common communication forms before preaching the Gospel among them. Like it or not, our lives are an integral part of the message. We need to be respected if we want the Gospel to be respected. This is especially true among peoples who have had little contact with the Gospel message.

The above five principles for enculturation will help the cross-cultural evangelist to move through the cultural screen and communicate the Gospel from within the framework of the host culture. This is called an emic position in the culture. It means an inside position. It does not mean that the evangelist has become 100 percent like the people he is evangelizing. They still recognize that he is from another culture, but they respect him because he has learned to follow, understand, and even improve upon the lifeway of the target people. He has learned to communicate the Gospel effectively in their culture.

It is very important that the cross-cultural evangelist make the effort to enculturate himself and use local communication forms. If he does not, he will remain in an etic or outside position on the wrong side of the cross-cultural screen. Only through achieving an emic position within the target culture can the evangelist hope to be effective in evangelizing a target people group!

SUMMARY: This chapter sets forth principles for understanding culture and for helping the cross-cultural evangelist to become enculturated among a people group other than his own. A good understanding of the basic communication process is helpful in discussing the principles for effective cross-cultural communication and evangelism. God is the source of the Gospel, and the evangelist is the secondary source. That means the life the evangelist lives before those he wants to reach is as important as the message itself, because he is God's way of channeling the message to the host culture. He must be certain the meanings he wants to communicate are appropriate and effectively transmitted by the linguistic and behavioral forms he uses.

The best way to do that is to follow the five principles for enculturation, assuring that he will be presenting the Gospel from an emic position within that culture.

QUESTIONS FOR UNDERSTANDING

1. What does encoding mean? Define "noise" in the communication process. What is the importance of feedback in the communication process?
2. What causes the greatest amount of noise in cross-cultural communications? Explain why.
3. According to figure 4.b, what should the evangelist do to communicate effectively to the people of another culture? If he is successful in his evangelism, which direction should the respondent culture move—toward AA or BB? Why are AA and BB different?
4. In the story about the African drums, why didn't the evangelist understand which drumbeats were "good" and which ones were "bad"? What does this teach about the evangelist's ability to judge the behavior of cultures?
5. Name seven categories of cultural differences. What relationship do they have to the cross-cultural screen? Why are they important to understand?
6. To which part of the communication process would language relate? Explain why words translated from one language to another do not carry the exact same meaning. What is the significance of this fact for cross-cultural evangelism?
7. Define what is meant by "social structures." Explain social hierarchy, and open and closed classes.
8. Explain the difference between forms and meanings. What mistake did the lady guest make in the African village when she saw the dance-drama? Why did she make that mistake?
9. Explain the meaning of "absolute meanings and relative forms." How does this idea relate to biblical principles? Why is it important for the cross-cultural evangelist to separate forms and meanings in his own culture? What about doing so in other cultures?

10. What is meant by "worldview"? Define "value systems" and "behavioral forms." Clearly describe the relationships between all three.
11. Describe "culture shock." List at least seven symptoms of culture shock. What should an evangelist try to do when entering another culture in order to avoid culture shock as much as possible?
12. At what level on figure 4.d does an evangelist enter another culture? What should he carefully try to learn at this level? How does spending time with the people in the culture help him to do this?
13. If the Gospel only changes the behavior patterns of a respondent culture, what will likely be the result? At what levels must the Gospel bring change to avoid this problem?
14. Describe a basic values profile and how to use it. How can it help cross-cultural evangelists to become enculturated in another culture?
15. What should a cross-cultural evangelist be certain about before he introduces important ideas, messages, and innovations in another culture? What is the danger of not following this principle?

QUESTIONS FOR DISCUSSION

1. Think of a time when you tried to communicate with someone from another culture and had a difficult time doing so. From what you can remember, analyze what problems you encountered. Use figure 4.a and figure 4.b to explain what happened.
2. Discuss communication forms in relation to the communication process. Decide which communication forms are the most highly valued in your own society. Which ones are most highly valued in your church? List at least three communication forms according to the highest priority in both your culture and your church.
3. Have there ever been any places in the world where Christians could be allowed to go naked in public? If not, why? If there have been such places, describe the cultural situation where

this would not be displeasing to God. Relate your discussion to forms and meanings.

4. Think of somebody you know who has entered your own culture from another one within the last few years. Discuss the symptoms of culture shock in relation to that person's behavior. When you have finished your discussion, describe how your attitude toward that person changed since you read this chapter.
5. Make a basic values profile of your own culture using figure 4.e. Describe the kinds of cultures which would be the most different culturally from your own. What kinds of behavior patterns, value systems, and worldviews would those cultures be likely to have?

CHAPTER FIVE

Principles And Tools For Language/Culture Learning

KEY POINTS IN THIS CHAPTER[29]

1. Language learning is a social activity more than a "study" activity.
2. In cross-cultural evangelism, language learning should not be separated from culture learning and ministry.
3. The language student role is not a very effective position for learning a foreign language.
4. Enculturation into a target people group is best accomplished by complete immersion into the culture, beginning the day a person arrives among that people group.
5. The nature of language learning is such that most of the meaning of person-to-person communication is carried by culturally learned behavior, not the word symbols themselves.

---

[29] Many of the principles and concepts in this chapter are adapted from the following two books by permission of the authors:

Thomas E. Brewster and Elizebeth S. Brewster, *Language Acquisition Made Practical (LAMP)* (Colorado Springs: Lingua House, 1976).

Brewster and Brewster, *Language, Exploration and Acquisition Resource Notebook (LEARN)* (Colorado Springs, Lingua House, 1981).

6. The life of Jesus Christ is the best role model for the language/culture learner.
7. It is best to emphasize oral communication above written communication during the first few months of language/culture learning.
8. Scientific evidence shows that the Life Language Learning System uses the most effective principles for learning foreign languages well.

In chapter four, we learned the importance of enculturation for effective cross-cultural ministry. An understanding of the culture of the people to be evangelized is very necessary. In this chapter, we turn to the important subject of language learning. Too many people are afraid they cannot learn another language. This is especially true of those who speak only one language now. Yet language learning is essential for effective cross-cultural ministry just as much as enculturation of the evangelist into his target culture.

Language learning and culture learning are actually two parts of the same subject. They have too often been treated separately. They are like the two wheels on a cart. If a cart has only one wheel, the best you can expect is to go around in circles. Culture learning (enculturation) is never complete or adequate without good language learning. Language learning is never complete without good culture learning. Cross-cultural evangelists must be effective in learning both. They are the foundation for reaching unreached people groups. That is why we use the term "language/culture learning."

This chapter presents some principles and methods for language and culture learning which are unique. They are based on the best understandings of language learning principles by some of the world's best experts on the subject. This system does not require expensive study in a language school. Neither is it necessary to hire an expert language tutor. Yet the system has been proven effective enough to help anyone of normal intelligence and education to learn any foreign language effectively and in the shortest possible period of time. By consistently applying the principles of this system, such a language learner should rapidly be able to learn to speak the language conversationally. Using this conversational ability, as a foundation, the learner should be able to learn to teach or preach effectively, constantly increasing the learner's ability through gaining even more experience in the language. Since effective ability in the mother tongue of the target people is necessary, the cross-cultural minister should learn the principles and methods of this chapter well.

Figure 5.a: Split-Image Spectrum of Learner vs. Student

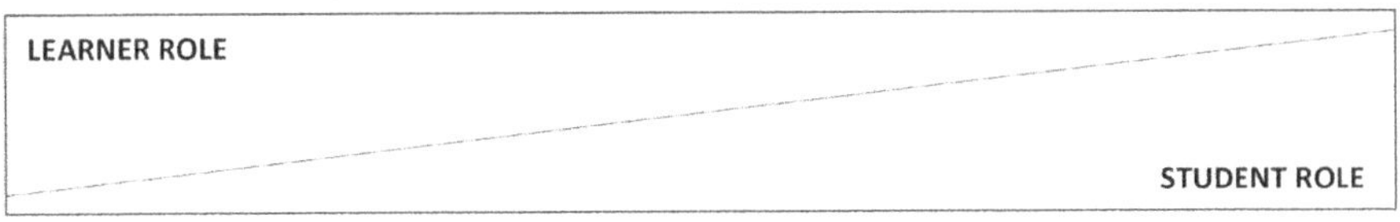

1. The learner learns the language in order to communicate his concerns and interests to people he meets every day.	1. Student studies the language with the hope of someday being able to communicate with the target people.
2. The learner's goal is to know the people and help them come to know him.	2. The student's goal is to get a good grade by which he is taught to think as he "learned" the language.
3. The learner uses the language to communicate with people.	3. Student learns how to "study" languages, not speak them.
4. Learner gets a little bit of the language, but uses it a lot in communicating with the target people group.	4. Student gets a lot of language, but uses it very little with target people.
5. Learner gets a feel for grammar by normal usage. He learns patterns of grammar by repetitious usage and observation.	5. Student memorizes grammar rules and technical terms of language and grammar.
6. Learner uses learned patterns of speech to generate new sentences and prepares his own practice exercise.	6. Student studies rules for generating new sentences, but done not learn intonation and inflection like native speakers.
7. Learner decides for himself what he should learn next.	7. Student becomes passive. Others decide what he should study next.
8. Learner learns material that he needs to use now. His motivation is high and he learns very fast.	8. Student studies material he may or may not use in the future. Hie desire to learn is diminished.
9. Learner is relationship oriented.	9. Student is task oriented.
10. Learner wants to establish a platform for learning the culture now. He wants to share his life as well as the message.	10. Student wants to learn in order to share the message in the future.

LANGUAGE LEARNING IS CULTURE LEARNING IS MINISTRY

Students or learners? There are millions of people who study foreign languages, but do not speak them fluently. And there are hundreds of millions of people who do not study foreign languages, but still **learn** to speak them fluently. Why is this true? Why should so many people study to learn foreign languages with very little success, only to see a world full of people who never formally study another language, but learn to speak it well? The answer lies in the nature of the differences between students and learners!

In most parts of the world, an education has come to be increasingly valued by greater portions of the populations of every country. Everyone wants their children to have better educational opportunities than they had themselves. Obtaining more and more formal education for their children is high on the list of goals for many millions of families. Such a desire to help our children is natural and should not be discouraged. Yet we must be careful not to lose sight of the fact that education does not only take place in formal schooling. It happens through learned experience as well.

For example, use the example of two fourteen-year-old boys. One had never been able to go to school. He worked from the time he was small in his father's corner grocery store. But his father taught him to read and write and do arithmetic. He learned how to do everything that needed to be done at the grocery store. Without worry, his father could leave him in charge of the store for several days when he was gone.

The other boy spent most of his life in formal schooling. He also could read and write and do arithmetic. He wanted to go to college, and he did. But he had never learned to stock shelves and make inventories. He didn't know the first thing about running a business of any kind. But when he got out of college, there were no jobs to be found. One boy we would call educated because he went to college. The other boy we could call uneducated. Yet both boys had learned many things. One had learned how to be a student. The other had learned how to run a grocery business. But they both learned!

Learning a foreign language is more like learning a grocery business than it is going to college. It is best learned by practical experience. That is the difference between learners and students. Students usually learn to **study** something. Students are learn-to-know oriented. Learners are learn-to-do oriented. Figure 5.a shows the basic differences between learners and students in learning a foreign language. This does not mean that most of the subjects that students study do not need to be learned, but they need to be learned in the right order and in the right way. Simply in some subjects, the most effective way of learning is by assuming the learner attitude, rather than the student attitude.

One big difference between language students and language learners is that the learner gets a little bit of a language before he uses it. But then he uses it a lot! It becomes a part of his thinking. He does not have to translate from one language to another in his mind when he wants to use what he has learned. The student, however, gets a lot of teaching about the language, the vocabulary, and the rules of grammar, but does not usually have enough opportunity to use the language. It does not stay in his mind. So he is forced to translate words and sentences in his mind before he can haltingly say something. But as we have already learned, it is impossible to simply translate straight from one language to another unless you know exactly what the words will mean in the context of the situation.

There are many stories of language students who thought they were saying one thing, but their hearers were actually hearing something much different. One student of an Asian language thought she was inviting her dinner guests to eat a special tasty food she had prepared for dessert. Though they had never seen a chocolate pie, they were interested to see it until she invited them to have some. She used the correct grammar, and all her words were combined in a manner to show that the food was desirable. But she did not realize her combination of a word and a normally desirable suffix in that language in this case signified that she was inviting her guests to join her in eating a slice of human dung! As we shall see, learning a language involves much more than simply learning lists of words and rules of grammar.

The emphasis on the learner role in language learning does not mean that learners will never need to "study" any language learning material. Actually, good learners create much of their own study material! They will eventually learn a great deal of material, but they will only "study" in order to use what they are already using in their daily lives. Also, do not mistake this emphasis on the learner role as an essay against formal language learning systems and trained language tutors. They can have great value for language learners when applied in the right order and using the right principles. But they should not be overemphasized above effective language learning methods. They have the best value **after** a person has learned using the principles outlined in this chapter.

Language Learning Is Culture Learning

Learning the language of another people really cannot be effectively accomplished without learning the culture. This is because linguistic communication depends on cultural behaviors as much as on the linguistic symbols themselves. Words are important, but how those words are spoken and the context in which they are spoken are equally important. It is the context in which they are spoken that contributes greatly to the meaning. Finally, the acceptability of the person speaking contributes greatly to acceptability of the message.

In actual fact, a person entering another culture needs to understand that he is part of the message and that his acceptability as a foreigner automatically means that the messages he conveys at that point are highly suspect, to say the least. The etic position from which he speaks makes his message much less believable.

This has been demonstrated by psychological research. There has been some important progress in understanding unwritten person-to-person communication. Every communicator wants his hearers to receive the messages he is conveying to them. It's accepted or rejected according to how people feel about the messenger. According to UCLA professor Albert Mehrabian, *only 7 percent of the positive feelings generated in language communication is carried by the words themselves*! Fully 38 percent is carried by the **way** the words are spoken—the intonation, the inflection of the voice, the appearance of the speaker, and the order and the emphasis given to the words.[30] That means an amazing 55 percent of the acceptance of messages in person-to-person communication is carried by the nonverbal behavior accompanying the speech! This includes the facial expressions, the gestures with the hands and body, and the position of the head,

[30] https://www.rightattitudes.com/2008/10/04/7-38-55-rule-personal-communication

hands, and body. It is no wonder that business and political leaders will get into a plane and fly around the world to negotiate with people of other cultures! And it should not be lost on us that the most effective means of communicating the Gospel is person-to-person and in the language using native intonation and nonverbal tools to make the message impactful and fully understood!

Since person-to-person communication is very important to cross-cultural evangelists, these findings have great importance for language learning in other cultures. Notice that traditional language instruction systems, which emphasize the "schooling" approach, are really concentrating mostly on the words and grammar. While such schools have the learning of pronunciation intonation as important goals, they fall short in this area because of the way words are used when we speak. We run words together in phrases and sentences when we speak. That very process changes and inflects how we say words. So we pronounce, inflect, and intone words differently according to what we are saying and what words we are using. Language "study" systems spend a lot of time drilling students and try to cover a lot of material. This results in far too little time in learning *how* to speak the words being learned and how to convey meaning through pronunciation, inflection, intonation, and nonverbal symbols that are commonly used while speaking. Yet the research shows that training in these things is probably **more important** than training in words and grammar!

More important, pronunciation, intonation, and inflection are much better learned in the use of the language in the community. It is often too artificial in the classroom. In the community, people speak as they do in their everyday language. The language learner's desire is to learn to communicate like the people in the community. In the classroom, learning the **how** of speaking a language becomes much less important than the **what** or **how much** of speaking the language. The **how** of speaking a language also varies geographically. Even the same language is spoken differently in different regions of most countries. For all these reasons and more, it is far better to learn language among the people you intend to evangelize, especially at the beginning of your time with the target people.

Since so much of acceptable personal communication is nonverbal, learning a language among the people you intend to evangelize is doubly important. People unconsciously communicate a lot to other people without really realizing it. There is a simple reason for this. When a person is talking, he learns to unconsciously adopt the use of certain gestures of the face, hands, body, eyes, etc. He learned these gestures by watching others of his group use them over a long period of time. But when a person in not talking, he is still thinking! As he thinks, his body responds with some or all of those same gestures he would use if he were talking. Since other people in his society have also become accustomed to those same gestures, they can watch him and understand much of what he is thinking. That is how other people know when we are listening to them, if we do not like them, or if we are uninterested in what they are saying. According to Mehrabian, fully 55 percent of positive feedback in personal communication occurs at this nonverbal level. Yet nonverbal communication is culturally learned behavior! It cannot be effectively learned outside a people group. For these reasons, language learning is vitally linked to learning the culture of the people. It is a social activity more than a classroom activity. Language learning really is culture learning!

PRINCIPLES OF LANGUAGE/CULTURE LEARNING

Before defining some important methods for language/culture learning, it is helpful to learn some basic principles behind this form of language learning. We call this system Life Language Learning (LLL) or language/culture learning (LCL). It requires daily living in the culture of the people to be effective. The best life language learners are those who become actively involved in the lives of people in the host culture. This system is as much a way of living as it is a plan for language learning. The principles underlying Life Language Learning are grouped under two important subjects: (1) Language/culture learning is not just preparation for ministry, it actually is ministry. (2) The best way to be successful in language/culture learning is to follow principles of bonding in the enculturation process.

Language/Culture Learning IS Ministry

The language/culture learning (LCL) system we are presenting emphasizes daily interaction with the people of the target culture. It requires that at least one-third of the learning time for each day be spent in actual communication with native speakers of the language being learned. As figure 5.a shows, it is relationship oriented. It is designed to help the learner become acquainted with people in the culture from the very first day. This daily interaction with people allows for valuable ministry to occur even when a person is in the LCL process.

One small group of cross-cultural evangelists decided to use this system to learn another language for a three-month period of time. Because of their daily interaction with the people, over thirty people came to accept Christ as Savior during that time. Most people in a typical language school would not be able to spend enough time around non-Christians to even meet thirty non-Christians, let alone introduce them to Christ! Yet this group of language/culture learners had not only made many friends, but also, they won thirty of them to the Lord while they were learning! Good LCL IS ministry!

LCL requires a special attitude on the part of the learner. He cannot enter another culture and think and act as he did when he left his own. He must follow Jesus' example. Jesus was really the first cross-cultural evangelist! He came all the way from heaven and left the glory and splendor he enjoyed there. He "made himself nothing, taking the very nature of a servant, being made in human likeness. And being found in appearance as a man, he humbled himself and became obedient to death…" (Phil. 2:7–8). Jesus emptied himself of the use of His divine glory, and assumed the role of a servant in human flesh. He enculturated himself completely into the Jewish culture and communicated his message primarily to Jewish people. Then He proved his love by dying on the cross for all peoples. He demonstrated His power through miracles and the resurrection. It was enough to change the world! That is an example of the potential power of true enculturation into the target culture.

The language/culture learner may have been a gifted and respected preacher and teacher in his own culture. He may be accustomed to preaching to hundreds or thousands of people at a time among his own people. But when he enters another culture, he must humble himself life Jesus did. If he wants to follow Jesus' example, he must be willing to assume three new roles: Learner, Servant, Storyteller.

The Learner Role: Jesus commanded us to "make disciples among every people" as we learned in the first two chapters. The word "disciple" means learner. Cross-cultural evangelists are called to make "learners of Christ" among the unreached people of the world. The evangelist certainly knows much more about Christ than those he intends to evangelize, but they know much more about their culture than he does. Therefore, it is important that he assume the role of a cultural learner when entering another culture.

People help people who need help! If an evangelist assumes a role of high status when he enters another culture, the people will not want to help him much. They will want his help instead. While this may help him feel important, he will not understand how to really help the people there because he will not understand their language and culture well enough to make any valuable impact on their lives. And after setting himself up as important without learning their language and culture, they will be more likely to use him for their own purposes, instead of becoming ready to receive his message. It is far better to assume the humble position and low status of a learner when entering another culture. This will remove the evangelist from the need to prove himself as an important person and allow him to demonstrate how much he needs the help of people in the culture to learn their language and their ways.

More important, it will allow him the opportunity to spend time with the people every day as a learner needing their help. He won't need to prove himself to them about anything except his humble desire to learn their language and culture. It will allow people he comes to know the freedom to help him. He need not try to prove himself in any way except as a learner. This way, he will learn much faster, and the people will become his friends much faster as he shows them gratitude for their help. Assuming the learner role shows the greatest respect for the people and their culture. It follows the example of Jesus. It is the best position from which ministry can be effective during the LCL process.

The Servant Role: Even though Jesus had all authority (Matt. 28:18) when he was incarnated as a human being, he did not assume the role of a king or ruler. He assumed the role of a servant (Phil. 2:7). In that verse, the Greek word "kenosis" is used. It means "to empty oneself." Christ purposely emptied himself of the right to use his divine glory and position as Lord of everything in order to identify with mankind. He assumed the role of a servant to be our example. He taught us to do the same when he washed the disciples' feet before the resurrection (John 13:1–8). He told us, "Whoever wants to be great among you must be your servant, and whoever wants to be first must be your slave—just as the Son of Man did not come to be served, but to serve, and to give his life a ransom for many" (Matt. 20:26–28). Just as Christ purposely emptied himself of the glory and position he had in heaven, so cross-cultural ministers must empty themselves of the glory and position they had in their own culture. They must never consider themselves too important to spend time with the common people in their new culture. They must learn to enculturate themselves in a humble-enough manner that God can use them to meet the spiritual needs of those people.

It is the attitude of the evangelist which is of great importance. The culture in which he is working may value ascribed leadership roles, rather than achieved leadership roles (see figure 4.e). If so, they will likely elevate the evangelist to a high status because he is a preacher, or because he is a foreigner. The evangelist may be tempted to assume that high status role, copying others in that society who are in that role. That is a mistake! His ability and knowledge in the language and culture will not be great enough to fulfill that role, and he will constantly need to prove he is something which he cannot yet be. If he refuses that role, assuming the role of a servant instead, the people will give him a better status in their hearts. He will be earning it as a servant and helper of the people. They will identify with him and come to be loyal to him because they care about him, not because he has status or power. If he has the attitude of a servant, he will have much more influence on the people for the Gospel's sake. If the people only respect him for his authority or foreign status, they may change their behavior, at least when he is near them. But when they respect his Christian love and service, they will consider changing their worldview and value system. They will want to be more like him. The servant role is the best position from which to evangelize the people of another culture. That is why Jesus came as a servant. It is also the reason he has taught us to assume the servant role.

Storyteller: Jesus taught people by telling stories (Matt. 13:34). He gained his reputation as a great master teacher mostly by telling parables or stories to the people. His stories helped the people receive Him as an important teacher. After they did, Jesus would often teach them more directly, like He did through the Sermon on the Mount (Matt. 5–7).

Jesus' example as a storyteller is not just valuable for learning to teach. It is also a valuable model for effective communication even while language/culture learning is taking place. Every culture tells stories in some way. Stories can simply be reporting something that is happening now, like when a language learner describes to someone his system for learning their language. Stories can also be in the form of proverbs or parables. Stories can be humorous, like jokes or anecdotes. They can also be stories from the Bible. One of the reasons this author obtained highest marks on his second-year language oral exam for a difficult language is the fact that he perfectly told a humorous story.

There is an African tribe which was reported to be closed to outsiders for years. But one cross-cultural evangelist entered their culture and assumed the learner-servant-storyteller role. He used storytelling as a tool for learning the language and culture. He learned to tell many stories that had been handed down in the tribe for generations. Because only the elders of that tribe usually told the old stories, they nicknamed him "the old man." This gave him greater respect before the people because older people were respected highly. When he started telling stories from the Bible, the people also listened. He became a successful cross-cultural evangelist by learning how to tell stories the way people were accustomed to hearing them. He used stories to preach the Gospel like Jesus did.

As the language/culture learner becomes able to tell stories the way the people do, he will come to understand what kinds of things children talk about, and what things young people talk about, and what adults talk about. It will also give him opportunity to hear many stories. That will help him understand more and more of the culture of the people. Storytelling also allows the language learner to make language mistakes without being so embarrassed. People are more tolerant of mistakes when they are listening to someone tell a story or describe something which happened. The only more tolerant setting for speaking to someone is in prayer. God knows when you are making a mistake in prayer, but He doesn't care! It is a good way to become fluent in the language—talk to God!

The learner-servant-storyteller attitude will free the cross-cultural evangelist from needing to prove that he deserves a high status. It will give him the greatest level of interaction with the people. It will provide him a position from which to learn the language and culture well. Most people who adopt these roles during language/culture learning find that their experience greatly enriches their preaching and teaching ministries when they begin to speak to larger groups. These roles also make language/culture learning a happy, fulfilling phase of their cross-cultural experience.

Bonding and the Language/Culture Learner

Many people have heard stories of animals which lose their mothers at birth, but survive by becoming attached to a substitute mother of another species. Ducks have been mothered by geese. Dogs have been mothered by coyotes. This has led to a scientific principle called *imprinting*. In researching this principle, one scientist gathered baby ducklings close to himself at the critical moment, right after they were hatched. From then on, the ducks responded to him as if he were their parent.[31] They would follow him wherever he would

[31] See Konrad Lorenz, Wikipedia.

go. Experiments have also been carried out with other animals. It has been learned that imprinting must occur immediately after birth. If an animal's mother is absent at that time, the infant may attach itself to a substitute mother. This could be a different kind of adult animal, or even a human being! The key element necessary for imprinting to occur is the timing. It must occur immediately after birth.

Studies show that imprinting occurs between human mothers and their children. A term for this which has been popularized by Dr. Brewster in the field of LCL is "bonding." Just after a child is born, there are God-given physiological and psychological forces interacting together to bond the child to its parents. At the moment after birth, a child is very alert. He is experiencing new smells, new sounds, and new sensations in completely new surroundings. The parents are also excited. Their emotional energy is very high, even though the ordeal of giving birth has just passed. Both parents and child are especially capable of close bonding during those minutes right after birth. Later, the child will become very sleepy and less alert. The mother will want to rest.

Infant-parent bonding is a good analogy for language/culture learning in another culture. The moment a language learner enters another culture, it is like being reborn. Just like a child newly born, his or her excitement and energy levels are very high. They are emotionally and psychologically ready to become a real belonger in the new culture. They want to begin the enculturation and language learning process. They are ready to become bonded with the people. It is a crucially important time.

In some cultures, infant bonding does not take place because the child is born in a hospital. As soon as the child is born, it may be shown to the parents, but then it is quickly taken to the nursery while the mother rests. There is no opportunity for bonding. This is often the case when babies are premature because the child needs special care. Studies show this can have a negative effect on the child-parent relationships throughout the child's life.[32]

---

[32] https://journals.sagepub.com/doi/pdf/10.1177/147470491201000311

The same thing too often happens when a cross-cultural worker first arrives in another culture. He typically will be greeted by someone from his own culture when he arrives. There will probably be a time of getting acquainted, perhaps during a specially planned meal. The new evangelist and his family meet others from their own culture who also live in that country. All conversations will be in the mother tongue of the cross-cultural evangelist. They will be invited to stay with such a family for a few weeks until they can get established in a place for their own family. They are grateful for the help of their countrymen and usually accept the invitation. So for several weeks, they live with members of their own culture. They continue to speak their own language. They are also immersed in an expatriate lifestyle—a pattern that removes them from constant contact with the people they came to evangelize. It also removes them from contact with the culture during that crucial first few weeks when they would have had the opportunity to become quickly bonded within the culture they came to evangelize. Like the child snatched away to the nursery in a hospital, they lose the opportunity to become immediately bonded to the local people and their culture.

The way the evangelist and his family spend their first few weeks will greatly determine their effectiveness in establishing a sense of belonging in their new culture. If they spend most of their time around their own countrymen, they will likely become bonded to a foreign lifestyle rather than having the opportunity to learn and value local behavior patterns. While they could learn about those patterns of behavior after a period of "easing into the new culture," they will probably not do it well and not do it with clear perspective on the value of the culture. Their perspective on how to live in their new country and culture will be too slanted toward an expatriate perspective and interpretation of the new culture. Becoming bonded to an expatriate lifestyle will greatly increase the impact and level of culture shock, plus diminish the level and speed of language/culture learning dramatically.

Those who try to enter another culture in a gradual way will usually fail to do so completely. They may also be denied the experience of belonging to the people and the local way of life. They likely will not experience the joy of real friendship with the local people really caring for them. It is far better for them to begin their very first day by living with the people whose culture they came to persuade to follow Christ and God's Word. After all, they themselves are the most visible message of the Gospel the local people will ever see.

They should learn right away to eat with them, go shopping with them, use their system of private or public transportation, and hear them speak their language. From the very first day, they should begin to develop relationships with local people in the target culture. They should immediately declare their desire to become a language learner. If they demonstrate a learner attitude, many people will try to help them. The Life Language Learning System we are encouraging you to follow provides guidelines for helping this kind of bonding with the local culture to occur.

THE LIFE LANGUAGE LEARNING SYSTEM

The best method for learning the Life Language Learning System (LLL) is to actually follow the procedures you are learning by using them in a practical situation. So the best way to learn these principles and methods is to use them to learn another language. It is the only way you will really understand the value of this system. Five practice days among native speakers of another language is enough to prove to yourself the value of this system. This is for you to practice before you even go to your target culture and prove to yourself that this system works. Here is a step-by-step procedure for getting started:

1. **Get Your Supplies:** You will need a small recording device, preferably one which has the following features: (a) cue and review, (b) a time or tape counter, (c) built-in microphone, (d) speed control, (e) earphones, and (e) loop tapes or their digital equivalent. You will also need a loose-leaf notebook or binder with divider tabs. If they are available, five-by-seven-inch (twelve-by-seventeen-centimeter) note cards that can be placed in a binder will be important also.

2. **Choose the Specific Language:** This is not the culture you are going to evangelize, though you may choose to do so, if you think that is what you want. This is for you to practice using the system. So think of a community near you which speaks a language far different than your own and which you know little about. In all the major cities of the world, there are communities of people from Asia, North America, Europe, Africa, or the Pacific islands. They speak many different languages, and their peoples usually live mostly in one area of the city. For your purposes, it is best to choose a language spoken by at least thirty or forty families which live fairly close together. Do not be afraid to choose a language which seems very hard to you. Choose one with virtually no words that you understand now. It will show you the value of this system better.
3. **Procedure:** The purpose of this exercise is to give you five days' learning experience in another culture and language. We strongly encourage you to follow this procedure well to gain the maximum benefit from this chapter for your future ministry in another culture. After you choose which language group you want to work with, you will follow what is called a Daily Learning Cycle (DLC). It consists of four parts: (1) getting your talk, (2) practice your talk, (3) communicate in the community, and (4) evaluate your progress. These procedures are explained in detail below. By following the Daily Learning Cycle for five days, you will actually be learning the same way you would if you were entering another culture to stay.
4. **Finding a Helper:** You will need someone to help you in step one of the Daily Learning Cycle. In the beginning, you should NOT use an experienced tutor. He needs only three qualifications: (1) he must be willing to help you for about one hour each day, (2) he must be a native speaker of the language who has lived in a metropolitan area for at least three years, (3) he must be able to read and write in his own language, and (4) he should be able to speak

your own language enough to understand simple conversations. There is good reason for not using an experienced language teacher during the beginning stages of using this system. Experienced teachers have their own ideas about teaching techniques. They will usually be accustomed to directing the learning process. But in this process, YOU will be the one to direct the learning experiences. It is also a good idea not to refer to your helper as your teacher to anyone. Though he will indeed be teaching you, if you use that term, he will be tempted to try to direct the learning experience, instead of letting you do it using this system.

The Daily Learning Cycle

The four steps of the learning cycle are explained in detail below. This is the procedure which you should follow for each day you are working to learn another language.

STEP ONE: GETTING YOUR TALK:

This is where you decide what you should say when you first speak to people in your target language. Your "talk" is the actual words you should say when you first speak to people in your target language. You don't want to say much—only what you can learn easily and with good pronunciation, intonation, and inflection. This is also the step where you will need your helper. There are six activities for getting your talk correctly:

OBTAIN: This is where you get your helper to tell you how to say your talk in his language. First, tell him what you want to say to the people you meet in his language. The first talk should be something like this:

> "Hello. I'm learning [name of language]. My name is [your name]. This is all I can say. Goodbye."

Your helper (let's call him Komo) should understand that you want to learn to say everything just like his people would say it to each other. Ask him not to translate everything word for word. The best way to help him (or her) keep doing this is to continually describe what you want him to say, instead of telling him words you want to translate. For instance, say, "I want to learn how to greet people. If I come up to someone, and want to give them a general greeting, what would I say?" Komo would then be more likely to give you the correct greeting, instead of just translating the word "hello" into his language. By continually describing what you want to communicate, rather than giving him words to translate, you will get the most common and appropriate ways of expressing those thoughts in Komo's language.

CHECK: As you get your talk, ask Komo to write it down in his own language without showing it to you. When the whole talk is written down, have Komo say it all out loud. Make sure he thinks it sounds natural, just like someone would say it in his own language.

TRANSCRIBE: Once Komo is certain the talk sounds natural, and could be used when you first speak to someone in his culture, then have him write it down. If his language uses the same kind of letters yours does, then you write it down as he has on your notepaper. If his language uses different symbols for writing, carefully write it down as best you can using your own letters or symbols. If the language you are learning is only a spoken language, with no written forms, simply write the sounds as best you can using your own language symbols. Have Komo help you by pronouncing the sounds slowly as you write. Do not worry if it is not exactly correct. In the beginning, you will emphasize listening to your talk, not reading and writing it. You can worry about learning to write in the language after you have learned to speak it conversationally. (You will be able to learn to write it much more rapidly and accurately at that time.)

UNDERSTAND: Now, make sure you understand the general meaning of each line. For your first talk, this is easy, but it will be harder for later days. You can ask questions about the meaning of certain words, but it is not necessary. You should simply know the meaning of the phrases and sentences so you will know what you are saying when you use them. The exact meanings of the words will come to you as you practice using the talks.

Note: This is your chance to notice where you might have problems in making the same sounds as Komo. You should note those sounds which are difficult for you to pronounce by underlining them in your talk if you write it down. You will want to practice these an extra amount during step two. Later, as you have experience with other talks, you will begin to notice things about certain words or patterns of saying things. For instance, you may notice that the last word always ends with a certain kind of sound when you are speaking to someone else. You would probably assume this is a verb ending for the first person, as in the sentence "I will go." As you learn more talks, you will make many discoveries like this, and you will want to make a note of as many as you can at this stage of getting your talk. This will begin to prepare you to "feel" the grammar rules in the language and eventually help you to know when it does not sound correct. When you get insights or questions about these types of things, you can ask Komo about them at a later session.

RECORD: It is time to record the talk on a digital or tape recording device. This exercise is very important. The better you learn the recording method, the easier it will be to learn your talk and be understood by those to whom you speak. You will be using three types of drills:

Whole Text Listening Drill: This is for listening to the whole talk at the same time. Have Komo record the whole day's talk on the first part of the recording device. Be sure he practices saying it a couple of times just like he would actually say it if he were talking to someone. Have him pause and envision someone is speaking back to him normally between what he says each time. Once he feels comfortable saying it in his language, record it.

Sentence Mimicry Drill: The purpose of this drill is to allow you to mimic each phrase and sentence in your practice session. Ask Komo to record each sentence three times at normal speed, pausing each time to allow you time to repeat the sentence after him. For example, if you were doing this in English, you would record your first talk like this:

"Hello."

(Pause)
"Hello."
(Pause)
"Hello."
(Pause)
"I'm learning English."
(Pause)
"I'm learning English."
(Pause)
"I'm learning English."
(Pause)
"This is all I can say."
(Pause)
"This is all I can say."
(Pause)
"This is all I can say."
(Pause)
"Goodbye."
(Pause)
"Goodbye."
(Pause)
"Goodbye."
(Pause)

After you record the talk with three repetitions, you should also record it with one repetition, like this:

"Hello."
(Pause)
"I'm learning English."
(Pause)
"This is all I can say."
(Pause)
"Goodbye."
(Pause)

You should continue using this process each day, adding new sentences each time. Later, when the sentences in your talk become longer, it will be hard for you to repeat the whole sentence at once. When that happens, you should ask your helper to repeat the sentences in phrases. Each time he does it, start with the last phrase in the sentence and work back to the front. This will make the sentences sound like a native speaker actually talks. When each phrase has been repeated, then Komo should do the whole sentence at once. For instance, let's say your third day's talk has this sentence in it: "I have been in Bengaluru for only three days." This is how Komo should record it:

"for only three days"
(Pause)
"for only three days"
(Pause)
"for only three days"
(Pause)
"in Bengaluru"
(Pause)
"in Bengaluru"
(Pause)
"in Bengaluru"
(Pause)
"I have been"
(Pause)
"I have been"
(Pause)
"I have been"
(Pause)
"I have been in Bengaluru for only three days."
(Pause)
"I have been in Bengaluru for only three days."
(Pause)
"I have been in Bengaluru for only three days."
(Pause)

Completion Drill: There is one more kind of drill that you should record for each talk. It will help you remember the talk easily, and it will improve your fluency. Ask Komo to say only the first word or first part of each sentence, giving you time to say the whole sentence after him. But only Komo's voice should be on the tape. The drill should be recorded like this:

> Komo: "I'm…"
> (Pause for you to say, "I'm learning English.")
> Komo: "I'm learning English."
> Komo: "This…"
> (Pause for you to say, "This is all I can say.")
> Komo: "Good…"
> (Pause for you to say, "Goodbye."
> Komo: "Goodbye."

Finally, have Komo record the full talk at normal speed once more, making sure he pauses after each sentence for a response from the person being spoken to. Then have him record only the first word, pausing for you to say the whole talk after he prompts you with the first word. This will be used during your practice time.

If you have a loop tape, the last thing you should do during your session with Komo is to have him record the whole talk on your loop tape. Time the seconds needed for him to say the whole talk. Get a loop tape that is twice that long, giving you time to say the whole talk after he does. If it is being recorded on another device, such as a mobile phone, follow the same procedure. If you cannot use a loop tape, you can also copy and duplicate the recording and the pause time on your device, repeating the process at least ten times in a row, so you can use the recording as a practice drill. Alternatively, if there is a command on your device to continually repeat the recording and the pause, set it to do so automatically just like on a loop tape. This will keep you from having to return to the beginning of the recording on your device so much in order to do your practicing.

STEP TWO: At this stage of the Daily Learning Cycle, you will practice listening, mimicry, and completion. It is best to begin this practice while you are still meeting with your helper. Go through each of the drills while Komo listens. He should be ready to tell you the places where you need the most practice on the pronunciation. For instance, he may notice that you say the "r" sound much different than his people do, making it hard to understand. Or he may notice one sound which you are saying which sounds almost like another in his language, confusing the listener about what you are saying. He should tell you about differences like these when he hears you do the drills. After making a note on those things, your session with Komo is finished. Now you are ready to practice by yourself.

This is how you should do the practice drills:

LISTENING DRILL: You should first listen to the talk from the recording device many times. Use the portion of the tape or recording device where Komo says the talk at full speed and clear through without stopping. The repeat function on your device is very valuable here. You can use earphones with your device, hang it on your body, and do some of your daily tasks while it is repeating your talk in your ear. You can listen while you are shaving, doing housework, or even when you are reading something else—even while lying in bed. Listening over and over again will train your mind to hear the exact sounds Komo has recorded. When you start to speak those sounds yourself, your mind will not be completely satisfied until you are saying those sounds correctly. That is why the repetition process is so valuable. Even if you do not have, and cannot get, a device that allows you to repeat the exercise automatically, you should still listen to the whole talk many times before going on to the mimicry drill.

MIMICRY DRILL: After you have listened to your talk twenty times or more, go on to the sentence mimicry portion of your recording. Repeat aloud after each time Komo speaks. Continue to do this until you can say each sentence without prompting and with complete accuracy and fluency, as much as possible, just like Komo. This drill will continue to improve your pronunciation. Be sure to work more on the sounds which are hardest for you to copy. This drill will not only train your tongue, but also, it will continue to train your ears. The better you imprint the sounds in your mind, the better will be your pronunciation, intonation, and inflection. Each part of the mimicry drill should be repeated at least fifty times.

COMPLETION DRILL: After you feel comfortable with your progress on the mimicry drill, move on to the completion section of the recording device. Say each sentence completely after it is started by Komo (see example above). Be sure to listen to Komo when he repeats the sentence after you say it. Be sure you are saying it right. Repeat this drill as many times as necessary to be sure you can complete each sentence, sounding like Komo. When you can do that, move on to the portion of the recording device where Komo says the whole talk at normal speed. Practice saying it with him each time, then say it again by yourself in the pause provided. Do this over and over at least fifty times. At first, it will seem like he is speaking much faster than you can, but you will be able to keep up after practicing with him the first few times. Finally, when you can do that, see if you can say the whole talk by yourself. Practice until you can do it by just quickly thinking of what you want to say. It should roll off your tongue naturally, with a complete and total mimicry of what Komo has recorded for the whole talk. You don't have to translate in your mind. You don't have to remember the first word. It just comes out naturally as Komo said it and as soon as you try to say it.

STEP THREE: COMMUNICATE: Now you are ready for the most important step of the Life Language Learning System. You are ready to begin communicating what you have learned to people in the target language group. You should go into the neighborhood where most of these people live. Then begin to say your talk to everyone you meet who looks like they should be able to speak your target language. You should say your talk to as many people as you can. Be creative about finding a way to speak to them. Boldness is a necessity. Try to say it to at least forty people, fifty if possible. Plan to spend three to four hours in the foreign language community speaking to people.

Every person you see is a potential person to say your talk to. You may be able to find people to speak to in stores along the streets. You can talk to the sales clerks, the customers, to children, or anybody who looks like they may be able to pause to listen. If there are no stores, you may need to visit places where people are not busy doing something important, like people at a park or waiting for a sporting event. If you have to go to people's homes, you should be careful not to break any local rules, such as visiting when the husband or children are not home.

Your first day will be the most difficult. You may feel a little embarrassed at first. The first time you try to say your talk to someone, it will probably not come out right, or you may not immediately remember the first word. But keep trying and keep saying it, regardless of the reaction of those you speak to. After the first few times, it will begin to come out right. By this time you will be able to notice the reaction people normally have. If they begin to speak back to you in their own language, you will know they understand what you said. You will also know you did well because they will think you know their language better than you do! When this happens, do not worry, just smile and go say your talk to the next person, though you do not understand what they say back to you (you will understand some).

You will learn to understand people as they speak back to you as you prepare and use more talks each day. By the time you speak to forty or fifty people, you will feel very comfortable in saying it. And you will not forget it—some of it for the rest of your life! You will be able to tell by the smiles and expressions on people's faces that the people are pleased that you are taking the trouble to learn their language. They will WANT to help you. And you will be able to say the whole talk without hesitation and with full fluency. You will be able to say each sentence immediately without thinking about it and whenever the thought to do so crosses your mind. This will prove increasingly valuable to you as you continue each day's learning cycle.

Even though you will not understand them when people speak back to you, do not let that threaten you. Be polite and let them speak to you. Recognize that they have probably never seen anybody do what you are doing. It may be funny to them. It may surprise them. Or they may simply be unable to respond at all. Just keep your own sense of humor and smile. Whatever you do, do not fear making mistakes. You will make some. Try not to repeat them. Once while the author was in Mexico, he one day told about fifty people that his HUSBAND was in

San Francisco! Your mistakes won't be worse than that one! By the time you have completed the first five days, you will be comfortable with the learning cycle. You will actually look forward to the time when you can put this system into practice among the people you believe God has called you to evangelize in the country where you are called to serve.

STEP FOUR: EVALUATE: When you get back from step-three fieldwork, you need to spend about one half hour evaluating your experience and progress while it is still fresh in your mind. The first thing you should do is write today's talk into your notebook. Do it by date on a separate page for each day's talk. This will be your permanent record of the talk. Do not worry about how the talk was spelled when you wrote it with your helper. Write it the way it sounds to you now. If you have practiced learning to write with phonemic sounds, use them. If not, just come as close to writing the exact sounds as you hear them in your mind using the letters in your own language. It is okay to combine letters together for a single sound if it helps you remember the way to pronounce it better. If you want to write the letter in the target language below your own words, and you know how to do that, you can do so. This should be written in a section of your notebook called Daily Talks.

Next you should use the Learning Cycle Evaluation Guide which appears in the appendix of this book. You can make copies of this guide for use each day during your evaluation time. Fill in the answers to the questions in the questions in the spaces provided in the form. This will help you get ideas to enter into your notebook for that day.

Now you should make notes about things which came to your mind while you were doing the field communication. You may have noticed that the older people did not act correctly or respond as positively when you spoke to them. This probably indicates that your greeting needs something more respectful than a general greeting in that language. You should make a note about it to ask Komo tomorrow. Maybe there is a better form for greeting older people. If Komo says there is, ask him to use that form in the next day's talk so you can alternate forms when talking to older people. Be sure to ask him if there are differences in greetings when talking to women also. If so, learn them also in the first few days. Also ask him when it is not appropriate to talk to a woman in that culture if you are a man, and vice versa. You should start a section in your notebook entitled Cultural Notes. You can put things like the variances in talking to people of different age or sex.

You should also have a section in your notebook entitled Method Ideas. In this section, you should write ideas about how you might expand your drills, talks, or communication efforts to give you more or better practice in areas where you see it is important. You might want to work up your own drills to use in addition to the basic ones given above. You might also want to make notes on ways to improve your practice time (step two). Any ideas that allow you to do any of the steps better should be written in this section of your notebook.

In a section called Pronunciation, you can note the sounds which you think you have the most difficulty pronouncing. This will alert you to work on those sounds when they come up again in future talks and when you review old ones.

Another section should be tabbed and entitled Grammar. This is an important section in your notebook. Over time, it will become very important. This is where you write down rules about the structure of the language as you learn them. At first, it will be difficult to understand the structure and you should not worry about trying to do so. So you should not try to say anything in the future or the past unless you have that as a part of your Daily Learning Cycle. But even after a relatively few days of saying what you need to say, you will begin to see similarities about verbs, nouns, and other parts of speech. When you see those similarities in the talks you prepare each day, you should write notes and questions about them in the grammar section of the notebook. After you have used them, you can ask the helper about them the next day. Do not let him give you present, past, future, past continuous, present continuous, future continuous, etc., verb endings in a list of ways to say a verb! Avoid that, for sure! Just allow him to point out what they are as you use verbs in your actual talk each time. Don't ask anything about them until after you have already used them fifty times in the field. Then write notes to yourself or look up answers to your questions in a grammar book, looking up only those forms which you have already employed in your talks. DO NOT study grammar beyond those forms that you are using!

Let's talk about this more deeply. By way of example, let's say you have a number of talks which use the future tense of the verb "to be"—the "I will do something" sense of speaking. Eventually you will notice that there is a part of the verb—usually the ending—which is the same for most of the words talking about the future. Ask Komo to give you several words (verbs) you have used already that have those same sounds in them. You will begin to see a pattern for making verbs that speak about doing something in the future. This will, first of all, help you recognize them when you hear them. After some time, you will begin to know how to make verbs in the future yourself. For the first four weeks or so, YOU SHOULD NOT DO THIS! There are too many variations in verb endings, especially for common words like the verb "to be." Just be patient. Keep learning your daily cycle. Eventually, you will simply know which endings to use because you will have heard them over and over. You will feel when it is right and when it is not.

You can follow the same procedure for learning how to say many other speech patterns, like "he did something" (past tense), "you have always" (past perfect), "we are going to do something" (present perfect tense).

There are many things you can learn by using your grammar section this way. It is not important that you learn every grammar rule exactly like it would appear in a grammar book. You are trying to learn as you use the language. Just like a child, you will make mistakes. People will forgive you, so you should be prepared to forgive yourself. You will get better at using correct grammar as you expand your ability to speak. Just DO NOT make up your own sentences when speaking to people at this stage! If you do, you will make habits of using bad grammar and they can take years to overcome, if you ever do! Just use your daily talks only with other people and keep asking questions about grammar the next day from your helper.

As time goes by, you will increasingly begin to "sense" the right way to say things. This is important. Every language uses grammar rules whether they are ever written down or not. Such rules may or may not exist in the minds of the people, but the habits of speech surrounding those rules are drilled into their children when they are young. You must become like one of those children absorbing those habits by repetition until you feel when it is right and when it is wrong. So even if you can dissect the language grammatically and perfectly before it is over, you will have learned how to use it well before you do—just like the target people did by speaking it, first like a child, then eventually like an adult. Even if you know all the grammar rules, they will never teach you how to say everything correctly in another language. The rules are not as important as knowing how things are said by learning to say them!

You must learn how things are normally said in a language. You cannot say them like you would in your own language. For example, let's say you are reading this book, and suddenly you find it on the floor. In North American English, you would say something like, "Oops! I dropped the book!" In most languages of the world, you would say something like, "Uh-oh! The book dropped!" Notice the first version uses active voice. The second uses the passive voice. Both versions are correct and polite according to the language being used. To a North American, it is important to use the active voice. It denotes a sense of responsibility on the part of the one holding the book. To most other languages, particularly those in Asia, it feels polite to use the passive voice in order to ascribe no fault to the person holding the book. To a North American, the passive voice sounds phony. To an Asian, the active voice sounds impolite and uncultured.

Knowing grammar rules perfectly will never teach you how things are said in another language. That is why it is better to concentrate on learning how things are said first, then figuring out as much grammar as is useful as you discover how to use it. After you have learned how to speak conversationally in the language, you can try to study the grammar rules more formally if they are available. It is important that you learn to sense when and how to express your thoughts the same way the target people do as you use the oral tools this book gives you to use. For at least the first four months or longer (depending upon the language and how diligently you are learning it), you must let your understanding of grammar come not from studying it, but from learned usage, not vice versa.

Your notebook should also contain a section called Comprehension Activities. This section is to be used later in your learning program to record ideas and methods for learning to understand more of what people are saying to you. For example, one such activity would be for your helper to listen as you say your talk, then respond by saying what a person should say back to you. Then you see if you can understand what he said by catching as many words as you can. Just recognize the words and let your mind put together what he probably said. Test yourself this way regularly.

After you have completed your Daily Learning Cycle for about three months, your fluency should be sufficient to begin what can be called the storytelling phase of your learning. This is the phase where you start learning to tell brief stories after greeting people. It is also a phase when you can start witnessing to those you meet each day or on occasions when you think it might be appropriate in a target culture. At this point, you should have a storytelling talk prepared as a part of your Daily Learning Cycle one time per week. The story can be something from your own life, something you heard about somewhere else, a joke you have learned, or a story from the life or words of Jesus. By this time, you should know the culture well enough to know what kind of story to tell. Above all, do not make it very long. Make it interesting to the people you will be with in your Daily Learning Cycle practice. All cultures love stories. Telling appropriate and good stories will increase your fluency and endear you to the target people more than anything else you can say.

Finally, you should now have eight sections in your notebook. They should be divided by tabs and easy to find. Each day you should also carry a small notebook to write down ideas when they come to you wherever you are. After thinking about them or asking your helper about them, you can write them into your permanent notebook that evening during the evaluation time. You can also use your small notebook for writing new words and phrases as you hear them during your field conversations.

You should follow the plan of the Daily Learning Cycle all the way through your language learning. There will be different kinds of talks you will use, some of which are discussed below. But this basic four-step procedure should be followed with a new talk each day. After two or three weeks of following this procedure when you are actually working within your target culture in the field, you will begin to notice that you are beginning to see rules forming in your mind about how to make verb endings when different people are speaking. You will begin to sense when to use certain words with certain kinds of people. You will begin to sense when to understand some of the feelings the people have in their hearts because of the way they say things and through their nonverbal communication. This process will continually expand as you gain more and more talks and ability to interchange the sentences you use between talks. Do not succumb to the temptation to make up your talk as you go! Even if they can understand you, succumbing to this temptation will damage your language learning! Use only what you have learned. Keep using the Daily Learning Cycle (DLC) only so you won't form bad habits. Remember that learning how to say something is more important than how much you can say! It is natural to want to communicate more. But if you keep using the DLC, your communication power will still multiply rapidly without losing your ability to communicate correctly. Later you will have enough communication power to speak what you want and have back-and-forth conversations with others.

This system's rapid expansion of your power to communicate well is a key to the tremendous value of the Life Language Learning System. Your ability to speak and understand the language is always built upon what you have already learned each day. By learning small amounts of language each day then using it a lot, you will see those sentences you learned used in many different situations as you become increasingly and rapidly more fluent. Your speaking power will multiply more and more rapidly. It will also expand your ability to comprehend what other people are saying to you. You will find yourself understanding words and phrases only at first. But still you will come to increasingly understand what you are hearing more often. Later, as you continue to generate talks, you will understand more and more of what you are hearing. By the time you have been following this system for three months, you should be fluent in your ability to speak well and understand everyday conversation. You will be able to buy things, travel where you want, give personal testimonies of your faith, and tell stories which help people want to listen to you. Better still, your pronunciation, intonation, and inflection habits will be so close to a native speaker of the language that you will feel very comfortable in almost any everyday circumstance in the mainstream of the culture. You will also have built a platform in the minds of the people to be heard!

Generating Learning Talks

Now you know the basics of the Daily Learning Cycle (DLC). It is the foundation of the Life Language Learning System. But you also need to learn how to make up talks that will help you the most in your daily application of the DLC. The basic principle behind generating talks is this: **get a little bit, then use it a lot!** Most people want to start with very large talks. This is a mistake. For the first two or three weeks, your talks should not be more than a few lines in length. The emphasis is on getting your talk correctly—not just the words you say, but the way your say them. This is best done with small talks in the beginning. Remember, you will be training your ear to hear sounds you have never heard clearly before. You will be training your tongue to use sounds it has never pronounced.

Beginning Talks: To help you complete your first week, sample talks for days two through five are listed below. You do not have to use these talks. If you think of something you would like to be able to say which is more important to you, simply make up your own talks when appropriate. But whatever talks you use, be sure to follow the DLC (Appendix A) and fill in the evaluation form (Appendix B) for each day.

TEXT FOR DAY TWO

"Hello! My name is [your name]. I'm learning [language]. This is all I can say now. Can I come back tomorrow? Thank you. See you tomorrow."

TEXT FOR DAY THREE

"[Greeting—learn the right greetings for different ages and sex]. My name is [your name]. I'm from [your home]. I have only been here three days. I want to find a place to stay for a few weeks. Do you know a family I could stay with? Could you write their address? Thank you. Goodbye."

TEXT FOR DAY FOUR

"[Greeting—variable by age and sex]. My name is [your name]. What is your name?

I am pleased to meet you. I am [or *we are*] looking for a family to stay with for a few weeks. Do you know a family I could stay with? I would help pay expenses. Could you write their address? How could I meet these people? This is all the [language] I can say. Could you help make the arrangements? Thank you very much!"

TEXT FOR DAY FIVE

"My name is [your name]. What is this?"
("This is a papaya.")
"Papaya?" (Repeat it and write it in your small notepad.)
("Yes. That is a papaya.")
"What is he?"
("He is a barber.")
"Thank you." (Repeat and write down *barber*.)

"You're welcome." (Try to write it down in notepad to check later.)
(Leave-taking. Learn different ways to take leave from Komo. Use correct one here.)

Notice that these talks build on material from the day before. That is a good way to expand your communication power while giving opportunity to review previous material. It also helps you become accustomed to substituting different sentences into different talks. When you do this, be sure you use only the sentences in previous talks. Don't try to make up your own.

Greetings and leave-takings deserve further attention. Each language has a number of ways to greet people and to depart from them after a conversation is completed. For instance, there is usually a general term to greet someone, a term for greeting which shows respect, as you would for an older person or one with authority. There is also usually a familiar form of greeting as you would greet a friend. The same is true of leave-takings. Polite leave-takings, casual goodbyes, and various ways of letting people know you are leaving are all common to most languages. The words used often do not make sense when they are translated literally. For instance, in some Asian languages, a common leave-taking literally means "I am coming." It has the polite connotation of "Do not be concerned. I am coming back." It is the equivalent in English of "See you later." It is important to learn the different forms of greetings and leave-takings with your helper. Be sure to understand exactly when it is proper to use each form.

Notice the talks for days three and four. They invite the hearer to help the learner find a local family with whom they can stay while beginning their language learning. Some people would feel uncomfortable asking for that kind of help, but it is probably the most important thing language learners can do during the first few days in another culture. Most people are really surprised how many people are willing to invite them to stay with them during the beginning of their language learning. Many groups of language learners have used this talk during the first few days in another culture, and almost without exception, they have received many invitations and found a family to stay with right away. This was true even when they had children with them. From the perspective of the host family, living for a while with a foreign family is often a fascinating way to entertain and learn from foreigners. And it can help their budget too! So it is good to offer a bit more than is needed to pay for expenses.

Staying with a local family during the first few weeks or months in another culture will greatly accelerate language/culture learning. It is by far the best single action you can take to ensure that you will get the full benefit of the bonding process. When you stay with a local family, you learn many things about the lifeway of the people. But you learn like an insider! Shopping, cooking, eating, washing, cleaning, doing various kinds of work—often the best ways of doing these things are learned in their natural context when you live with a local family at the beginning. You will find yourself understanding many of the behavior patterns and values of the local people without any cultural rejection on your part. Instead of seeing some of their ways as inferior because they are different, you will begin to openly adopt most of their behavior patterns. You will see why they make good sense in that culture. You will grow to love and appreciate your "family" as they are allowed to share hospitality with you. You will learn to work alongside them in everyday tasks and learn from them. They will accept you and appreciate you in that role as in no other when you first enter a new culture. It is a bonding experience you should not let yourself be denied. If it is possible, try to stay with your host family for at least six weeks.

Power Talks: You can create power talks to greatly expand your communication and understanding ability in another language. Power talks are prepared in such a way that other people help you expand your word usage, vocabulary, ability in the culture, or speaking ability. For instance, a power talk might contain the question "What is this?" People will be happy to tell you the name of whatever you are referring to. "Text for Day Five," which is written above, is a power talk. Can you find the two "power sentences" in the talk? Here are some examples of power sentences which can be used to make power talks:

"What are these called?"
"Do you use these like this?"
"How do you spell _______?"
"Could you repeat that and let me say it until I say it right?"
"Please help me to write that down."
"Which bus do I take to go downtown?"
"What do you call this part of my arm?"
"Which train will take me to ______ [place]?"
"If I point like this, which direction am I pointing?"
"How many of these do I have? How many do I have now?"
"What time is it?"
"What is the date today?"
"How much does this [or *do these*] cost?"
"Can you tell me any other words that have the sound _____ ?"
"I'm going to do something. [Raise hands, turn around, etc.] Please tell me what I did."

By thinking about these sentences, it is easy to see how much help you can get even when you are talking with people during the DLC. By carefully mimicking (and LATER writing down their answers), you can quickly and accurately learn to say many common things. When someone tells you something, be sure to write it down, talk about it with Komo to fully understand, then practice it before you see them the next day. After you have been doing your DLC field practice for several days, you will probably establish a routine where you talk to many of the same people every day. Most people will be delighted to help you and will be amused by both your rapid progress and even your mistakes. If they help you with something one day, then you go back and show them what you have learned the next day, they will want to help you a lot more!

Learner Talks: Up until now, most of the talk material which has been introduced would be in the category of Learner Talks. They help you to assume the role of learner in another culture. You can make up many other talks like this.

Servant Talks: Here are some sentences to help you assume the servant role during the beginning part of your enculturation. They can be inserted into other talk material which you have already learned. Or you can put them into new talks you make up yourself. Here are two examples:

> "I hear you are not feeling well. I am visiting to let you know we are praying for you. I brought these sweets [or *flowers*, *books*, *food*, etc.] for you. I want to help you with the housework [or *care for the animals* or *with the farmwork*] while you are sick. I hope you are feeling better soon."

> "I want to spend one day each week working with someone to help you. Of course, I won't get paid, but I will learn a lot. This way I can learn about different kinds of work while helping you. And I can get to know you better. Do you know someone I could work with tomorrow? What time do we start? Good. I'll come tomorrow."

Storyteller Talks: Every people group has individuals who tell stories. Sometimes these stories are told mostly by older people. Sometimes people of all ages tell stories. Many cultures have stories that are like proverbs. They tell a story which shows the truth of certain principles or values accepted in that culture. The language learner would do well to learn the types of stories people usually tell in the target culture, then try to use those same stories or other stories that would fit into that pattern. Be sure the stories you tell are positive ones.

You can tell stories about thousands of things. Just describing something which has happened to you is telling a story. The more skillful you become in telling stories, the more people will want to listen to you. You will eventually gain more opportunities to spend time with the people in the host culture. You can also use storytelling as a tool for generating power talks, like in the first example below. Here are two different kinds of stories and suggested talks for each type. You can make up many more:

STORYTELLING POWER TEXTS

I want to learn to tell about this article in the newspaper. I don't understand this sentence. What does this word mean? Have you read this? I want to try to tell you about this in my own words. Please help to correct my mistakes when I am finished.

OTHER SUBJECTS FOR POWER TEXTS (TELL HOW TO)

- Make tea or coffee.
- Catch a bus and go to the train station.
- Make a phone call.
- Fix a bicycle.
- Drive a car.
- Buy food in the market.
- Hire a taxi.
- Plant a field.

EVANGELISM STORYTELLING TEXTS

- Your personal testimony about accepting Christ.
- The origin of sin (to distinguish Satan from the many types of evil spirits).
- The creation story.
- The story of the flood.
- The Ten Commandments.
- Prophecies about Jesus.
- The birth of Jesus.
- Jesus feeds the five thousand.
- The rich man and Lazarus.
- The woman at the well.

- The story of Zacchaeus.
- The story of the Prodigal Son.
- Jesus predicts His death and resurrection.
- The Last Supper.
- The story of the crucifixion and resurrection.
- The story of Jesus' ascension into heaven.
- The coming of the Holy Spirit.

You do not need to learn and tell these stories all at one time. People will understand and look forward to your next visit even if you tell it like this:

> There is only one true God. You and I are both part of God's creation. Sometimes different people don't get along with each other. Neither do different nations sometimes. Some people don't get along with God either. This is all I can say today. I'll come back tomorrow.

NEXT DAY

> It did not please God that people don't know how to get along with each other. He decided to appear on earth as a man so we could learn about God. He was born of a virgin by a miracle, and was called Jesus [or local name for Jesus] which means Savior He chose twelve men to learn about God from Him. He taught them how to be forgiven from their sins and live a new kind of life. This is all I can say for today. I'll come back tomorrow.

This same process can continue day after day until you have filled in the details and completed the story. You can include a testimony of what God has done in your own life or whatever you think should be in the story. At first, this seems like a foolish way to tell a story. But after the people whom you are seeing every day get used to your coming, they will accept this method very easily. There will often be other people there to listen next time. It is wise to get advice from Komo before telling a Gospel story like this during language learning. It may be better to wait until you understand the culture very well and speak the language fluently before sharing a Gospel story in a Muslim or a Hindu culture. But it can be effective because the people know you are just learning the language and they will often forgive you for not understanding their culture yet. One language learner finished telling her story similar to what is demonstrated above. And the person listening wanted to accept Christ. Another learner more experienced in the language came to help, and the man became a Christian!

MAKING EXPANSION DRILLS

There is one more kind of activity that you need to learn—how to make drills to expand your learning speed and communication power. These drills can help you expand your vocabulary, learn to use the correct verb endings, and give you practice at interchanging the sentences in your talks. We will discuss three basic kinds of drills.

Pronunciation Drills: In your daily practice with your helper, let's say you find that you are having trouble pronouncing the sound "b" the way they do it in your target language. It sounds like a "p" to you, and you tend to pronounce it that way, according to Komo. The pronunciation drill will help you learn how to pronounce it correctly.

Step One: Ask Komo to give you six to eight words which have the difficult sound in them. Write them down by separating them according to whether the sound is in the beginning, middle, or end of a word. Now write them in your notebook like this:

Pronunciation Drill "b"

Beginning	Middle	End
Boy	Habit	Rub
Ball	Library	Jab
Barber	Labor	Globe

Use this pattern in substituting words from your target language. Make sure each word has the sound "b" (or whatever sound you need to use) in the right place for each column.)

You can make notes on the front of the card or page about things you should remember when pronouncing the sound. For instance, you might not have noticed that you should release more air when you pronounce the sound in the middle of the word, or that you should shorten the sound at the end of the word. You should make up a card or page in your notebook for each sound that you have difficulty pronouncing. Then you should practice pronouncing each of those sounds by substituting words into sentences you already know. You can also have Komo put them on tape, one word at a time, with a pause for you to practice mimicking them. If you do this, end the practice by using the words in a sentence each time. That will help keep it like the sound used in the language.

Substitution Drills: These drills can greatly expand your communication power and your understanding of the structure of the language. Substitution drills are made by simply substituting words or phrases for those in a talk line. These drills are the best way to learn numbers, dates, time, and days of the week, for instance. They are also useful for learning personal pronouns and verb forms. You will think of many ways to use substitution drills as you master more and more of them. You should be preparing these drills regularly to increase your communication power. Here is a sample of a typical substitution drill notebook entry.

Substitution Drill				May 21
Structure:			"to be"	
Pronouns, Numbers, Pattern:	I	am	twenty-five	years old
Substitutions:	You	are	thirty	years old
	He	is	twenty	years old
	She	is	sixteen	years old
	They	are	both fifty	years old

This is how you should have Komo put the drill on a recording:

> "I am twenty-five years old."
> (Pause)
> "You are thirty years old."
> (Pause)
> "He is twenty years old."
> (Pause)
> And so on.

After you have practiced these using the recording, with you repeating Komo after each sentence, you should practice changing the pronouns and the numbers around yourself, varying the pronouns and the numbers back and forth. This will make you comfortable in making your own substitutions as you learn the patterns. Feel free to learn the numbers one to one hundred during this exercise, then practice substituting all the numbers as well. This will be very valuable in helping you become comfortable in making substitutions when talking with someone.

Comprehension Drills: This method of drilling can help you remember things very quickly. It can be used many ways. You will probably think of many, after you see the examples. It can also be a good chance to stand up and move around some while you are working with your helper or even when you are doing your DLC in the field.

This is how you would make a typical comprehension drill page in your notebook:

Comprehension Drill: Moving Hands	May 27
Lift your hands	**high**
Lower your hands	
Stretch your hands	**out forward**
Put your hands	**on your eyes**
Etc.	

To use this drill, first have Komo instruct you with the commands on the card by showing you what you should do as he gives the command. That means when he tells you to lift your hands, he also lifts his own. After you have mastered all the commands that way, he should tell you the commands, and you alone make the movements with your hands. Finally, after you have mastered that, you give him the commands in the target language, and he does what you say. Keep practicing until he is doing everything you think you are telling him to do. Practice each command at least twenty times.

Comprehension drills can be used to learn numbers, parts of the body; bending and jumping movements; turning left or right; looking up, down, and sideways; and describing the use of objects and many other things. The language learner should make up and master at least two comprehensive drills each week.

What you have learned in this chapter is the method for patterning your language/culture learning. You should feel free to make modifications in drilling and making talks if you see the change can help you in your target culture. But the basic system should be followed even into the advanced stages of learning. If you stop using this system too soon, as most people are tempted to do, then your pronunciation will decline rapidly, your sentence structure will be incorrect more and more, and people will understand you less. Worse still, you will begin to form habits of speech along those lines that will be very difficult to overcome later when you realize they are incorrect.

After you have become fluent and comfortable in daily conversation, you should begin a reading program in the language. Ordinarily, this should begin about three to four months after the beginning of language learning—a bit longer if you have to take time to learn a foreign language symbol system that is completely foreign to you. If the language has not been reduced to writing yet, you should have a trained linguist on your cross-cultural evangelism team. One of his main tasks will be to devise language symbols for that language so the Bible can be translated into a form they can eventually learn to read. The alternative is to find an oral linguist who can accurately work with them to translate the Bible into their language and make recordings for them to hear the Word of God. If their language is written, the linguist can also teach you much about the structure of the language even as he learns it and prepares to translate the Bible. It is best not to try to reduce a language to writing yourself, unless you are a trained linguist.

Some languages use symbols unlike our westernized alphabets for writing their languages. Korean, Chinese, Japanese, Hindi, Arabic, Bengali—these are only a few examples of many such languages. These symbols need not scare us just because they are different. Writing is only symbols of the sounds in a language. After you have become fluent in using conversation in your target language, it will be much easier for you to learn to match the sounds with the symbols.

It is at this point, and not before, that you can greatly benefit from an experienced language tutor, if one is available. Whether you use an experienced tutor or Komo, you need to drill yourself in connecting the sounds with the symbols (letters). After you have memorized the different letters or symbols, one good way to drill is to try to listen to your helper make the sounds, then you write it down. This is called dictation. You should emphasize this form of drill in the beginning. It helps keep the emphasis on using your ears. Do this until you can identify those sounds with the letters or symbols they represent. It is also important for your helper to use the sounds in a common word you have learned after you speak the sound. After mastering your ability to hear the sounds and write them down correctly, you can begin to read the words from paper out loud. They will sound correct when you read if you follow this plan. Remember, the most important tools in language learning are your ears!

If the language you are learning uses the same Western symbols like in English, you will have an easier time learning to read, but a more difficult time keeping your pronunciation good. When we read symbols we are accustomed to in our own language, we want to pronounce them according to the habits we formed in our own language. But no language pronounces the same symbols the same way. That is why we emphasize learning by listening so much. It is also why we encourage you to become fluent in conversation before beginning a reading program. When you read the language, it is important for you to pronounce the words in your mind the same way the native speakers do. If you emphasize reading (using the eyes) in language learning, you will automatically slide into pronouncing the sounds much more like you do in your own language. If you use the Life Language Learning System, you will be emphasizing the use of the ears. The sounds will not be connected to written symbols in your mind. Therefore, you will be much less likely to mispronounce the sounds by confusing them with those in your own language.

If there are radio or television programs in your target language, you should start listening or seeing them on a limited basis after six weeks of using the DLC. This is for comprehension only. You will begin to understand more and more as you continue your DLC. You will also be training your ear to use the sounds you are hearing and the words you are learning. After about six months, this will also greatly have expanded your comprehension and vocabulary.

If there are books available in the target language, begin by reading simple ones. Do not be ashamed to read primary-level books. By doing so, you will quickly fill in some gaps in your learning. After you begin reading, do not be afraid to read a lot. It will help you increase your ability to think in the language, and it will greatly expand your vocabulary. The key warning point is this: **Do not let your reading keep you from communicating with people! Keep using the Daily Learning Cycle!** The power of the DLC to increase your learning speed should not be underestimated. You can vary your DLC topics to include things you are reading about, or things you found in a newspaper, or even things you are hearing on the news. This is very important to learn to keep refining your pronunciation, intonation, inflection, proper usage, and fluency.

As your reading material becomes more advanced, increase the time given to reading in the language. Emphasize newspaper and news magazine reading. These will be printed with the more widely understood vocabulary. Just make sure all your reading is in the target language. By this time, it should also include your Bible reading, if that is available in the target language. This author learned much of his fluency by praying and reading Scripture in one target language he learned. Eventually you should be able to read and enjoy books on many different subjects. Keep a dictionary nearby if one is available, even if it is only available in the target language. All this will help you to increase your vocabulary rapidly. Do not be afraid to read to yourself out loud. Continuing your DLC and reading out loud will help refine your pronunciation and fluency even further.

THE FINAL PHASE OF LANGUAGE/CULTURE LEARNING

There will come a time in your language learning when you should discontinue using the Daily Learning Cycle. Most people want to discontinue using it far too soon. They are tempted to use it until they can converse fluently with people about most common subjects, then they stop using it. That is a mistake. The DLC is an important source for continuing to learn new material on different subjects and learning to use it with good pronunciation, intonation, inflection, and good phrasing. It is an important method to continue learning new subjects and refining a witness for Christ. You should continue to use the DLC until you have completely reached level 2.5 on the speaking proficiency checklist in the back of this book (Appendix C). It may take you ten months, or it may take you two years, depending on your dedication and ability in using the Life Language Learning System. Only after reaching that high level of proficiency should you consider stopping the Daily Learning Cycle. In the meantime, it is okay to modify the content to suit what subjects you want to learn better.

That is the point to begin the important final phase of language learning. This is the phase where you work on polishing your language usage into a thing of beauty to those who listen to you. It is a refining phase where you personally determine to sift out of your usage the little mistakes and habits which distinguish you from a native speaker of the language. The author knows personally a man who continued this refining process until he entered and won a national speech contest in a target language. You can do that well also if you are determined to never quit learning how to refine your speaking ability without ever stopping.

Even after learning the language well, one of the best ways to keep learning is to sit down with a friend who is a native speaker for an hour or so each day, and just talk about different subjects in his language. It will help if you are sure he is educated and understands the grammar rules of his language. The main thing is that he practices the same kind of speech commonly heard in public, and on radio or television in that language (if it exists). If he is a good friend, ask him to stop you periodically to show you how to phrase an idea better than you do. If it is important and hard to remember, you should ask him how to say it better and write it down. If there is a consistent mistake you are making using the wrong grammar, such as verb tenses, he should show you how to correct them. All these conversations should be in his language. You may want to keep a grammar book near you to refer to, if there is one available. Refining your language usage will greatly increase your effectiveness in cross-cultural evangelism. Never stop increasing your ability to speak and communicate better in your target language!

THE IMPORTANCE OF THE LIFE LANGUAGE LEARNING SYSTEM

You now have a thorough introduction to the Life Language Learning System. While there are many more things about language learning you could learn, you actually have enough to learn any language well. If you consistently apply this system and use new ideas for improving what you are doing as they come to you, you should be able to learn any language fairly well within one year. Appendix C gives you a widely accepted standard for measuring how far you have progressed in your language learning. You should look at it before you begin language learning so you will know what kinds of goals to strive toward. You should also use it to check your progress as you learn. As you continually expand your communication power, you will find new ways to learn more.

Others who have learned or taught schooling or classroom systems of language learning may not appreciate this system of language learning. Do not let that discourage you. It is a far different system than that which has traditionally been used in many parts of the world. But remember, it is much closer to the way people who really speak foreign languages without going to school first learned to do so. You can be certain this system will work, if you work it!

A scientific experiment was conducted in Guatemala to test this system of language learning against traditional language courses. The church headquarters of one denomination was training cross-cultural ministers to learn Spanish. Some of the trainees were in a traditional language school, and a similar number was using the Life Language Learning System. Those in school followed the normal language study curriculum, and the other group which were called LEAP participants was out in the field learning the language in the community as described in this chapter. A twenty-page report was filed with the church headquarters after both groups had been working on the language for eleven weeks. Here are some of the comments in the report:

- "Each of them [the LEAP participants—LP]...feel relatively 'at home' in the Latin culture. The language schoolers [LS], even those who have been here for many years, do not."
- "The LPers have not only learned some Spanish, they have learned how to continue learning by relating to people. Most LSers, when asked about further Spanish learning, have ideas of 'taking an advanced course' or 'working through a grammar book on my own'" (page 18).
- "Those in the control group [LS] have, on average, one Guatemalan friend. The LP group has 15 or more" (page 18).
- "Each LPer has had contacts with dozens of people in Guatemala. There are at least 1,000 Guatemalans who have had positive experiences with the LPers during the 12 weeks of this program" (page 19).
- "The development of relationships, not 'vocabulary' learning, was in focus for these LP learners. Yet, when their core vocabulary usage was compared with LS students..., the study revealed a 74% recognition/production score for

> the LP group while the LS group scored 56%. When both groups of individuals [LP and LS] were matched up with 'the same' (or equivalent) grammatical knowledge, phonetic skill, etc., the LP person knows 32% more vocabulary!" (page 19).

The organization which conducted this study is not being revealed here. An interesting footnote about this study revealed a notable fact. Some of those who were in the LEAP (LP) group were trained like you are taught in this chapter. Before they ever entered Guatemala, they practiced using the Life Language Learning System in another culture at home. Just like you are being encouraged to do—practice the system before you go! The other section of the LP group received their training after they had already arrived in Guatemala. Those who received their training before they entered the country did twice as well on the tests compared to those who took the training after going to Guatemala. This demonstrates three important principles: (1) Language/culture learners should be trained in the Life Language Learning System before they enter their target culture. (2) The bonding principle is valid and very important (those who were trained in the country had little chance for early bonding in the culture). (3) This confirms that *language learning is culture learning.*

There are many more benefits to this system which you can discover for yourself. This system can help you learn any language. It will even help you learn a language which is not in written form. It will also help you learn a language where there is no formal language school. It is a superior system of language learning compared to traditional language school systems. That does not mean language schools have no value. Some language schools have already, or are in the process of, adopting the principles of the Life Language Learning System. Some are learning to effectively combine these principles with more traditional ones. But there are no language school textbooks written for many thousands of languages, yet millions of people learn those languages without studying them. The lack of a language school should not stop you from learning any language. With the Life Language Learning System, you can learn any language and evangelize any people group God calls you to reach!

A Final Word About Translation Devices: There are currently new translation devices and programs coming onto the marketplace which automatically translate speech from one language to another. Unfortunately, none of them are likely to have translation systems that work for the languages of unreached peoples. However, there are translators that work for the national languages of many countries. If the cross-cultural evangelist is working in a country where these programs are available in the national language, it can be a great help to avoid a major problem. Many cross-cultural missionaries have thought they must learn a country's national language before they can learn the target language of a people group within that country. They can avoid this temptation by using one of these translation programs of the national language to help them function in that country while they concentrate on learning the language of the target people group. That must remain their main focus, so such translation tools can be very valuable in a practical way. They must remain focused on learning the target language well. That is the only way they will ever be able to start an autochthonous and explosive movement of church multiplication within the mainstream of a target culture!

QUESTIONS FOR UNDERSTANDING

1. Why is it best to think of language learning as a social rather than a school activity? How is learning another language linked to learning another culture?
2. Contrast the differences between students and learners. List at least five ways the learner role is the best for language learners.
3. In language communication, what percent of the acceptance of the communication is carried by the words alone? What percentage is carried by the pronunciation, inflection, and intonation? What does this tell you about the best way to learn a language?

4. In language communication, what percentage of acceptance of the communication is carried by nonverbal expression? What significance does this have for language/culture learning?
5. If you were asked to defend the learner-servant-storyteller roles as good language/culture learning attitudes, how would you do it? Use Scripture in your answer.
6. Describe the learner attitude. Write how it can encourage others in the local culture to help you with your language/culture learning.
7. What is imprinting? What does it have to do with language/culture learning?
8. What does "bonding" mean in language/culture learning? When must bonding occur in order to be effective? List some benefits of bonding and give an example from the text of a group of language/culture learners who proved its benefits.
9. List and describe briefly the four parts of the Daily Learning Cycle. For how long should you use the DLC when learning another language? Why?
10. List and briefly explain each of the six activities of the "Getting Your Text" step of the Daily Learning Cycle.
11. Match the activities on the left with the correct step of the Daily Learning Cycle on the right. Write the correct step number behind each activity in the space provided.

a. Listen to the text twenty times. ____	1. Step One: Getting Your Text
b. "Future Texts" section. ____	2. Step Two: Practice Your Text
c. Record text on a device. ____	3. Step Three: Communicate
d. Talk to fifty people. ____	4. Step Four: Evaluate

Explain the differences between (a) power texts and evangelism texts, and (b) servant texts and storyteller texts.

12. Describe how to make (a) a substitution drill, and (b) a comprehension drill. How does each one help you to learn?
13. Describe the procedure for beginning to read in another language. How long should you wait before you begin? Why?
14. Explain why cross-cultural evangelists should be trained in the Life Language Learning System before they enter another culture. Also, explain how this will help them to be "bonded" better than any other time for training.

QUESTIONS FOR DISCUSSION

1. Discuss the advantages of the Life Language Learning System as opposed to what you know about language school systems in general. Which one do you think you would like to use if you enter another culture to do cross-cultural evangelism? Why?
2. Discuss the learner versus student roles in language/culture learning. Which role is the most effective for language learning? Does this mean you should never assume the role of a student? Name some things you think you can learn better as a student, and some of the things you can learn better through the learner role. For both roles, tell when they should be used in the language/culture learning process.
3. Discuss the principles for becoming "bonded" in another culture. Why are they important? How does bonding help the enculturation process? What kinds of personal sacrifice in your behavior might be necessary to have an effective bonding experience?
4. Discuss the percentages of the acceptance of the communication carried by each of the following in ordinary language communication: (a) the words only; (b) the pronunciation, intonation, and inflection; and (3) nonverbal signals. What

are some of the implications of these figures for communication in your own language? What does this mean for those who intend to learn another language?

5. Discuss the statement "Language learning is culture learning is ministry." What are the dangers of separating language learning from culture learning and ministry? How does language learning help culture learning when done right, and vice versa?

CHAPTER SIX

Principles Of Cross-Cultural Ministry

KEY POINTS IN THIS CHAPTER

1. Effective cross-cultural preaching presents the Gospel in such a way that it can be received without cultural interference. This places great responsibility upon the evangelist.
2. There are different levels of trust established between people in a target culture and the evangelist. The evangelist must reach the higher levels of trust before he can be effective in his ministry.
3. Standards of Christian behavior vary from culture to culture because they are symbols of biblical principles. They change like words change when the Bible is translated into another language.
4. The cross-cultural evangelist must learn to distinguish between biblical principles and cultural forms in his own culture, in biblical cultures, and the culture he hopes to evangelize.
5. Judging the validity of people's conversion by behavioral standards is not effective in cross-cultural evangelism.
6. The Centripetal Model of Conversion is the most effective way to view conversion in cross-cultural evangelism. It emphasizes the direction of growth rather than behavior patterns in people's lives.

7. Conversion is best viewed as a process with many steps, rather than an event which occurs at a particular time within each target culture.

INTRODUCTION

Some cross-cultural workers labor long years in the field without seeing any significant results. Why? What problems arise and how can they be overcome? Jesus said he would "build" his Church and the "the Gates of Hell will not overcome it!" (Matt. 16:18). In biblical times, leaders gathered at the gates of each city to plan the affairs of the whole community. That included planning strategy for war and conquest. Jesus was strongly indicating that the Kingdom of Heaven has a strategy to overcome anything planned by Satan to stop the penetration of the Gospel into the mainstream of each culture. That means we must learn principles and strategies from Scripture, the Holy Spirit, and sociological sciences when targeting another culture for the Gospel.

Before going on to learn some important methods for planning cross-cultural ministry strategies, it is necessary to discuss some additional principles for evangelizing target peoples. We need to learn how to develop a strong platform of trust within a target culture. To accomplish that, we must focus on the felt needs of the people in the target culture while learning how to teach biblical truth in a cross-cultural setting. To facilitate that effort, it is important to learn the dynamics and nature of conversion from both a biblical perspective and a perspective on the nature of conversion itself. These understandings will lead us to some important principles for effective cross-cultural church planting.

EVANGELISM FOCUSED ON THOSE WHO ARE LISTENING

Remember how we discussed Matthew 28:19–20 in previous chapters. We established that the responsibility to "make disciples" lies squarely on the shoulders of the one who proclaims the Gospel as much or even more than it does on the people who hear it. We cannot be satisfied with simply proclaiming it in a manner that sounds good to us, then blame those who don't accept Christ because it is their fault. We cannot just "throw the Gospel up in the air" using our own way of thinking, speaking, illustrating, and preaching. Then if it is not accepted by others, consider it their own fault. We must do everything necessary to remove every cultural and linguistic barrier to accepting the message so that those who hear are confronted with full understanding that they are lost and in need of a Savior who is Jesus Christ. It is the responsibility of the cross-cultural evangelist, according to Jesus' own words, to present the Gospel in a manner that every person in every culture has an adequate opportunity to accept Christ as Savior and serve Him in the mainstream of His own culture. Our task is not complete until the only barrier to accepting Christ is the challenge of gaining forgiveness for sin and following after Jesus. Jesus came to build His church in every cultural mainstream to that level. And we are His co-laborers in that task.

We must remember that Jesus himself showed us how to cross barriers. He purposely chose to give up the use of his divine power and operate on this earth as a human being. He fully "enculturated" himself, leaving His heavenly home where He is worshipped by angels. He assumed the role of a humble servant, sacrificing himself in every way, including death, in order to bring us salvation (Phil. 2:1–11). Though He could have called twelve legions (about seventy-two thousand) angels to rescue Him from the cross, he chose to die alone for each one of us (Matt. 26:53). Is it too much for us to be willing to die to our own cultural behavior patterns and learn others in order to become the only kind of good news unreached peoples will ever see and hear? Evangelism focused on those who hear in the mainstream of a target culture involves the attitude of the evangelist as much as it does on the methods he uses.

This kind of evangelism focused on those who hear requires a certain amount of courage on the part of the evangelist. He must be willing to leave the comfortable language and culture of his own people and his Sending Churches. He must be willing to humble himself like a child to learn the language of the target people. He must be willing to labor at the task of enculturating his family into the mainstream of a target culture. He must learn a new language with all its nuances, expressions, stories, parables, behaviors, and value system so he can communicate the Gospel in a manner that can be accepted in the mainstream of the target culture. That takes sacrifice, and it takes the kind of love that Jesus had to do all that for the sake of humankind!

THE IMPORTANCE OF MUTUAL ACCEPTANCE AND TRUST

It was common for the men of a certain tribe in Brazil to structure their social life around imbibing a local alcoholic drink made from the yucca plants that grew there in abundance.[33] It was made by their tribe as a group activity, but mostly by the women. They would pound the manioc into a powder, mix it with oil and the women's saliva in a pot. Then they would let it ferment in the tropical heat. They would occupy hours sitting around in a group to get the drink just right, then add water before they let it ferment. It took days to attain the maximum fermentation they desired.

The men gathered together all the time around pots of the fermented concoction. The main purpose was to get drunk. The drink so painstakingly prepared by the women of the tribe was used by the men as mental lubrication to tell all kinds of wild drunken stories about their past escapades.

One day a cross-cultural evangelist arrived in the village. He had been called by God to evangelize this particular tribe. He did not know the language or the customs of the tribe. The elders of the tribe offered the evangelist a drink of the fermented mixture. The evangelist realized immediately that this offer of the drink was an important form of hospitality for the tribe. But he also understood that it would intoxicate him and set his stomach on fire.

The evangelist noticed that the children of the chief of the village were the ones holding the cup and that it had to be a test of his manhood and trustworthiness. He did not know whether to take it or not. Would it be helpful to the cause of Christ or not? Could he

---

33 https://en.wikipedia.org/wiki/Cauim#Preparation_and_customs.

overcome the smell enough to take a sip, or did he need to take two or three large swallows? Holding the cup to his lips for a moment, he had a concerned look on his face. Obviously, the village leaders were making this complicated. They were nodding their heads affirmatively as they saw he was about to drink from the cup.

Would it be good for him to take a drink? Should he? Would it be a sin? Once he took some, he could never take it back. And his family would have to live there for many years. This was an important decision. By this time, a major portion of the village was watching him. He took some of the drink. Two big swallows, noticing the approval of the chief and the men. He tried not to wince from the strong pungent taste. The chief grabbed his arms, and the men of the village nodded their approval. It was their welcome into the village.

That was the last time the evangelist ever drank the drink, though. As his family lived there and learned the language, they quickly noticed the behavior of the men of the village. They saw how destructive it was to the way of life of the tribe. Eventually, some of the villagers began to accept Christ as the evangelist, and his family became more and more proficient in the language. The villagers also noticed how the evangelist and the new converts treated their families. They did not get drunk and beat their wives. Their children were respectful and learned their school lessons well. They were not mean when they played with the other children.

One of the young girls who had accepted Christ was betrothed to one of the young men. As they began to prepare for the wedding, the couple agreed not to have any yucca drink at the wedding. They felt the drunkenness would detract from the importance of the wedding and take the attention off their sacred vow to serve God as husband and wife. They prepared for a different kind of celebration. At first, the leaders and men wanted to shun the wedding. But everyone knew and loved the young couple, so they came anyway. There was good food, and nobody drank the yucca liquor. Everyone did have a good time, though there was a lot of grumbling by the men.

The other young couples started adopting the Christian wedding rules even before they became Christians. Eventually, the men saw the value of Christian weddings. Over time, this was the door that led to almost everyone in the village and tribe becoming Christians. When the chief became a believer, almost everyone else followed him and became followers of Jesus. Everyone saw the value of the Christian way of living, and the men eventually quit making the alcoholic beverage. They realized it had been destroying their village. Yet it had also been the primary test of the evangelist's acceptability to become a member of the village. He wisely chose to pass that test in order to win the people there to Christ.

This story brings up an important lesson that must be emphasized. When we enter another culture, everything about us looks, smells, and acts like we are foreign to the target people. They have no way of judging us except by the ethnocentric standards of their own culture. Whatever we do or say and however we act before them will always be judged by what it means in their own culture, not ours. In the beginning, we will have no way of knowing what we say or do means to them.

So when you enter another culture, it is like you are below zero (figure 6.a) in the minds of the people in the target culture. Everything you are—your behaviors, dress, way of thinking, what you want to talk and think about—all look, feel, and smell foreign and undesirable to the people in the target culture. You are at the bottom looking up! You speak and act like a child in their minds. You don't know their cultural cues, and so you don't laugh when they do. That makes them laugh at you! And they laugh at you behind your back also! Your gestures are foreign, and you don't understand why they think you are saying things you are not. Your behavior looks foolish. At first, they can only judge you by all the negative things they have heard about the behavior of people from your country. And their behavior shows they have dismissed you as not important, a curiosity at best.

Figure 6.a: Working Up to Zero

All this makes you want to run away to be around people of your own culture who also live in their country (your teammates, business people, diplomatic core people, retirees). That is a strong temptation, and it is a serious mistake when it comes to your enculturation process. It will cut you off from learning what you must learn.

So the first task is to become a humble learner of culture and language among the target people. Learn to laugh at yourself and your mistakes when they do. Apologize when you make one. Jesus took a long time to learn the culture he was born into. He learned it well, humbled himself when He did not have to do so (Phil. 2). If you love the people God calls you to evangelize, you will be willing to endure a lot of misunderstanding, some of your own doing, and some by the target people, in order to become capable of influencing them in a positive manner toward accepting the Gospel. You will be willing to "work your way up to zero" in the minds of the target people and enculturate yourself. Then they will be able to witness your life and hear your words with the value they should place on them as though you were a cultural insider.

There are basic steps to being accepted by a target people in cross-cultural ministry: (1) the prior question of trust, (2) mutual acceptance, (3) mutual respect, and (4) mutual trust. These steps are progressive. Each one builds upon the other. When a relationship of mutual trust develops between the evangelist and the local population, the effectiveness of his witness reaches the highest level.

1. ***The Prior Question of Trust:***[34] When we meet another person in any culture, we are asking a question inside our heads. "Can I trust this person?" This is especially true when we meet someone from another race or culture. When we enter another culture, people will be asking themselves a lot of questions about who we are and where we came from. They will be guarded in their acceptance of us in many ways. If they are willing to interact with us, they will be probing about us to learn about our families, country, maybe even our education, profession, and level of resources. Their questions are more likely to be accusatory than accepting of us. They want to know if they can trust us and how far! They are deciding what they can tell us about themselves, and whether it should be true or deceptive. They are also deciding if there is any benefit to allowing us to be around them. They are deciding very quickly about many categories of people that exist in their minds and where to place us. Their first response is to trust us very little or not at all. So the first category that must be overcome in the minds of a target people is the issue of trust.

    When the chief leaders of the Brazilian tribe mentioned above came in contact with the cross-cultural evangelist, they offered him a drink of the Yucca plant beverage. He sensed its importance. If he had refused the drink, they would have reject him and his presence in the village. It was central to their social interaction. It was used in puberty celebrations and every other major event in their culture. It was the most important act of hospitality in the culture. By accepting the drink, the evangelist demonstrated his acceptance of the leaders and the tribe, while demonstrating a humble position as their guest. If he had not done so, he and his family probably would not have been allowed to live with the tribe. After gaining the confidence of the people, he later demonstrated with his own life and fam-

[34] https://www.reachinginternationals.com/establishing-trust/.

ily the superiority of not using the yucca drink. In time, this attracted many people to his family and their way of life. And most of the tribe accepted Christ and eventually quit using and centering their lives around the yucca drink. Instead, they centered their lives on the teachings of the Bible.

When an evangelist enters another culture, it is very important for him to demonstrate that he can be trusted. If he shows confidence and respect toward leaders in that culture, he will gain respect for himself. It will open doors to him and his family.

One of the most common symptoms of culture shock is the inability to trust the local population in the target culture as much as one of the evangelist's own countrymen. It is not just the target people not trusting the evangelist. It is also the preconceived ideas about the target population which may be in the mind of the evangelist. These can be instilled in his mind before he even gets to the country, or they can be planted in his mind by his own countrymen after he arrives in the country. Just as a member of the target population can mistake the meaning of the evangelist's behavior, so the meaning of the target population's behavior can easily be mistaken in the mind of the evangelist. People in that country from the evangelists own country who are not well enculturated will make a whole host of judgments about the behavior of the target population. Many of them will be incorrect.

We must remind ourselves that Jesus came from heaven to earth, gave up the use of his own divine attributes and power, and entrusted His message to a group of fishermen, tax collectors, and rebellious rebels, intending to use them to change the world! We also must learn not only to trust people in the target culture, but also do what is necessary to help them trust us! Even Jesus lost one of his disciples and it cost Him his life. We must offer trust to people in the target culture, even if they prove to be traitors to us and the Gospel. It will be worth it because of how God will use those who do prove to be trustworthy. Eventually, they can learn to evangelize their own culture, and others as well.

One cross-cultural evangelist lived in an Asian country that underwent a military coup. He had dedicated his entire life to that people and country. There was fighting in the streets in many parts of the city. Many of the Christian homes were confiscated by the military. Finally, there was a call for foreigners to leave their homes and go to a safer part of the country. The cross-cultural evangelist was told to abandon his home for a few weeks.

He decided not to leave. He and his family lived on the bottom floor of the house, and he allowed a local pastor named Amal and his family to live on the second floor. The cross-cultural evangelist decided not to give the keys to the downstairs to Amal. He was afraid that if anyone found out he had them, the soldiers might come and force him to open the downstairs so they could loot it. They thought it could lead to the death of Amal and his family. But Amal thought the real motivation not to leave the keys with him was that he was not trusted. He was one of the most respected pastors in the city, and he was humiliated by the lack of trust. It created a great distance between them that never healed. Now Amal works for the Lord independent of the cross-cultural evangelist.

This story demonstrates the importance of gaining and keeping the confidence of the local population, but it also demonstrates the importance of one of the principles we discussed in chapter four: the social, moral, and religious behavior of the cross-cultural evangelist will be judged by the norms of the host culture. The cross-cultural evangelist should have considered more deeply the impact the key had on Amal. He was worried about Amal's security and wanted to spare him the very real possibility that military looters might make him open the evangelist's bottom floor. But Amal and his people viewed his actions as a glaring demonstration of mistrust.

It is difficult to exaggerate the importance of developing trust within a target people group. It is the first step in creating a base from which to communicate the Gospel of Christ effectively. In contrast to the above story, one cross-cultural evangelist was visiting with a pastor named Ranjit, who was the pastor of the largest church in the country. They had spent time together in ministry and knew each other well. Once, when visiting in the capital city, the cross-cultural evangelist noticed that Ranjit was looking tired. He spoke to him and asked how he was doing. It became apparent that he was exhausted and suffering from high blood pressure. The evangelist was very concerned for him and told him so. He invited Ranjit to get out of the city where he pastored and visit the place where the evangelist lived in another city. He told him that he was going out of the area for meetings, and he urged him to use his home to rest for as long as he liked. He insisted that he do this for his health's sake. At first, Ranjit said, "No, thank you," in a culturally appropriate manner. The evangelist knew he was just being polite and that no meant no only after being repeated at least three times. So he insisted that he go to rest at his home. He said he would leave the key with a trusted person and that he should accept the invitation. Finally Ranjit said thank you, but never committed to go. The evangelist knew he would because rest was very necessary.

When the evangelist returned home, he learned that Ranjit had accepted the invitation and stayed a few days at his home while he was away. He was glad, but thought nothing more about it. It was months later, while visiting the capital city, that the evangelist went to church services where Ranjit was preaching. As an illustration, Pastor Ranjit used the offer of hospitality by the evangelist as an example in his sermon about trust. He stated that no other foreigner had ever offered their home to him and his family ever for any reason. That bond of trust proved to be providentially important in the years that followed in the ministries of both men.

2. ***Mutual Acceptance:*** It is only after we are confident that people accept us totally as we really are that they will consider our message seriously. We need to be sure that the hospitality being

offered to us in another culture is based on a genuine desire to welcome us and nothing else. Given enough interaction with the people, it will become apparent whether they are just curious about us, want to benefit from the presence of a foreigner in some way, or if they genuinely enjoy being around us for who we are! They must not only accept our presence, but also, they must value our presence for the right reasons.

The degree of acceptance of the evangelist also depends upon the degree to which he accepts the people and their culture. He must demonstrate that he accepts their culture and their way of life. He cannot condone or copy the elements of their culture that are obviously sinful. He cannot show acceptance of those parts of the culture that are obviously against biblical principles, but it is certainly not his job either to attack those unbiblical activities in the very beginning. He must first demonstrate an interest in the people and their culture as important.

Too frequently, people who enter another culture notice the things the people do that they do not like or are against their understanding of Christian behavior. And they speak out against it. This is a symptom of serious culture shock (see chapter four). The evangelist cannot afford to display such behavior when he enters another culture. He does not know what a particular form of behavior means in that culture and is not qualified to judge it from a biblical perspective until he truly understands what it means to the local people. The last thing he should try to do is think about changing their behavior only. He should focus on what is required to change their worldview and values from a biblical perspective, as we discussed before. If successful in doing that, they will change ungodly behavior themselves! Until he is fully enculturated, he is not qualified to judge what a specific behavior means in the hearts of the local population anyway. It is only after being enculturated that he will be qualified to demonstrate a better way through the principles of the Word of God. Demonstrating acceptance of the local culture will open a door of acceptance to a biblical way of life in their hearts also.

3. ***Mutual Respect:*** Respect is based on trust and acceptance. It is important that the cross-cultural evangelist present a message that he lives out himself, so that he can gain the respect of the people he is called to evangelize. His listeners will not value his message if they do not appreciate and respect who he (or she) is.

A target people group can believe that the motives of an evangelist are good and that he is a sincere person, but they can also totally reject his message. The cross-cultural evangelist must also live an "incarnational" Christian life! As much as possible, he must learn to eat, sleep, work, speak, and fellowship with the target people just like they do. As he demonstrates an identification with the way of life of the local people, he (or she) will gain the platform to be heard and to fully proclaim the Gospel of Jesus Christ.

In order to demonstrate how they can live a Christian life, he must be sufficiently enculturated to understand the norms of their behavior and what they mean. He must know the worldview and values upon which they are based. That will give his family the ability to correctly model a way of life that is more appealing than the way the people are living. That is how the evangelist among the Brazilian tribe discussed above was able to show the value of Christian living with his family. And it allowed him to win most of the tribes to Christ!

Evangelists must become well advanced in their third step in trusting before they can be very effective in making disciples. Acceptance is as important as establishing trust. The amount of respect that we have for the culture is demonstrated by the respect that we show for the people of that culture. If the evangelist's family accepts the people's social hierarchy and customs, and works within them, they will make great progress in demonstrating the necessary respect for the target culture. And the people of that culture will greatly respect and admire the evangelist and their families for doing so.

It is not enough to show respect only to the one or two people who are in charge of the decisions made by the people. Give respect to those in authority, but also show special love and respect for those who are least respected in the society of the target people. When people at all levels of society are given respect and dignity, the Gospel can be transformational for that society.

4. ***Mutual Trust:*** The final step in establishing an increasingly effective trust relationship within a target culture is to develop interdependent and mutual trust. This is the level where both respect and trust are mutual. Both the cross-cultural evangelist and the people in the target culture trust each other deeply. The basis of such a relationship is mutual trust. At this stage of progress, the people know that the desires of the evangelist's family are not just focused on their own goals, but also on the goals of the target people. They know their motivation, and they trust them completely. They know their loyalty to the people's needs and desires is sincere. They understand them completely and trust their efforts to help them. They are not threatened by their presence in any way. They know the family is not there for their own personal gain, but for the benefit of their people. They have come to understand that they are not there under deception and can be trusted within their own culture. This loyalty to each other allows the people and the evangelist to pursue common goals.

We haven't actually told the whole story about the Brazilian tribe that we related to you at the beginning of this chapter. We can analyze further some of the factors relating to the success of the cross-cultural evangelist working among them. He passed the test of initial trustworthiness by taking the traditional yucca plant drink. That allowed the tribe to approve his request to live among them with his family. Even though it was difficult, his family was allowed to live among the people, and learn and study the language and culture for an extended period of time. It was the major effort needed to show the people of the tribe the benefits of living for Christ in that culture. They never took another drink of the yucca plant beverage. They showed how much better it made their lives in contrast to the local people around them. The women in the tribe noticed that the evangelist, though a man, did not get drunk and mistreat his wife.

The cross-cultural evangelist sat with the men as they drank from the yucca plant beverage. He told them the stories of the Bible without condemning what they were doing or their way of life. As time passed, some of the men began to sit with the evangelist to ask his advice. Some accepted Christ. And when they got together to talk about it, the believers decided to meet regularly to pray and translate the words of the Gospel into their own language with the help of the evangelist. More of the unconverted tribal members began to join the group instead of sitting with the men to get drunk. They also accepted Christ.

After a period of time, the believers decided to construct a shelter where they could meet without being in the rain. They also began to use it to conduct their puberty ceremonies and the weddings. One of the women who got married decided that nobody could come to the wedding unless they pledge not to drink the yucca beverage at the celebration, as was the previous tradition. Before, the men would get so drunk, it would disrupt the celebrations and distract attention from the bride and groom. When the people saw what a different and wonderful wedding the girl and her husband enjoyed, they all wanted to have the same kind of wedding. This brought more people to accept Christ. The puberty ceremonies also became free of the yucca drink. The respect for the way of life of those who accepted Christ grew rapidly. They began to work hard and sell some of their fruits and cassava in the town markets. They came to be wealthy and became leaders of the village. They translated the Gospel stories in a booklet called "Way to Life," and they sent evangelists to other villages and even to other tribes. They sent their own cross-cultural evangelists who were trained by the one who brought them the Gospel. They determined to do what he had done among their own people. They were effective and fruitful.

During the years when the evangelist lived among the target people, he and his family moved progressively through each successive step of developing trust relationships with them. They learned the language and normal patterns of behavior of the people. He learned all their customs, but participated only in those that were worth keeping. And he did not condemn the people for them. He simply showed them a better way until they began to copy his behavior. They respected his family because they knew they loved the people deeply.

Eventually, the people in the tribe prospered enough that they built a church building. By this time, most of the tribe was converted, and a great celebration was scheduled to dedicate the building. They invited everyone from their tribe and dignitaries from the government. By this time, they had fully translated the four Gospels in the Bible and displayed them proudly during the celebration. And there were no drinks from the yucca plant allowed! They had also brought the Gospel to the other villages of their tribe. Just as important, they successfully evangelized other tribes nearby whose language was similar to their own.

The most important evidence of mutual trust was the transformation of the work of the tribal chiefs who became unified in their efforts to help the community as their primary reason to get together. This kind of trust cannot develop when the evangelist enters a culture with only one objective in mind. He cannot simply be pursuing his own self-interest. The objective of establishing such mutual trust is not just for the people involved, but also for the wider population as well. It is the kind of relationship necessary to reach the broader spiritual objectives of his presence in the village. It is the kind of relationship necessary to fan the flames of evangelism—the kind necessary to establish autochthonous churches.

LEARNING TO DISTINGUISH BETWEEN BIBLICAL PRINCIPLES AND CULTURAL FORMS

Consider the power of the Word of God to communicate His nature and His intention to transform lives. That power does not reside in the actual words of the Scriptures themselves. It resides in the meanings the words represent. For example, to a real Christian, the words "Jesus Christ" can be of great significance. They can engender a great faith and comprehension of the nature and power of God. But to unbelievers within the same culture, that term can mean nothing more than a curse word. But to people in another culture, the words can mean a foreign inferior God!

The power of the words "Jesus Christ" is not in the words themselves, but in the significance they have to the believer. It is the same in respect to all the Scriptures. The words are simply representative symbols of meaning. They are NOT the same as the meaning itself! Remember our discussion of communication theory in chapter four.

It is important for cross-cultural evangelists to learn to transmit the pure meanings of the Scriptures using culturally appropriate forms—appropriate words or symbols of the target culture! We must look deeper into the importance of this concept as it relates to the spread of the Gospel inside a target culture. As the evangelist studies the culture he wants to reach, it becomes increasingly easy to communicate the basic principles of the Gospel in a way that is understandable and important to the local people. There are biblical principles—eternal biblical meanings—that apply to every culture and to all people. On the other hand, there are biblical forms (practices and behaviors) that obviously apply specifically to the culture in which they were practiced in biblical times. The effective cross-cultural evangelist must learn to distinguish between them. If he fails to do so, his ministry will suffer greatly. He must learn how to distinguish between biblical principles which apply to every culture, every language, and every people and those forms of behavior that represent biblical truth only in a specific culture.

Just like the culture of today, the peoples of the cultures in the New Testament established normal and accepted behaviors of conduct for their daily lives. Different behaviors were positive in the minds of their people and accepted by their societies. Others were not, just like in every culture today. For example, the Jews of Paul the apostle's day considered the meat that was offered in the Greek marketplaces of the Roman world to be contaminated because of the manner in which they were killed. They thought the meat killed represented a sacrifice to pagan gods. They even insisted that Gentile believers not eat anything sacrificed to such gods (Acts 15:29). But Paul taught the believers in Corinth to "eat anything in the meat market without raising questions of conscience" (1 Cor. 10:25). But he went on to caution them not to offend the conscience of another person. He told them, "Everything is permissible—but not everything is beneficial…if anyone says to you 'This has been offered in sacrifice' then do not eat it. Both for the sake of the man who told you, and for conscience' sake—the other man's conscience, I mean, not yours…So, whatever you eat or drink or whatever you do, do it all for the glory of God. Do not cause anyone to stumble" (verses 23, 27–29, 31).

Here is a classic case of a clash between two cultural norms of behavior. To people of Jewish background, it was anathema to even think about eating something that MAY have been in some way killed in honor to a pagan god. To new believers with a Gentile (non-Jewish) background, normal meat in the marketplace, regardless of origin, was made clean and covered with the blood of Jesus' sacrifice (see Acts 10). Two cultures. Two norms of behavior. Both acceptable to God.

Notice, however, that Paul was clearly pointing to an overriding biblical principle that applies to every culture: "Do not cause anyone to stumble, whether Jews, Greeks or the Church of God—even as I try to please everybody in every way. For I am not seeking my own good, but the good of many, so that they may be saved" (verses 32–33). He had already told them, "I have become all things to all men, that by all possible means I might save some" (1 Cor. 9:22). Paul was a man of high education and a product of many cultures. He was able to sort out the differences between cultural norms and biblical principles. He was not willing to impose upon the Greek believers the cultural norms of Jewish believers. He knew the principles were the most important, but the behavioral norms were specific to time, place, and culture. Learning how to make such distinctions is absolutely critical for the cross-cultural minister of the Gospel!

So it is not right for a cross-cultural evangelist to impose an outside code of culturally based behavior upon the new believers in his target culture. (Just as it was not right for Jewish believers to impose their cultural norms on Gentile believers.) Doing so in the most common mistake made by cross-cultural evangelists early in their careers. Taking the norms of Christian behavior from one culture and imposing it upon the new believers in another culture can cause great damage. It can cause serious damage to the believers and greatly diminish the power of the Gospel to spread in that target culture. What is considered holy and positive in one culture can be considered just the opposite in another culture.

Let's take an example from the idea of what is normal clothing in each culture. Each culture defines what is desirable and what is lude or lascivious when it comes to women's clothing. For the Muslims of the Middle East and Asia, virtually any part of a woman's body is sufficient to incite lust in the minds of males of those societies. As a result, when a woman is out in public, they are required to wear a "burka"—a robe-like cloth that covers their body completely, with only a small opening so they can see. This is considered proper "protection" for the women.

In the subcontinent of Asia, such as in India, it is considered improper for a woman to be uncovered from her waist to her feet. But it is proper and acceptable for her to be uncovered, or partially covered from her waist to her breasts. Her arms can also be mostly uncovered. But in many tribes of Africa, it was traditional and normal for women to wear nothing in the way of clothing above their waists. To do so was considered an insult to tribal leaders and to men in general. (It also allowed for unhindered breast feeding.) For women to wear clothing above the waist was considered unnatural and immoral (no longer the case now). Only a person of low reputation who wanted to show off, such as a prostitute, would do such a thing at that time.

So what biblical principle applies to women's clothing? 1 Timothy 2:9 and 1 Peter 3:3–4 gives us the answer to that question. Paul encourages women to dress modestly with decency and propriety. He wants their beauty to shine from an inner beauty and a quiet, gentle spirit, not from the accoutrements of outward beauty, such as gold and jewelry. He shows that such beauty lasts for life, not just for the young. Notice that Paul is not condemning a particular form of adornment for women. He is simply pointing to the more important biblical principle of seeking beauty based upon a spiritually empowered heart. Such a beauty could be found in women dressed like any of the examples of clothing valued in the parts of the world discussed above, if they have been born-again as Christians.

Women's clothing is only one example of many that illustrate the principle we are discussing here. We are not sent by God to other cultures to change their norms of behavior ourselves. We must learn to distinguish between cultural norms of behavior and biblical principles that apply everywhere to everyone. If our ministries emphasize the latter, the Holy Spirit will help the new believers of each culture change their behavioral norms in a way that appeals to the people of that culture and is pleasing to God.

Everyone needs practice in learning how to distinguish between cultural forms and biblical meanings. Figure 6.b lists some biblical events and behaviors. Put an X in the column that you think is correct. Is each scripture an example of a biblical principle or a cultural form?

Figure 6.b: Biblical Principles and Cultural Forms

Biblical Principle	Cultural Form	Scriptural Example
________	________	"Let us not give up meeting together" (Heb. 10:25).
________	________	The believers met together on the first day of the week (Acts 20:7).
________	________	The believers gave their offerings for the work of the Lord on the first day of the week (1 Cor. 16:2).

________	________	Believers are warned to "avoid every kind of evil" (1 Cor. 5:22).
________	________	Timothy was encouraged to "use a little wine because of your stomach and frequent illnesses" (1 Tim. 5:23).
________	________	Men are to pray with their heads uncovered. Women are to pray with their heads covered (1 Cor. 11:4–7).
________	________	"Salvation is found in no one else, for there is no other name under heaven given to men by which we must be saved" (Acts 4:12).
________	________	"Then they drew lots, and the lot fell to Matthias; so he was added to the eleven apostles" (Acts 1:26).
________	________	"All the believers were together and had everything in common. Selling their possessions and goods, they gave to anyone as he had need" (Acts 2:24–25).
________	________	"I don't permit a woman to teach" (1 Tim. 2:12).
________	________	"Does not the very nature of things teach you that if a man has long hair, it is a disgrace to him, but if a woman has long hair, it is her glory?" (1 Cor. 11:14–15).
________	________	"Greet one another with a holy kiss" (2 Cor. 13:12).
________	________	"Pray continually" (1 Thess. 5:17).
________	________	"As in all the congregations of the saints, women should remain silent in the churches. They are not allowed to speak, but must be in submission, as the Law says" (1 Cor. 14:33–35).
________	________	"the law of the Spirit of Life set me free from the law of sin and death" (Rom. 8:2).

If you marked more of your answers in the "Cultural Form" column, then you have learned to distinguish between biblical principles and cultural forms well. If you marked in the "Biblical Principle" on half or more, then you need more practice in thinking about this principle. An effective cross-cultural evangelist will put the majority of his X marks in the "Cultural Form" column. For some of the examples in figure 6.b, it is easy to discern which column is correct. Most of them are not so easy, depending upon the culture you live in. For example, it is not difficult to see why we do not choose our leaders in the church by "drawing straws," or letting chance be the determining factor. Most cultures do not practice such a thing today in English-speaking countries. But that is not true in Africa. What would you say if African believers decided to follow that pattern? It was common in the early church, and it is in the Bible! God used that form of selection to choose the twelfth apostle!

In the same way, it is easy to recognize that greeting one another with a "holy kiss" was common in New Testament times and is common in some cultures today. But it is not so easy to recognize the practice of going to church on Sunday as a cultural form. It is so common in so many cultures today following the custom of the New Testament believers. This brings up an important point. Even cultural forms often illustrate a biblical principle, and that is why they can be confused. The cultural form of going to church on Sunday represents a way to fulfill a biblical principle—"let us not give up meeting together" (Heb. 10:5). Going to church is the biblical principle. Doing it on Sunday is a cultural form. That is why believers in countries like Bangladesh meet together on Friday—the only day off of the week in a Muslim country. So copying the cultural form of meeting on the first day of the week is a good practice, but meeting on any day is fine with God, so long as we do not quit meeting together! We meet together to worship God! We also use the time to learn from his Word together. Both are vital to the Christian life. Jesus purposely chose to repeat every one of the Ten Commandments to his followers except one: "Remember the Sabbath to keep it holy." If He had taught his disciples that one, we would all feel obligated to meet on Saturday!

Do keep this principle in mind that cultural forms do reflect and serve as examples of biblical principles. For example, in New Testament times, it was commonly accepted in the culture that women should have their heads covered in public, not speak publicly when men are present, and have long hair. This was not just a custom for the church, but for whole societies of the time. For a woman to break one of those common customs would bring a bad name to the Church and to the Gospel. Paul knew he was not laying down a law, but was encouraging the women to behave in a manner that gave the Gospel a positive influence in the societies of the peoples they were trying to reach with the Gospel. That was behind most of the decisions Paul made about the behavior of believers, both men and women (1 Cor. 10:33). Cultural forms represent biblical principles (meanings), but they can vary from culture to culture according to what they mean within each culture. That is why the ability to distinguish between the two in biblical times, our own cultures and in the cultures we are called to reach for Christ is so important.

LEARNING TO DO CROSS-CULTURAL EVANGELISM SKILLFULLY

It would be easy to present biblical truth in other cultures if biblical principles and cultural forms were the same everywhere. We could simply tell everyone everywhere in the world to follow the same practices as the people in the New Testament. But to do so, we would have to tell the believers that they cannot worship in churches, only in Jewish synagogues or in people's homes. We would have to teach believers to greet each other with a "holy kiss" and "take a little wine for the stomach's sake." Believers would only be able to meet for worship on Sundays. The leaders would need to be chosen by "casting lots." But it would not be that simple. The believers would spend a lot of time trying to decide whether to follow the cultural forms of the Greek believers or those of the Jewish believers.

God never intended believers to all be tied to specific cultural forms, whether Greek, Jewish, or our own! Cultural forms are only symbols of meanings just as the words of Scripture are symbols of meaning. The words used in a specific language are not significant in themselves. They are only linguistic symbols. They are significant only insofar as they convey the meanings of Scripture. It is the meanings themselves that are significant and holy. The words (forms) can be translated into any language, and the meanings will stay much the same if done correctly. It is the same for cultural forms. They have their validity to the extent that they convey and demonstrate the actual scriptural meanings of living a Christian life in the language and culture where they are used.

There is another reality which is important to add to this analysis. Cultures do not remain the same! They change over time. Nothing is permanent in terms of behavior. A specific behavior or linguistic form now will take on new meanings over time. Nothing remains the same. So both in our own culture and the people groups we are trying to reach behaviors will change over time.

Some cultures change rapidly, others slowly. But all cultures are in a process of change. Over the years, they find new and better ways to take care of the necessities of life, depending upon what is available to them to do so. As they interact with other cultures, they adopt some of the methods of other cultures as they become available to them. So we cannot let the forms we use to communicate significant and permanent biblical principles to remain static. We must allow the forms to change as the culture changes. If we demand that the forms that have become standard for believers in our culture remain static, over time, they will be positive only for believers. They will increasingly become negative for unbelievers as the culture at large continually changes. This diminishes the value of our Gospel message greatly over time in the minds of the unbelievers of our culture. It also keeps believers from having a positive impact on society as a whole. If we want the Gospel to be effective in winning unbelievers in our own society, we cannot try to keep the forms we use to convey the meanings of the Gospel the same over time. We must be willing to change the forms in order for the meanings of the Gospel to have a positive and maximum impact.

We can summarize the process required of a cross-cultural evangelist in order to have an effective ministry:

1. **Step One: Separate Forms and Meanings in Scripture:** Study the behaviors of different cultures in the Scriptures. Focus on the New Testament. Identify the different cultures and take note of their behaviors that differ from those of other cultures. (We will give examples below.) This will help you to refine your ability to distinguish between biblical principles and the specific behaviors of the cultural norms themselves. The important "supra-cultural" meanings, or biblical principles, are for everyone everywhere. The cultural norms are valid only as they reflect the correct meanings in a specific culture.
2. **Step Two: Separate Forms and Meanings in Your Own Culture:** There are many normal patterns of behavior in your own culture that are representative of important biblical principles. Learn to distinguish between them. For example, the Bible encourages believers to be hospitable, kind, honest, loving, and many other positive attributes (Gal. 5:22–23), which we can easily identify with specific behaviors in our own cultures. Can you learn to hold lightly your culture's methods for displaying those positive biblical attributes in order to learn behaviors in another culture that convey those same biblical meanings?
3. **Step Three: Clothe the Gospel in the Correct Cultural Forms of the Target Culture:** The challenge is to unclothe the Gospel in the New Testament from the cultural forms that were used to convey the biblical meanings, then do the same in your own culture, and finally, reclothe the Gospel in cultural forms of the target culture that correctly convey the exact same biblical meanings you found in the Bible. That is easier said than done, and it will require concerted effort on your part to make the distinctions of this three-step process.

Most of the illustrations that show mistakes in this book up to this point relate to cross-cultural evangelists who did not learn to leave their "cultural baggage" at home. They did not know how to separate forms and meanings, cultural behavior from biblical principles. This whole discussion is to show the importance of learning how to do that.

THE DYNAMICS AND NATURE OF CONVERSION

One cross-cultural evangelist visited the country of Japan to preach the Gospel. He did not know the language or the culture. He hired an interpreter to help him convey the Gospel message. At the end of each message, he would ask the people listening to "raise your hands if you want to accept Jesus." The interpreter simply said, "He wants us to raise our hands." Everyone did that without understanding what he was asking them. This was repeated each time he spoke. The evangelist got excited. He cancelled his meetings back home and told everyone that he could not leave because so many people were being "saved." This went on for a long time until the evangelist came to realize that the people were not raising their hands for salvation, but were just raising their hands because they were asked to do so. This made him mad at the interpreter. But it was eventually explained to him that the interpreter had only done what his culture required him to do. Japan is a "shame" society, and it is considered very impolite to embarrass someone, particularly a foreign guest, by refusing what he asked them to do. In their minds, they could not refuse his "request" without shaming him dramatically and causing him to lose "face." They were not accepting Christ. They were only doing what they were asked to do in order to help the evangelist not lose "face."

The Centrifugal Model of Conversion versus the Centripetal Model of Conversion: It is biblical to expect the behavior of new believers to change after they accept Christ as Savior (Luke 3:8). "Therefore if anyone is in Christ, he is a new creation, the old has gone and the new has come" (2 Cor. 5:17). When people genuinely accept Christ, it changes them—they want and do different things than before. The changes may come quickly or over time, but being "born again" changes things. It is easy to recognize those changes and their value in our own culture. That is not so easily done when we see people converted in other cultures. This problem is illustrated in figure 6.c. The large rectangle represents the whole culture and all its people. Those in the smaller rectangle where there is a cross represent Christians and "Christian" or biblical behavior. Those outside the small rectangle represent unbelievers and non-Christian behaviors. It is common for Christians to learn to recognize the validity of a person's faith by the behavior displayed in their lives.

The problem of focusing on behavior becomes multiplied enormously when a cross-cultural evangelist gains converts in another culture. Forms of behavior which have positive meanings in one culture can have negative meanings in another culture. The evangelist in Japan, for example, was enraged when he found out the interpreter had simply been asking people to raise their hands in order to be polite to the foreigner. But it made perfect sense to the interpreter! One thing is for certain: until the cross-cultural evangelist knows the nuances of meaning and behavior in a culture, he is not capable of correctly judging the meanings of specific behaviors in that culture. And he should never make it his job to do so. If left to their own knowledge of what is good and bad behavior, people who really accept Christ will change their behavior in a manner that brings a positive name to the Gospel and is accepted by other believers as genuine.

Figure 6.c: Behavioral Model of Conversion

In figure 6.c, those who are saved are judged by their behavior. Those within the box are considered to be following behavior that is Christian. Those outside the box are judged to be following behavior that is not Christian. Therefore, the O people are not saved and the X people are saved in the mind of those observing. There are three deficiencies surrounding this basic model of conversion. First, it places an undue emphasis on behavior, implying that salvation is a result of good behavior. But salvation is by grace, and we can never obtain it by good behavior (Eph. 2:8–9). While this is biblically valid to observe people's behavior this way, it is dangerous to judge other people simply on the basis of their behavior. People can act like Christians without actually being Christians. Far too many people try to act like they are good people and assume their salvation is assured by such efforts. They think their good behavior within the box assures them that they are safe (see figure 6.c). They find themselves in danger since they rely on their behavior to feel like they are saved. The need to feed their spiritual lives with biblical truth is not recognized. When their sin reemerges, they feel condemned and give up. That is no way to live, and that is why Jesus did everything necessary to eradicate the guilt of our sin. He knew we could not measure up to the standard of God's holiness and justice. That is why He died for us. Our good works must result from a solid relationship with Jesus Christ (Matt. 7:21–23), not an effort to look like a Christian.

The second deficiency in the Behavioral Model of Conversion is that it is too static. It focuses on maintaining a certain code of conduct in the life of a believer. That idea is contradicted in the words of the apostle Paul in Ephesians 4:13, "Until we all reach unity in the faith and in the knowledge of the Son of God, and become mature, attaining to the whole measure of the fullness of Christ." Our knowledge of Christ and the resulting behavior that honors him is progressive. It is not a static set of behaviors turned on like a switch after we accept Christ As we learn more of Him, we become more like Him. The sanctifying power of the Holy Spirit helps us continually be in the process of becoming mature believers following Christ's teachings and example. The Behavioral Model of Conversion focuses on the boundaries—what you can get away with and what you cannot. It focuses on what other people think, not the principles of "take up the cross daily" (Luke 9:23). It can easily dishonor the sacrifice Christ made and deceive people into thinking they are saved just by acting like what society says is adequately good behavior. Focusing on behavior makes people think about what they can or cannot do as Christians, rather than focusing on the cross and becoming more and more like Jesus in their hearts.

Finally, let's turn to the deficiency of the Behavioral Model that is most important for cross-cultural evangelism. The evangelist comes from an outside culture and cannot know the complete details of what is and what is not good Christian behavior within his target culture. Remember that he or she must learn to distinguish between biblical principles and cultural forms within that culture. He knows the Bible prohibits antisocial conduct—killing others, adultery, robbery, etc. He also knows Christians are to live holy and virtuous lives. But he does not know all the details of what behaviors clearly demonstrate and conform to biblical principles within the target culture (see figure 4.c). Too often, he would try to impose the norms of Christian conduct in his own culture upon the believers in his target culture. That can cause very significant errors within the churches he is starting and become a very significant barrier to the spread of the Gospel.

<u>The Centripetal Model of Conversion</u> (figure 6.d): The centripetal model is a better picture of actual conversion than the Behavioral Model (figure 6.c). That is especially true for doing cross-cultural evangelism. The Old Testament Hebrew word *shuv* and the New Testament Greek word *epistrepho* are the primary words used in the Bible to denote the concept of repentance. Their essential meaning is "to turn around" or "reverse course." The principle meaning of the biblical concept for repentance is to reverse the direction your sinfulness is taking you. Turn away from sin and move toward God. Figure 6.d illustrates this concept. Each X in the drawing represents a born-again believer. Each O represents an unbeliever. The distance from the cross represents how closely the behavior of each is "Christian" behavior in a given culture. Notice that it is possible to act like a Christian should act in that culture, but still not be a real Christian. As indicated by the term *repentance* in the Bible, it is the direction we are moving, the desire of our hearts, the determination to be the person God wants

Figure 6.d: Centripetal Model of Conversion

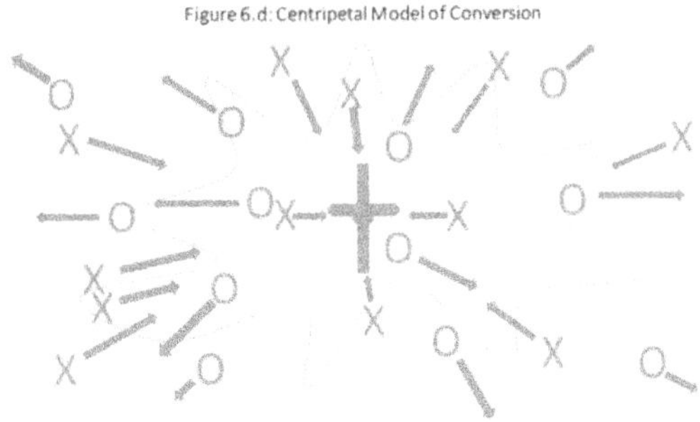

us to be that determines whether we are real Christians. It is not our words, or even our behavior. It is the direction our hearts are taking us.

Look at the illustration carefully. Notice that there are quite a few real believers whose behavior does not look nearly as Christian as some of those who are unbelievers. They may have recently become believers and are still wrestling with old unchristian ways of behaving. Or they have not yet learned to trust the Holy Spirit as He gently tries to guide them toward the cross. But their hearts are turned toward God, and if they continue in that direction without compromise, they will please God and increasingly have better lives. Their salvation is not dependent upon their behavior, but rather on the sacrifice of Christ and the direction their hearts are turned. This uneven line that is different distances behaviorally from the cross is a better picture of people who have truly repented and are on their way to heaven. Since their behavior will never get them to heaven anyway (man's greatest deception is to think it will), it is better to be concerned about the direction and intent of people's hearts when judging whether they are followers of Christ.

All this leads to an important principle for cross-cultural ministry. The best judge of Christian behavior in a culture not our own is the believers in that culture we are working to evangelize. It is not the evangelist. It is easier to judge the direction of a person's heart in another culture than it is his behavior. Without doubt, that is also most important to God (Matt. 15:8, 1 Sam. 16:7). A person who is genuinely saved with his heart totally turned toward God may display behavior that looks very unchristian in our own culture, or even the target culture. If and when that happens, we must ask ourselves some questions: (1) What does that behavior mean to the people of the culture we are targeting? Is it positive or negative behavior to the people of the culture in general? Over the long term, will it likely bring a positive or negative reputation to the Gospel (1 Cor. 9:19–23)? (2) Does the behavior violate God's direct commandments? (3) Does the behavior work (in that culture) at cross-purposes against a principle of God's word? If the answer to all three of those questions is no, then it is best to let leaders in the culture decide when and if to change the behavior. If the answer is yes to any one of those questions, the cross-cultural evangelist should then decide what priority to place on changing the behavior. Then he should encourage the leaders in the new churches to think about the behavior, comparing it to the words of the Bible. Then they will change to more appropriate behavior themselves. They will best know how to do that.

The Centripetal Model of Conversion leads to some important advantages to the cross-cultural evangelist. First, it calls attention to the fact that the primary objective of a new believer is to draw closer to God, not just look good to other people. It avoids the establishment of a minimal code of conduct by which even the believers in the target culture use to judge the salvation of their own people. Instead, it focuses on the potential for a believer to achieve maximum growth in his relationship to Christ and to serving Him.

The most important advantage to this model of conversion is that it allows room for the Holy Spirit to change the new believer's value system and grow more rapidly in the Christian life (see figure 4:d). In Jesus' time, the religious leaders' determination to focus on the system of religious behaviors that had built up in their culture over time kept them from developing a true devotion to God. They thought following their behavioral codes proved they were close to and accepted by God! (See Matt. 23:13–28). Their relationship to God was superficial at best. Over time, they had abandoned the values of God's law and substituted their behavioral norms for them. The correct approach in any culture is to focus on our relationship to God, his principles and standards in his Word, not the traditions of any culture.

For those who are far away from God when they accept Christ, it is necessary to grow closer to the ways of the cross and mature in Christ over time. We have to learn to let the Holy Spirit have the time to show us that our lives are much better when we assume the obligations of following him before we can see it for ourselves. When the author accepted Christ, he did not know what kinds of behavior were appropriate for a Christian. Wisely, none of the mature believers told him what he could and could not do as a Christian. They just loved him and trusted the Holy Spirit to teach him. Over time, because he did want to grow closer to God, the things in his life that were destructive to his faith and harmful to his witness simply melted away over time. The people around him who knew Christ simply lived exemplary lives around him, and he wanted to follow in their footsteps as they grew closer to God themselves. That is an effective way for believers in any culture to win others to the Lord and help them mature in their faith.

This Centripetal Model of Conversion is so important because it helps the cross-cultural evangelist avoid a too common mistake in ministry within another culture. If he or she does not focus on letting believers in the target culture decide what biblical norms of behavior should be, he will almost automatically start guiding them toward the norms of Christian behavior in his own culture. The more he is successful in doing that, the less effective will be their Christian witness within their own culture. It will make the Gospel look and feel foreign and unattractive to unbelievers in that culture. And it will move the new churches outside the mainstream of that culture. Following the principles of the Centripetal Model of Conversion will avoid such problems and will help the churches reproduce effectively within the mainstream of their culture.

2. **<u>The Dynamics of Conversion:</u>**: When we search the scriptures on the subject of conversion, we quickly find the examples of people like Paul the apostle (Acts 9), the Ethiopian eunuch (Acts 8), and Philippian jailer (Acts 16:16–34). Those are among the most amazing events in the New Testament.

   Sensational conversions also occur in our own time. Many accept Christ even today as a result of miracles, healings, and deliverance from demonic power. In fact, the majority of people who accept Christ in India today do so as a result of witnessing or hearing about physical healings or deliverance from demons. Evangelists in that country deal with such issues on a regular basis. So let me state very clearly that miracles DO happen today and that does play a significant role in the conversion of the lost. In the English-speaking world, there are many cultures who have been almost inoculated against belief in the supernatural, miracles, and spiritual gifts. This must be dealt with if we are going to fully represent the Gospel of Christ in any culture.

The Excluded Middle: Professor Paul Hiebert, an eminent expert in anthropology, wrote an article that should be read by every cross-cultural evangelist in the English-speaking world. He developed an important model that describes the best way to describe the interplay between a culture and its worldview, how the culture looks at reality in the physical and nonphysical worlds (see figure 6.e). In his "Framework for the Analysis of Religious Systems," he creates a model for the way cultures view reality on three levels. In addition, he divides all three levels into two separate ways of viewing reality, either as a Mechanical Analogy, on the one hand, or an Organic Analogy on the other hand. We should look at each of these levels closely.[35]

Figure 6.e: Hiebert's Flaw of the Excluded Middle

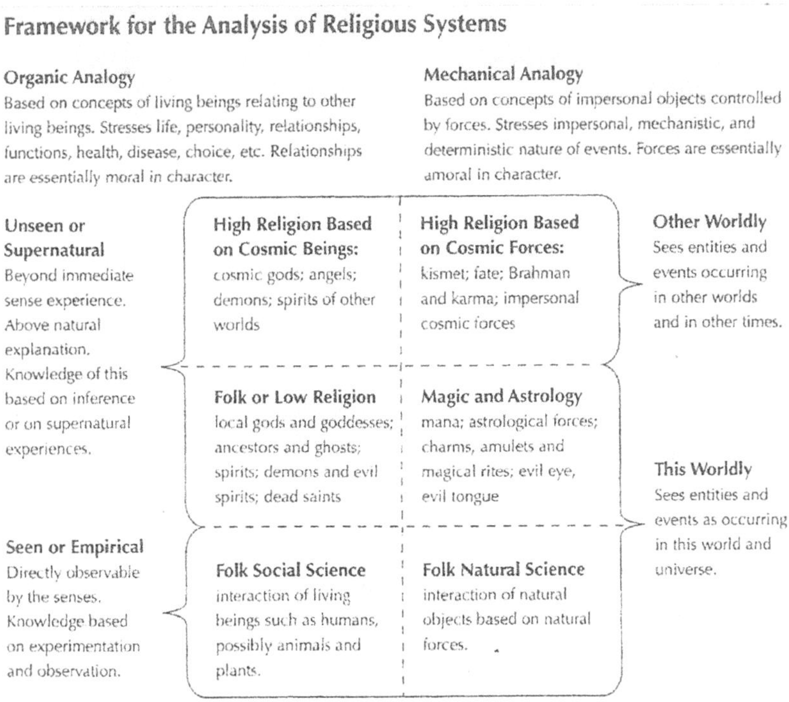

Framework for the Analysis of Religious Systems
Organic Analogy
Based on concepts of living beings relating to other living beings. Stresses life, personality, relationships, functions, health, disease, choice, etc. Relationships are essentially moral in character.
Mechanical Analogy
Based on concepts of impersonal objects controlled by forces. Stresses impersonal, mechanistic, and deterministic nature of events. Forces are essentially amoral in character.
Unseen or Supernatural
Beyond immediate sense experience. Above natural explanation. Knowledge of this based on inference or on supernatural experiences.
High Religion Based on Cosmic Beings:
cosmic gods; angels; demons; spirits of other worlds
High Religion Based on Cosmic Forces:
kismet; fate; Brahman and karma; impersonal cosmic forces
Other Worldly
Sees entities and events occurring in other worlds and in other times.
Folk or Low Religion
local gods and goddesses; ancestors and ghosts; spirits; demons and evil spirits; dead saints
Magic and Astrology
mana; astrological forces; charms, amulets and magical rites; evil eye, evil tongue
This Worldly
Sees entities and events as occurring in this world and universe.
Seen or Empirical
Directly observable by the senses. Knowledge based on experimentation and observation.
Folk Social Science
interaction of living beings such as humans, possibly animals and plants.
Folk Natural Science
interaction of natural objects based on natural forces.

[35] https://journals.sagepub.com/doi/10.1177/009182968201000103.

COSMIC BEINGS VS. COSMIC FORCES: Human beings in every culture look at "other worldly" reality either through a high religion lens of natural laws that govern the universe or through an additional high religion lens of supernatural forces that include cosmic beings, such as gods, angels, demons, and spirits of other worlds. The former can be called a mechanistic worldview. The latter can be called an organismic worldview. Unseen organismic beings are thought to be the cause of many things that exist and interact at all levels of reality. Mechanistic views of reality insist that all that is known in the universe is a result of natural cause and effect, absent any supernatural forces whatsoever.

FOLK RELIGION VS. MAGIC AND ASTROLOGY: Those who believe in the effect of cosmic beings on the natural world see local gods and goddesses, ancestors, ghosts, demons, etc., as capable of interaction with the physical world. Evidence is based on various kinds of supernatural experiences in the physical world. Magic and astrology advocates base their hopes on manipulation of reality through charms, amulets, magical ceremonies, evil eye, and other mechanistic methods of determining reality and events in the physical world. The former views the forces manipulating events in the physical world as coming from the supernatural realm. The latter sees such events as emanating from practices in the physical world.

Figure 6:f

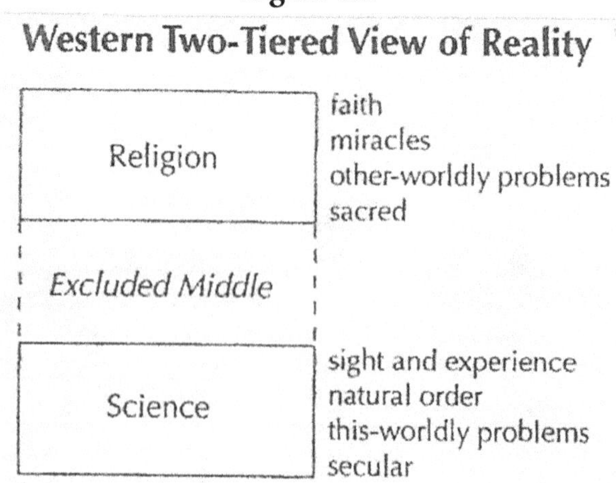

FOLK SOCIAL SCIENCE VS. FOLK NATURAL SCIENCE: Folk Social Science focuses on the interactions of living beings including humans, animals and plants. This is based on observed or perceived interaction between supernatural forces and physical beings. It is based on perceptions of how the supernatural interacts with the natural world. Folk Natural Science is based on observed or perceived interactions between natural objects based on natural forces that are not impacted by anything supernatural. The emphasis here is on the "folk" view of reality, not that based on scientific proof. On the mechanistic side, old wives' tales about pregnancy, the sex of an expectant child, or how to ensure that your cow did not give birth to a stillborn calf are examples of the mechanistic view of reality. So are astrological signs and places you feed your cow to be sure she keeps giving milk. On the Folk Social Science side, it was the color of a bride's dress or "something borrowed, something blue" and other forms of superstition that are examples of traditional folk social science in the Western world. But in other non-Western cultures, there can be spiritual forces that are unseen and live in plants, trees, and houses. For example, in many cultures, it is important to have the front of a house pointed in a certain direction so that it will be protected from and blessed by unseen spiritual forces. In Korea and some cultures in Asia, it is important to sacrifice a chicken at the intersection of two roads in order to protect the family from evil spirits. Efforts to make sick people well suffer from many folk science beliefs on both the mechanistic and the organismic sides of the spectrum.

There is a strong bias toward the mechanistic worldview in Western education. Over time, Western education has worked hard to eradicate any folk social and natural science that has existed over the centuries. This has increasingly moved the worldviews of countless millions of people around the world ever further from anything approaching an organismic worldview. The mechanistic worldview has increasingly become the only reasonable way to look at reality. The scientific method has become the only acceptable yardstick for measuring reality, and nothing else. If it cannot be understood and explained by the scientific method, then it is not real. Or so we are told. This has left a significant flaw in the minds of those trained by Western education, according to Hiebert as demonstrated in figure 6.f.

Western educated people often know very little about the unseen yet real supernatural world and how its elements interact in the seen world. If it cannot be analyzed and measured by our Western analytical scientific tools, it is not considered real. Yet using such tools can be like trying to measure the distance around the room you are in with a handful of Jell-O! The tools of science cannot measure unseen spiritual forces.

Scripture confirms over and over again that spiritual forces do operate in this world. Angels and demons do exist. God is real, and so is his authority and power over the whole world! No matter how much we learn about the universe, we know only a small fraction of what is real. We have mathematicians smart enough to calculate how many atoms must make up the whole universe so far as we can see it in the Hubble Telescope. Yet they cannot tell us anything about 72 percent of those atoms! That means that almost three-fourths of the reality that they so proudly proclaim must exist mathematically is totally unknown to them. They can only speculate about what it might be! Scientists are increasingly coming to mathematical conclusions that there are possibly ten dimensions of reality that exist—nine more than our own! (Yet it was a monk in the thirteenth century who prophesied that there were ten.) That means there are realities beyond the length, breadth, height, and space-time that we know about. Is it not possible that angels, demons, and even God himself exist and operate in those dimensions also, choosing to interact with our dimension according to God's own design? It is arrogant and foolish for mankind to assume that his knowledge is sufficient to define all reality. It is equally as arrogant to say that our science proves there is no God or anything else that is supernatural and organismic in the universe. Even small children in many cultures have enough experience with the supernatural to know that cannot be true. Those trained in Western educational systems might wish to rethink how much they think they know about reality!

For the cross-cultural minister, it is essential to gain more knowledge and experience from the non-Western world using the Bible as a guide concerning the supernatural. Western-educated cross-cultural ministers must realize at the outset that they are handicapped by the worldview of Western education. And they must study the Word and their target cultures to discern where they need more enlightenment. That means they must not dismiss out of hand the perspectives on reality held by people in their target cultures. It is probably closer to a biblical perspective than their own! As a stark example, just think about the fact that Adolf Hitler experimented in sorcery and Spiritism. The unspeakable horrors of the World War II death camps where six million died were doubtless inspired by demonic forces. Hitler is dead, but those demonic forces still exist in the lives of other people on earth. The Bible says that is our primary enemy: "For our struggle is not against flesh and blood, but against the rulers, against the authorities, against the powers of this dark world and against the forces of evil in the heavenly realms" (Eph. 6:12). The effective cross-cultural minister will not just be well trained in how to cross cultural barriers with the Gospel. He will also need to be well-versed in understanding how to do battle with supernatural forces that are not of this world!

CONVERSION AS A DEMONSTRATION OF GOD'S POWER

Conversion is a supernatural event. It requires the power of God's Spirit to be active in the life of an unbeliever. The apostle Paul, a man of great learning, proclaimed to the Corinthians, "My message and my preaching were not with wise and persuasive words, but with a demonstration of the Spirit's power, so that your faith might not rest on men's wisdom, but on God's power" (1 Cor. 2:4–5). If anyone needs to understand and be used by God's power, it is the cross-cultural evangelist. Some people accept Christ as a result of physical healings. Others do so as a result of people being delivered from demonic oppression. The renowned expert on church growth, Dr. Donald McGavran, wrote openly about how divine healing and deliverance from demonic oppression figured heavily in conversions and church growth in country after country.[36] Others are convinced of the truth of the Gospel by witnessing such demonstrations of God's power. More than one study of conversions in India assert that as many as 90 percent of conversion in India have occurred as a direct result of someone being healed of diseases or delivered from demons. When Western-educated believers hear such numbers, they immediately begin to wonder if people were really healed of diseases, or if they just thought they were healed. But while it is true that many people in India cannot name the disease they were healed from because of the lack of medical care, they can certainly tell when the symptoms of those diseases disappear. And so can the people who know them. There are two reasons why healing is so attached to conversions in India. First, Indian peoples often cannot afford allopathic doctors trained in Western medicine, so they cannot always identify the disease with a medical term. Second, their friends can see when they have been healed because peoples of India tend to not be concerned about normal aches and pains. Their lives are often difficult, and they are concerned only about the things that hinder their ability to function and perform their work which must be done. So when someone is healed, it is usually obvious to everyone who knows them. Second, God shows mercy on the poor and needy more than those who can find medical help in the Western world (Luke 5:31).

The issue of demonic oppression also needs to be addressed here. Western education, as we are discovering, is deficient in its ability to believe, let alone comprehend, the reality of demonic power and oppression. The author's friend who has since passed away was a well-known evangelist in Brazil. His name was Bernard Johnson. Some have called him the Billy Graham of Brazil. His crusades filled huge soccer stadiums up to two hundred thousand people for years. Raised in Brazil by Pentecostal missionaries, Bernard was well acquainted with the Spiritist practices in that country that were brought over from Africa by the slaves imported centuries before. Macumba and Umbanda Spiritism (black and white magic) have been practiced in

[36] https://renewaljournal.com/2012/05/19/divine-healing-and-church-growth-by-donald-mcgavran/.

Brazil for centuries clear into the highest levels of society. According to his wife, Doris, Bernard was having a crusade in Northern Brazil, in a city of about fifty thousand people. About ten thousand showed up at the soccer stadium the first night of the crusade. At the end of the message, an altar call for salvation was issued. During that time, a very thin woman with long unkempt hair began screaming at the top of her voice. She began running down the steps toward the platform, screaming curses and epithets directed at Johnson. When she reached the platform, the crusade team gathered around her to pray for her, but she did not relent, and her cursing grew even louder. Johnson realized he would have to deal with her personally. He came down from the platform and began to speak to the demons as he approached her. He demanded first that they name themselves, which they did. There were seven of them. One by one, he cast them away from her. After they all left her, she slumped to the ground like she was dead. Within a minute or two, she woke up and shouted for joy, praising God and thanking Johnson for the deliverance he brought to her.

That is not an unusual event at all in Brazil. One Episcopalian leader in America asked his Brazilian counterpart, "Do we need to send any more missionaries to Brazil, or do you now have enough leaders there to help the work now?" The Brazilian bishop who led the Episcopalians in that country replied, "Yes. We do need more missionaries, but please, do not send any more who do not know how to cast out demons. They are useless to us."

There is an important and real end of that story about Johnson that is worth mentioning. It was about eight months after that event at the crusade in Brazil. Johnson was in California preaching in a church in Modesto and challenging the people to be involved in missions. At the end of the message, a woman in the back of the audience stood up and began cursing and shouting at Johnson, "We know you, Bernard Johnson, and you are not going to cast us away again!" Then they proceeded to name the city, place, and date when he had cast them out of the woman at the crusade in Brazil. Johnson remembered some of their names, and he began to once again speak to them and cast them away from the woman in Modesto with the same result as in Brazil. This story is true, and it is alien to our "excluded middle" Western mindset. Yet it is at the heart of some of the things we must learn to become successful and effective cross-cultural evangelists. "Greater is He that is in you than he that is in the world" (1 John 4:1–4). Yet as foreign to Western thinking as it is, this story fits perfectly with Jesus' own words in Matthew 12:43–45: "When an evil spirit comes out of a man, it goes through arid places seeking rest and does not find it. Then, it says, 'I will return to the house I left.' When it arrives, it finds the house unoccupied, swept clean and put in order. Then it goes and takes with it seven other spirits more wicked than itself, and they go in and live there. And the final condition of the man is worse than the first." It is essential that the cross-cultural evangelist learn to practice spiritual warfare using the power of God's Spirit. No amount of study or learning will be an adequate substitute for that spiritual power. For help with that effort, it is recommended that cross-cultural evangelists study carefully the content of a book entitled *Doing What Jesus Did* by John and Lori Decker.[37]

CONVERSION AS A PROCESS

We encounter many experiences in Scripture of people being converted to Christ. We can learn from them, and it will help us to think through what happens in the mind of a person who hears the Gospel. We encounter three noteworthy examples in several chapters of the book of Acts: the apostle Paul (9), the Ethiopian eunuch (8), and Lydia (16). They are among the most astonishing events in the New Testament.

Conversion is an important life-transforming experience. We often think of it as a single event, when in reality, it is a part of a process. We remember when someone confesses Christ as Savior, but we do not often think about the path of their thinking that led them to that conversion event. It can happen quickly as a result of witnessing a miracle as we have discussed, or it can happen over a period of time. Whether short time or long, conversion is a process that involves a change in thinking. Figure 6.g represents a description of that process.

---

[37] Published by Christ's Ambassadors International, Bend, Oregon, 2003.

Figure 6.g

DOMAINS OF BELIEF							LEVELS OF COMMITMENT		
	-5	-4	-3	-2	-1	0	+1	+2	+3
SPIRITUAL	Faith in no or another religion	Little or no interest in Christianity	Knowledge of personal need for help	Belief that faith in Christ may solve problems	Faith in the work of Christ and truth of Gospel	**FAITH THAT GOD WILLL ACCEPT PRAYER FOR SALVATION**	Faith that God wants us to serve Him as part of the Church	Sanctification	Reproduction
MENTAL	Knowledge of teaching against Christianity	Little or no knowledge of the Gospel	Some under-standing of the Gospel	Full understanding of the Gospel	Concludes benefits of Gospel outweigh the risks	**DECISION TO ACCEPT CHRIST AS PERSONAL SAVIOR**	Decision to join a local church	Decision to live a life that is pleasing to God	Decision to make disciples among unbelievers
EMOTIONAL	No desire to leave security of religion	No desire to know anything about Christ	Desire to find greater spiritual help	Desire to learn more about Christian life	Desire for a strong relationship with God	**DECISION TO REPENT OF SINS AND FORSAKE THEM FOREVER**	Desire to serve God in fellowship with other believers	Desire to learn how to live well from the Bible	Desire to help others find freedom in Christ
Decision to Reject Christ									

As can be seen by studying the chart, different people and whole cultures have a different starting point on the path to conversion. They also have decisions to make about their commitment to Christ and His church after conversion. In addition to their spiritual response to the Gospel, different individuals and cultures also vary in their mental and emotional processes on the path to redemption.

It is normal for sin itself to blind people and make them incapable of responding to God spiritually. But the life and works of Jesus has prepared a pathway that allows the Holy Spirit to convince people of "sin, righteousness and judgment" (John 16:8). It is the Holy Spirit who works on human conscience to compel people to respond to God's invitation to live life with Him. The Spirit enlivens a person's spirit to respond to God. "As many as are led by the Spirit of God, they are the Sons of God" (Rom. 8:14 [KJV]).

People respond to the Gospel mentally as well as spiritually. Their minds embark on a constant search to learn more about Him. We have the ability to reason, and we are always trying to use it. Our quest to learn more about God engages our mind, straightens out much of what is wrong with human thinking, and gives a greater capacity to serve God faithfully. It helps us learn to think more like God does. Over time, the Holy Spirit teaches us to start from wherever we are and progress in our thinking toward the point of accepting Christ and then learning to serve Him in the fellowship of other believers.

People also respond to God based on their emotions. Emotions are tied to our relationships with our family and the people in our culture. They provide most of the things that make us feel secure. That is important. Our emotions can often become a barrier to embarking on the path to salvation. Even when someone mentally accepts the reality and truth of the Gospel, emotions can keep a person from progressing down the path toward salvation. Fear is the opposite of faith, and it is tied directly to our emotions. Interest in the Gospel and its reality must become strong enough to overcome emotional reticence and the fear that comes with it. In addition to understanding the Gospel and experiencing the drawing power of the Holy Spirit toward Christ, a person must come to believe that the risk they are taking to come to Christ will be overshadowed by the benefits of the Gospel. One of the ways to do that is to find ways to lessen the emotional stress of making that decision.

The author once lived in a country that was mostly Muslim. Together with other leaders, he discussed and decided on ways to minimize the emotional fear of following Christ. There was a strong effort to separate cultural forms from biblical principles so that the forms that were cultural and not religious could be used to help believers be attracted to the Gospel. Yet the use of culturally appropriate, but not religious, forms of behavior were used to keep those accepting Christ within their cultural mainstream. Biblical meaning was poured into those cultural forms. Some mistakes were made and had to be adjusted. But as believers learned how to do it, using culturally appropriate forms to convey Gospel truth, many people in the culture became believers in Jesus. This helped those people realize that they did not have to leave their culture to follow Jesus. It was not simple, and it involved many challenges and dangers to new believers. But they knew it was worth it because they came to know the power of the Holy Spirit and the value of following Jesus. Cross-cultural evangelists should pray and work hard to help new believers remain within the mainstream of their own cultures without compromising Gospel truth. Clothing Gospel truth within nonreligious cultural forms is a powerful way to accomplish that purpose.

So our spiritual, mental, and emotional capacities are essential parts of our progress toward the point where we accept Christ. When we seek to win individuals or groups of individuals to Christ, we must be aware of their status on all three levels. It is not adequate to bring a person all the way down the path of mental progress, for example, without also paying attention to their spiritual and emotional progress. One of the three can lead the other two, but not by too much. All three paths must progress to the point where they are at least somewhat in harmony as a person or group of people accept Christ.

The progress on these three levels of belief can be unequal in a person or people group. A person can be at -1 in terms of spiritually perceiving his need for salvation. But at the same time, he could be at -3 in terms of understanding the Gospel, and at level -2 in terms of feeling that need emotionally. This refers to a person who does not know much about the Gospel, but is a good candidate to learn more. Let's go into this subject a little deeper to learn more specifically how to use the "conversion as a process" chart.

There are unreached people groups in the world who have no knowledge of the Gospel and no desire to learn anything about it. In fact, though they may have heard something about the Christians and the Gospel, they have been trained to think of both in negative terms. They are against both and are at -5 on the scale of figure 6.g.

Let's consider the case of Abdul. He is a Muslim and lives in a Muslim country. He has often been warned to stay away from Christians and has been told that they are of the devil. As he grows older, he is told that the Christians are "immoral, sleep with other people's wives, and dance naked in the streets when they get drunk" (a common tale told by Muslim teachers). Furthermore, he is told that the Christian Bible has been "changed and corrupted" or else it would agree with the Holy Koran about the blessed prophet Muhammad. He is challenged to memorize the Holy Koran, and he spends a lot of time trying to do that. He must memorize it in Arabic, though he speaks another language at home. So it is very hard. He is sent to a Madrassah (Islamic school) in the afternoons and on Friday to learn the Koran. As he memorizes the Koran, he also learns what it means in his own language. Abdul is smart. As he is memorizing the Koran, he notices that there are a lot of Koranic verses, especially in chapter 3, that refer to another prophet named Nobbi Isa. He is curious about him and asks questions from his teachers. But they have few answers that satisfy his fascination with Issa, who is treated with great respect in the first part of the Koran.

As Abdul reaches his teenage years, he is a hardworking son of a normal Muslim family. He studies diligently and is obedient and respectful to his parents. One day, he notices another young Muslim man in the marketplace wearing his "tupi" (Muslim hat) and performing an interesting and mesmerizing chant on the street in front of the marketplace. In Abdul's language, the man is using the sing-song, rhythmic, and rhyming communication form so highly esteemed among Abdul's people. And he is telling a story about Nobbi Issa as he is rhythmically singing with beautiful words about the value of knowing about Issa. Fascinated, Abdul waits and listens a long time. When he is done, the singer greets Abdul, and they strike up a conversation about Nobbi Issa.

Abdul asks questions of the singer, whose name is Rafique. That is when Abdul begins to hear the Gospel for the first time. For Rafique is actually a believer, and Nobbi Issa is the name used for Jesus Christ in the Koran. Rafique looked, acted, and spoke just like any other Muslim, but his words about the Koran and Issa were new. Fascinated to learn more about Issa, Abdul asks the same questions of Rafique that he had asked his teachers in the Madrassah. And the answers he received amazed him. As he left for home, he had many questions in his mind. And he had progressed from -5 to -4 on the spiritual scale of Figure 6.g. But he had progressed to -3 on the mental and emotional scales. He wanted to know more!

When he returned home, he asked his father what he knew about Nobbi Issa, but his father seemed to know even less than Abdul had been taught in the Madrassah. So in fascination, he returned to the marketplace the next Friday afternoon, and was happy to see that Rafique was there again, using that sing-song, rhyming, rhythmic communication form so highly prized by his people. And he was singing more wonderful things about Nobbi Issa! After several weeks of going to the market on Friday afternoons, Abdul began to understand the wonderful truths of the Gospel. Eventually, he reached -1 on all three scales of Figure 6.g. He came to the point where he believed what Issa had said and that he wanted to have the salvation Nobbi Issa had come to bring to the peoples of the world. So he asked Rafique what to do. Rafique invited him to the home of a friend who also followed Issa. While there, they led Abdul in prayer to accept Issa as his Savior. Then they cautioned him not to tell anyone about his new faith, but to come to the house again every Friday to learn how to serve Issa and help others to know him. They also promised that they would help him share his new faith with his family when the time was right. They never told him that Issa was the one whom Christians worship. That would come later.

They focused on preparing him in his faith, and they helped him in his desire to bring his family into the same faith. At that point, the thought that he had become a Christian did not occur to Abdul, and nobody ever called him one. They knew it was just a word that had a negative meaning to their people and that they should not use it. (Remember that words are symbols of meaning, not the meaning itself.) The seasoned believers would not use the word "Christian" because they knew the imams constantly blasted Christians as people who got drunk, danced naked in the streets, and slept with other people's wives. Therefore, it never occurred to Rafique to use the term "Christian." He did none of those things.

Over time, Abdul kept up his studies in school and in the Madrassah. But his eyes were now open because he had been born-again. His insides hurt because he wanted to tell everyone about his new life serving Allah and being set free through Nobbi Issa. But he was cautioned to wait by Rafique and his friends. Eventually, others in his town heard Rafique and had secretly became believers also. When Abdul's father heard about it, he decided to go hear Rafique on Fridays also. At first, he was mesmerized by the beauty, rhythm, and power of Rafique's culturally prized singing. But as he listened to the words, he also began to wonder about the message of Nobbi Issa. He began to think about what the Koran said about Issa. He was the highest prophet next to Muhammad himself. He was born of a virgin miraculously. He worked miracles. Abdul decided to wait until Rafique was finished one day so he could ask some questions.

Sensing his interest, Rafique took him to a park away from the marketplace. During the course of their conversation, Rafique asked Abdul's father a question, "If we were in the marketplace and I was speaking to a group of people, what would you think if I told you, 'I am the way, the truth and the life. No one comes to Allah except through me.' What would the people say? What would you say? You would think I was crazy, a lunatic! Right? But those are the exact words Nobbi Issa told to people in a crowd in his day! Yet the Holy Koran states that Issa was a great prophet! So He had to be telling the truth, right?" Abdul's father could not argue with that logic. So he quickly moved from -5 to -3 on the spiritual scale, and it was not long before he reached -2 on the mental and emotional scales. It took about three weeks, but Abdul's father also confessed his faith in the work of Issa to die for his sins and bring him salvation. And he pledged to learn how to serve him for the rest of his life! Eventually, under the guidance of Rafique, Abdul and his whole family came to be followers of Issa, and they worshipped him as God and Savior.

These kinds of experiences among Rafique and Adbul's family were repeated many times over until many thousands of people became followers of Issa. They learned how to be discreet and wise in their witness, but persecution did finally arise as the Muslim leaders began to investigate. But by that time, there were so many followers of Issa that they could stand together and withstand the persecution, praising God like they found in Acts 3:23–31 and Mathew 5:11–12.

It is important to note that the subject of a people group's attitude toward the Gospel can also have an important impact on the decisions we take to target unreached people groups. As an important example, consider the choice of what Muslim people groups should be targeted first. While all people groups deserve a chance to know Christ, and they should all be targeted, it is best to target the people groups who are most likely to respond to the Gospel first. So if a cross-cultural evangelist wants to win Muslims to the Lord, he should study which groups are most likely to be most responsive to the Gospel and target them first.

It is a fact that Islam penetrates deep into the cultures of the Middle East. But the further away from the Middle East they live, the more thinly does the Islamic worldview penetrate the hearts of the people. Many other animistic beliefs, for instance, pervade the thinking of Muslims in Indonesia much more than in Saudi Arabia. And since the vast majority of Muslims in the world live outside the Middle East, it makes perfectly good sense that the "Lord of the Harvest" would first have us target the people groups among Muslims who are most likely to receive the Gospel and face less persecution for doing so. In Indonesia, for example, there have been whole people groups who turned from Islam to Christ. So the fact is that most Muslim people groups live outside the Middle East in the countries of Indonesia, Bangladesh, India, and Pakistan. And they are more receptive to the Gospel the further you go from the Middle East, as a general rule. Such people groups should be prioritized without neglecting those in the Middle East!

EFFECTIVE CROSS-CULTURAL EVANGELISM

A group of cross-cultural evangelists worked for a number of years to evangelize a people group called the Dani in Eastern Irian Jaya, New Guinea. The Dani were resistant and hostile to the Gospel and to outsiders. They were a Stone Age primitive tribe who had little contact with outsiders. The main part of the tribe lived in the valley surrounding the Baliem River. When a great deal of effort had been expended to evangelize this people, they demonstrated a great resistance to the Gospel. One part of the tribe lived on the other side of a high plateau that was four days away from the main river valley. After the cross-cultural evangelists had communicated the Gospel for about two years in that area, the whole group of about two thousand Danis decided to burn their fetishes and convert to follow Christ all at the same time!

Later, they thought about the Dani people they were related to in the Baliem River Valley. They endured the dangerous four-day journey in order to tell everyone what happened to them, "Become believers like we did. Decide to follow Christ Jesus! Decide which of you should be pastors and teachers. The evangelists came to us, and they will teach you too. Give them food so they will be free to teach. God will bless you like He has blessed us!"

After a short period of time, eight thousand members of the Dani Tribe in the Baliem Valley also assembled at a central place. They had decided to burn their fetishes and declare their allegiance to Jesus Christ. Together, they declared their faith and allegiance to the Lordship of Jesus Christ as a community. The cross-cultural evangelists didn't know what to do. They were accustomed to people accepting Christ individually. Some of the evangelists argued that conversion was not valid unless it was done on an individual basis. But the majority of them argued that all the decisions of those Dani on the other side of the mountain were made by consensus of the group. They realized that the decision had great merit and that it was an opportunity to teach the people the principles for living a Christian life and follow the teachings of Christ. They started by teaching the leaders of the Dani Tribe, and instructed them on how to teach others (2 Tim. 2:2).

Today, tens of thousands of Danis are Christians.[38] They have also sent Danis to other tribes who live in other parts of the islands of New Guinea. Many thousands of them have become believers also! This is the Gospel going full circle as God intended. If every culture sends evangelists to other cultures, who in turn do the same, the world will have an adequate chance to know Jesus in every generation!

Principle One—Group Conversion: The story of the conversion of the Dani Tribe is a classic example of a people movement. It represents cases where whole people groups, or a major portion of a people group, decide to accept Christ and follow His ways collectively within a short period of time. To people in individualistic cultures, this seems strange, but not to the people who live in that kind of tribal culture. They are highly dependent upon the group and its leaders when making important decisions. That is because the group acts and thinks in terms of how their decisions affect everyone. They are individually dependent upon the whole group for their very survival. In such cultures, taking an individual decision that works against the well-being of the group, whether that is perceived or actual, will inevitably separate an individual from the group and cause him or her to be an outcast. It is far better if the whole group can be convinced to take the decision at the same time. It is not less valid than when we convert individually. And in a group-oriented culture, it is a powerfully effective occurrence.

Remember the story in chapter four about the intercultural evangelist who stayed in the African village for two years, building suspense about why he and his family were there?

Everyone was anxiously awaiting his explanation that he promised them at the end of two years. They threw a feast when it was time for him to tell them. Then the chief himself accepted Christ

[38] Scoville, 2007.

and in effect gave everyone else permission to do the same. That is another story of group conversion.

When you stop to think about conversion as a process, you must also remember that people who are converted also must subsequently experience a process of deeper and deeper commitment to Christ. The Dani Tribe Christians who lived across the barrier of the high plateau immediately began to think about the members of their same tribe who live on the other side of the plateau. They had friends, relatives, and even enemies whom they wanted to tell about the power of God to stop the wars and gain freedom in Christ. That natural desire to help others they know among their own people outside their own area is the next step to be taken after uniting as a worshipping community of believers in Jesus. It is the "Judea" of the last instructions given by Jesus just before ascending into heaven.

We should also consider the social dynamics existing when the innovators of a society are reached first. They may or may not have a significant position as leaders in their society in terms of age or position. But if they are respected in the mainstream of their society, they can still have a significant impact at all levels of their society. A good example is the Muslim man who simply chanted the story of Issa in the highly respected singsong, poetic, and rhyming poetry of his people. As we have stated in numerous ways, the message of the Gospel is not separate from the one who tells it. The more they respect him or her, the more valuable will be the message people are hearing.

The principles concerning the Centripetal Model of Conversion also helps us understand this important principle. Repent means "turn around" away from sin toward something better—a new life in Jesus Christ. So everyone who has turned around, progressing closer and closer to the point where they embrace the Gospel message as truth and decide to follow Jesus, is participating in that process we call conversion. He or she is learning more, wanting more, and feeling more like following Christ as a lifeway. Each step before and after conversion requires increasingly greater depths of commitment toward God. As long as we work to move people, whether as individuals or also as groups, in that direction, we are being the effective evangelists we are called to be.

Principle Two—Reaching Peoples in Networks: A good part of the world's population is in a rapid process of transition to an extent never seen before in history. Right now, over 55 percent of the world's 7.9 billion people live in urban centers, not rural areas. By AD 2050, that percentage is expected to rise to more than 68 percent of an expected 9.8 billion.[39] People are invading the cities of the world in record numbers in virtually every country of the world. This means individuals and cultures are in significant transition. We need to understand the implications for cross-cultural ministry. This urban population explosion creates rapid cultural transition in urban settings. Many of them are poor. They often do not know how to balance their need for work in the city with the costs of living in the city. Even if they learn how to earn more money in the city, many have difficulty handling the changes between rural and urban life. They still occupy hovels in impoverished areas of the city. In spite of their poverty, however, they are also more likely to listen to the Gospel and accept it. For them, change has been rapid. Rural traditions are being questioned in their quest for survival in the city. They are more open to change, and our strategies to reach them should include help on how to adapt to urban life effectively.

Principle Three—Urban People Movements: We have learned that it can be a good strategy to work toward the conversion of tribal peoples as a collective group. That can also be a good strategy in cities. The interwoven relationships between people groups who move to the city provide a strong emotional and economic interdependence among their populations. They are inclined in the rural areas they come from to be interdependent. In a rural setting, the hostilities and competition they face from outsiders can make them band together even more closely. The realities of working in different jobs and locations can mitigate their ability to stay close to one another, but their language and rural history also make them want to stay close to one another. A good strategy to reach them would include finding a central place where they can meet and socialize together, much like they did in their villages. This is especially a good strategy when their

[39] United Nations Department of Economic and Social Affairs, News.

language or dialect is not spoken in the city by other groups. People movements in the cities can happen very fast. When they do, it is best to help provide a place where particular people groups can meet regularly and have an opportunity to interact in their own language and cultural norms. Even if they all speak the major language of the city, they should still have opportunity to have separate meetings if there are other language or cultural groups in the churches that are formed after their conversions.

In many cities of the world, single churches or evangelistic centers may house church services in many different languages. There may be translations from one major language to another prominent language in the same service. Or there may be separate services conducted in a single less prominent language that has a lot of believers. Being able to worship in your own language is essential for believers to feel comfortable before God and one another. There is nothing that touches the emotions and mind more than being able to express ourselves in a language that we are comfortable using. This in no way reflects in a negative way concerning the fact that we are one body unified under the sacrifice of Christ for our salvation. We must remember that it was God who confused languages in the first place (Gen. 11:9). He could have dealt with man's rebellion against him in many ways, but he chose to confuse the languages of the people. That was the beginning of people groups, and God knows the advantages they can present for evangelism.

After people live a long time in the city, they will become more accustomed to using a more commonly used language, such as a national or even an international language. As this happens, it is natural for them to gravitate toward using that language more of the time. This especially happens as children grow up in the city. It is also natural for parents to desire that their children retain their mother tongue even though they live in the city. But inevitably, the children gravitate toward the majority language and culture. No amount of visits back to the village will change this desire and process. It is better to help parents to teach their children the value of retaining both their own culture and also gain the value of adopting a major language and culture of the city. The parents can take pride in their children as their ability to function in both cultures lifts the family economically. There is a natural "redemption and lift" (see McGavran[40]) that take place as people become believers in all parts of the world. The principles of honesty and integrity taught by Jesus and his followers make believers more desirable both as employees and employers. This phenomenon lifts whole people groups out of poverty in cities over time. That is inevitable and should be encouraged even as being bicultural is encouraged.

Principle Four—Small Groups: It is a very effective strategy in urban evangelism to encourage the establishment of small group ministries. Evangelism in fast-growing cities can very often be so effective that it is almost impossible to build enough facilities to house worshippers all at the same time. Land rapidly becomes so expensive and conversions so numerous that buildings to house worshippers cannot be built fast enough even if there is enough money. Equally important, church growth experts who have studied the growth of churches around the world have demonstrated that the use of small group meetings increases the growth of churches dramatically.

There are three main structures needed for churches to grow consistently over time.[41] By structures, we are not talking about buildings, though they may also be built. By structures we mean the *types of meetings that Christians participate in on a regular basis*. The first structure is **celebration**. People who know the Lord need a regular time and place where they can meet together primarily to worship and celebrate their freedom from sin as believers. It may take place openly or in secret, depending upon the degree of freedom enjoyed by citizens of a given country. Usually this is accompanied by singing and other forms of Christian celebration together with the preaching of the Word of God. Growing churches emphasize the benefits of the Gospel and the principles for living a victorious and appealing Christian life in such a celebration. This is attractive to new believers and those being drawn toward the Gospel, as well as those who are already believers. This outward focus of celebratory meetings is most

40 McGavran, 1990,185.
41 See Wagner, 1976, 97–109.

common on Sunday mornings, but can also be at other times in the week.

The second structure common to consistently growing churches is called congregation by Wagner (see bibliography). It is a separate and regular set of meetings designed to teach Christians to become leaders or better leaders. This is the "teaching them" function of the Great Commission (Matt. 28:19–20). It involves training meetings based on God's word that help believers become mature examples of Christ's way even as they learn to be used by God to minister to others also (2 Tim. 2:2). Those churches that train leaders consistently with a high quality are the ones that can grow rapidly.

The third structure common to consistently growing churches is small groups. They may be called cell groups, life groups, Bible study groups, or a host of other names, but they have these things in common: (1) they openly invite believers and unbelievers to the meetings; (2) they focus on the Word of God, what it says, and what it means for everyday life; (3) they serve as a place where unbelievers and new believers can increase their interaction with one another and pursue their interest in or their commitment to Christian living; and (4) they serve as a halfway point to reach people who would not ordinarily go to a church, but will accept an invitation to a home or more public place to meet with people they know.

The size of small groups is limited, usually to no more than thirty or forty people, depending on the culture involved. In most Western cultures, for instance, the ideal size is not more than fifteen people because it gives time for all the people in the group to discuss the ideas and topics that are the focus of each meeting. The size of the group can vary a lot, but the group should be ready to split into a second group as soon as it reaches a size when most leaders agree it is time to do so. Those who lead such groups should be trained as discussed in the teaching or congregation structure above. That is where leaders of small groups are trained. The better the training and commitment, the more rapid will be the growth of small groups.

It is common for people to be able to go to a church building in cities only once a week. Transportation can be expensive and difficult. This makes small groups even more vital. When the training and commitment to small groups is sufficient, the number of people in small groups can (and should) eventually exceed the number of people who are attending the celebration and worship services in the church building. In other cases, it can be illegal or dangerous to attend worship services. This is true in a number of Muslim countries and in China. That makes the multiplication of small groups, even secretly, to be a great benefit to the spread of the Gospel. History demonstrates that Christianity actually can grow much faster under significant persecution! In such situations, small and even secret meetings are necessary. The church grew rapidly under such conditions during most of the first three centuries of Christianity!

When the number of people attending small groups exceeds the number of people attending church worship services, the continued rapid growth of the church is assured. When growth is dependent upon small groups more than a church building, any building-based growth of Christianity such as is common in Western cultures has been overcome. The church will continue to grow in spite of external, ecclesiastical, or government issues.

Perhaps the best example of this three-structure principle is found in Seoul, Korea. The Full Gospel Central Church is located on Yoido Island right next to the Parliament Building of the South Korean government. With multiple auditoriums serviced with closed-circuit television, a total of twenty-five thousand people have met at one of many worship services each weekend for many years. The church is now pastored by Young Hoon Lee. For at least forty years, this has been the largest church in the world by far. It currently has over four hundred thousand members and has been instrumental in founding several thousand other churches throughout Korea.

Seoul is within shooting distance of the thousands of North Korean artillery emplacements lined up along the southern North Korean border and pointed at the city. Everyone knows that the whole city could be under attack and their church could be destroyed within minutes. To plan for that contingency, Dr. Cho, founder of the church, established tens of thousands of cell groups consisting of one or two dozen believers meeting in homes. When the groups get large enough, they split into two groups (like the cells of a human body). To prepare for these groups to split, leaders are prepared in advance to assume responsibility for those groups at a new location. There are tens of thousands of such leaders with more being trained all the time. The members obviously cannot all attend services at the Central Church each weekend, so they were asked to do so only once per month. So the church would continue to grow even if the main building were to be destroyed by North Korean artillery, as it surely would be in the advent of an outbreak of open war between North and South Korea. This is a good example of a church that operates all three ministry structures very effectively.

SUMMARY

In this chapter, we analyzed the importance of the cross-cultural evangelist establishing confidence in himself within the people group he hopes to evangelize. He must take the time and effort necessary to establish mutual acceptance and trust among those people in order to establish a position from which he will truly be respected. That way, his message of the Gospel will also be respected.

The cross-cultural evangelist must also learn to distinguish between biblical principles that apply to every culture and the biblical forms that express those truths in culturally appropriate ways. That will give him the understanding necessary to find the culturally appropriate forms necessary to convey those biblical principles in his target culture. Biblical principles are "supra-cultural," and they apply to every culture. But guided by the Holy Spirit, the evangelist must learn how to convey those principles and truths of the Bible using linguistic and behavioral forms that best convey the importance and impact of those principles. Learning to do that well will elevate the value his hearers place on Gospel truths.

Seeing conversion as a process is better than seeing it as an event. Even though a person must come to the conclusion that he needs to seek forgiveness in Jesus' name and commit his life to serving Him, the spiritual, mental, and emotional processes that lead him toward that conclusion must be firmly in the mind of the evangelist. Otherwise, he may "vaccinate" more people against the Gospel than the converts he gains. People must be encouraged and allowed the time necessary for them to come to a genuine, well-developed sense of their need for salvation and the fact that Jesus' work on the cross is the only way to obtain it. All this should take place, quickly or over a long period of time as needed, before they make the life-changing decision to follow Christ. Sometimes people come to such a decision together and make their decision as a group at the same time. This should not be discouraged, but welcomed by the evangelist.

The increasingly urban population of the world presents both challenges and opportunities. Effective cross-cultural evangelists in urban centers should become very aware of the unique needs of people groups who have migrated to the cities. They should work in cooperation with others to help these people in transition meet their unique needs while showing them the power of the Gospel to satisfy their spiritual needs. City life can be cruel and corrupting without God. People in cities still interact and get their emotional and social needs met primarily in their own people groups, even though there are many such groups in every city. Evangelizing them, helping them survive, and leading them toward God can be accomplished better by respecting and working within the boundaries of their people group. Over time, they can be encouraged to become truly capable urban dwellers, perhaps even multicultural citizens who excel in their endeavors through following the principles of God's Word.

QUESTIONS FOR UNDERSTANDING

1. Why should evangelism be focused on the target people group? Why is it the responsibility of the cross-cultural evangelist to be sure that is the focus? What can result if that does not happen?
2. What are the four steps necessary to establish a trust relationship with the people of a target culture? Which step is the most necessary for a cross-cultural evangelist? Why?
3. Describe the ways a people of another culture will almost always judge the behavior of a cross-cultural evangelist when he first enters their culture. Describe how and why their judgment

about the evangelist can cause serious problems. What should the evangelist do to avoid or overcome such problems?

4. What is the first question the people of another culture will ask themselves concerning the cross-cultural evangelist who enters a target culture? What steps should he take when he senses that question is on their minds? Explain the significance of this principle by using the example of a cross-cultural evangelist in Africa.
5. At what point in the process of establishing trust within his African target culture did the cross-cultural evangelist feel free to communicate the Gospel with the greatest effect? Why is it so important to live an exemplary and culturally appropriate lifestyle in order to be able to take this final and effective step?
6. Distinguish between biblical principles and cultural forms. What is the relationship between the two?
7. In your own words, defend this statement: "There does not exist an absolute set of cultural norms of conduct that mean exactly the same thing in every culture everywhere." Give biblical examples in your answer.
8. Give at least three examples each of biblical principles and cultural forms in the Bible using figure 6.a.
9. In what sense do we use words as cultural forms when we translate the Scriptures from one language to another?
10. Enumerate three important steps that the cross-cultural evangelist must take to effectively learn to distinguish between biblical principles and cultural forms. Tell why each one is important.
11. What is the major weakness with a Behavioral Model of Conversion. Give examples of the kinds of problems this model can cause in cross-cultural evangelism.
12. What are the benefits of the Centripetal Model of conversion for a cross-cultural evangelist?
13. Why is it better to look at conversion as a process more than an event? At what three levels does a person progress on the path to conversion? Explain the terms "sanctification" and "reproduction" as a part of the process of conversion.
14. Explain why strategies to encourage group conversion can be best when trying to evangelize tribal groups who live in closed

societies. Explain why an emphasis on individual conversion can create serious problems in such people groups. Can you think of any group conversion events in the New Testament?

15. Explain the significance of reaching peoples in networks. How can this be effective in cities? Give two examples.

QUESTIONS FOR DISCUSSION

1. Analyze the methods of the cross-cultural evangelist who lived among the people of a tribe in Africa before telling them the reason he was there. Why do you think he was effective in winning the tribe to Christ? How many reasons can you give? Do you have the determination and dedication to do what his family did if God calls you to do it?
2. Analyze the steps that lead to a trust relationship in a target culture. In what ways and with what people should you seek a mutual trust relationship? Why is this important for a cross-cultural evangelist?
3. Explain how different cultures use different forms to communicate the same messages. List some biblical principles that form the basis of behavioral norms in your own culture. How has your attitude about the behavior of Christians in other cultures changed as a result of studying this chapter?
4. Analyze figure 6.g, "Conversion as a Process." What is the relationship between the steps in the process and the domains of belief as they relate to your own conversion experiences? How do you think this chart relates to people you know who accepted Christ, then decided not to serve him? How can you apply the principles found in figure 6.g to making plans to evangelize an unreached people group?
5. As best as you can, analyze the strategies you have observed for rural evangelism and urban evangelism. Can you give any examples of group conversion that you know about in today's world?
6. Do you know of any effective evangelism among those in transition from rural to urban life? Are there any principles in this

chapter being used in your own culture to help such people come to Christ?

7. Can you think of any other strategies in your own culture that have been effective in rural or urban settings? How might these be adapted to cross-cultural ministry?

CHAPTER SEVEN

Planning Strategies For Cross-Cultural Evangelism

KEY POINTS IN THIS CHAPTER

1. Failing to plan is the same as planning to fail. Like any other large important task, evangelizing unreached people groups requires effective strategy planning.
2. There is no single strategy which will work to reach every people group. Some part of a strategy may be useful among more than one group, but no part of strategy is useful for reaching every people group.
3. Good strategy planning requires good skills in setting long-range and intermediate-range goals.
4. Other than specific direction from the Holy Spirit, receptivity is the single most important factor in choosing which people groups to evangelize first. The Holy Spirit does direct the work of evangelism through human reasoning.
5. It is possible to measure the receptivity of a people group to the Gospel message with a useful degree of accuracy.
6. The beginning point for understanding a target people is an analysis of their needs.
7. Cross-cultural evangelists should be well trained before leaving to evangelize another people group.

8. Selection of leadership in the emerging churches of a target people should primarily be the responsibility of the local believers.
9. There is a direct relationship between our level of faith and our willingness to set goals for future cross-cultural evangelism.
10. Strategy planning is a process which continues from the beginning to the end of our work to evangelize an unreached people group.

If you plan to start a garden,
You can reap for a season.
If you plan to plant fruit trees,
You can reap for a lifetime
If you plan to plant churches,
You can reap for eternity.

We now begin a section of three chapters to discuss ways to plan and implement strategies for cross-cultural evangelism. In this chapter, we discuss principles for planning, making strategies, and setting goals. These principles will lead us to a step-by-step procedure for designing our own strategies for cross-cultural evangelism.

THE IMPORTANCE OF GOOD STRATEGY

We all make plans every day. We make plans to do the work we need to accomplish each day. We plan special occasions. We plan to take care of the needs of our families. Carpenters make plans for the things they build. Farmers make plans for the crops they plant and harvest. Parents make plans for meals. Many of the plans we make are made only in our minds. They are usually plans which deal with things we can do in a short time, and do not need much details.

But when we need to make long-term plans, we must write down each part of the plan, or we will forget some things that need to be done in the correct order. When a carpenter wants to build a chair like he has already built before, he already has the plans in his mind. He knows how much wood he will need, and he knows the tools which will be required. He knows how long it will take also. So he promises the customer that he can have the chair at a certain time. But if a carpenter wants to build a big building, he must write his plans down in detail. He must figure out how many pieces of wood in what sizes he will need. He will have to calculate also how much cement will be needed and how to get it prepared and poured. He has to decide if he will use bamboo, cinder blocks, or bricks, and if so, how much. There will be a long list of things he must write down and how much it will cost him and the customer. Finally, he must calculate how much time it will take him and how much to charge for his labor and expertise. He needs a long-term plan to build the building.

Strategies are long-term plans. We already know it takes years to effectively evangelize a people group. Therefore, we need effective plans to guide our work and check our progress. Some people think it is not a good idea to plan to do Christian work. They say it might interfere with the leading of the Holy Spirit. But that mistake can be avoided by doing two things: (1) invite the Holy Spirit to help you formulate your plans and (2) make your plans flexible so they can change as new information and spiritual insight become available while you are implementing the plan. Good plans are never set in concrete. They are made in such a way that adjustments can be made as needed while they are being put into practice.

The apostle Paul constantly made plans during his missionary journeys. He planned where he would go next and the kinds of ministries and priorities he would pursue when he got there. Most of the time, he followed those plans because God had helped him to make them. But sometimes, like when he wanted to go to Bithynia, the Spirit helped him change his mind (Acts 16:6–10). So the Spirit can help us make good plans, and he can also help us to change them if needed while we are carrying out those plans. That is the perfect way to plan and the perfect way to implement plans, under the Spirit's guidance when doing so.

TYPES OF STRATEGIES

There are a number of ways to approach strategy planning. Let's discuss three of them: the Standard Pattern Strategy, the God-Will-Help-Us Strategy, and the Unique Pattern Strategy.

Standard Pattern Strategy: This strategy arises from a carefully worked-out plan for evangelism which arises through planning and testing in the field. Then the plan is applied to every country and location. Every Home For Christ (EHC), a worldwide ministry based in North America, is an example of this kind of strategy. Their goal is to put at least one piece of literature containing the Gospel in every home in every country of the world. To date, they claim to have reached 2 billion homes and recorded 211 million decisions for Christ and started 349,000 groups of believers who meet in small groups or as new churches.[42] This strategy is not a bad one, and it has reached a lot of people in a positive way. But it does not do much for the 16 percent of the world's population that cannot read. It also assumes that everyone will have an adequate chance to accept Christ if they are simply exposed to the right literature. It also assumes that people paid to distribute literature actually do so. The author has personally seen EHC literature scattered across the countryside in abandoned bundles and heard of it being used for toilet paper!

We must not just think about the impact of our strategy upon the small percentage that value the message we broadcast, whatever the form, but also what message it gives to those who are not Christians. Muslims, for example, consider God's messages to man (which they think is holy and contained in the Koran) as so holy that it cannot be dishonored in any manner. So to see the words of Christ (especially when He is called Nobi Issa in tracts for witnessing) mistreated in any way becomes a mockery of God's majesty and holiness. So this strategy can have a positive result, but it is possible to have an even more widespread *negative* result in many parts of the world! It must be used carefully, and it is still limited as a strategy.

Crusade evangelism is a strategy which arose in the mid-twentieth century, primarily in North America, and it spread to many other parts of the world. It was popularized especially by the Billy Graham Evangelistic Association. When done well, crusade evangelism uses different kinds of radio, television, and printed advertising to announce and broadcast crusade meetings. Sometimes, with today's

[42] https://www.ehc.org/about.

technology, it has been simulcast around the world in churches and other meeting places, even as it is being broadcast from one location. This type of strategy has proven effective in some ways and in some parts of the world. Especially if there are local churches to follow up in their communities after a broadcast. Many thousands have come to Christ as a result of this strategy over the years. But it does not effectively evangelize every people group in those areas where it is used.

Many indigenous Indian people groups in Latin America were virtually unaffected by this strategy even though crusade evangelism has been held in virtually all parts of Latin America. Studies have shown also that crusade campaigns held in Guatemala, Colombia, and the Dominican Republic revealed disturbing news. Overall growth in Protestant churches in those countries did not occur and attendance actually declined in those churches after major crusades were conducted there. Though the churches' growth increased during the year of the campaigns, they declined in growth in the years after it. In fact, their rates of growth were lower after the campaigns than they were in the years prior to the campaigns! This raises serious questions about the dynamics related to crusade evangelism. It also demonstrates that it will not, by itself, give every culture in every location an adequate chance to accept Christ and serve Him as Savior.

In Muslim cultures, even the word "crusade" is anathema. The Holy Crusades of European Christians in the eleventh, twelfth, and thirteenth centuries made that word a lasting negative historical memory in the minds of virtually every Muslim. Many thousands of Muslims were slaughtered under the banner of the Crusades. Every Home For Christ was previously called Every Home Crusade. The name had to be changed. The word is so negative to Muslims. Just as one strategy cannot be used everywhere, so every label or translation of words cannot be used everywhere. Remember our discussion of words as symbols of meaning, not the meaning itself.

Let's take a moment also to consider broadcast television as a means to spread the Gospel. The largest global networks for such ministry include Trinity Broadcast Network and Daystar Television. Daystar broadcasts now to 200 countries and households totaling 680 million people. It is a popular broadcast medium for Christianity in many parts of the world. It clearly presents the Gospel on an interdenominational basis.

But Daystar's audience is mostly people who speak English as their first language. Some can understand English as a second language. It is an effective ministry as far as it goes. But it does not go nearly far enough! We have already made the case for the need to effectively present the Gospel in every language to every culture, to every people group. So we must not assume the world is being reached with the Gospel by Daystar Television or any other international ministry that uses television as its means of communication. We will never see all languages and peoples confronted with a clear Gospel message in the mainstream of their culture until we see cross-cultural ministry dedicated to each one of them.

While a certain strategy or method of evangelism can prove to be very effective in certain places and cultures, it is often a mistake to try to export that strategy to other people groups in other parts of the world. It can cause wrong messages to be heard very quickly. It can actually "vaccinate" people figuratively from even wanting to listen to the Gospel.

God-Will-Help-Us Strategy: This strategy is based on the idea that little or no planning is necessary to do God's work well. It may focus on the necessary planning for getting a work started—deciding where to go, who will go, and how they will be supported. But it emphasizes little or no further planning. The rest is "left up to God." People who use this type of planning generally believe that long-term planning is God's responsibility. This type of planning is too often followed by too many people because it is safe. There is little chance of failure because long-term goals are few. Goals are focused on getting started, not accomplishing specific purposes. Success is defined by how many people are sent, not how many peoples we reach. So most anything can be classified as success with this kind of strategy. It is akin to the problem we pointed out in chapter one—emphasis upon the one who goes rather than the one who hears the Gospel.

Christ taught us that being his disciple is risky. He also taught us the value of long-range planning. He gave examples of a man building a tower, and another going to war (Luke 8:28–33). Before doing either, He said, it is important to make plans and have the right resources to finish the work. He was saying that if it is necessary to make good plans for earthly tasks, how much more important it is to make plans for spiritual tasks! People who plan little achieve little. Or, as one cliché aptly puts it—those who aim at nothing usually hit it. Remember that the last thing Jesus said and the first thing the Holy Spirit did in starting the Church is to declare that we are God's instruments to evangelize every people group on earth (Matt. 24:14)! God wants to do it through us, not in spite of us! He wants us to have the joy of full participation in what he is doing. To do that, He wants to bless our planning just as he will the outcome of that planning.

Unique Methods Planning: This strategy understands that each situation is different and that every people group requires a special strategy designed especially for that people group. It assumes that there is no standard approach which will effectively evangelize all people everywhere. It also assumes that designing a special strategy for each people group is important and necessary for effective evangelization of each people group. Matthew 24:14 establishes the fact that God Himself is focused on people groups: "This Gospel of the Kingdom will be preached in the whole world as a testimony to all nations [nations or ethnos or people groups], and then the end will come." It is impossible to improve on what God is focused to achieve! This is the most effective basis for planning strategies for cross-cultural evangelism. It emphasizes strategies that respond to the unique needs and context of each people group. The overall goal of evangelizing each people does not change, but the planning and methods for reaching each people group must vary greatly.

This strategy planning assumes that God will lead those who plan, as well as those who act on those plans. It assumes the Holy Spirit is able to help them discover the special keys that will open the door to the heart of each people group. It also assumes the Holy Spirit is able to help them adjust their plans as needed during their implementation. Every culture is constantly changing, and the Holy Spirit knows how to handle changes and adjust plans as needed. Overall principles for planning and evangelizing can remain the same for all people groups, but the methods and practices used must be specifically designed to meet the needs of each people group.

LEARNING TO SET GOOD GOALS

Planning good strategies requires learning the skill to set good goals. Learning to set goals skillfully not only has a powerful impact on the quality of strategic planning, but also, it has a wonderful effect on the lives of those who practice good goal-setting principles. Some people live in cultures which are oriented toward the past and present more than toward the future. Most African cultures, for example, tend to be oriented that way more than Western cultures. The less future-oriented our culture, the less likely we are to be goal-conscious (see figure 4.e).

It is important to see that the Bible is future-oriented and goal-conscious. From the beginning, God had as his primary goal the redemption of mankind from the penalty and effects of sin. Christ died and rose again so that all who would believe in Him in the future would be saved. His teachings were goal-oriented. Consider the parable of the talents, the wise and foolish virgins, the sheep and the goats in Matthew 25. Jesus gave specific goals to His disciples, the most important being "make disciples of all peoples" (Matt. 28:19). He also showed them how, where, and among whom to do it (Acts 1:8). Paul the apostle understood the future orientation of the Christian life, and the power of setting specific goals. He said, "Forgetting what is behind and straining toward what is ahead, I press on toward the goal to win the prize for which God has called me heavenward in Christ Jesus" (Phil. 3:12–14).

The most successful people in every society are the ones who have overcome great difficulties or adversity to accomplish great things. They did so because they were willing to set goals and pay the price to achieve them. Down through the centuries, Christians have been willing to endure suffering and even martyrdom in order to achieve God's goals for their lives, and eternal rewards in heaven. Sometimes their goals were written only in their hearts, but they were willing to give up that which they could not keep in order to gain what they could not lose! To be effective, cross-cultural evangelists must have the same kind of dedication and orientation toward achieving the goals that are primary to the Kingdom of God!

Goals Must Be Clear and Precise

The more clear and precise a goal is stated, the better chance it has to be fulfilled. Jesus understood that. That is why He not only told us to "preach the Gospel to every creature" (Mark 16:15), but He also told us what that means in Matthew 28:19: "Therefore go and make disciples of all peoples." The International Lausanne Committee on World Evangelism has declared:

> Our manifesto at Manila is that the whole church is called to take the whole gospel to the whole world, proclaiming Christ until he comes, with all necessary urgency, unity, and sacrifice. (*Luke 2:1–7, Mark 13:26–27, Mark 13:32–37, Acts 1:8, Matthew 24:14, Matthew 28:20)*[43]

We can help make this declaration clear by defining the term "make disciples" as *"to persuade men and women to accept Jesus Christ as Lord and Savior, and serve Him in the fellowship of His Church."*[44] This definition helps us understand Jesus' words even more precisely. If we are to obey His command, we must make strategies and plans which prove to be effective in persuading men and women from every people group on earth to accept Christ and Lord and Savior, and serve Him in a local church or group of believers of some kind. As we have discussed (chapter two), this is to be the primary ministry function of the Church. Therefore, it becomes the primary overall purpose of cross-cultural evangelism. It is a clear and precise goal. Everything we do in cross-cultural ministry, both strategy and implementation of strategy, should directly aid the fulfillment of that goal.

Making goals clear and precise requires a little practice. If we say our goal is to reach the Yakmal Tribe with the Gospel, it is not clear enough. We could broadcast radio programs in the Yakmal language

---

[43] https://www.lausanne.org/content/manifesto/the-manila-manifesto?_sfm_author_alias=Theology+Working+Group.

[44] See the twofold ministry function of the Church in chapter three.

and say we were reaching them. Even if few people had radios, we could say that. We could put a Gospel tract in each home and say we are reaching them, even if most of them don't know how to read. We could send evangelists to evangelize them, and say we are reaching them, even if there are no conversions. While this may sound ridiculous, it is not far from exactly the kind of approach taken by some cross-cultural evangelists.

On the other hand, if we say our goal is to persuade members of the Yakmal Tribe to accept Christ as Lord and Savior, then determine to serve him in autochthonous churches, then our goal is more clear and precise. As we carry out our plans to reach this goal, we automatically must ask ourselves if any of the Yakmal people have accepted Christ, and if there is anything we can do better to help more of them do so. If so, we must also ask if they are actually serving Him in fellowship with other believers of their tribe.

Goals Must Be Measurable

Good goals are measurable in terms of quantity and time. Our example above of stating a goal well can be made even better by making it measurable in terms of quantity: "Our goal is to persuade 20 percent of the Yakmal Tribe to accept Christ as Lord and Savior, and serve Him in autochthonous churches." If we think the believers in the tribe can evangelize the rest of their tribe without outside help, then that is a very good goal. It tells us when our task is complete. Then we can leave a few of our people to train leaders, and move the rest to another unreached people group. But we will know that our task is not finished until 20 percent of the tribe are disciples serving him in some kind of church. Making measurable goals helps us check our progress as we go, make mid-course corrections, and lets us know when the task is complete.

Making goals in terms of time is equally important. We can further improve our example by stating it like this: "Our goal is to persuade 20 percent of the Yakmal Tribe to accept Christ as Lord and Savior, and serve him in autochthonous churches within the next ten years." This will force us to check our progress regularly to see if we need to adjust our goals. It also helps encourage us by celebrating the points of progress along the way toward that goal. Making goals measurable greatly helps us manage our task and encourage those doing the work.

Intermediate Goals

What we have just described above is really a long-range goal, sometimes called our purpose or overall goal. By looking at that goal, it becomes obvious that we must make smaller goals which will lead to the completion of the long-range goal. Using our example, we might make intermediate goals like this:

1. Within two years, train, equip, and raise support for six cross-cultural evangelists who will be sent to evangelize the Yakmal Tribe.
2. Help the whole team of evangelists and their families become enculturated, be fluent in the Yakmal language to a level of 4.0 on the NDSL scale, and establish positive trust relationships among the Yakmal people within three more years.
3. Make disciples of 7 percent of the Yakmal Tribe in their primary locations with seven autochthonous churches within two more years (end of seven years). Establish a Bible-training system available to all leaders within this period.
4. Make disciples of at least 15 percent of the Yakmal Tribe who serve God in at least twenty autochthonous churches by the end of nine years on the field.
5. Make disciples of at least 20 percent of the Yakmal Tribe who serve God in at least thirty autochthonous churches by the end of the year ten of the project. By this time, at least 80 percent of the teachers in the Bible school should be Yakmal leaders.
6. At the beginning of the tenth year, two-thirds of the cross-cultural evangelist teams should transfer to work among another target people group. The remaining two

> teams should remain to help train Yakmal leaders in the Bible training system, working there for a maximum of five more years before moving on to target another people group.

Notice how these intermediate goals accomplish the stated overall goal or purpose of the work. Notice also how making good long-range and intermediate-range goals help in planning strategy. Even with our good overall goal (purpose), it is sometimes difficult to decide how to reach that goal. We could simply send two cross-cultural evangelists, then trust God to bring results. But that would be following the God-Will-Help-Us Strategy. It is far better to trust God to help us make good goals and then make good strategy to reach those goals.

By looking at the examples of possible intermediate goals, it is easy to see that evangelizing the Yakmal people would take a lot of planning and effort. Six experienced evangelists would need to heed God's call for cross-cultural ministry. They would need to be trained. Their churches and friends would need to raise enough prayer and financial support to send them to the Yakmal Tribe and sustain them on the field. They would need to concentrate first on language/culture learning and building trust relationships with the Yakmal people during most of the first three years. They would need to devise the best strategy and timing to present the Gospel to the tribe. They would need to continually evaluate their plans and progress to see if adjustments of any kind are necessary. There would need to be a regular process of evaluating their plans and progress, while making necessary adjustments each step along the way where necessary. They would need to be sure all adjustments were for the benefit of reaching the long-range goal, rather for their own benefit or "looking good" to supporters.

Good long-range goals are stated as purpose. They point to the need for intermediate goals which guide strategy at each step along the path to fulfilling that purpose. In the rest of this chapter, and in chapters eight and nine also, we will discover principles and methods for planning effective strategies to evangelize unreached people groups.

Making a Planning Strategy

Planning a strategy for cross-cultural evangelism is an act of faith. It is seeing the future through the eyes of faith, under the guidance of faith and the help of the Holy Spirit. It is faith and reason interacting with the future. If a farmer plants a crop, his faith and reason are interacting with the future. Faith and hope say his field will produce a bountiful harvest. Reason says planning the right crop, preparing the soil, planting correctly, and caring for the crop as it grows are all necessary to see the farmer's faith rewarded.

It is the same for reaping a spiritual harvest. If we believe God wants us to evangelize an unreached people group, we must use His help and our God-given ability of reasoning to plan a strategy to reap the harvest. We must know the condition of the field, the context of the people we want to evangelize. We must decide who best can do the sewing of seed, training of converts, and nurturing of believers. We must count the cost of planting the crop. Are we willing to invest the time, money, and lives into the project in order to reap the greatest spiritual harvest? If so, we must have the courage and faith to actually undertake the task and all it requires. It takes both faith and reason to plan for cross-cultural evangelism. Human reasoning is a very powerful gift from God. When combined with God-given faith and vision, Spirit-led human reasoning has a wonderful potential to reap bountiful harvests for the Kingdom of God.

Planning strategy is a tool to help us get from where we are to where we want to be. It is a tool for breaking a task down into individual steps which will help us reach our goals. Secular institutions such as governments, businesses, and armies spend a great deal of effort planning strategies. It is not just a secular activity, however. Jesus said, "I will build my Church, and the Gates of Hell will not overcome it" (Matt. 16:18). In Old Testament times, the gates of the cities were the place where the elders of each city would meet to discuss important affairs. They would gather there in the evenings, discussing whatever seemed to be important to the city and to them. But if there was a war being planned, it was at the gates of the city where the leaders would meet to plan their strategies for the upcoming battles. So Jesus was referring to this practice of planning strategy at the city gates. Today we plan strategies in group meetings also. But they may take place in person, online by computer, or in other ways. When Jesus promised that the strategies of the Gates of Hell would not overcome the strategies of the Kingdom of Heaven, he was giving us encouragement to believe we will prevail against the enemies of men's soul (Satan and his minions). And we already know that it is central to his kingdom's strategy to give every people group on earth a chance to know Christ and serve Him only.

There is no single strategy which will work for every people group. That should be obvious to you by now. There are simply too many different kinds of people in different cultures with different kinds of needs for one strategy to work among every people. Each people group needs a strategy designed for them. Some strategies may use some methods which have been used among other people groups, but there will always need to be some elements that are planned specifically for each people group.

Though there is no single strategy for every people, **it is possible to design a system for planning strategies which will help us reach every people group**. Such a system would help us know what kinds of information we need, questions we should ask, steps we should take, and errors we should avoid. It would not tell us what to do in order to evangelize a specific people, but it would tell us how to decide what to do. It would not allow for a Standard Pattern Strategy to develop. It would encourage a strategy to emerge which takes into careful consideration the differences in language, cultural differences, felt needs, responsiveness to the Gospel, and location of the group to be reached. Though there should not be a Standard Pattern Strategy, there can be a **standardized system for designing a strategy to reach every people group**.

A STRATEGY PLANNING MODEL

A system for planning strategies should help us to make plans and decisions on a number of important subjects. We must decide which people to evangelize. We must decide who can best do the different phases of the work. We must determine the cost and plan ways to raise the funds. We must design a step-by-step plan of action. Then we must actually carry out those plans, adjusting them as necessary while we do so. These are the basic steps to planning an evangelism strategy. They are illustrated in figure 7.a. In the rest of this chapter, and also in chapters eight and nine, we will examine these steps in detail. But first, we should briefly describe the dynamics of this planning model in order to see how the different steps are related to one another.

Figure 7.a: Strategy Planning Model

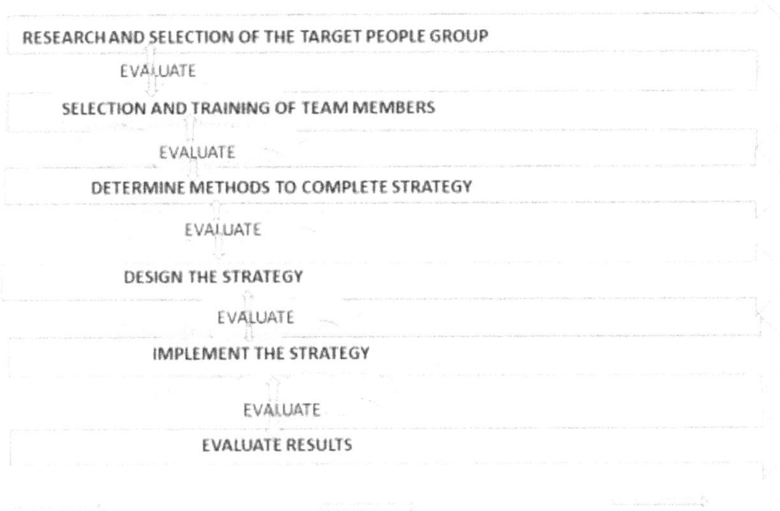

Target People: This is the first level of planning strategies. It includes two important stages of planning. First, the people targeted for evangelism must be selected from among other groups of unreached people. There are some important principles for deciding which group to evangelize first. Second, there is a great need to understand the people which have been selected. An analysis of their society, culture, and needs will help strategy planners greatly in designing a specific strategy to reach the chosen people group.

Evangelism Personnel: When enough information is known about the target people, some tentative decisions can be reached about the kinds of ministries which should prove most effective in reaching them. Cross-cultural ministers must be selected, trained, and equipped to do the work. They should be chosen according to the kinds of ministries which appear to be the most desirable. But they will not be the only ones who will be active in the project. As members of the people group accept Christ, many of them will also become active in evangelizing their own people. A good strategy must include a plan for selecting and training local leaders.

Deciding Methods: After the target people and the cross-cultural evangelism team have been selected, it is time to begin the process of deciding which methods can best accomplish the goals for each stage of the evangelism effort. On the one hand, specific methods for involving and inspiring the Sending Churches (churches, organizations, and individuals who will support the cross-cultural evangelist team) in the vision to reach the target people must be decided. Funds must be raised, lines of authority must be established, and evangelists must be trained in the dynamics of cross-cultural ministry (if they are not already). On the other hand, information about the target people should lead to specific methods for attempting to evangelize them. Those methods should be discussed by experienced leaders and by the evangelists selected for the target people. This process can take some time, and should continue throughout the evangelist's training and/or fundraising period. Indeed, this process continues even throughout the process of evangelistic effort. As methods are prayerfully agreed upon, they should also be given priority in relationship to each other. They should be set as goals to be monitored in terms of their progress. But they should also be subject to change as information and experience show they should be modified. By agreeing on methods and their priorities, the human, financial, and time resources of those involved will become more clear and used most effectively.

Designing the Strategy: This is the stage where specific, measurable goals are decided for each step in the cross-cultural evangelism process. As discussed in the section on setting goals above, each necessary activity is stated as a goal, together with the necessary intermediate goals and objectives to accomplish that part of the strategy. The amount of time needed for each step is estimated, and projected by faith as a part of each goal. Specific plans as to who is responsible to lead in accomplishing each goal and how they are to do so are incorporated into this strategy statement. Policy statements and organizational lines of control are also included in this strategy. Those chosen to lead for each part of the strategy are also responsible to report to others and those who lead the efforts. Each person being supported by churches and individuals are responsible to report progress to those helping to fund the efforts. The purpose statement (overall goal) should be general enough to include everything being pursued to achieve success, yet specific enough for everyone to know when the project has been successful. The intermediate goals and objectives should be specific enough so that every person knows his or her responsibilities, and has guidelines for completing them. Yet they must remain flexible enough to be changed on the field as the need to do so becomes clear. Everyone should feel confident that their own responsibilities will contribute directly to the completion of the purpose.

Implementation: Implementation of the strategy begins as soon as the target people and the evangelists are chosen (in that order). If they are already trained as cross-cultural evangelists, they should undergo specific training related to the target people. The better they are trained before going to the field, the better will be their success in achieving the overall goal to effectively evangelize the people group chosen. They must also raise funds. All these things must be part of the overall strategy. They can be standardized to reach any group of people. Therefore, implementation—carrying out the specific target people's strategy—really begins when the evangelists leave their own country or region of the world to enter the target culture. From that moment forward, the methods and activities will differ according to the strategy for that people group. Strategy planning continues even during implementation of the strategy. Good strategy planning allows for and plans for those actually carrying out the strategy to make changes on the field when there is agreement that it is necessary.

Evaluate Results: During the implementation process, it is important to be able to evaluate and measure progress. This is not only helpful for adjusting strategy in reaching one people group, but it can also be used for making strategies to evangelize other people groups. Evaluation is important for checking progress against intermediate goals and objectives, plus calculating the amount of time necessary for their completion. The information accumulated will be useful in adjusting the tactics used and the time necessary to complete each phase of the intermediate goals and objectives. There are standard ways to measure the growth of Christian believers and projecting that growth into the future. That in itself will help the evangelists plan for leadership training and church planting, plus other needs of the target people group. Measuring and projecting progress is an essential part of the planning and implementation processes.

In the planning model, notice how each step is staggered below and to the right of the step above it. This is because each successive step continues through the process. While one target people is chosen, analyzed, and prepared for, leaders can use the information gained to refine the selection of the next target people and their needs. While one cross-cultural evangelism team is being selected, trained, supported, and sent to the field, another team for another target people can follow in their footsteps. But also consider that each step of the Strategy Planning Model should also continue as the team progresses. More information is constantly gleaned to study and research the target people group during the whole time the team is being selected, trained, and deployed to the target people, and while they are implementing the strategy. Gaining new knowledge about the target people is important for everyone involved. The methods for doing so are also important and can help other teams and other target peoples. Information and insight in each succeeding step in the process helps everyone involved in the task and everyone involved in planning the next steps in detail. This mutual sharing culture should characterize each team on the field and at home.

There is a constant process of evaluation occurring during the whole process. That is why "Evaluate" appears between each stage of the planning model. For instance, the evaluation of the target people should suggest the qualifications of the people being selected to implement the strategy. Information may also flow in the opposite direction. Those responsible for the ministry on the field may need to help change parts of the strategy that was devised earlier. They may also ask for help in determining additional intermediate goals for the target people based on their time with them in the field. So the whole process must be flexible and iterative. Information and suggestions must flow freely between those responsible for the planning process and those responsible to implement the strategy. Both overall strategy and methods for completing that strategy must be subject to modifications when it is apparent they are needed by those closest to the target people. The needs of the ones who "hear" the Gospel are predominant over the desires of those who proclaim it.

TARGET PEOPLE SELECTION

Figure 7.b: Strategy Planning Model

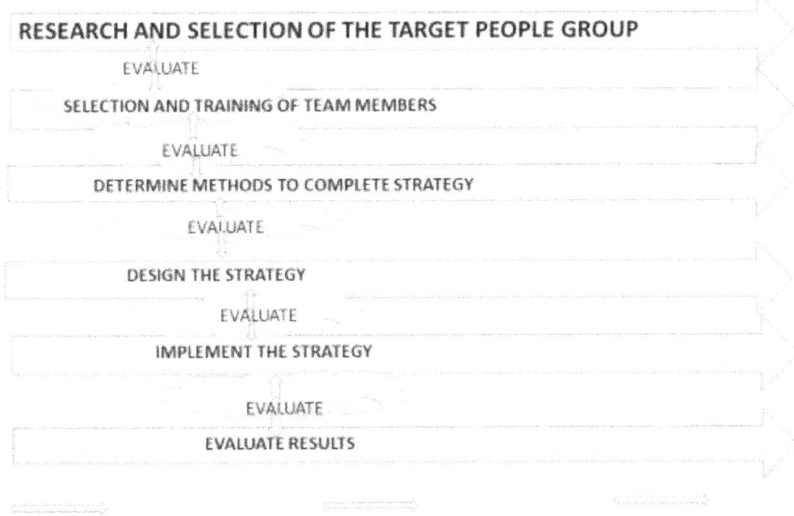

Every people group deserves an adequate chance to accept Christ as Savior, serve Him among their own people, and worship Him in their own language. There are approximately seventeen thousand unreached people groups.[45] How do you decide which one to evangelize first? We need to combine our common sense with the guidance of the Holy Spirit to answer that question.

The Harvest Principle: A rich farmer had three fields of orange trees. At the beginning of harvest season, he went to town to hire workers to harvest the orange crop. He hired forty-five men that day. He sent fifteen men to each of his three fields with instructions on how to harvest the oranges. After the first hour, the foreman reported back to him. The men in the first field were only able to pick one basket each in the first hour. Most of the fruit was still green and could not be picked yet. The ripe ones were scattered in the trees. The men in the second field did better. In their field, though much of the fruit was still not ripe, they were able to pick three baskets in the first hour. But the men in the third field found the fruit very ripe and almost ready to fall off the trees. They each picked six baskets in the first hour. The farmer told his foreman to take fourteen men from the first field and ten men from the second field and go help the pickers in the third field before the fruit fell to the ground. So one man worked in the first field, five worked in the second field, and thirty-nine worked in the third field that day. After the third field was picked, most of them went to the second field which was ripe at that time. Finally, after picking the second field, they all went to the first field because it had also become ripe by that time.

The farmer was following common sense. He knew the fruit in the field which was fully ripe would be lost if he did not put most of the workers there. Later, when the other fields became ripe, he put the workers there. This is the same principle Jesus taught us when He said, "The harvest truly is plentiful, but the workers are few; ask the Lord of the Harvest, therefore, to send out workers in His harvest field" (Matt. 9:37–38). Jesus teaches us to focus our attention upon fields which are "white unto harvest" (John 4:35). He understood the

[45] Joshuaproject.net/resources/articles/how_many_people_groups_are_there.

importance of sending workers to harvest souls when they are ready to listen.

This is the basis for **the Harvest Principle: concentrate evangelism efforts toward reaching the most receptive peoples first, while they are responsive**. This does not mean we should fail to send evangelists to people groups which do not seem responsive. We should send a small number to such groups so we will know when they become responsive. But we should concentrate our personnel and resources toward those groups which are "ripe unto harvest." We must win the winnable while they are responsive.

We already mentioned the principle that Muslims are generally more receptive to the Gospel the further they are away from Saudi Arabia. The further away they are geographically from the theological centers of Islam (Saudi Arabia and Egypt), the more the teachings of Islam covers over deep traditions of animism. This makes them more receptive of the Gospel message in general, and less hostile to those who turn to Christ. Indonesia is an example we talked about earlier. But there are also opportunities to reach Muslims due to political and economic reasons. In Bangladesh, for instance, there was a period of time, 1971 to 1980, when Muslims were receptive to the Gospel as never before. Their Muslim "brothers" from West Pakistan killed at least one million Bengali Muslims in the war of 1970–'71 that gave birth to Bangladesh as a nation. That left a bitter cultural and spiritual vacuum in the hearts of Bengalis, and they became much more open to non-Muslim ways of life. Many of them became Christians through the efforts of dedicated cross-cultural missionaries who loved them and quietly helped them come to know the power of God in the name of Nobbi Issa—Jesus Christ. This is a good example of "ripe unto harvest" cross-cultural ministry.

People groups have different levels of receptivity to the Gospel message. Even if the Gospel is communicated effectively by good principles and methods of cross-cultural evangelism, different groups will prove to be more responsive than other groups. The Harvest Principle says we should evangelize the most responsive groups first. That means we need an effective method to determine which groups are the most responsive.

One method which has been suggested is to send evangelists to every unreached people group then send in more workers to those groups where there is a good response. That is an excellent beginning point, and not unlike our illustration of harvesting oranges. But it is also inadequate because it depends too much on the ability of the cross-cultural evangelist working almost by himself to determine the receptivity of each people group. Because a lack of training, a lack of experience or spiritual qualifications, accountability procedures, or a failure to use good principles of cross-cultural evangelism, or even just have enough help, a worker may fail to be successful among a responsive group of people. The sending group of believers and churches may decide that it is an unresponsive people group, and send their other workers to more responsive groups. This can cause a ripe harvest field to be neglected. In addition to that, some churches will want to send their workers in groups. They cannot send an evangelist to every unreached people, and they cannot wait several years to decide which groups are most responsive before sending their workers. There needs to be a method to determine which groups are likely to be most responsive before sending full-time workers.

MEASURING THE RECEPTIVITY OF PEOPLE GROUPS

The first step in measuring the receptivity of a people group to the Gospel message is to clearly define who those people are (see chapter two). For instance, the target people may be the Tramuhari Indians of Northern Mexico, or the 31 million Muslims in Algeria or the 7.6 million Mongolians who live in Mongolia and China or the 22 million Amhara in Somalia. The unreached people must be described specifically enough that it is obvious as to who is part of the group. Remember, people groups are not just about geography. They are also about language and ethnicity.

Once a people group is clearly identified, it is possible to measure their receptivity to the Gospel by using some sociological and anthropological principles. Using these principles, evangelists and church leaders can become fairly accurate in identifying the most responsive people groups. The following measuring techniques are designed so almost anyone can investigate the receptivity of a specific people group. It consists of three parts: (1) the Cultural Distance Rating, (2) the Degree of Change Rating, and (3) the Validity of Religion Rating. The results of each of these rating scales are combined to yield a **Receptivity Quotient**.

The Cultural Distance Rating (CDR): One important way to tell in advance how receptive a people group will be toward the Gospel is to measure the cultural distance between them and those who bring them the Gospel. Generally speaking, the greater the cultural distance between the evangelist and the people group, the greater the resistance the people will feel toward the Gospel message. This is not the only factor that determines receptivity. Indeed, this whole book is about learning to overcome cultural distances. But cultural distance still remains a factor in determining receptivity. The messenger is part of the message as we discussed in chapter four. The people will be more likely to view the Gospel as an unimportant foreign religion if the messenger is from a culture much different from their own. Perhaps more important, the people will be much more likely to think they must change their own culture in order to become Christians when the evangelist's culture is far different from their own.

Figure 7.c[46]

Category	Many Extreme Differences 1	Many Differences 2	Moderate # of Differences 3	Minimum # of Differences 4	Cultures Mostly Alike 5
WORLDVIEW					
VALUE SYSTEM					
BEHAVIOR PATTERNS					
LINGUISTIC FORMS					

[46] For an alternative set of categories that help define cultural distance, and with deeper discussion, see Hesselgrave (1991), page 192.

SOCIAL STRUCTURES					
COMMUNICATION FORMS					
COGNITIVE PROCESSES					

To find the Cultural Distance Rating: First, put a check in the box which best describes the people group for each category in terms of how different they are from your own culture; second, add the values of all the categories using the numbers at the tops of the columns marked; and finally, divide the total by 7. The answer is the CDR score.

CDR Score _____

When we speak of cultural distance, we are not speaking about geographical distance. People groups which are very close to us in geographical distance can be very far from us in cultural distance. For instance, the seven thousand Chinese expatriates living in India are far different than the cultures in India, though they live next to each other geographically.

Figure 7.c shows the scale of cultural distance. The seven areas which are measured are those we discussed as the major categories of cross-cultural differences in chapter four. The purpose is to estimate how different the target culture is from the evangelist's culture in each of the seven categories. One way to do this is to question people from that culture, or at least someone who has spent a number of years in that culture. The best way would be to spend years among the people yourself. But that is not possible when you are trying to learn the cultural distance receptivity in order to plan strategy.

Another way to get information about people groups, as we have already discussed in chapter two, is to study information available through organizations that have already studied them and published information about them. The Joshua Project, Global Mapping International, the Ethnologue of Wycliffe Bible Translators, and the SEED Company are among the very best sources for such information. The anthropology sections of university libraries are also an excellent source.

Even if you do not have detailed information available to you, there will be enough information available that you can make good estimations of the degree of cultural differences on the scale. Simply do the best you can. The more you can learn about potential target cultures, the better will be your cultural distance assessment and also the challenges you face when targeting a specific people group.

After you have rated the cultural distance between the evangelists' culture and the target people group, follow the instructions at the bottom of the chart to obtain the CDR score.

The Degree of Change Rating (DCR): A very important factor in determining the receptivity of a people group is the amount of change which is occurring in their society. Those people groups which are experiencing rapid transitions from one way of life to another are almost always more receptive. People groups can range from very traditional and rigid in their opposition to change to being very desirous of change, with their people in the midst of rapidly changing their way of life. The more rapid and highly valued change is, the more receptive a people group will be.

Examples of peoples who are highly open to change would be (1) peoples who have been dispossessed of their land through war, governmental action, or natural disaster. These people are often refugees. (2) Peoples who have recently moved into a city from rural areas. (3) Peoples who are poor for any reason and are seeking changes in living conditions. And (4) university students who are questioning traditional values and pursuing ideas that are open to change.

Acculturation and mobility are important indicators of rapid change in people groups. If the people travel back and forth between their people and mix with other cultures while pursuing their livelihoods, their mobility is high. When they have a lot of contact with other people groups on a business or social level, it is an indication that acculturation is taking place between the two groups. Some groups discourage contact with other groups, and most such groups discourage intermarriage between people groups, class, and race. The more that is the case, the more they are traditional societies. These are more traditional people groups. Their level of mobility is usually much less, and there is little acculturation between them and other groups. Those people groups with greater mobility and acculturation are usually the most open to change.

FIGURE 7.d: DEGREE OF CHANGE RATING

DEGREE OF CHANGE RATING	Tradition Oriented	Change Tolerated Some	Change Tolerated Moderately	Change Moderately Desired	Change Highly Desired
	1	2	3	4	5

DCR SCORE: _______

______ 1. Tradition-Oriented: Society is rigid in its observance of traditional patterns of living. Change is highly resisted. Little mobility or acculturation.

______ 2. Change Somewhat Tolerated: Small degree of mobility and acculturation. Change opposed by all but a few who are not leaders. Traditional pattern of life is not seriously threatened.

______ 3. Change Moderately Tolerated: Mobility and acculturation growing and common among a minority of the people group. Some change tolerated on a practical basis by the group as a whole, but opposed by the leaders.

______ 4. Change Moderately Desired: Mobility and acculturation common among a sizable portion of the people group. Change only tolerated by leaders, but the need for change valued by the majority of the people.

______ 5. Change Highly Desired: Mobility and acculturation are very high. There is a general dissatisfaction with traditional patterns of living and values. The need for embracing change seen by leaders and the group as a whole.

The Degree of Change Rating scale is shown in Figure 7.d. For each people group you wish to measure, put a check beside the number which best describes the people group.

The Validity of Religion Rating Scale (VRR): No group of people lives in a complete religious vacuum. Even people who profess to have no religion actually gravitate toward religious ideas and faith in their assumptions even while they deny having any religion.

For example, the author traveled to Asia with a renowned electrical engineering professor and scientist named Jim who professed to his belief in evolution. After discussing all the scientific issues related to the assumptions of evolutionary theory, and how tenuous they actually are, the author finally said, "You know, from all our discussion, it seems clear to me that it takes more faith to believe what you believe about evolution than it does for me to believe what I do about God's creation of mankind." After pondering that for a moment, the professor said, "I think you are right, but I still believe it." Without going into a discussion here, humanism and the many forms of secularism that result do increasingly have all the traits of a religion. Every people group practices some kind of belief system that requires faith in their assumptions about reality. Even those who say they do not believe in God display some kind of system of beliefs which they use to guide their lives. That is the essence of any worldview and belief system.

The issue here is the degree to which a person's religion or belief system satisfies the questions about reality that exist in the mind of every person. Even in societies where religion and politics are inseparable, such as in many Muslim cultures, religious ideas do not always satisfy the longings of the human heart to know truth. That is a major reason why there are millions of Muslims around the world who are turning to Christianity to answer their need for a satisfying view of reality.

Whatever the dominant religion of a people group, it is important to learn how highly the people regard their belief system. Does their religion help them meet their daily needs, or is it mostly just traditional practices which have little value for everyday life? Or are their traditional beliefs a hindrance to their daily lives? Does their religion penetrate to the level of solidly supporting their worldview and value system? Are their religious practices meaningful internally with the people placing great faith in them, or are they mostly traditions which the people follow and succumb to societal pressure to do so? All these are important clues as to the validity of the religion followed by a people group. The more highly valued a people's religion, the more resistant they will be to the Gospel.

Figure 7.e: VALIDITY OF RELIGION RATING

VALIDITY OF RELIGION RATING	Religion Highly Valued	Religion Somewhat Valued	Religion Moderately Valued	Religious Frustration Apparent	Religion Being Ignored
	1	2	3	4	5

VRR Score: ______

______ 1. Religion Highly Valued: Religious activities are very meaningful, and participated in regularly by almost every member of the people group. Religious leaders are the most highly respected members of society. The religion has penetrated the deepest level of their worldview and value system. The people believe the religious practices are absolutely necessary to meet the needs of their daily lives.

______ 2. Religion Somewhat Valued: Most religious activities are meaningful to the people, and the majority of the people actively participate in them regularly. Religious leaders are among the most highly respected members of the communities. Worldview and value system are mostly a result of the teachings of the religion. Most of the people feel that their religious practices are necessary to meet the needs of their daily lives.

______ 3. Religion Valued Moderately: Some religious activities are meaningful to the people, but some of them have become rituals practiced out of duty, legal requirement, or more of a social activity. Some people rarely participate in religious activities. Religious leaders are respected some, but not as much as political or sports figures. The effect on worldview and value system is mixed, with some people preferring a more secular view of reality. Many people are not sure about the importance of some of their traditions. It is increasingly clear to some people that their religious practices do not meet the needs of their daily lives.

______ 4. Religious Frustration Apparent: Most religious activities are considered a ritual performed mostly from a sense of duty. Less than half the people participate regularly in religious activities. Religious leaders are respected little more than the average person. The religion has penetrated the people's worldview and value system, but outside forces are putting pressure on people's perspective to change them. There are many practices and values that contradict the teachings of their religion. Many of the felt needs of the people group are left unmet by the activities and teachings of their religion.

______ 5. Religion Being Ignored: Only a small minority of the people place importance any more on the practices of their religion, most of which have lost much of their original meaning, and are performed mostly for financial reasons and to keep in contact socially. Religious leaders are considered greedy fakers by many, and they have little power to persuade people toward deepening their faith. The people's worldview and value system are changing rapidly to what the people consider to be a modern perspective. Few people believe the basic teachings of their religion any more. There is a strong feeling that the old religion does not help the people as much as it hurts them.

By combining the average score of the three scales (total scores divided by 3), then multiplying by 20, we obtain a **RECEPTIVITY QUOTIENT**. For example, let's assume your team of strategists are trying to decide whether to send their missionaries to the Lampung Abung Tribe on the island of Sumatra in Indonesia or to the Maguindano Tribe who live on the islands of Mindanao in the Philippines. Both tribes are animistic, but consider themselves Muslims. The Lampung Abung number about 200,000 and the Maguindano number about 1.1 million. Both tribes are less than 1 percent Christian and are unreached in the mainstream of their populations.

So our imaginary team of strategists and cross-cultural missionaries decide to study both groups to determine their receptivity. After finishing their research, the scores for measuring receptivity might look like this:

Figure 7.f: CALCULATING CULTURAL DISTANCE

CATEGORY	LAMPUNG ABUNG	MAGUINDANO
WORLDVIEW	2	1
VALUE SYSTEM	3	2
BEHVIORAL SYSTEM	2	1
LINGUISTIC FORMS	2	2
SOCIAL STRUCTURES	2	3
COMMUNICATION FORMS	3	2
COGNITIVE PROCESSES	2	2
TOTALS:	16	13
DIVIDE BY 7 FOR CULTURAL DISTANCE (CDR):	16/7 = 2.29	13/7 = 1.86
DEGREE OF CHANGE RATING (DCR):	3	2
VALIDITY OF RELIGION RATING:	2	1
TOTAL VALUE OF RATINGS:	7.29	4.86

DIVIDE TOTAL BY 3 FOR AVERAGE RATING:	**7.29/3 = 2.43**	**4.86/3 = 1.62**
MULTIPLY TIMES 20	**x20**	**x20**
RECEPTIVITY QUOTIENT:	**48.60**	**32.40**

By carefully finding the information and filling in the scores to evaluate the three receptivity rating scales, and then figuring the totals, it will be easy to measure which people group will be most receptive to the Gospel. This does not mean strategists and leaders should necessarily decide to send all their cross-cultural evangelists to the Lampung Abung Tribe. They might want to send a smaller team to the Maguindano also, praying for the day they will show evidence of becoming more receptive. Then more cross-cultural evangelists can be sent to them also.

There are so many unreached people groups (fields white unto harvest, laborers few [Matt. 9:37]), it is important to make the best effort to discover which ones are most receptive. More and more, leaders and researchers are giving more attention to this matter. Experienced cross-cultural evangelists and missiologists are researching the different unreached people groups around the world. Much of the information is being made available through the organizations mentioned above. The information now available through such organizations and university libraries will be very helpful in analyzing the receptivity of people groups. This will help leaders make their decisions about the people groups they want to evangelize. The Harvest Principle demands that we make the effort to know which are "white unto harvest" and use our resources wisely to target them first. The effectiveness of our efforts to obey the Lord of the Harvest depends upon it.

DESCRIBING THE TARGET PEOPLE

After the target people group has been chosen, further study is needed to help plan the best evangelism strategy. A short-term and a long-term analysis of the felt needs of the people group is very important. An analysis of the felt needs will include different levels of the needs people in the target culture know they have as well as those they may not know. Survival needs, social needs, intellectual needs, and spiritual needs should be investigated. Understanding the needs of a people group will lead to important insights for planning strategy.

Needs Analysis: The beginning point of planning strategy to reach a particular people group is an analysis of the needs felt by the people in their daily lives. The key principle for learning the needs of the people is to let them be defined by the people themselves. A common error of cross-cultural evangelists and strategy planners is that they try to present a Gospel which meets human needs according to the culture of the evangelist, not the target people.

Every culture has demonic influences. But every culture also has beneficial qualities. In every culture, people are drawn together for survival needs, social needs, mental needs, and spiritual needs. Because mankind is in a fallen sinful condition, no culture meets all the needs of its people. People are constantly frustrated in their attempts to have their needs met at different levels. Tensions between people or groups of people occur when one person or group appears to gain an advantage over others. In many cultures, just the physical location of the people group can cause many needs. For instance, some Indian tribes high in the Andes mountains and also those in the high mountains of Tibet have a custom to rarely, or never, bathe their bodies. This is due to the cold climate, frozen water, and the cultural customs which have resulted from those conditions. This can cause medical problems, and threaten the survival of whole people groups. People may learn to live in situations where they are disadvantaged by their environment or many other kinds of difficulties. They feel the fears, frustrations, anxieties, and tensions of their challenges. An effective needs analysis of a specific people group should penetrate to the true sources of those frustrations.

Survival Needs: Even from an outsider perspective, people give a lot of thought and attention to meeting physical needs. If the people group as a whole is having a struggle just meeting the basic needs necessary for survival, this will be visible by the way they live. People seek basic survival needs—food, clothing, shelter, and health, in that order of priority. The author has ministered where all of those needs were not being met for some people. Food is the last to go when all else is gone. That need is immediate, and you cannot proclaim the Gospel to people who are literally starving and dying in front of you. First, you meet their need and do so as a means to open the door to their hearts to hear the Gospel. Using donated sorghum grits and local vegetables and spices, we did that for up to thirteen thousand people in Bangladesh for a long time until the need went away.

Even the results of scientific breakthroughs can be used to help a people group at the level of their felt needs. For example, one of the felt needs of the people of Bangladesh years ago was their frustration with the monsoon rains that would cover their rice fields with water so fast that it would cover the tops of the rice shoots, destroying crops and causing starvation. But the scientific breakthrough of the International Rice Research Institute solved the problem for them. A strain of rice was developed that would grow five inches a day, even eight feet tall if necessary, and that allowed the rice to grow faster than floodwaters would rise. It has saved a lot of lives over the years and met a very strong felt need.

A word of caution should be stated here. It is important to keep in mind that even after those basic human needs are met, people will always seek the security of having more material possessions. More than one cross-cultural evangelism strategy failed because it included providing emergency materials to people whose survival needs were already met. This can too often breed greed and corruption, a very unhealthy environment for creating a hunger to meet spiritual needs. An evangelist must never confuse the level of survival needs in his own culture with those in the target culture, which may be less. Survival needs ministries must remain just that without extending beyond what is truly needed according to the standards of the target culture, not the evangelist. Otherwise, corruption will often be the result. This is simple wisdom in order to use God's resources wisely and to avoid creating "rice Christians"—people who are only interested in material benefits when they need spiritual benefits even more. Christ told us to help people with their material needs when it is in our power to do so (Matt. 25:31–46). But we should not give materially if it is not needed and replaces a desire for spiritual truth with a desire for material gain!

Social Needs: People have social needs at different levels. Everyone has a need to be loved, appreciated, and accepted by other people in every culture. How those needs are met are determined entirely by the culture of the people group. Some cultures frustrate those needs greatly. A common area of strongly felt needs in many cultures is the customs controlling the status and role of women. Some people groups simply do not give their women the respect and status commanded in the New Testament. Before Christianity was introduced into a number of tribal groups in Indonesia, for instance, the women had a very low status in the society. Their roles were mainly to grow and prepare food plus have and take care of children. In some of those tribal cultures, if a man died in a war, it was commonly believed it was because some woman who knew him had "eaten his spirit." So in the midst of their sorrow about losing a loved one, many times women were set upon and killed by the men to punish them for being the "witch" who had eaten the soul of the man who died! In such tribes, the need to increase the status of women was a survival need. Thank God that there has been a move of God among those tribes, with tens of thousands of people becoming Christians. They no longer hunt down and kill "witches" when a man dies. They rejoice that both men and women who die have gone to heaven!

The need for social interaction and fellowship is a very strong drive in all cultures. It should not be overlooked in planning strategies. Often people have problems in interacting with others of their own culture because the level of trust among those in the group can break down over time, or because environmental or external circumstances of the group changes. When this happens to a strong degree, people tend to withdraw, trusting only close relatives or friends. The ability of the Gospel in people's lives to build strong bridges of trust is well-known. Good strategy will seek to demonstrate trust in exactly those ways where it has been lacking within a people group. A believer's simple, pure desire to obey the Lord before everyone is well-known as a builder of trust in the minds of other people in every culture. Trust is a basic social need. The Gospel is powerful enough to change whole groups of people rapidly when strategy focuses on helping the first converts prove their trustworthiness in their own society.

Mental Needs: The human needs to understand reality is universal. Mankind has a deep sense of need to gain more knowledge about his world and the forces that control it and himself. The fact that every culture has developed a worldview, a way of explaining reality at a cosmic level, is sufficient evidence of this human need. Since cross-cultural evangelism must penetrate to the level of Worldview to be effective, our strategies in presenting the Gospel must satisfy mankind's need to reason about such issues. Whatever kind of system of reasoning a culture uses, the Gospel must invade that realm at a deep level. It is important to realize that different worldviews cause people to seek the answers to different questions. To be sure, the Bible contains those answers, but good strategy will seek to give people biblical answers to questions they are really asking in their hearts.

Baht Singh, the famous evangelist of India, was once interviewed about the Christian message he preached. He was asked, "Do you talk about the wrath of God?" He replied, "No! All the gods of India are angry!" The next question was "Do you talk about love?" Singh answered, "No! People in India mostly relate the word *love* to the subject of sex!" Then he was asked, "Do you talk about the death of Jesus?" "No," came Singh's reply, "my people already have many martyrs!" "Well, do you talk about eternal life?" Singh's reply, "Not often. The Hindu's concept of eternity is cyclical. Eternal life is not something to be desired as they understand it. It is something to be endured." "Well, then what do you emphasize in your preaching that is so effective?" came the final question. "We emphasize forgiveness of sins, inner peace, and tranquility. That is what Hindus seek most. That is where God meets them first."

Baht Singh had a powerful ministry in India through which tens of thousands of people accepted Christ. He was wise enough to use a strategy which focused on preaching the part of the Christian message which met the needs the people felt in their minds and hearts. That does not mean he did not preach the whole Gospel. He would teach other Bible truths after people were believers. But in order to evangelize them, he emphasized the parts of the Gospel which gave the people answers to their felt needs.[47]

Spiritual Needs: There are many kinds of spiritual needs. To discover which ones are most important in a target people, look for needs which involve the emotions of the people. What do people fear most? What causes them to feel guilty, or bad about themselves the most? Every society spends time and energy on trying to meet their spiritual needs, though it is not always clear to outsiders. Planning good strategy requires that we gain insight into the spiritual needs of the people.

Perhaps the most effective and rapid way to gain insight into a people's felt spiritual needs is to examine their rituals. Whatever a people's religion, or lack of outward religion, there will be some ceremonies or rituals they follow to have their spiritual needs met. Even those who profess no religion participate in secular-oriented practices or gatherings to reinforce their lack of religion and the practices they use to substitute for religion (which have religious overtones of their own). Anthropologists know that people will usually spend a lot of time and energy performing rituals, ceremonies, magic, or institutional practices in those areas where they feel they need spiritual help or institutional reinforcement of their beliefs. In those societies where people can use modern machinery and digital technology, they do not always perform their rituals so much in public. But they often do so by developing secretive societies like the Masons, Shriners, and similar fraternities. It is not uncommon, for instance, to discover all sorts of Spiritist practices and even Satanic rituals among those who profess to be secular humanists! If the things done in secret in many such societies, the extent of their spiritually oriented rituals, sexual practices, and political aspirations and goals to gain power would resemble tribal societies in almost every respect.

Do not think that large-scale urbanization and the modern momentum toward secular education will eradicate the spiritual needs of any people group. It will simply make it less visible outwardly. More of the people's felt spiritual needs will be less visible

---

[47] David Hesselgrave, *Communicating Christ Cross-Culturally* (Grand Rapids: Zondervan, 1978), 169.

and talked about. There will be less ritual performed outwardly, but they will be adapted to modern city life and performed more secretly. One of the most insidious strategies of the Evil One, the devil himself, is to convince people that he does not exist. He has succeeded infamously to do that outwardly in many Western cultures, mostly through secular education. Yet people in all cultures are regularly influenced to greater and lesser degrees by sinister evil spirits. Even some of the high level political and economic leaders in many Western countries secretly carry out ritual forms of Satanism and sexually deviant and predatory practices (they exist in concert with each other). Cross-cultural evangelists must learn and be equipped spiritually to combat these forces in prayer and personally as they perceive the need to do so.

This kind of ministry has been a key to the rapid growth of evangelical Christianity in the country of Brazil. Spiritist practices of all kinds have been openly dominant in all levels of Brazilian cultures for scores of years. Because the cross-cultural evangelists who started churches there realized they would have to battle those spirits from the beginning, they did so directly. Uncountable numbers of people had to be delivered from demonic oppression. Because the evangelists and believers faced this need directly, many people were delivered from demonic control and tens of millions of people accepted Christ as a result. That was their greatest spiritual need. Planning effective strategies to evangelize unreached peoples must include the spiritual dynamic necessary to overcome the spiritual forces that try to control every people in every culture.

Long- and Short-Term Needs Analysis: In order to plan strategies before sending a cross-cultural evangelism team, it is important to do a preliminary analysis of the needs of a selected people group. This may involve a short-term visit to the people group by one of the planners, such as the team leader or a missionary sending leader. In many cases, a search for written materials online and in libraries will yield enough information to make an initial needs analysis and strategy. But the first needs analysis necessarily must be short-term, tentative, and preliminary. The conclusions reached by this effort will be an important help in making the first strategy and help to save effort, time, and resources. It will also indicate the kinds of cross-cultural workers that will be needed.

When the preliminary needs analysis is ready, it is time to begin step two of the planning model—selecting evangelism personnel. But that does not mean that discovering the felt needs of the target people is finished. It has actually only begun. There will be a continuing need to study the culture of the target people. As the evangelism group is chosen and trained, one of their most important areas of responsibility will be to continue studying the target people more closely. Their worldview, value system, behavior patterns, social ties, and a host of other things will need to be clearly understood as time goes by—both before and after the team is deployed to the field. Long-term study and investigation will be needed, and strategies must be adjusted accordingly. Like other steps in this model, analysis of the needs must be a continuing process throughout the planning and implementation of the strategy.

EVANGELISM PERSONNEL

Figure 7.g: Strategy Planning Model

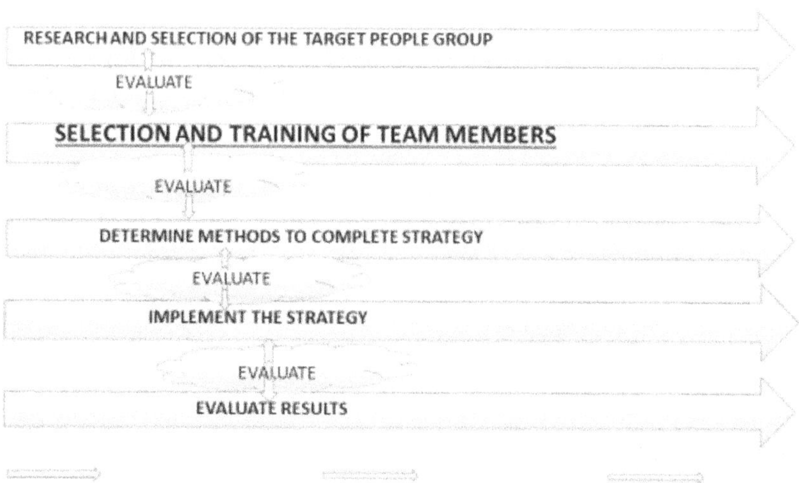

After the preliminary needs analysis of the target group is available to the strategy planners, it is important to begin selecting those who will become the members of the cross-cultural evangelism group. The most experienced leaders available should be involved in strategy planning at this point. The preliminary needs analysis should give the planners an idea of the kinds of people needed for the team. Their basic principle for selecting the members of the group should be to find people who can best minister to the felt needs which were revealed in the needs analysis. If the people group's economic survival is threatened, a person might be selected who has training or experience in economic development. If the people often suffer from serious physical diseases, a member of the team might be a trained or experienced medical worker. If the people live in constant fear of evil spirits, an evangelist with demonstrated gifts and experience in confronting such forces with the power of the Holy Spirit should be a member of the team. People should be purposely selected for the team who are experienced, or who can be trained, to meet the kinds of needs felt the most by the target people.

QUALIFICATIONS FOR CROSS-CULTURAL EVANGELISTS

When choosing cross-cultural evangelists, the most basic principle to remember is that it is God who really does the choosing (John 15:16). God will place a burden for cross-cultural ministry upon those whom he calls to this kind of service. Furthermore, they will not be novices in evangelism, and they will already be working for God. They must prove their gifts and ministries in their own culture before they are selected for cross-cultural evangelism. As the leaders in the Antioch Church did (Acts 13:1–3), strategy planners and church leaders must learn to recognize God's call to such ministry. We should do what we can to lift the vision for cross-cultural ministry in the minds of the people in all our churches. But when we select them, we must recognize that we are really just ratifying and recognizing what God has already done in the lives of those He has chosen.

God does not choose the wrong people and He empowers those He chooses. There are some basic qualities common to good cross-cultural ministers. Learning these will help us recognize God's call to this important kind of work in people's lives. It may also help us recognize a call on our own lives.

Spiritual Vision and Experience: Cross-cultural ministry is a spiritual task to accomplish a spiritual work by spiritual means and methods. It requires that only genuinely spiritual people be entrusted to do this kind of work. Only people who are born-again, knowledgeable in the Scriptures, and experienced in ministry should be considered for cross-cultural service. This does not mean a person must reach a certain age limit or have a high level of training. History shows that the most effective cross-cultural workers have been those who started fairly young in life. Neither does it mean that a person must possess a specific amount of formal education, though it can be very helpful. It does mean that the candidate for cross-cultural service must have a proven ministry in their own culture before they will be qualified to serve in another culture.

Candidates should be people who have *pure motives*! Their lives should demonstrate that their primary purpose in life is to see the Kingdom of God on Earth expand in number and spiritual impact. They must not be seeking cross-cultural ministry in order to escape their present problems and responsibilities. They must not be wanting to work somewhere else in the world in order to gain some personal advantage financially, or for any other self-centered reason. They must have demonstrated a love for God and dedication to His work that is above their own personal interests.

Faith and vision are also prerequisites for candidates who want to enter cross-cultural service. Faith is a spiritual gift which comes from God (Eph. 2:8–9). Faith is a way of thinking like God does about human need. It opens whole new horizons of thinking and creative ability in a person's life. It makes a person dissatisfied with things as they are. It includes a knowledge that God will help anyone who will have the courage to work to do things for God. Jesus once instructed his disciples to cast their net into the water on the other side of the fishing boat. When they did, they caught many fish. As

God's "fishers of men" on earth, we must have faith to cast our nets outside our own people group to bring the news about the grace of God to the many unreached people groups around the world—one group at a time.

People with faith are willing to cast their net into the future, trusting that God will help them win souls and establish churches in other cultures. In order to accomplish God's work, a person must have a vision for what God wants. Then he must have faith in God to consistently pursue the goals of that vision. This kind of faith and vision should have already been demonstrated in the lives of those who are selected for cross-cultural service.

The candidate should especially be a person of self-discipline and have a strong personal devotion to God. The stress and strain of working in another people group, often separated from one's own culture, people, and family for years, requires a strong personal relationship with the Lord. Cross-cultural workers cannot often depend upon others to help them make decisions, solve problems, and grow spiritually. They must constantly be able to give out spiritual strength. This requires that they know how to gain that strength and faith from God through personal devotion and learning at the foot of the cross in prayer.

Most important, the candidate for cross-cultural service must be personally convinced of God's call to the unreached peoples and is willing to go where God enables him to fulfill that call. Problems always arise in ministry everywhere. He must know in difficult times that God called him to be there and that He will help him through difficulties. If Paul had given up the first time he was stoned and left for dead at Lystra (Acts 14:19–22), we would not have most of the epistles of the New Testament! Paul would not give up no matter what happened because he knew God had called him. He knew it was a privilege to obey that call, even if it cost him his life. That same resolve to obey God's call is a primary spiritual qualification for cross-cultural service.

Personal Qualifications: There are also a number of personal qualifications which are desirable in candidates for cross-cultural service. First, it is important that the candidate (husbands, wives, family) be in good physical health. A physical examination and medical history should comprise a part of the screening process for cross-cultural team members. This is true because this kind of work requires physical stamina and health. It is also true because a considerable amount of money will be needed to send and support cross-cultural workers. If their health will not permit them to fulfill their duties well or for a long period of time, the money, training, and other resources will have been expended with little return for the Kingdom of God.

Cross-cultural candidates should also be people whose personality traits are mature enough to work well with other people in the pressure of a cross-cultural setting. This involves much more than simply being a likable person in one's own culture. The author is convinced that problems in relationships with coworkers is one of the greatest single tools Satan uses to hinder effective cross-cultural teams. A small weakness in one's personality at home quickly can become a major problem when that person is working in another culture. This can quickly lead to dissension and become an avenue to vent upon coworkers all the frustrations a person feels when working in another culture. A person should have experience working with other people well over time before being accepted as a candidate for cross-cultural service. He or she should have a demonstrated ability to work, plan, discuss, and cooperate well with others. A loving and tolerant spirit is one of the most important qualifications a candidate can possess.

Flexibility is another important qualification. There will always be many unforeseen problems and opportunities which arise in cross-cultural work. A person needs to be able to make rapid adjustments, approach new situations without feeling personally threatened, angry, or frustrated. Opportunities need to be utilized. Problems must be overcome. An ability to be flexible and positive in outlook will greatly aid cross-cultural workers.

In the final analysis, a person who consistently demonstrates the ***fruits of the Spirit*** in his or her life has the best personal qualifications for working within other people groups. "Love, joy, peace, patience, kindness, goodness, faithfulness, gentleness and self-control" should be a basic list of personal qualifications for cross-cultural service (Gal. 5:22).

Cross-Cultural Training: Once an individual or group of candidates for the cross-cultural team are selected, they should be given an opportunity to receive adequate training. This book should be a central part of that training. It is also at this point that work should begin on the third step of the planning model—deciding methods (see chapter eight). Even as training and preparation to field the team begins, discussions and planning should begin on which methods will best bring the important message of salvation to the mainstream of the target culture. The team members preparing to go to the field should be involved in key portions of the planning.

The training of the team should be intensive and full-time for at least three months. Study and work in the following subjects should be considered as a minimum: (1) biblical theology of missions, (2) cross-cultural training and enculturation strategy, (3) principles and practices in language/culture learning, (4) autochthonous church planting, and (5) organizational relationships in cross-cultural ministry. It is easily recognizable that this book provides extensive training in all five of these subjects. The team should learn theoretically and practically. For instance, they should be given actual practice in learning another language following the principles and methods in chapter five of this book.

This book can form the foundational textbook for training the cross-cultural evangelism team. But other materials should be used to supplement what is in this book. In that regard, the notes, bibliography, and websites referenced in this book can be useful to provide additional training material as time and resources permit. Cultural materials from universities and government archives can be helpful as well. It is not unreasonable to hope that leaders from different churches, denominations, and mission agencies from different regions of the world will work together to prepare and share even more specific information and training insights for specific target people groups.

Perhaps the most important factor for training cross-culture team members is the people who actually do the training. They should have a number of years' experience in actually doing cross-cultural work. They should be gifted teachers and have a strong desire to multiply their expertise by training others. Last, but not least, they should be well trained in the theory and practice of at least one of those five subjects delineated above. Such people are not always easy to find, but it is worth the effort to gain their expertise. There are still many cultures that must be targeted effectively. The trend toward independent churches with loose organizational ties to one another in Western cultures makes good trainers harder to find. That makes the value of such trainers even more important. The effectiveness of cross-cultural evangelism and the lives of those who go are strongly dependent upon good training.

It is impossible for this author to conceive of much long-term effective involvement in cross-cultural ministry unless adequate opportunities for training are developed to help those who go to reach unreached people groups. Every regional Bible school or seminary that trains ministers should have a division of cross-cultural ministries or a major in international studies that teaches the subjects in this book.

The Value of a Team Approach

There is a strong value placed upon individual achievement in English-speaking countries. People have a desire to strike out on their own and work independently. It is one of the reasons business in English-speaking countries has thrived compared to the rest of the world. We must not confuse leadership with independence, however. Leaders will never accomplish their full potential working alone. Success in any endeavor is never accomplished without teamwork. That is especially true of cross-cultural ministry. We will approach this subject in depth in chapter ten, but it is important to emphasize teamwork here while still giving room for individual initiative.

When working for the Lord among our own people, we are responsible to those people. We learn what we can and cannot do in ministry. We also know how to do it. In other cultures, working individually is much more difficult. It takes at least two years to learn a language and culture sufficiently to have significant results in another culture. One person cannot learn everything well or fast enough to be effective. It takes a team effort plus open and honest discussion and planning. In teams, everyone can learn from the experiences of others. Rather than competing for recognition from others, good team members share their mistakes and their successes openly and learn from one another. It is also an opportunity to receive suggestions to improve the ministries of each team member. It is the responsibility of team leaders to keep such open interaction and helpful communication flowing within team meetings.

Cooperative Planning: One important reason to use the team approach as much as possible is that effective strategy planning is impossible without it. Planning strategy must continue even during the implementation stage of doing cross-cultural evangelism. The strategy planning methods we are suggesting in this book require continuing research, group consultation, and planning, even while the team members are engaged in their ministries. The team approach allows this to happen effectively. One person may agree to research the worldview and the value system of a target people. Another can agree to investigate the key locations for starting churches and locating members of the team. One person may be in charge of taking care of the logistical needs of the team as a whole. The group will need to assign tasks to several members which are too large for one person to complete. There are many benefits to planning and working together in teams to do cross-cultural ministry.

The one caution worth mentioning at this point is the need for team members to be unhindered in their language/culture learning process. All team members will be anxious to learn the language and culture quickly so they can get into full-time team ministry. Such members who are still learning will not be qualified to judge when they are ready to enter full-time into team ministries. There will be a temptation to do so before sufficient language/culture learning is completed adequately. This early desire to short-circuit the language/culture learning process will inevitably diminish the long-term effectiveness of a team member. Senior leaders must place requirements and sufficient standards upon the activities of new team members until they are measurably capable of full ministry responsibilities *while carrying them out in the target language*, not English. They should achieve at least 3.0 on the NDSL scale of language ability before moving into ministry as their primary focus. Furthermore, their status, input, and integration into team meetings and strategy sessions should be limited until they reach that level. They must spend their time among members of the target culture, not the foreign members of their team. Such limitations, focus, and standards will be the best blessing to new team members they can ever imagine.

Accountability: Since much of the planning for specific tasks needs to be done in the field among the target people, the success of those plans should be measured and evaluated in the field. While we are all accountable to God for what we do on earth, we also need to be accountable to people who help us in our work. Cross-cultural team members will benefit greatly by submitting their plans and progress in ministry to one another for approval and advice. There is truly wisdom in "a multitude of counselors" (Prov. 15:22). Conferring with one another provides a degree of safety in planning to do the work (Prov. 24:6). Super-individualism is out of place in cross-cultural evangelism and in the Kingdom of God in general! When team members submit the details and progress of their ministries to others for advice and approval, everyone's ministry will be better than it would without the help of the team.

That does not mean team members must spend all their time around one another or live in the same location or work on the same tasks. Not only would that hinder the need to deepen language/culture learning capacity, it would lessen the abilities of people assigned to specific types of ministry. It does mean that there should be regular times for the team to meet, pray for one another, and share concerns and successes with one another. By submitting their ministries to one another and strategizing together, the cross-cultural ministry team will be more effective in evangelizing any people group. It will also help them report to those "back home" who are supporting the ministry. As more and more governments around the world have access to online media, exactly how much and what is shared with the supporters back home needs to be agreed upon in team meetings. In some parts of the world, especially in Muslim and Hindu areas, that is extremely important.

SELECTION AND TRAINING OF LOCAL LEADERS

No evangelization strategy can ever be really successful if the only people doing the evangelism are members of the cross-cultural team. The apostle Paul recognized this and told Timothy to teach "faithful men" who learn to "teach others also" (2 Tim. 2:2). As people come to Christ in the target culture, the evangelists must place a priority on selecting and training leadership among those converts. As those converts learn by doing evangelism and other ministries, they must also be equipped to teach others to do the same as they have done. Most of the people in the target culture will need to be won to Christ and taught to be disciples by their own people. This means leadership training and selection must be an important part of the strategy from the very beginning.

Principles of Leadership Selection: There are some important biblical principles for choosing leadership. Selecting leaders occurs at different levels as churches are planted and their ministries expand. There is much available material for training leadership in the English language, but there will likely be little if any available in the target language. An effort to adopt or develop such training materials in the target language will become a priority at the same time the first converts are coming to Christ. The biblical principles for selecting and qualifying leaders in the church are found in Ephesians 4:11, 1 Timothy 3:2–7, and Titus 1:6–9. These should always remain a guide for selecting leadership at all levels of the Church in every culture. These guiding principles should be adapted to the context of the people group being targeted as we have discussed earlier. Our purpose here is to discuss some principles which are normally not available in other study materials, and which apply specifically to choosing leadership in a cross-cultural ministry situation.

The Pyramid Principle: Those of us who study the growth of churches know there is an important principle which demonstrates the need to effectively choose, train, and multiply leadership in any church growth movement. Briefly stated, the church growth principle states that *a church cannot grow spiritually and numerically beyond the size of its base of leadership* (see figure 7.h). Building a pyramid, like the Egyptians and Indians in some parts of Latin America did years ago, requires a large-enough base to support the weight and size of the structure. The taller the pyramid, the larger and wider the base must be. Similarly, more and more leaders are needed to do evangelism and help teach new converts as the church expands in a target culture. If that does not occur, the growth will slow down dramatically and may even stop. That is why Paul gave the instruction to Timothy, cited above. He knew the base of leadership must continually be expanding in all the churches that had been established. He also knew that the only way for that leadership base to expand as rapidly as needed is if each person who receives leadership responsibility and training will train others to learn as he himself has learned. It is also good pedagogy. If you know you will be responsible to immediately train someone working under you exactly what you are learning, you will pay much better attention and find a way to prepare to train others.

Figure 7.h

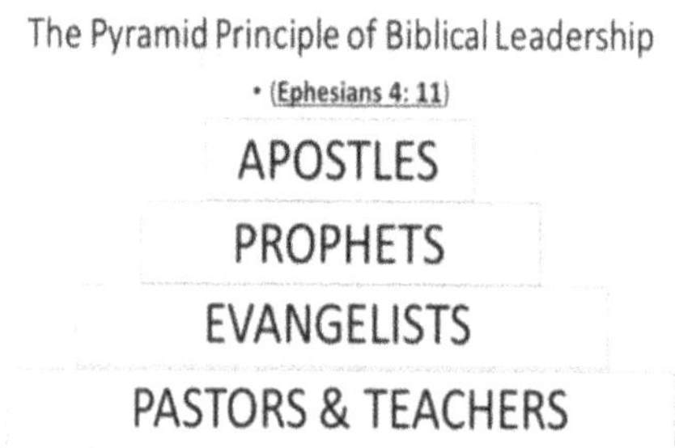

Who should do the choosing? In almost every situation, cross-cultural evangelists and team members should not be the ones to actually pick the leaders in the churches they start. This is true for choosing leaders to oversee churches. It is also true for choosing people to receive leadership training. The cross-cultural evangelist should ask the group of new believers who among them most exemplifies the leadership qualities found in Ephesians 4, 1 Timothy, and Titus above. He should be careful to counsel the believers not to choose people just because they are older or financially more powerful when they choose their leaders. He should counsel them to choose their leaders according to whom they would choose to effectively lead the work God wants to accomplish. If the believers need deeper instruction before choosing their leaders, it should be given to them.

To accomplish this level of maturity, believers must come to truly believe that the church being established belongs to God and to them, not to the foreigners who brought the Gospel to them. Otherwise, they will feel they must answer to the leadership of the foreigner. They will perceive that the church belongs to the foreigners, not to God and themselves. Second, the local believers will know the true motivation of the people in their group. The Holy Spirit will help them to know it, and the cross-cultural evangelist must encourage them to make leadership decisions themselves. The people in the church and the evangelist (in that order) should both be convinced that the leaders they have chosen are the ones chosen by God.

Local leadership patterns should be respected. It is important to choose leaders in a way which will be in step with local leadership forms. This applies to the method of choosing leaders, the kinds of leaders chosen, and the way the leaders lead. In choosing leaders, do not tell the people anything about how leaders are chosen in your own culture. Simply talk about the needs they feel for leadership in doing God's work. Ask them what kinds of leaders could best fulfill those needs from a spiritual perspective. Discuss the biblical examples with them. Then let them choose the people who should lead at every level.

Do not elevate leaders too high too soon. Encourage the people to set different levels of leadership which they feel comfortable with. Help them to establish their own rules for qualifying, training and appointing leaders, based upon biblical examples. Ask them more questions than you make statements to them. Teach them the scriptural principles, and ask them to decide how evangelists, teachers, pastors, elders, etc., should be qualified and appointed. Always encourage the people to base their selection of leadership on the needs they want met, and on the ability of the leaders to help meet those needs. Do not allow the selection process to be based solely on a person's position in society, but on spiritual qualifications. Let advancement in leadership be based on clear delineations of leadership standards and the successful performance of those standards. Help the believers to write those standards down and make accountability an important part of them.

In training leaders to do the work of God, it is important that the evangelist emphasize the **what and why** of leadership responsibilities, not the **how and where** of carrying out their duties. This is especially important during the beginning of leadership selection and training. Well-chosen leaders will know the best ways of communicating with their own people and bringing up leaders under themselves. They will be better at telling Bible stories and giving illustrations from everyday life than the evangelist will be, at least in the beginning. The leaders will likely model what subjects should be communicated and taught because they know the issues that are most important to the people. The evangelist can learn from them to use the best forms for communicating biblical truth by watching how these leaders do it and discussing the what and why with them. The Holy Spirit will help them communicate and lead their people in the way most effective for their culture. The evangelists will do well to minister to them at a personal level to keep the spiritual tenor of their leadership in sync with the Holy Spirit. Over time, the evangelists will learn the best leadership forms utilized by leaders in that culture. They can then begin to emphasize more of the how and where for leaders and believers alike to carry out their spiritual responsibilities. This pattern of leadership development will prove to be effective for generations.

PRINCIPLES FOR TRAINING LOCAL LEADERS

There are many important principles for training leaders in churches. There is no space to discuss them all here. But there are three basic principles that are so important that they must be emphasized when training leaders cross-culturally.

Make the Training Practical: Too many of the world's educational institutions have concentrated on simply teaching people knowledge. But knowing **what** does not necessarily mean knowing **how**. Too many people have been given a lot of knowledge, but too few have been trained to use that knowledge effectively. The best kind of education unites training to know with training to do. This is especially true of Christian education. We cannot afford the luxury of simply challenging the minds of our students. They must also be motivated and capable to use what they learn to challenge the world with the knowledge of God. That means practical learning must be a part of every phase of training in cross-cultural evangelism.

Jesus trained the disciples in practical ministry. He gathered them together for sessions of training. Then he sent them out to minister the Word of God, practicing the principles of what He taught them. They alternated between getting knowledge about God from Him, then going out to use it in practical work (see Mathew 10). This is the best principle for training in a cross-cultural situation. No matter what level of training is being given, let the training alternate between learning and doing, between gaining knowledge and using that knowledge. While you are training people to evangelize, periodically send them out to evangelize, then come back to discuss it and learn more. If you are training people to teach the Bible, let them actually teach as part of their training. If you are training people to be pastors, help them learn to start churches and pastor them while they are taking their training. No matter the level or place of training, the more the training can be united with the practical use of the training, the more effective it will be.

Follow the same principles when evaluating the progress of the trainee. Do not simply test people's knowledge. Also test their ability to use that knowledge in ministry. Let people's success in their training be measured by how well they can practically and usefully demonstrate their learning. If you are teaching, then teach others to teach also. Test them by evaluating their actual teaching plus what the people do with that teaching. This keeps the focus on doing ministry rather than just knowing about ministry. If you are teaching evangelists to plant churches, do not let them complete their training until they have actually planted or helped to plant a church. Walk with them along the path of doing so. Use this principle of learning to do, not just learning to know from the very beginning. It will make an enormous difference in the effectiveness of your work. It will greatly multiply the power and effectiveness of the churches among the target people groups for years and years to come.

Another benefit of using this principle is that it helps keep the training at the correct level. When you are teaching a subject which will be tested in fieldwork very soon, your teaching will be much more likely to be at the correct level. It will not be "over the heads" of the people. It will, of necessity, remain practical. When trainees know they are going to soon use the knowledge and teach others to do the same, they will be motivated to learn well. Their questions and ideas will be practical and lead to useful information. They will not allow the teacher to become too far removed from practical training. They will learn at the level where they can use the training. Train to do, not just to know.

Balance the Training: In chapter three, we discussed the two-fold primary ministry function of the Church: making disciples and teaching them to obey the commands of Christ. We discussed how everything the churches do in ministry can be listed under one of those two ministry functions. We also discussed how there must be a balance between the two. A church which emphasizes teaching, but not making disciples will stop growing. A church which emphasizes making disciples, but not teaching them will not grow effectively either. Too many converts will backslide because they were not grounded in their faith.

When starting churches cross-culturally, this means we must balance the kinds of training we do right from the beginning. Experts in church growth have labeled those whose work for the Lord to plant churches are primarily making disciples as class 2 workers. Those whose work is primarily teaching believers in the churches are called class 1 workers. That does not mean that one kind of work is more important than the other. They are both equally important. But it is a useful way to classify the work and workers because it shows the need to have and evaluate both kinds of workers in every church.

Since churches which are balanced in their ministries are healthiest and grow the fastest, we must be sure to provide training from the beginning to multiply both class 1 and class 2 workers. We should not just train new believers who are emerging leaders to simply teach Bible classes. We should also train them to lead others in evangelizing their communities and starting other churches. When planning strategy for training programs, the plans must balance the need for workers and trainers in both of these primary areas of ministry function.

Build Infinitely Reproducible Leaders: You may recall that we discussed a scale for measuring the reproducibility of churches in chapter three. We stated the importance of making sure that everything we do in starting autochthonous churches is reproducible. This is especially true in training leadership. We also cited the instructions the apostle Paul gave to Timothy in 2 Timothy 2:2. He actually gave us a formula for reproducibility in this scripture. The passage contains four generations of leadership training:

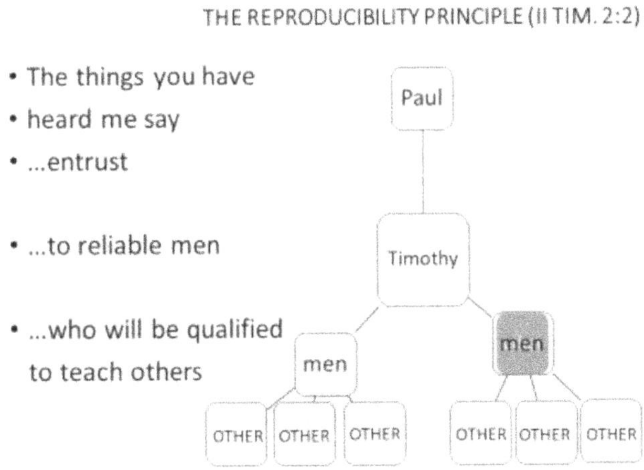

This passage shows the power of reproducibility. Paul did not simply tell Timothy to teach to others what he had learned from Paul. He told him to teach it in such a way that they would "be able to teach others also." We must not only make our training practical, but also, we must make it reproducible! We must not just teach people to know and do the work of God. We must teach them to teach others to know and do the work of God. This principle should be incorporated into our training programs at all levels. When we teach people to teach Bible classes, we must also teach them how to teach others to do the same. When we teach people to make disciples, we must also teach them to train others to make disciples.

The power of this principle cannot be overemphasized. Following this principle at every level of training will greatly multiply the power of the churches we start. They will grow spiritually and numerically much faster. To give you an idea of the power of this principle, just think of applying it to making disciples. If you were to dedicate yourself to making one disciple every month for the rest of your life, you could win twelve people to the Lord every year. That would be good. But it would be far better if you determine to make one new disciple every month, but then you also teach each disciple to do the same for every month of his life also. If each succeeding disciple would determine to do the same thing and succeed, many more people would be won to Christ. The total number of believers (assuming every disciple did the same thing) would double every month! In the first year alone, there would be 4,096 new believers. And if the process continued, with every new believer winning someone else every month, the growth would be amazing. By the end of the second year, there would be at least 16,777,216 believers. And by the end of two years, eight months and two days, every person on earth would be a Christian! Now the chances are slim that everyone would continue to win someone each month, but it certainly demonstrates the power of the Principle of Reproducibility. We must make everything we do in training leaders within the target people group as reproducible as we possibly can!

We have now discussed the first two steps of the planning strategies model. It is important to remember that there is no single strategy to evangelize every people. But this model for planning strategies can help you plan a strategy to evangelize and reproduce churches within any people group. Selecting the target people is the first step. This requires the short- and long-term investigation into the needs of the people. After the people group has been selected, defined, and evaluated, it is time to begin the second step in the model—selecting, training, and deploying the personnel for cross-cultural evangelism. Even after they are working among the target people, they should continue to use good principles for selecting and training leadership among the believers of the target people. In the next chapter, we will examine the two next steps in the planning model.

QUESTIONS FOR UNDERSTANDING

1. According to this chapter, why do we need good strategies to evangelize unreached people groups? Name two things we can do to keep human planning sensitive to the leading of the Holy Spirit?
2. Name the weaknesses of the Standard Pattern Strategy and the God-Will-Help-Us Strategy. Why is there no single strategy which will work to reach every people group?
3. Tell what is wrong with this statement as a goal: "We will try to reach the people of the city of Bangalaru with the Gospel." Give examples of how this goal could be improved.
4. Name two important ways in which good goals are measurable. What are the advantages of making goals measurable?
5. Explain the relationship between long-range goals and intermediate-range goals. Why are intermediate-range goals necessary? How do they help you think through specific tasks in carrying out a strategy to reach your goals?
6. According to the Strategy Planning Model, list six important steps in strategy planning. Briefly explain the purpose of each step.
7. Explain the process necessary for selecting the target people group. When should the second step in the planning model begin? How long does each step last? Why?
8. Why does the word "evaluate" appear between each step of the planning model? Why do you think the arrows are pointing in two directions?
9. Define the Harvest Principle and why it is important. What does it mean for cross-cultural evangelism?
10. Explain the process for obtaining a Receptivity Quotient for a people group. What three measuring scales are involved? How are the answers combined to give the Receptivity Quotient?
11. Why is it worth measuring the degree of change in a society? Give some examples of the type of people groups

where rapid change would be likely to occur. Describe a people group which is given a 4 on the DCR.

12. What four kinds of needs should be investigated when trying to discover the felt needs of a people group? Briefly explain the meaning of each. Explain the difference between long-term and short-term needs analysis. Why are both necessary?
13. List five subjects that cross-cultural evangelists should study before leaving to enter another culture. What are the qualifications for those people who should train them? What are the implications of this for regional Bible institutes and seminaries?
14. What is the Pyramid Principle in regard to leadership? What does it mean for training leadership in the churches of other cultures?
15. Name three important principles for training leaders in the churches of a target people group? Briefly explain why each one is important.

QUESTIONS FOR DISCUSSION

1. Discuss the relationship between faith, the future, and making goals. Use biblical examples in your discussion. Do you think the Bible is future-oriented?
2. Discuss the principles for setting clear, precise, measurable goals. Together with some friends, decide on a simple goal which you would like to reach together. State the goal correctly and write intermediate goals and objectives for reaching your main goal. Discuss all the parts of the goal together as you make them.
3. Discuss the people of your own culture who are not Christian believers. Using the principles of this chapter, analyze the felt needs of that group. What insights do those needs give you about methods to better evangelize your own people group?
4. Discuss the members of another people group who live close to you. Using the principles of this chapter, analyze

the felt needs of that group as best you can. What insights do these needs give you about methods for evangelizing that people group?

5. Discuss the team approach to cross-cultural evangelism. How do you feel about it? Does it fit your culture? Do you think it is a wise approach? Why? Can you think of examples in the Bible where the team approach was used?

CHAPTER EIGHT

Planning Strategies For Cross-Cultural Evangelism II

KEY CONCEPTS IN THIS CHAPTER

1. The selection of good methods for cross-cultural evangelism will not guarantee success. But the selection of poor methods will limit the amount of success possible.
2. Methods are ways of applying practical knowledge to accomplish specific goals. They are the "how to do it" part of strategy planning.
3. The Holy Spirit is creative, using different methods for different cultures. Methods play an important role in evangelizing unreached people groups. It is possible to measure the appropriateness of specific methods for evangelizing a particular culture.
4. We can learn much about the methods we should use from the people we are trying to evangelize.
5. Strategy planners have faith that God has a special strategy for each people group. They see their task as discovering that strategy and joining in partnership with the Holy Spirit to see it become effective.
6. Good strategies are goal-oriented and process-oriented. They use specific, measurable goals. They are flexible and changeable as the strategy is being implemented.

7. Good strategies are oriented toward the needs of the target people. They are also balanced in their efforts to meet those needs.
8. Good strategies are oriented toward group change. They emphasize individual conversion, but they also emphasize moving the whole target society closer to Christ on a continual basis.

DECIDING METHODS

Figure 8.a

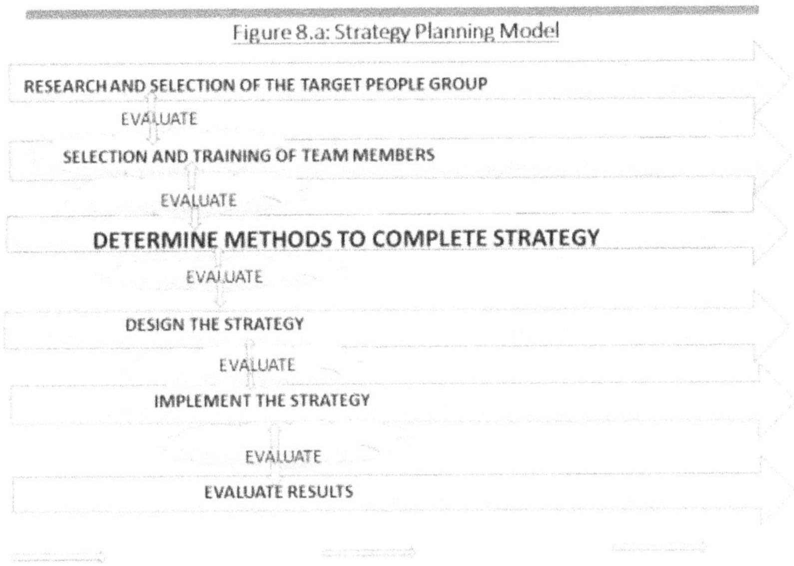

In chapters four and six, we discussed the difference between biblical principles and cultural methods. The principles apply to all cultures. The methods and forms must be changed to correctly communicate the same truths in an autochthonous way to each people group. This requires that we learn the characteristics and importance of good methods. We also need to understand how to use them as a part of the planning model.

THE IMPORTANCE OF GOOD METHODS

Learning good methods is like a farmer learning to grow crops in a new field. He has to learn what kind of soil is in the field before he knows the best crop to plant. According to the crop he will plant, he will decide what kind of furrows, the spacing, and how deep to plow the ground. That will tell him what kind of equipment he can use to prepare the soil. He must decide how deep to plant the seed and if he will need to add something to the soil to prepare the ground before and after he plants. He must decide if there will be enough water from the rain or if he will try to irrigate the field by some method. He may have to decide how to best rid the field of weeds or pests as the crop grows. He also must decide when and how to harvest the crop and sell it. All these decisions require knowledge and experience. Sometimes the farmer does not know the answers to all his questions. He needs to find other farmers who are experienced in farming fields like his. By learning from other's experience as well as his own, the farmer will be much more successful in gaining a good crop and selling it for a good profit.

Deciding methods for cross-cultural evangelism is much like farming. It is a process of deciding many things. What kind of field does each people group represent? What methods can best be used to plant the seed of the Gospel in the hearts of people so it will grow? What are the best methods for a specific people group and how much time and resources will be needed to see that seed grow until a spiritual harvest is ready to be reaped?

Like farming, choosing methods requires experience and learning from others. It is a process which can improve results greatly as evangelists become more experienced in choosing the right methods. Just as a farmer would never use the same methods to grow wheat as he would to grow rice, so an evangelist cannot use all the same methods to evangelize one people group as he does another.

We can carry this farming analogy a little further. Even if the farmer uses all the right methods for plowing, planting, nurturing, and harvesting his crop, he can still lose the crop. Storms, floods, insects, wild animals—any of these problems can destroy or diminish a crop. There are some things the farmer cannot control. He can use every correct method, but he must still rely on God to assure that the field is fruitful. Still, one thing is certain. If he uses the wrong methods, barring a miracle, he will definitely have a poor crop! Even with God's blessings on poor methods, the best the farmer can reasonably hope for is a poor crop. This is also true of cross-cultural evangelism. God can bless poor methods the same as he can bless good methods. But the difference will be in the size of the spiritual harvest. Since souls are more valuable by far than crops, it is far better to learn to choose good methods. It is the only way to be certain that none of the spiritual harvest is needlessly lost.

Good methods are very important to good cross-cultural evangelism. But it should be mentioned that there are other factors which also determine the effectiveness of an evangelism strategy. You may have the best methods in mind, but it also takes sufficient financial resources to carry out those methods. So good methods should include ways of raising the necessary finances to carry them out. The spiritual gifts, qualifications, and dedication of the cross-cultural evangelists are also important factors in success. The direction and blessing of God throughout the process of planning and implementation is the single greatest factor that determines the success of cross-cultural evangelism. There is a reason farmers pray for rain. God can take control of the things that we cannot control in order to ensure a fruitful and bountiful spiritual harvest in our work. Since He is "not wanting any to perish" (2 Peter 3:9), we can trust Him to help our methods bear much fruit!

DEFINING METHODS

A method is a regular or systematic way of doing something. It is a standardized procedure for accomplishing a desired result. It is not a haphazard attempt to accomplish something. It is a way of proceeding in a task which is based upon knowledge and experience. The better the method, the more it will prescribe exactly what needs to be done and how a task should be accomplished.

No method is sacred. It is not a principle. It is a form of accomplishing a goal. In doing cross-cultural evangelism, the value of a method is limited to its usefulness in accomplishing the intended task in a particular culture. Even in doing spiritual work, methods are basically human creations. They can be changed, improved, or discarded according to their usefulness. Though the Holy Spirit may prompt a person to think of methods for one people group, that does not mean those methods must necessarily be used in any other place for any other people group.

Methods are a grouping of procedures for accomplishing a task. In farming his field, the farmer mentioned above has to perform quite a number of tasks. One of them is to plant the seed. There are a number of methods for planting seeds. What is the best kind of seed to use? How deep and with what should it be planted? How wet should the soil be? The best answers to all these questions would yield the best methods for planting that kind of crop in the field.

Similarly, in doing cross-cultural evangelism, there are a number of tasks that need to be performed. A method needs to be developed for performing each task the best way among a target people group. For instance, one of the important tasks for a team of cross-cultural evangelists is to learn to communicate well in the tongue of the target people. Chapter five teaches methods for doing this. Spending a maximum amount of time with the target people, using the Daily Learning Cycle, using the learner-servant-storyteller approach—all these are methods for learning a language well. These methods not only help us to accomplish our goal to communicate well in their language, but they also help us to learn their culture and minister to people at the same time. Those are important methods to reach important goals. Each need to be met (goal) should lead to methods that accomplish those goals the best way. The goal to learn the local language well leads to the development of several methods that help the learner reach the goal most effectively.

Here are some methods which have been used to reach evangelistic goals among some people groups:

Temporarily living in homes of local people	Street evangelistic meetings
Door-to-door witnessing	Crusade evangelism meetings

Small house churches	House-to-house visitation
Internet chat sites, YouTube, Christian movies	Bible correspondence courses
Bible translation into other languages	Apologist teaching on TV, DVD, and YouTube
Small group meetings in homes	Starting Christian Schools
Target language music festivals	Medical clinics
Kinship evangelism training	Media advertising

The above examples of methods are directly related to specific goals. By looking at each one, could you write a possible goal they would help accomplish? Notice how adopting some methods can lead to long-term commitments and large expenditures of resources. That is a good reason to consider carefully which methods will best reach the goals for each target people group. We should not adopt methods used elsewhere unless we are firmly convinced they are the very best way to reach our goals within a target people group strategy.

In using the planning model, it will be necessary to use good methods for each step along the way. That means good methods must be used for choosing a target people, selecting evangelism personnel, and implementing each element of the strategy. That is why this book concentrates on principles for each step of the planning model. Though some suggestions are given as examples, the people who will be most qualified to choose good methods will be those who are actually following the steps of the planning cycle. They will need to decide such things as (1) best methods for gathering the required information about unreached people groups and deciding which one to target, (2) a method for screening candidates to be appointed to the team, (3) methods for training team members, (4) methods for deciding which goals to pursue as priority in the overall strategy, (5) enculturation methods, (6) methods for starting the first churches, and (7) methods for training leaders among the new believers. These are just examples of the many methods which will need to be selected to provide a good cross-cultural evangelism strategy for each people group.

PRINCIPLES FOR SELECTING GOOD METHODS

Methods are tools for accomplishing chosen goals. They are a specific set of patterned activities designed to accomplish particular tasks. If we send a carpenter to build a building, he would need to be equipped with the correct tools. He would not cut boards with a hammer. When he is ready to drive a nail, he would not use his pencil. He must select correct tools for specific tasks. Similarly, when planners select methods to include in their strategy for cross-cultural ministry, they must learn to pick the right methods to accomplish their goals.

The first principle for selecting good methods is to decide if they are in harmony with scriptural principles. Methods which clearly violate biblical principles should not be considered for becoming part of a strategy. For instance, in some parts of the world (such as in a Hindu or Muslim country), there is a strong cultural prohibition against conversion to another religion. In such situations, converts may be beaten or even killed. A wrong kind of method for helping new converts in such places would be for all Christians to take up weapons to defend those who become believers. Though it is not right to harm people because they change their religion, it is also against the principles of the Bible to harm those who persecute us because of our faith (Matt. 5:11).

Remember also that methods that were used in the Bible are not necessarily better than other methods for reaching a particular people group. When we refer to a method as being biblical, it means that method is in harmony with biblical principles, not biblical methods. (See the discussion of "Principles vs. Methods" in chapter three). There are many effective methods which are used in evangelism today which did not exist in Bible times. Many of them, such as some of those listed above, were not even possible then. Though methods used in the Bible may be good examples of important principles, they are no more appropriate to evangelism today than any other method might be. There is nothing sacred about any method, but they do serve as good examples of the creativity of the believers then and the power of the Holy Spirit. As long as a method is in harmony with the principles of the Bible, it should be judged according to its own merits as a method for accomplishing a good goal. If it is not opposed to biblical principles, any method should be considered a possibility for use in cross-cultural evangelism.

Planners need some good principles for choosing good methods. Without such principles, they may not be able to agree on which methods are the best. One person may suggest a method he has already used himself. Another planner may think another method is best for his own reasons. Planners need a way of deciding the best methods without being so dependent upon their own personal experience or opinions.

Figure 8.b: SCALE OF METHOD SELECTION

PRINCIPLE	VERY LITTLE	SOME	VERY MUCH
Meets Stated Goals	1 2 3	4 5 6 7	8 9 10
Culturally Appropriate	1 2 3	4 5 6 7	8 9 10
Follows Autochthonous Principles	1 2 3	4 5 6 7	8 9 10
Laity Involvement	1 2 3	4 5 6 7	8 9 10
Financially Appropriate	1 2 3	4 5 6 7	8 9 10
Technologically Appropriate	1 2 3	4 5 6 7	8 9 10
Timing Is Appropriate	1 2 3	4 5 6 7	8 9 10

Total of all scores equals **Method Selection Quotient**: _______

Figure 8.b shows the **Scale of Method Selection**. The chart shows seven different principles useful for deciding the correctness or appropriateness of particular methods. These principles are explained below. To use the scale, it is only necessary to circle one of the numbers to the right of each principle listed, according to what you know about each method being considered for use within a specific target people strategy. This should be done for each method a group of strategy planners are considering. After circling the best number for each category, simply add all the numbers you circled. Your answer will be a number you can compare with the scores for other methods you have considering. This final score is called the **Method Selection**

Quotient (MSQ). By comparing the MSQ for one method with those of other methods, it will be easier to see which one will be the most appropriate to meet each of the stated goals.

There are different ways to fill in the Scale of Method Selection. You may want different people to fill in the scale for each of the different methods being considered. Then the average score for each method can be calculated by totaling all their MSQ results, then dividing by the number of people who filled in the scale for each method. This should be limited to planners and researchers who have studied the target people group as thoroughly as possible. Another way to use the scale is for the planners to simply sit down and discuss what scores should be given for each category until they agree on each score and then add them up. Whatever method is used, the final MSQ for each method will be the result of a mutually considered assessment by the whole planning group. Whatever system is used for filling in the scale, including one you think will work better than either of these two, the scale is a useful tool to help you more effectively reach your strategy goals.

Each of the principles on the Scale of Method Selection are explained below. This will help you decide how to score each category when filling in the scale.

Meets Stated Goals: Methods must be directly linked to reaching the stated goals in the strategy. Though this cannot be the only principle for selecting methods, it is among the most important. Methods should result from well-stated long- and intermediate-range goals. The more probability that a method will be effective in helping to reach a goal, the higher the score for that method on the scale. As we discussed in chapter seven, intermediate goals are designed to meet long-range goals. Methods help to reach intermediate goals like is shown in figure 8.c.

Figure 8.c

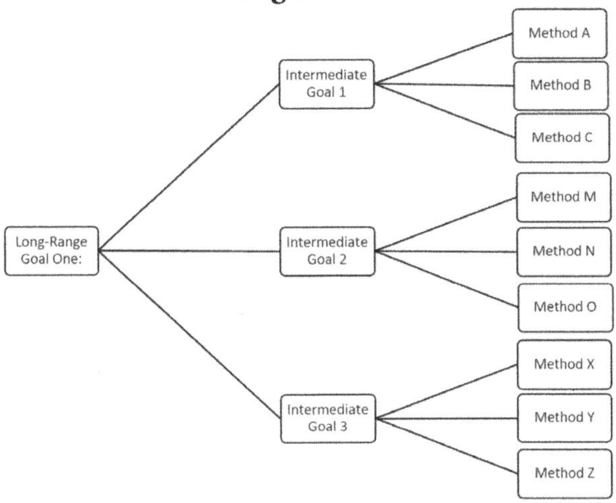

According to the chart, Methods A, B, and C should be effective in helping us to reach Intermediate Goal 1. Similarly, Methods M, N, and O will help us reach Intermediate Goal 2; and Methods X, Y, and Z should help us reach Intermediate Goal 3. Intermediate Goals 1, 2, and 3 should enable us to complete Long-Range Goal One. This shows how good methods should be tied to good goals. The more planners agree that a particular method will be effective in reaching the stated goals, the higher the score it should be given on this category of the scale.

Culturally Appropriate: The method being considered should be measured as to its compatibility with the culture of the target people. A method may look appropriate in the eyes of the strategy planners. But they must be careful not to judge its effectiveness according to how it has worked in other cultures or even their own. It must be assessed according to how effective it will be in the target culture.

This can be demonstrated by looking at two church groups who decided to send cross-cultural evangelists into China many years ago. The first groups sent a team of two women evangelists. They were dedicated workers who spoke the local language fluently and labored many years to plant churches in one region of China. After many years, they had a small group of believers meeting in one church. But most of the congregation were women and children. There were hardly any men present at all. The children would attend the Sunday Bible class and other meetings, but they would fall away when their fathers would refuse them permission to be baptized when they were older. The ladies asked their supporting churches back home to pray for that part of China because the people's hearts were hard, and they were slow to receive the Gospel message.

Then another group of churches decided to send a cross-cultural evangelism team to that same area of China. But they did not send only women. They sent a number of families to start churches. Many people in the Sending Churches sold property and sacrificed greatly to send the families. The Chinese people in the area quickly identified with those families and their positive witness in the area. Within just a few years, there were dozens of congregations of new believers springing up over the entire area which was supposed to be so hardened against the Gospel (Chua 1975, 968).[48]

The basic difference between outstanding success and little results in that area of China had little to do with the dedication and ability of the evangelists. All were capable and dedicated to their work for God. The difference was in the method for making the cross-cultural evangelism teams. Within the target people group, it was the men, not the women, who led the decision-making processes. According to their culture, it was not appropriate for the men to receive teaching from women. That is similar to the cultures of Asia Minor in Bible times (see 1 Tim. 2:12). So there were little results until the Gospel came to be represented by dedicated families. The culture was very family oriented. As the Gospel message grew, many times it would spread through family ties. Many times families would evangelize new areas through kinship ties. The Chinese there could only relate to God in terms of dedication to Him as whole families. That led to the conversion of many people in that region. The basic difference did not lie in the spiritual dedication of the women who were sent, but in the method for choosing members of the cross-culture evangelism teams. Only sending unmarried women

---

[48] https://www.sermoncentral.com/sermons/social-hindrances-in-cross-cultural-evangelism-paul-fritz-sermon-on-evangelism-fear-of-38299.

as the team, regardless of how dedicated they were, proved to be a culturally inappropriate method to evangelize that people group.

Many times the most culturally appropriate method can be learned by studying the methods of the target people. How do they convey important messages? In what kind of circumstances? Who can best do it in their culture? How and when do they do it? Why are some messages given importance and others not? Choosing the best methods will prove to be very important and greatly affect the success of the whole evangelism effort. If the wrong kind of method is used, it can cause a negative response by the people.

This is especially important when the message is first communicated. Remember the cross-cultural evangelist in Africa who waited two years before he told anyone why he and his family came to live in their village? Planners should ask themselves questions like, who should hear the message first? When, where, and how should the message be first communicated? What kind of trust relationships must be established first, and what will be required on the part of the team to create those relationships? What communication forms would be best? These kinds of questions can best be answered by studying how important messages are conveyed and by whom in the target culture. The more the initial Gospel message conforms to the behavioral norms of the target culture, the greater will be its potential long- and short-term.

Follows Autochthonous Principles: Each method should also be examined to determine how much it is in harmony with autochthonous principles. A particular method may have some potential for reaching stated goals and be culturally appropriate, but still not conform to some of the principles for starting autochthonous churches.

One team of Mexican cross-cultural evangelists was sent to minister to an unreached people group in Mexico. Their preparation and training were very good. They were dedicated to their work, and they loved the target people. For the most part, they used good methods in their evangelism. But they made the mistake of following a method they had in their own culture. In their culture, only ordained ministers were allowed to baptize people and officiate at the ceremony of the Lord's Supper. And in their churches, before they could be ordained, they had to have many years of experience and training. The team was very successful at first in starting new churches. But after they started about a dozen churches, the growth began to slow down rapidly. Each church had their own local leaders and a pastor who was licensed to preach, but he was not ordained. He was not allowed to baptize and lead communion services. This was culturally accepted due to the influence of the Catholic Church and the traditional role of priests. So every time there was a need to have a communion service or baptize new believers, the cross-cultural evangelists were called to travel to all the churches to lead in these ceremonial services. This kept the evangelists so busy, they had too little time to work on starting other churches and training local leaders. It also discouraged the licensed pastors from taking much initiative to start new churches because they felt they were second-class ministers.

That is an example of using a method that worked against the Principle of Reproducibility. At first it appeared the cross-cultural evangelists' work was very successful. They used good principles for starting the churches. They trained people in evangelism. But their method for training leadership was not ***infinitely reproducible***! It proved impossible to qualify enough leaders for the external concept of qualifying for ordination fast enough to keep pace with the growth of the churches. The cross-cultural evangelists should have taught local leaders how to examine candidates and baptize them! They should also have authorized them to hold their own communion services, teaching clearly the symbolism of the elements of the Eucharist. This also illustrates why Jesus instructed his followers to make disciples and baptize them themselves (Matt. 28:19–20)! The evangelists had confused a cultural form with a biblical principle! Jesus' own teaching shows that the one who makes a disciple is quite qualified to baptize that disciple like Phillip did the Ethiopian eunuch (Acts 8:26–39). The principle is that new believers be baptized. The cultural form that is flexible is who does the baptizing. Since local believers should be making most of the converts, they should also do most of the baptizing.

Involvement of the Laity: Whether it is in the target culture or in the evangelist's own culture, methods which encourage the involvement of nonpaid workers are the most reproducible and effective. It is important to remember that pastors, teachers, evangelists, prophets, and apostles are gifts of ministry given by the Lord to the church. Their primary responsibility is to "equip the saints for the work of the ministry" (Eph. 4:11–12). That means it is the nonpaid lay members of the church who should be actively involved in every phase of the church's work. It does not imply that those who are ministry gifts to the church in those five roles have to be paid to do it. They have to be called to do it. If they can find a way to be supported without being paid, that will not diminish their importance or the value of their ministries. Methods which involve reproducing nonprofessional normal people into ministry should be given a high priority. In many rapidly growing and multiplying groups of churches around the world, most of the people called to be one of those five ministry gifts to the churches are not paid to do so.

The apostle Paul chose many times not to be dependent financially on the churches he planted, such as in Acts 20:34. Yet he was sent to work cross-culturally by help of offerings by the people in Antioch where he had a large part in building up that church (Acts 13:1–3). The principle is to do the work God calls us to do. How we are supported to do so is variable. It can result from the offerings (the labor) of others, or it can result from our own labor. Neither method is holy. Yet the labor of people who are not paid to spread the Gospel is usually more respected in the minds of those we try to reach because it requires sacrifice on the part of the one who does it. *This book is being written by a fellow cross-cultural laborer who has almost completely supported the ministry he does by the labor of his own hands for twenty-seven years! And that has allowed him (me) to labor for the Lord in sixty-nine countries!*

In the target culture, it is important to choose methods that involve strong participation by laypeople—people who do not get paid to work for God. Any method that elevates those chosen for leadership above other leaders in actually carrying out the ministries of the churches should be avoided as much as possible. That is true whether they are paid by offerings or work for God using their own resources. These paid or unpaid workers at the local church level should be involved in making the decisions concerning the ministries of those churches as much as possible. Being paid does not automatically elevate one's status before God or before people. Yes, it is biblical to teach believers to give! But the more that giving can be used to start other churches and help the needy, the better. Culturally appropriate ways of making decisions about ministry, planning, and carrying out plans for evangelism, building churches, and supporting God's work should all involve strong input by those involved in doing those ministries—with or without pay to do so. Methods which encourage widespread involvement by all the local believers who can and will participate sacrificially should be given higher priority than those that do not.

Financially Appropriate: Methods must also be judged in terms of the amount of money they will cost. The key element in determining the financial appropriateness is balance. While it is more common not to have enough money to carry out a cross-cultural ministry strategy, it is also possible to use too much money to carry out parts of that strategy, making the effort unbalanced and ineffective. Also, some methods are more important than others because they have greater potential for reaching the most important goals. A certain method may appear very effective when judged by itself. But if it requires that most of the money for implementing a strategy would be needed for using that method, it is probably an indication that the method should not be used. It would rob too much money away from other important methods.

For instance, let's assume a team of evangelists enters a target people group which is very interaction-conscious and event-oriented. The team wants to plan the best method for using a certain amount of money they have available for evangelism goals. They see the need to provide money for three needs: (1) evangelism literature, (2) funds to help pay travel for local people who want to evangelize relatives in a distant area, and (3) money to purchase a speaker system for large evangelism meetings. They want to decide between three methods for literature distribution: (1) print many thousands of copies of several Gospel tracts and drop them over the villages from an airplane. This would cost all the money they have for evangelism. (2) Print many thousands of copies of one tract, and quickly leave one copy at every home. This will cost only 10 percent of the money available to them. Or (3) print fewer copies of several tracts to meet different kinds of needs, and include a Bible portion in a packet of literature. This would also cost 10 percent of the money available. They would make those packets available for local believers to use as they visit friends and relatives.

Which method do you think would be most financially appropriate? In an interaction-conscious culture, the literature would be more highly valued by those who receive it if they receive it from friends and relatives. So the third method would be the best to choose. The first two methods would be culturally much less appropriate. The first method would also cost too much. Using the third method, the literature distribution would also be the most effective, and those who receive it would be targeted for witness through already established relationships. They would value the literature more highly because it came from people they know. It would also allow other funds to be available for methods to meet other goals in the evangelism strategy for the target people. The cost of methods to meet one goal should be weighed against the cost of financing methods to reach other necessary goals.

Technologically Appropriate: Every culture has its own kinds of technology. This refers to the way people use tools to take care of their daily needs and wants. In highly industrialized countries, the technology is based upon highly developed machines, like automobiles, airplanes, electric appliances, computers, televisions, and handheld electronic devices. In lesser-developed countries, the people may have a different set of technologies to meet their needs. They may use more human labor than they do machines. They may plow their fields with draft animals or different kinds of less expensive machines. They may not have community water and sewer systems, but make do in other ways. They may cook in earthen ovens with wood fires, and travel with carts, bicycles, or motorbikes. The danger here is in using methods for evangelism that are foreign to the target people. The technology used must be capable of reproduction by the evangelists of the target people.

An evangelist from North America was working in a poor country in Asia. One day, he received an invitation to preach to the people of three villages in the interior of the country. He was from a country with a very highly developed base of machine technology. He was one of the first to buy the (then) new wristwatches which tells time with a digital display of the numbers. He also had a speedboat to travel into the many areas of that country which could only be reached by waterways. So when he received the invitation to preach to the people of those three villages, he remembered they were located on the banks of a small riverway into the interior of the country. To save about one day's travel by regular boats, he used the speedboat to get to the villages. The people had never seen such a boat or heard such a loud engine. They were only a little less frightened than their cattle, which ran away at the roar of the engine.

The evangelist preached to the people for over two hours. It seemed the people were very interested to hear what he was saying. Finally, he asked the crowd if they had any questions. At first they said nothing. Finally, one older man asked the two questions most on the minds of everyone. How much did that boat cost? What did you pay for that wristwatch?

The evangelist was surprised. It seemed as if the people had heard little of the message he preached. Slowly he began to realize that his North American technology was causing "noise" in the communication process. From then on, when he travelled to evangelize in a new area, he left his watch and boat at home. He began to use the local methods of travel and telling time. This made his work much more effective.

It is important that we use technology that is appropriate for the target culture. In many countries, even poor people now have cell phones. Yet they do not have computers and high-tech machinery. Cell phones are bypassing the industrial revolution. While they represent a danger and destabilizing factor for many cultures, they also represent an opportunity to communicate the Gospel more effectively and encourage new believers. Effective evangelism and training in almost any target culture must include methods to use locally available technologies effectively. That includes cell phones. While most developing countries do not yet use 4G telephone systems, they will be arriving there soon enough. Eventually, they will even have 5G or 6G capabilities or better. Strategy planning should include advanced planning on how to use such technologies for spread of the Gospel, communication between believers, encryption technology, and training.

Timing Correct: Methods should be correct in their timing in two ways. First, they should be placed in the overall strategy at the right time in relationship to other methods. To state it another way, they should meet the goals which are placed in the best order in the planning strategy. They should neither be too soon or too late. To the greatest degree possible, they should be planned in advance enough to be used at the right times with the appropriate resources during the implementation of the strategy. When planners agree on goals, the order and timing of the methods that reach those goals may seem correct to them. But as they begin to examine the best methods more closely, they may decide that they should change the order of some of those goals and methods.

Another way the timing of a method should be correct is in how long it actually takes to implement the method. If one goal must be completed before beginning another goal, it will be important to estimate the amount of time different methods will require to help complete that goal. If the time is too long, either the method should not be used or the timing of the goal must be changed. The time needed to carry out particular methods should be in harmony with the timing of the steps in the planning strategy. This will become clearer by reading the strategy planning example at the end of this chapter. The more compatible the amount of time needed for a method, the higher the score it should be given on this category of the scale.

The Scale of Method Selection can be a very useful tool for those who plan strategies to evangelize target people groups. It helps planners weigh the value and benefits of different methods against their goals and against one another. It helps them select those methods which are best suited for use among a specific people group. It also helps them to organize the priority and timing of their goals and methods. When using methods everyone can agree upon, the scale provides a very useful checklist for planners. And when decisions are more difficult, the scale can become a very important way to bring objective analysis into the planning process.

One thing this scale is not capable of doing is giving people ideas for possible methods. It can help planners weigh methods against one another, but the power of the Holy Spirit is required to help planners find and devise effective methods. The scale can help refine the methods and make them better, but the One whom Jesus has sent to "teach you all things" (the Holy Spirit [John 14:26]) is the one upon whom we must depend for creative ideas about useful methods. By using the scale to examine those ideas, we will learn which ones can best be used to reach each people group.

DESIGNING THE STRATEGY

Figure 8.d: Strategy Planning Model

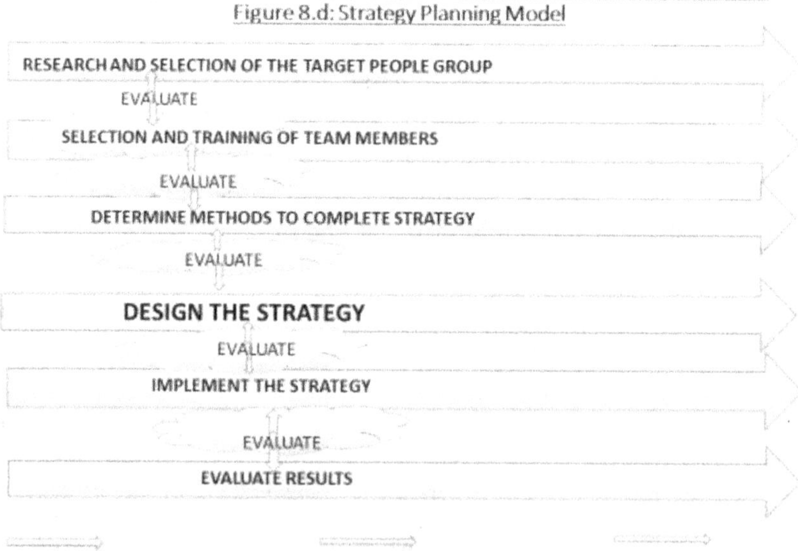

Designing the strategy is a crucial stage of the planning model. It is the stage where the spiritual insights, ideas, research, goals, and faith of the whole strategy planning group comes together to form an effective guide to all those involved in the effort to evangelize a specific people group. It should be usable for years as an effective tool for that purpose. In this section, we will first discuss the characteristics of good strategy planning. Then we will investigate the levels of strategy planning. Finally, we will use a case study to actually plan a strategy.

CHARACTERISTICS OF A GOOD STRATEGY

We have been studying the needs and benefits of planning strategies throughout chapters seven and eight. But before we move into the details of actually designing a strategy, it is valuable to summarize the nature and characteristics of good strategy planning to guide us in our task. Five characteristics of good strategy are listed and explained here.

Receptor-Oriented: In chapter six, we discussed the need for all phases of cross-cultural evangelism to be receptor-oriented. Goals and methods must fit into the value systems and behavior patterns of the target culture. The communication of the Gospel to the people group should be in their own mother tongue and use their own communication forms. Evangelists and converts should be trained not to disrupt the social system except to bring kingdom change which is positive in the eyes of most of the people. Such social change should only result from the converts' growing understanding of biblical principles and the needs of their society. Goals and methods of the strategy should be designed to bring people to a decision for Christ according to autochthonous decision-making processes. The whole strategy should be designed to help the target people make deep, worldview-level, life-changing decisions for Christ. It should be receptor-oriented in terms of using culturally appropriate organizational forms in the new churches being established. It should also be receptor-oriented in terms of guiding new believers on how to build a positive image for themselves and the Gospel in their whole society. Receptor-oriented thinking should guide team members as they develop their goals and methods throughout the church-planting process.

Needs-Centered: Good strategies base their goals on the needs of the target people. Every unreached group has a great spiritual need to find Christ real in their lives. They need to have opportunity to see the Lord meet their needs through prayer and following scriptural principles for living. That must always be the primary need for which strategies are designed.

But each people group also has social needs. Goals and methods for meeting spiritual needs often lead to opportunities to meet social needs. As people begin to accept Christ among a target people, they should be trained and encouraged to be a blessing to their communities and society as a whole. Societies which are not based upon Christian principles will have many needs. After becoming Christians, members of the target culture should be encouraged not to turn their backs on their society. Jesus definitely expects his followers to have an impact on their society (John 17:14–16, Matt. 5:13–15). If research shows there are glaring social needs among a target people, the strategy should include goals which help the local believers change their society in the areas of need.

We related earlier how the tribal peoples of the mountains of Eastern Indonesia became Christians. One of the changes the believers brought to society was to stop killing women as "witches" after a man would die. This is an example of how believers can change their society for the better. Good strategies pinpoint those areas where need for societal change is the greatest, and they include those changes as part of the goals. The key is to be sure new believers are taking the initiative to make those changes.

Good evangelism strategies also pay close attention to survival needs. If large portions of the target people are not capable of meeting their needs for food, clothing, shelter, or medical help, this should be an important subject in the strategy planning. When a person's survival needs go unmet for very long, it becomes almost impossible for him or her to hear and receive the Gospel effectively. The human impulse for survival is very strong. When people are experiencing great difficulty in surviving, they will view everything that comes into their lives according to its potential to help them meet their survival needs. Such need introduces an unacceptable level of "noise" in the communication process. Simply preaching the Gospel to people in such a situation is cruel. The Gospel must first be demonstrated by helping meet survival needs before people can listen with open hearts. That is why Jesus commands us to help meet their needs (Matt. 25:31–46).

The author labored as a cross-cultural evangelist in the country of Bangladesh just after the war between East and West Pakistan resulted in East Pakistan becoming the country of Bangladesh. During the war, almost all the leaders of East Pakistan were slaughtered, including military, university students, political leaders, teachers, and wealthy businesspeople—about one million people. The country had been stripped bare right down to the motor vehicles, tractors, and even the microscopes in laboratories. Millions were thrust into total poverty within a two-week period of time.

Those of us there for cross-cultural evangelism could not ignore that fact. When a person is destitute, the first thing lost is housing, then clothing, then food, and finally health. Those who had lost all those things could not hear the Gospel from us. They had to see it! At one point, we were feeding thirteen thousand people every day just to keep them alive! We also ran a medical clinic to help survivors get well. We would use donated USAID sorghum grits plus a few vegetables from the market to give them six hundred calories a day to keep them alive. We could not feed everyone, but we could tell who was most needy by the condition of their clothes and how their bodies were wasting away. I have gotten up at 5:00 a.m. in the morning only to discover that a starving baby who had been brought to our gate had died just before I arose from sleep. While we were able to save every baby who came to us alive, I was haunted by those who died!

In that kind of situation, you have to show people the love of God by helping them. After they have recovered, then they will have a good witness and an opportunity to hear the Gospel without fear of coercion or needing to become "rice Christians" to survive.

A word of caution should be given concerning survival needs. The strategy should try to meet survival needs, but resources should be balanced between meeting those needs and the spiritual needs of the target people. The need for evangelism must remain primary. It would be a tragedy to help many people survive tragedy physically only to see them lost spiritually due to our own neglect of their spiritual needs. The numbers of people who are experiencing survival needs, the amount of help the people are receiving from other organizations, the amount of money available to implement the whole strategy—all these factors must be considered in deciding how to include the meeting of survival needs in a strategy.

As a general rule, it is best not to start ongoing institutions such as hospitals and clinics to meet such needs in rural areas. It may be necessary in an urban area where the needs will be continual due to urbanization and poverty, and so long as the funds and personnel will be available as part of a long-term strategy. While funds for such ministries will generally be easier to raise in the short run, that is not necessarily true in the long run. The resulting shortage of funds and vision for evangelism can actually detract from efforts to win specific people groups to the Lord if it is not a balanced effort. Instead of starting large long-lasting institutions, it is often better to concentrate on meeting survival needs on an emergency basis and/or developmental basis. Development refers to methods of helping the people supply their own needs within their own culture by introducing new or improved methods for earning money. Examples would be training and improving methods for farming, fishing, raising animals, or starting new businesses. The goals and methods of good strategies balance the resources available to help meet spiritual, survival, and social needs of the people in that order!

Process-Oriented: Good strategies are not static. Goals and methods should not be set once, then considered unchangeable. Good strategies emerge through a process over a period of time. At each level and step of the planning process, new and important information and insights will become available. Strategies must be kept flexible enough to allow for change as the planning and implementation progresses. Evaluation of strategies and striving to make them flexible as circumstances and needs change must remain paramount.

As an example, let's assume a strategy has already been agreed upon for evangelizing a certain target people. Their needs have been analyzed, and the cross-cultural evangelism team has been selected and trained. The strategy is in place, and the team has been sent to the field to enter the target culture. After arriving, the team immediately begins to notice that there are people without shelter and clothing. They soon learn that there was a devastating flood the week before they arrived. It destroyed a large percentage of the crops and washed away many homes and food supplies. Since there was not an apparent need at the survival level, the planning team did not set goals to meet survival needs in the planning process. So the evangelists quickly inform their leaders and supporters back home of the situation, and goals and funding are quickly established to meet survival needs. Resources for meeting other goals are also quickly transferred to meet survival needs because of their emergency nature. After the period of the emergency was over, funds were reallocated back to the original strategy purposes. This is an example of the kind of flexibility needed throughout the process of planning and implementing evangelism strategies.

The best strategies provide for the flexibility needed to deal with unforeseen circumstances and needs that can arise during the implementation of the strategy. They include good organization for efforts on the field and at home to make good decisions smoothly and wisely. Because strategy requires constant evaluation of planned results, and because there will always be unforeseen circumstances, good strategies are process-oriented. They are flexible enough to allow for quick and appropriate changes as needed. There must also be enough clear and consistent communication between all those involved to allow for adjustments to be made efficiently. This will become even more evident through the case study in the last part of this chapter.

Oriented Toward Group Change: Good strategies aim for conversion of the whole target people and their society, not just individuals. Strategies which overstress the individual nature of conversion often develop methods which are only effective for reaching a small percentage of the target people. Strategies should contain goals and methods designed to bring the mainstream of the target people closer and closer to embracing the Gospel.

The **"conversion as a process" chart** (figure 6.g) is a good tool to use in designing group-oriented strategy for goals and methods. Part of the research about the target people should focus on where on the chart the majority of the target people would fit. For example, research may show that the mainstream of the target people's society would fit at -4 on the **Spiritual** and **Emotional** tracks of the chart, and at -3 on the **Mental** track. That means that, as a people, they would have some knowledge of the Gospel, but little interest in knowing more about Christianity. With such an evaluation, strategy planners should include goals and methods which are designed to move as many people as possible to the right of the chart beginning with where they are. They should be brought along in the conversion process from -4 to -3 to -2, etc., until they come to the -1 level as a group as much as possible. Then they will be in a position as a people group to have an adequate chance to accept Christ and the good news about him in greater numbers. The goals and methods developed to accomplish this would also be those necessary to begin the first group of believers as a church. But they would also be designed to help the new converts become very inclusive in their attitude toward reaching the mainstream of their society. The purpose would not just be to help more people become believers, but also to help the new believers become more capable of winning people to Christ in the mainstream of their society. They would enhance this process by such things as helping to meet community needs, and actively identifying with the community as a whole. It is the opposite of isolating themselves from the mainstream of their society as believers. These concepts were discussed in chapter three as well as chapter six. The key is to design a strategy that as much as possible helps the whole society gain an increasingly positive attitude toward Christians and Christianity. As the witness of the evangelists and believers increases, this will keep the mainstream of the society aware of the dynamic and positive Gospel witness.

Goal-Oriented: The most effective strategies use specific goals to guide the direction and progress of the whole cross-cultural evangelism effort. Well-stated and well-implemented goals are at the heart of the true benefits of strategy planning. Usually, the better the goals and methods, the better will be the harvest of souls. Good goals help orient people to specific needs and tasks. Good goals demand positive action by those involved. When everyone agrees on goals, they are committing themselves to action to fulfill those goals.

Good goals also provide an excellent basis for checking the progress of the work. The primary goal of those who are in business is usually to make money. People who work for businessmen know their purpose is to help the business make money. Though there will be other guidelines for their work, the employees are given responsibilities, promoted, or dismissed according to their ability to help the business make money.

Good strategies for church reproduction also provide goals which help those implementing them to know exactly what kinds of work they should be doing and why. Their success can be measured against the goals they are pursuing. For instance, let's assume one of the goals in a strategy is to train six local leaders as pastors who are capable of leading their churches without direct help from outside. This goal is to be met within two years after the first church chooses their pastor. Whatever person assumes the responsibility for reaching that goal knows he must have a training system operating very soon after the first group of believers start meeting together. At least six leaders will be needed to help start those new churches. They will need to be trained in starting churches as well as in pastoring them. If two years are needed to train these pastors, the training program must be prepared ahead of time. If the training program will require only one year, the evangelist knows he can plan the program and begin the training after the first church is formed. Goals are specific and time-oriented in order to guide directly in the work. They also provide a standard to measure our progress. Just as important, they help us feel more accountable to the Lord for the work we undertake for him.

LEVELS OF GOOD STRATEGY PLANNING

Planning strategies for cross-cultural evangelism need not be a complicated task. But it is helpful to get a structural overview of the method for designing a strategy. Figure 8.e shows the flow of the overall structure, with five different levels of planning. Each successive level requires a more detailed and specific set of goals and methods.

FIGURE 8.e: PLANNING PROCESS OBJECTIVE FLOW

PRIMARY PURPOSE ⟹ SECONDARY GOAL ⟹ INTERMEDIATE GOAL ⟹ METHOD ⟹ OBJECTIVE

Level One—Primary Purpose: This is the beginning level of planning strategy. It simply requires one specific, measurable statement of the total purpose of the cross-cultural evangelism work among a target people. It is the overall primary goal of the work. It must be stated specifically, and be measurable in terms of quantities and time.

The primary purpose should be established sometime toward the beginning stages of the planning process, and it should become the anchor that defines the project clearly. It could be established immediately after the beginning of the research on the target people is completed. It could be set after the cross-cultural evangelism team is chosen. The team members should be in agreement about the goal before it is finalized. Whenever the primary goal is set, it must become the foundational goal upon which all the other goals and methods will be based.

In the beginning of chapter seven, we discussed methods for setting good goals. The example used to demonstrate how to make a goal specific and measurable was actually an example of stating the primary purpose of an evangelism strategy. The final goal we cited was "Our goal is to persuade 20 percent of the Yakmal Tribe to accept Christ as Lord and Savior, and serve him in autochthonous churches within nine years." This is a good example of how to make a statement of primary purpose. It meets all the requirements of good goals, and it is broad enough to describe the overall goal we intend to reach.

Level Two—Secondary Goals: The second level of goals includes the goals needed to be sure the primary goal is accomplished. The primary goal needs to be divided into the major kinds of activities needed to successfully fulfill the primary purpose. In figure 8.c, the secondary goals are those represented as Goal 1, Goal 2, and Goal 3. Like all goals, the secondary goals should be specific and measurable in terms of time and quantity. When we discussed methods for goal setting, in the first part of chapter seven, we discussed secondary goals. Looking in that section, you will find six secondary goals which are tied to the primary purpose we discussed above.

Notice how those secondary goals almost give an outline of the major kinds of activities necessary to fulfill the primary purpose. By successfully completing each of those six major activities, it should be possible to meet the requirements of the primary purpose. Secondary goals provide a broad strategy statement of what needs to be accomplished.

Level Three—Intermediate Goals: Intermediate goals break down secondary goals into more specific and manageable goals. They define what specific smaller goals must be met in order to reach the larger secondary goals. As before, these third-level intermediate goals flow out of the second-level goals. They specifically define the kinds of activities necessary to reach those second-level goals.

Let's continue with our example by writing some intermediate goals for Secondary Goal One in our above example:

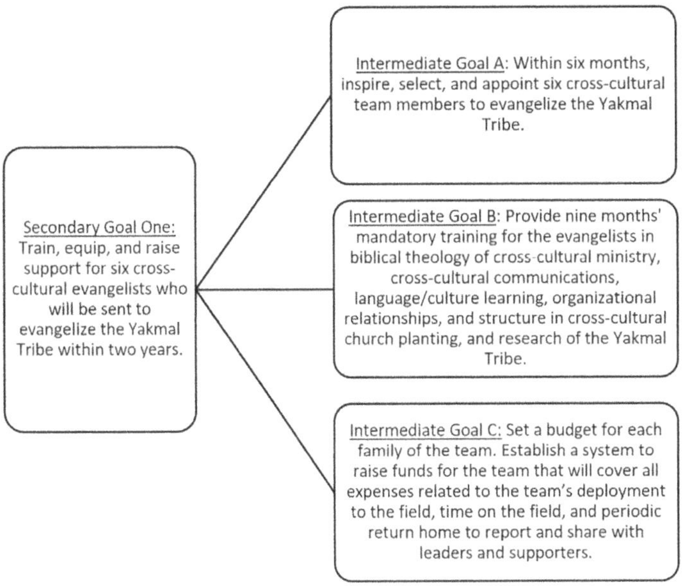

Secondary Goal One: Train, equip, and raise support for six cross-cultural evangelists who will be sent to evangelize the Yakmal Tribe within two years.
Intermediate Goal A: Within six months, inspire, select, and appoint six cross-cultural team members to evangelize the Yakmal Tribe.
Intermediate Goal B: Provide nine months' mandatory training for the evangelists in biblical theology of cross-cultural ministry, cross-cultural communications, language/culture learning, organizational relationships, and structure in cross-cultural church planting, and research of the Yakmal Tribe.
Intermediate Goal C: Set a budget for each family of the team. Establish a system to raise funds for the team that will cover all expenses related to the team's deployment to the field, time on the field, and periodic return home to report and share with leaders and supporters.

From the above example, it is easy to see how intermediate goals further define the activities necessary to reach secondary goals. By following this system, the third-level goals become very useful. They point the people involved toward the specific kinds of activities necessary to make the strategy successful. As a general rule, it is usually best to plan strategies completely through this third level before beginning to implement any of the strategy. This will give those involved specific direction concerning what roles they will plan in completing the project. Those who are appointed to the cross-cultural evangelism team will be able to understand the exact nature of their preparation and the goals they will work to reach. Those responsible for further planning will have the framework firmly in place for finishing their tasks. It is helpful for at least the one who will become team leader of the cross-cultural evangelism team to be part of developing these three levels of planning.

Level Four—Methods: The first three levels of strategy statements serve to precisely define the goals of the plan. At this fourth level, it is necessary to determine which methods will be the most effective for reaching those goals. We discussed methods at length in a previous section. You are familiar with their purpose and method of selection. Remember that methods emerge from the goals they are designed to fulfill, as well as the culture and needs of the peoples being reached. Using our continuing example of evangelizing the Yakmal Tribe, some possible methods based upon Intermediate Goal C might look like this:

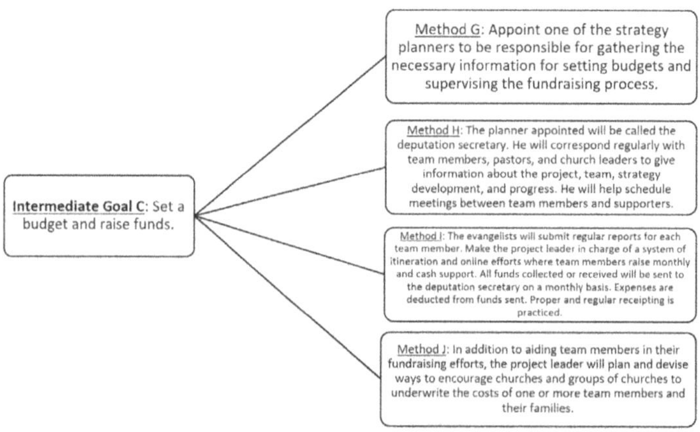

Intermediate Goal C: Set a budget and raise funds.
Method G: Appoint one of the strategy planners to be responsible for gathering the necessary information for setting budgets and supervising the fundraising process.
Method H: The planner appointed will be called the deputation secretary. He will correspond regularly with team members, pastors, and church leaders to give information about the project, team, strategy development, and progress. He will help schedule meetings between team members and supporters.
Method I: The evangelists will submit regular reports for each team member. Make the project leader in charge of a system of itineration and online efforts where team members raise monthly and cash support. All funds collected or received will be sent to the deputation secretary on a monthly basis. Expenses are deducted from funds sent. Proper and regular receipting is practiced.
Method J: In addition to aiding team members in their fundraising efforts, the project leader will plan and devise ways to encourage churches and groups of churches to underwrite the costs of one or more team members and their families.

Level Five: Objectives: The fifth level of strategy planning emerges from both the third and fourth levels. The methods and intermediate goals need one more level of planning. Objectives are precise statements of specific tasks which need to be completed. They combine the purposes of intermediate goals and the methods into small clearly defined tasks. This can best be understood by illustrating one step further in our example above. Using Intermediate Goal C and Method G, we could write objectives like these:

Objective 1: The strategy planners shall appoint a budget committee of four people to meet with the strategy leader at least once a month to approve or change budgets for the team and the ministries they plan to complete.

Objective 2: The strategy leader, together with the ministry team leader and deputation secretary, will gather all the necessary information for establishing the monthly living costs, travel costs, training expenses, field ministry project expenses, etc., for each evangelist and his family. This information, together with recommended budgets for each family, will be submitted to the supporting churches' budget committee for approvals. This must be available before the team members have completed four months of the nine-month training program.

Objective 3: Before the cross-cultural evangelism team has completed one month of their training, the strategy leader shall have prepared copies of each of the following forms for use in supervising the fundraising activities of team members:

a. **Monthly Deputation Report:** Lists all travel, postage, online communication, and other deputation (fundraising) expenses related to raising budgets. These expenses are to be balanced against offerings received, and unused funds are to be sent to the deputation secretary for deposit in individual accounts for the future expenses of team members.
b. **Deputation Policy Manual:** The strategy leader and deputation secretary, or someone they designate, shall prepare a policy manual that defines the rules of conduct and work of the team members during their training and deputation while they are preparing to go to the field where they will minister. The duties and obligations of the evangelists will be clearly stated concerning training requirements; travel,

> housing, and living allowances; plus relationships with supporters and leadership. Each person involved shall be given this manual to use as a guide to all their activities in preparation to depart for field ministry.

Notice that these objectives describe the specific tasks necessary to fulfill those parts of Intermediate Goal C, which is also related to Method G. From each method emerges several objectives which help to reach the intermediate goal. There may be only a few objectives, or a large number for each method listed. Notice also that these objectives are really narrowly defined smaller goals. They are precise actions which must be taken, and they are measurable in terms of time and quantity.

This fifth level of strategy planning provides specific tasks which must be completed in order to fulfill the larger goals of the strategy. It is a very big help to planners and to those responsible to meet specific goals and objectives of the strategy. It also keeps everyone informed concerning how their own work fits into the overall strategy and work of others.

It is in the fourth and fifth levels of planning that much of the daily decision-making is required. These are the "what to do and how to do it" levels of the strategy. Accordingly, these levels should be developed with the participation of the team members as much as possible. They will be the ones actually doing the work. They should be part of the planning process at this level. This is especially important when the objectives are refined in the field of ministry.

A STRATEGY PLANNING CASE STUDY

The best way to learn how to plan strategies for cross-cultural evangelism is to practice doing so where there is an actual need. This section takes you through an actual case of planning a strategy to reach a real unreached people group. Because we have only limited space here which we can devote to this case study, we cannot show the development of the total strategy. We will concentrate on the first three levels of strategy planning—primary purposes, secondary goals, and intermediate goals. We will include in our strategy planning to the first four stages of the planning model: (1) the target people, (2) evangelism personnel, (3) deciding methods, (4) designing the strategy. The implementation and evaluation stages will be discussed in chapter nine. It will be helpful to refer to figure 8.c as you read through this case study. In order to show as much of the strategy as possible, we will explain only those parts that seem to be most necessary. From the above discussions, it should be easy to follow the development of the strategy.

Let us suppose that you have been appointed to be part of a five-person strategy planning committee which we will abbreviate as SPC. This is a committee appointed by, or agreeing to work with, your group of churches in your own country. You have been selected to be a member of that committee, so this describes the work you and your SPC members need to perform. You are to plan, organize, prepare, and send a team of cross-cultural evangelists to plant churches among an unreached Muslim people group. The SPC will do the research and select that group.

One member of your SPC is an experienced evangelist who feels that God has called him and his family to cross-cultural evangelism within an unreached people. His name is Paul. In the first meeting of the SPC, Paul is selected to research Muslim people groups who would be most likely to be receptive to the Gospel, and who are unreached.

Paul remembers his training in cross-cultural evangelism. His professor taught that Muslims who live furthest away from Mecca are much more likely to be receptive to the Gospel. So he studied the Muslim groups in Indonesia. He knows from his training that the Joshua Project probably has the latest and most accurate information on Muslim people groups. He downloads a number of Muslim people groups in Indonesia. He finds that the largest group, the Sundanese, has a population of over 37 million, of which there are approximately 181,000 Christian believers, 0.49 percent of the population. Paul tells the committee that even though the Sundanese are not a total pioneer field because there are some Christians, they still represent a huge need because of the number of people without the Gospel. He also tells the committee that no more than 15 percent of the people have heard the Gospel or about Jesus in any form. He also tells them that the Sundanese are more receptive to the Gospel because Islam forms a thin layer of religious loyalty that covers or shrouds over thousands of years of animistic beliefs.

At the first meeting held to select a target people, the SPC decides that Paul should continue to do more research on Muslims in Indonesia. So Paul went back to work. His research led him to the island of Lombok to the east of Java and Bali. He discovered that whole island is populated mostly with the Sasak people group. Joshua Project information shows there are at least 3.266 million Sasak on the island, of which only 325 call themselves Christians, of which only 130 can be considered evangelical Bible-believing Christians. This people group is truly unreached, and the strategy needed will almost surely need to be independent from existing Christians, at least in the beginning. This was decided because the existing evangelical believers are obviously not reproducing effectively.

In further research, Paul discovered that both the Sundanese and the Sasak were still using the Wajang Kulit, a highly developed and dramatic form of puppet play. These puppet performances began centuries ago during the influence of Hinduism and Buddhism on the Indonesian islands before the Muslims arrived. They have become a very important form of communication to Indonesians. They are used to tell literally hundreds of stories. Every conceivable moral and ethical situation is taught by the skilled use of these flat puppets made of leather. The worldview of the puppets (and therefore, the Sasak) is very evident in the performances. The Wajang Kulit performers are accompanied by a small group of musicians called the gamelan in most parts of the country. Virtually every important event in the lives of the people is accompanied by a performance of the Wajang Kulit. Events such as birth, marriage, circumcision, or community crises are all accompanied by the Wajang ceremonies. Both the Sundanese and the Sasak have a highly developed artistic sense.[49]

The committee accepted Paul's report, but could not sense a specific direction from the Lord as to which group to evangelize.

---

[49] https://asiasociety.org/new-york/wayang-kulit-indonesias-extraordinary-shadow-puppetry-tradition.

They decided to use Paul's research and information on these groups to figure the Receptivity Quotient for each one (see chapter seven). The scores they agreed upon looked like this:

	Sundanese	Sasak
CDR =	2.14	1.86
DCR =	2	2
VRR =	2	3
Average =	2.05	2.29
Receptivity Quotient =	41.0	45.8

Though the higher scores was given to the Sasak, the SPC realized there was not enough in-depth information to make an accurate judgment of the Sasak. Therefore, since the scores were so close, they decided to pray and meet again in two days. Returning after that time, they finally reached an agreement. They decided to target the Sasak people group. Though there were many things they discussed, the one deciding factor was that their hearts were burdened because there were almost no evangelical believers and those who were there were not effectively reaching out to evangelize others. So since the receptivity was a little better, and since there is existing Christian work being attempted by others among the Sundanese, they decided God wanted them to target the 3.2 million Sasak. That was their unanimous decision.

At that same meeting, Paul was approved to be the team leader for the effort. He was asked to work full-time on the project beginning as soon as possible. He also agreed with the SPC that further research on the Sasak would be part of his assignment. Paul knew there were two groups within the Sasak. The Waktu Telu are the minority. They live in the more rural areas on the worst land. They are Muslims mostly in name only. Though they expect their priests to follow some of the rituals of Islam, the common man does not regularly practice Islam. The exceptions surround major events in people's lives, such as marriage, puberty ceremonies, etc. They think the Waktu Lima who are the majority have left their ancestral ways by becoming more openly Muslim. Both groups speak the Sasak language.

The Waktu Lima are separated into two classes—the higher-class land-owning or business-owning group, and the second-class landless artisans and peasants. Many of the Waktu Lima travel to cities in order to find work, but there are no reports of Waktu Telu living outside of Indonesia. The Watku Lima are more accustomed to meeting outsiders and are more aware of the world outside the island. They also participate more in the outward forms of Islam compared to the Waktu Telu. They see performing the hajj (pilgrimage to Mecca) as an ideal. They view the Waktu Telu as more backward and pagan.

After three more weeks of research and prayer, the SPC met to set some goals and discuss evangelism personnel. They agreed on the following as a statement of their primary purpose:

> "With God's help, and within the next twenty years, we intend to persuade at least 20 percent of the Sasak people on the island of Lombok, Indonesia, to accept Christ as Lord and Savior, and serve Him in a fellowship of autochthonous churches."

Evangelism Personnel

The SPC also asked Paul to research the felt needs of the Sasak. This is a preliminary list of needs Paul was able to discover:

1. <u>Survival Needs:</u> There appears to be only a small percentage of the population which is experiencing survival needs. Most of them are among the Waktu Telu who have been misplaced by unscrupulous landlords. They contract to provide needed fertilizers which they sell on credit to them, only to withhold it at the time it is needed. This causes their crops to fail or underperform and allows the landlords to take the land from them. The Waktu Lima have devel-

oped a group strategy to never let that happen, controlling the purchase and distribution of fertilizers collectively. The majority of the population still lives in the country and practices extensive home gardening and market produce. Unlike the majority of Indonesians, maize is used as their primary food starch. Only 2 percent of the island grows rice. Overpopulation is not so much a problem as it is in Java, and the people are generally able to provide a frugal living for themselves. A large percentage of the land is farmed by tenant farmers, but nobody knows how much because it is often obtained by using abuses like the one mentioned above. Lack of adequate health care is probably the greatest survival need. Government hospitals relieve some of the need in the larger towns and cities. Outside aid by the Red Crescent and other organizations also provides some medical help.

2. Intellectual Needs: There is a curiosity about the outside world among the young people, and also some of the older people of the Waktu Lima. The mixture of Islam and animism has left a lot of questions in the minds of some of the young people, especially with the growing availability of TV, telephones, and smart media. It is not certain what percentage of people can read their own language. But there is pressure in the schools to learn Bahasa Indonesian, the national language. There has been some resistance to "Indonesianization." This is the government policy to spread the national language, and de-emphasize the importance of ethnic identity among the country's many ethnic groups. Most of them resent the pressure. They see it less in terms of national identity and more in terms of the largest ethnic group, the Javanese, as trying to force their ways on other groups. The Sasak were conquered by their Balinese neighbors until the Dutch freed them in 1894. Still, the Sasak identify more closely with their Bali neighbors than with their Javanese countrymen. The New Testament has been available since 2007 in the Sasak language. The atti-

tude against Bahasa Indonesian makes the Bible a positive influence in the Sasak struggle to retain their own identity. In spite of all this, there is a class distinction between the educated and upper class because they are fluent in Indonesian (Bahasa), a necessity for business and leadership. This will require two different strategies to reach both classes of Sasak.

3. Social Needs: There are many inequities in Sasak society. The upper-class Waktu Lima control the politics and institutions of the society, and speak Bahasa. They clearly do not want to change the status quo if it threatens their position of dominance. Over time, the majority of the Waktu Lima lost their land as described above, but they have a strong desire to obtain land of their own. They also strongly resent those in power who obtained wealth by unjustly taking the land of their fathers. Any strategy which includes increasing their ability to earn wealth to buy back their land with God's help will be accepted in the most positive way. Since they have been told they are not respected in numerous ways by those in charge, any strategy which emphasizes unified action as the Body of Christ will produce an effective witness in the lower classes of the Waktu Lima. People movements in other countries demonstrate that large numbers of conversions in a people group automatically reforms the behavior of believers for the better. It increases their ability to succeed financially as well as spiritually. This should be included in the teaching about following Christ.
4. Spiritual Needs: The daily lives of most of the people are controlled by a strong belief in the forces of the spirit world. Mixing teachings of Islam with ancient animistic practices, the people feel the weight of their fear of spiritual forces on a daily basis. The Muslim teaching about fate (almost everything that happens is predetermined by Allah) does little more than dull the concerns of animistic belief. Divination, witchcraft, and sorcery are commonly

> practiced, but are usually mixed with Muslim teachings about such things. The accommodation to Islam by the Waktu Lima is strong enough to alienate them from their Waktu Telu brothers, who live remotely in the south and in the mountains. Increasingly, many of the Waktu Lima have migrated to the cities to seek work. Their exposure to the media there is becoming increasingly confusing to them. The attractiveness of media exposure and the onslaught of Western forms of entertainment and video games is challenging their views of reality. A strategy which includes reaching these new city dwellers as a priority can be effective. The strategy would be even more effective if it could combine some of the new media tools with traditional forms such as the Wajang Kulit to demonstrate the power of Gospel messages.

In light of the preliminary needs analysis, the SPC has decided to initially appoint four cross-cultural evangelists and their families to work among the Sasak. All should be experienced in evangelism and dedicated to a lifetime of service. In addition, one family member in the group should have special experience in agribusiness. Another should have skills in starting businesses. Another should have special ability in music and art. Experience in these areas will prove more important than academic certifications. These skills should prove useful in meeting the felt needs of the Sasak as well as in using culturally appropriate forms of communication.

Each of the four families of the team should spend some of the time during training to do research in their additional areas of specialization. They should seek to learn how God might want to use their skills to build trust relationships among the people, as well as help meet their felt needs.

Secondary Goals: The SPC decides to meet again in two weeks to plan secondary goals. They have already established the level-one or primary purpose goal, which is stated above. Each member of the committee prayerfully writes out the secondary goals he thinks should be included before the committee meets again. After comparing their goals, they list those they agree upon first. Then they list each remaining suggested goal individually for discussion. Finally, they agree on the number of their goals and their wording. This is their list of secondary goals:

1. Within two years, select, train, and raise support for four cross-cultural ministry families to evangelize the Sasak people group. Send more in later years as need and opportunity arise.
2. Each team member (both husbands and wives) shall become enculturated and fluent in speaking and writing the Sasak language to at least a level 3.5 on the NDSL scale within two years after arrival on the field. In addition, the group shall submit a list of updated methods and objectives describing future goals and work for each team member in the area of his or her specialization within that two-year period.
3. The team will work to make disciples at key levels of society among the Waktu Lima first. They will work to see six thousand believers serving God in at least twenty autochthonous churches within five more years of work (nine years from project inception).
4. Within six more years, they will work to see at least 50 percent of the Sasak people at -3, 15 percent of the people at -2, and 10 percent at +2 on the "conversion as a process" scale (CAPS). This requires a major movement of the people toward Christianity, and hundreds of thousands of people becoming believers within fifteen years of the start date. It will require individual miracles and the miracle of a people movement toward Christ. It will require mobilizing massive prayer everywhere possible.
5. Within five more years (total of twenty years), work to see 40 percent of the Sasak people at -2 or better, and 20 percent at +2 on the "conversion as a process" scale. Within this time, Bible training schools will be established as

needed locally, regionally, and online at three levels to train established leaders and Gospel workers.

To some people, it might seem impractical, if not almost impossible, to expect such large numbers of Muslims to become believers, and do so in such a short period of time. But things are not as they have been in the past in Muslim countries. Even in Iran, a strongly Muslim Middle-Eastern country, at least a million Muslims have turned to Christ, many of them secretly. The Lord of the Harvest has strategies and timings to bring large numbers of Muslims to the Lord, and this has been demonstrated in Indonesia as well. Indonesia has only a thin crust of Islamic belief covering a largely animistic worldview among its tribal people groups. It would not be dreaming to expect a major people movement toward Christ among the Sasak. It has already happened in other parts of Indonesia. And the Lord has a plan to give an adequate opportunity to every people group to know Him. To see such a movement have the best chance of happening, however, will require a well-trained spiritually powerful team of evangelists who are bold and courageous. And they must use culturally appropriate methods in their Christian witness.

Intermediate Goals

Before deciding the methods the team will use, it is necessary to understand our secondary goals better by breaking them down into **intermediate goals**. These third-level goals will lead us to a preliminary list of methods the team should emphasize.

The SPC decides to meet two weeks after setting the secondary goals. As before, each person is to write the intermediate goals for each of the secondary goals adopted. In the meeting, the same system as before is used to agree on intermediate goals. Except for Secondary Goal One, those adopted are listed below. Those for Goal One are about the same as the ones listed in the example of the previous section. So only the intermediate goals for Secondary Goals Two through Five are listed here. We will code each intermediate goal to correspond with the secondary goal for which it is written. So the codes for the intermediate goals related to the second secondary goal would be 2A, 2B, 2C, etc. Here is a list of intermediate goals agreed upon by the SPC, beginning with those for Secondary Goal Two:

2A: Each evangelist and his family will spend a minimum of six months living in a Sasak home with a Sasak joint family unit. It will be in an area where people speak the most widely accepted form of Sasak with a good accent. They will follow the principles of the Life Language Learning System to learn the Sasak language. They will live at least two hours' journey away from other members of the team, and shall meet together with team members no more than once a week for the first four months.

2B: After six months, team members will decide the best locations for each family to begin their full-time ministries. They will relocate, if necessary, and finish a program to improve reading and writing skills in the language throughout the following eighteen months. Unless the team receives written approval otherwise, three couples will be located in towns or cities among the Waktu Lima. The other couple will work in a more rural setting among either the Waktu Lima or the Waktu Telu as the team decides.

2C: During the last eighteen months of the first two years, each team member will spend about 25 percent of his time doing local research in his area of special training or ministry, focusing mostly on written materials in the Sasak language. At the end of that time, a fully updated and revised set of methods and objectives will be submitted to the SPC at home for approval. The revised plans will include assignments to specific areas of responsibility for each team member. Evangelism will remain at the heart of all efforts to serve the people's needs.

3A: In the beginning, the team will concentrate its ministries mostly toward the lower-middle and middle classes among the Waktu Lima. These are people who are influential members of the community, but not generally a part of the ruling and official classes. These people are the shopkeepers, travelling laborers, and tradesmen among the Waktu Lima. They make up a large segment of the population. They will look for breakthroughs to the upper and ruling classes, but not concentrate on them at first. Above all, the team members must present the Gospel in autochthonous ways and teach new believers to be inclusive and appealing members of the mainstream culture as witnesses. By faith, at the end of the fourth year in the field, there will be at least five established churches and twenty home groups among these people, with at least one thousand believers.

3B: By the end of the seventh year in the field, an extension system of Bible training will be in place to train leaders at a minimum of the beginning level. There will be at least seven courses available in the local language and sixteen courses available in Bahasa. A translation program will begin at the end of the first year of field ministry. All local churches will train believers of all ages with local believers as teachers. By the end of five more years of work in the field (project total of nine), and by faith, a total of twenty churches with one hundred outstation groups will have been established with six thousand believers.

3C: By the end of the ninth year of the project, seventh in the field, at least an additional ten cross-cultural evangelism families will have been deployed to the field and will have completed two years of the LLL system like their predecessors.

3D: By the end of the seventh year in the field (total project nine years), all churches will be led and governed by local leaders with autochthonous forms of government. Each church will be sending at least two church planters to start churches in other places. At least three evangelists will be sent to start churches among the Waktu Telu. At least one trained cross-cultural evangelist from the Waktu Lima shall already be sent to start churches on other islands.

4A: By the end of the third year on the field, radio, television, and online media programs will be under production focused on community development and spiritual truth. Emphasize the Wajang Kulit communication form as a major tool to communicate the important messages. Seek time on government stations as a ministry of the local churches, not the cross-cultural evangelists. Regular programming should be on the air no later than the end of the fifth year (project seventh year).

4B: By the end of the ninth year on the field (project total of eleven years), and by faith, there will be a total of one hundred churches and twenty-five thousand believers on the island. By that time, the church leaders should have a specific strategy for establishing churches in every city, town, and village on the island. The strategy should depend on foreign resources only in the areas of developing advanced training, technical online and broadcasting assistance, and Bible training materials. By this time, advanced training equivalent to a two-year Bible school will be available online in the Waktu Lima language and in the Bahasa language.

4C: By the end of the thirteenth year on the field (fifteenth year of the project), and by faith, a genuine people movement for Christ will be well underway among the Waktu Lima. There will be four hundred churches and over one hundred thousand believers. Regular Wajang Kulit community development and Gospel programs will be broadcast online and through the Internet. Every city and at least half the towns will have at least one local church. There will also be village churches in many locations. All churches will have local leadership.

4D: By the end of the fifteenth year on the field (seventeenth year of the project), local leaders will have conducted a research project to learn how many locations still have no church. They will plan a strategy to plant churches in each remaining location. By this time, everyone will have heard about the churches, and there will have been significant spiritual opposition which had to be overcome. They will also survey the attitudes of the people toward the Gospel to determine how to overcome misinformation about the Gospel message. The churches will be encouraged to have regular prayer meetings to overcome the efforts to keep people in spiritual bondage and free them from the influence of evil leaders.

5A: By the end of the eighteenth year (twentieth year of the project), the work should have reached the proportions of a genuine people movement toward Christ and Christianity. There should be at least 2,200 churches among the Waktu Lima, totaling 600,000 believers. There should also already be 180 churches among the Waktu Telu, totaling 50,000 believers for a total of 650,000 believers in the country.

5B: The system for training pastors and leaders should be operating at four levels fully: (1) training lay leaders for local churches by extension courses, (2) training local pastors by extension with at least six courses in the local language, (3) at least sixteen courses in the local language available by extension for training local and regional leaders, and 4) an in-country university for training leaders on-site and by extension in a variety of subjects including spiritual leadership, medicine, agriculture, and the arts.

5C: Working with leaders of the Waktu Lima and outside translation organizations, by the end of the eighteenth year on the field (twentieth year of the project), publish the first five books of the Bible, plus psalms and proverbs, plus an updated common language version of the New Testament in the Waktu Lima language. Within the same period, produce a complete children's pictorial storybook training system on the entire Bible using the Wajang Kulit picture format as the storytellers.

5D. By the end of the eighteenth year (twentieth year of the project), the cross-cultural ministry team remaining on the island should be fewer and they should be specialists in teaching the highest levels of leaders in needed areas. All the top teachers and leaders at all levels of training should be respected, seasoned, and well-qualified Waktu Lima or Waktu Telu.

5E: By the end of the eighteenth year on the field (twentieth year of the project), the Waktu Lima church leaders should initiate another survey of the island, comparing the results with the first survey three years before. These results should meet or exceed the goals listed in Secondary Goal Five, and there should be at least one church in every city, village, or town over five hundred in population.

After completing the list of intermediate goals, the SPC realizes the importance of including all the members of the initial cross-cultural evangelism team in planning for the fourth and fifth levels of the planning model. They have many possible methods for accomplishing these intermediate goals in mind, but they do not want to approve those methods until the evangelists have had ample opportunity to discuss them together with the SPC. They decide they should begin these discussions after the team has completed their first six months of pre-field training.

DESIGNING THE STRATEGY

By this point, it is time to develop the strategy to the level that it can be implemented effectively. As prerequisites for strategy design, recruiting, and selection of team members, the beginning of the cross-cultural evangelism training and the beginning of the fundraising activities are all in process. One member of the SPC is designated to work with the team leader to supervise these activities. Both husbands and wives are enrolled in training courses. It is at this point when the development of strategy design can begin in earnest.

After four months in training, the SPC begins to include the evangelists and their instructors in regular planning sessions. It is time to consider specific methods and objectives needed to accomplish the goals in the first three levels of the planning system. This planning will benefit from research being done by each team member as a regular part of his training course assignments. Each secondary goal, together with its intermediate goals, are assigned to specific groups consisting of at least one member of the SPC, the team leader, and at least one other team member. Each group is assigned the task of bringing back proposals for methods and objectives in its assigned area. They are also encouraged to write methods and objectives for other goals being investigated deeply by other teams. By the time the full six months of training courses are completed, a full set of agreed-upon and approved primary goal, secondary goals, intermediate goals, methods, and objectives are adopted. All of these levels of planning continue to be refined as planning groups continue to meet periodically, in person and online, while funds are being raised to send the team to the field.

The evangelists also continue their research during the remainder of time they spend helping to raise the funds necessary to depart for the field. There is a final meeting two months before the team departs for Lombok. Together they suggest, discuss, and approve any final changes they think are needed in the strategy plans. The major goals are published in the supporting churches, and prayer support is enlisted among the church believers. The goals are ambitious, and the prayers must match that intensity to break down the spiritual forces that will align themselves against such a spiritual breakthrough among the Sasak people group. Prayer is where the battle will actually be won!

There is not space here to list all the methods and objectives adopted by the SPC and team members. But by looking at the previous sections which show the process for selecting methods and writing objectives, it is easy to imagine what kinds of activities and ministries they would include. They would be similar to the examples already given in the previous sections. Each of the intermediate goals lead to specific methods which lead to specific objectives. The methods and objectives are designed to complete the intermediate goals.

When the cross-cultural evangelism team left for Lombok, there was a large group of friends and loved ones to see them off at the airport. Church leaders, remaining members of the strategy planning committee, relatives, and friends, all experienced a joyful sense of excitement and faith as a new chapter of God's work began. The excitement of the team members and their families was matched by their determination to make whatever sacrifices necessary to implement the strategy plan and see the Waktu Lima and Waktu Telu have an adequate chance to know Christ and serve in their own churches worshipping in their own language.

Everyone knew there would be times of discouragement and loneliness away from all they had become familiar with at home. They knew there would be times when they would need to adjust the strategy by changing their methods and objectives. They knew the vision might have setbacks, and some of the limitations of the goals might need adjusting as the need to do so becomes clear. But they also knew they had a good well-planned strategy established in partnership with the Holy Spirit and with the guidance of the Lord. They had faith in a big God who is not willing that any should perish. They were ready for the challenge and the commitment, the frustrations, and the victories of doing what nobody before them had done effectively—evangelize the unreached Sasak people for God!

QUESTIONS FOR UNDERSTANDING

1. Write a definition of methods. What questions do methods answer in cross-cultural evangelism strategy? What is the relationship between methods and goals?
2. What kind of methods should not be used in planning strategies for cross-cultural evangelism? Give at least three examples of methods which might be used in cross-cultural evangelism.
3. Describe the process for finding the Method Selection Quotient. Describe two ways an SPC could use the Scale of Method Selection.
4. What are the dangers of using evangelistic methods which are not culturally appropriate? List three questions planners should find answers to when seeking good methods for a cross-cultural evangelism strategy.
5. List five characteristics of good strategy planning. Briefly define each one.
6. How do survival needs which go unmet introduce a high degree of "noise" into the cross-cultural communication of the Gospel? How should spiritual needs be balanced between other human needs? Which should remain primary? Why? Is there any time when survival needs should be emphasized over spiritual needs? Why?
7. Explain the reasons for making a strategy process-oriented. Explain how to use the "conversion as a process" chart (figure 6.d) to make strategies process-oriented.
8. List some advantages of making a strategy plan goal-oriented. Name at least two main characteristics of good goals.
9. Describe the relationship between primary, secondary, and intermediate goals. Which are the most detailed goals—secondary or intermediate goals? Which levels of goals should be completed before implementing even the first part of the planning strategy?
10. What is the difference between methods and objectives? How do they relate to intermediate goals? Why are objectives so helpful and necessary?

11. What people should be involved in planning methods and objectives? In a normal strategy plan, which would be more numerous, methods or objectives? When can we be certain intermediate goals have been achieved?
12. Using the description of the Sasak people group in the case study, write some possible methods which could be included in the evangelism strategy without copying what is in the text. Use your own analysis of the needs and culture, according to what has been given to you in this chapter.
13. Using the description of the Sasak people, tell why it was decided to appoint an agriculturalist and a person skilled in drama and music to be on the cross-cultural evangelism team.
14. Why do you think the strategy in the case study targeted the lower-middle and middle-class Waktu Lima? Why didn't the SPC start with all classes? Why didn't they start with the upper class?
15. Why should goals, methods, and objectives be flexible in a strategy plan? What are some advantages for revising the methods and objectives after the cross-cultural evangelism team has been working among the target people for two years?

QUESTIONS FOR DISCUSSION

1. Discuss the priority of evangelism in planning strategies for cross-cultural ministry. What are the dangers involved in an unbalanced strategy? Discuss situations when spiritual needs might be temporarily made secondary to other kinds of human needs. Are we ever justified in trying to meet spiritual needs without also trying to meet survival, social, and intellectual needs? Relate your discussion to the "conversion as a process" chart.
2. Discuss the value of measuring the receptivity of people groups. Discuss some of the reasons the Receptivity Quotient may or may not be very accurate. Upon what factors is the quotient based? Under what circumstances might you feel that the quo-

tient could be somewhat inaccurate? Under what circumstances would you feel confident that the quotient is very accurate?

3. Using the intermediate goal for secondary goal two in the case study, discuss possible methods and objectives which could be included in the planning strategy at levels four and five, or methods and objectives levels. Write at least three methods and six objectives which you think would help accomplish Intermediate Goals 2A to 2C. Use the Scale of Method Selection to find a Method Selection Quotient for each of the methods you choose.
4. Discuss the different levels of technology in different cultures. What kinds of mistakes have you noticed cross-cultural evangelists often make in the use of technology in other cultures? How do you think this makes the target people feel about the evangelists and their message?
5. How do you feel about the methods for planning and designing strategies contained in this book? How much are they different from what you might have expected? How much do they fit into your own worldview and value system? Do you think God can use this system to help us evangelize unreached peoples? If you could change the system to make it better, how would you do it?

CHAPTER NINE

Planning Strategies For Cross-Cultural Evangelism III

KEY POINTS IN THIS CHAPTER

1. Implementation and evaluation of good strategies is a cyclical process which is repeated over and over during the use of the strategy.
2. The major purpose of strategy implementation is to use the best possible means to reveal the value of serving Christ to the target people.
3. A team approach to working in other cultures has the greatest potential for successful strategy implementation.
4. Churches grow by multiplying into new units faster than they do by simply trying to make existing units grow.
5. Helping local leaders among the target people adopt their own strategy for growth is an important part of good strategy planning and implementation.
6. It is important to evaluate the growth of the target people society as a whole while they are moving closer toward acceptance of Christ.
7. Tools for numerical growth evaluation are very helpful for the planning and evaluation of cross-cultural evangelism strategies.

8. In measuring numerical growth, the rates of growth are at least as important as the numbers of growth of new people.
9. Evaluation of numerical growth can serve as an evaluation of both quantitative and qualitative growth.
10. The nature of good strategy planning and implementation requires periodic evaluation and adjustment of the strategy to make it most effective.

IMPLEMENTATION OF THE STRATEGY

Figure 9.a: Strategy Planning Model

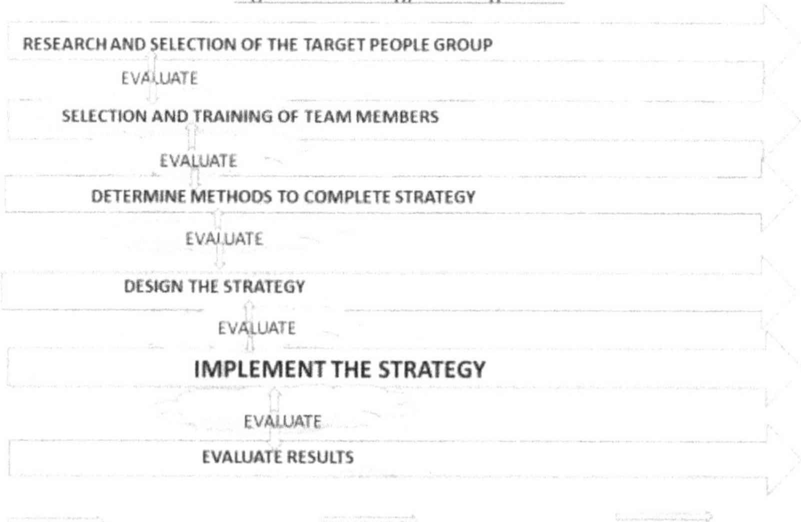

Over four thousand years ago, before Confucianism, Taoism, or Buddhism ever appeared in China, the people of that land had a concept of the greatest of all gods whom they called **Shang Ti**—"the Lord of Heaven." In Korea, he was called **Hananim**—"the Great One." Over a period of centuries, he became so exalted in the minds of the people that eventually, only the emperor was permitted to worship him. Even that was permitted only once per year. The people were not allowed to say his name or worship him directly. Eventually, even the emperor would not say his name, out of respect. Over a period of centuries, this caused the worship of this God to be forgotten. The people still remembered his name, but they only talked about this god in terms of the one who had left them. He became unknowable to them—even to their kings and emperors.[50]

Down through the centuries came the great religions of China listed above. But the people never really forgot about Shang Ti / Hananim—the great unknowable god of their past. When Catholic priests came to work in China, they adopted the Chinese phrases **Tien Ju** or **Tien Laoye**—"Master of Heaven" to refer to the true living God. When they went to Korea, they used the Tien names also, because it was readily understood by Koreans. But when Protestant cross-cultural workers went to Korea in the 1880s, they did some research to find out the best name to use for God. After much discussion, they finally agreed that **Hananim**—translation "One True God"—was the best term.[51]

They immediately began to preach about Hananim to the Korean people. Immediately, that age-old longing was awoken in the hearts of the Koreans. Legend said Hananim had a son who wanted to live among men. The Protestants preached about Hananim's son. These foreigners, it appeared, knew more about Hananim than even their emperor!

The message began to shake Korea! Converts soon began to pour into Protestant churches. It was also during that period when John L. Nevius (see chapter three) began to convince others of the importance of the "three-self" method of cross-cultural evangelism. He spoke about giving the converts maximum freedom and responsibility to lead and expand God's work. They followed Nevius's plan. The Koreans were reaching out to find that the unknowable god had become knowable through His Son, Jesus Christ. Thousands began coming to Christ.

---

[50] https://www.utpjournals.press/doi/pdf/10.3138/uram.9.1.17 —IP Address:173.126.8.245.

[51] Samual P. Yang, "The Legacy of Horace Grant Underwood," *International Bulletin of Missionary Research* 39, no. 3: 151.

The Catholics in Korea, meanwhile, were gathering a very meager number of converts in Korea compared to Protestants. They had chosen to use the Tien forms for God which the Koreans identified with the Chinese. The dominance of the Chinese over the culture down through the centuries caused much resentment. Using the Chinese terms for God became a part of what the Koreans felt was a Chinese invasion of their culture.

Eventually, the Catholics realized their mistake and began to use the term Hananim for God. After that, they began to gain more converts. But that was not until a genuine Protestant people movement of the Korean people toward the God of the Bible was well underway.

In addition to the use of the term Hananim for God, a political situation in the twentieth century changed the attitude of Koreans toward Christianity. In the year 1910, the Korean peninsula was captured by the Japanese, who dominated the region until the end of World War II. The domination was cruel, and standing up against the Japanese rulers was very dangerous. The leaders of the most effective groups forming the resistance to that domination were Christian believers. This was widely known, so after the Japanese were defeated and left the peninsula, Christian leaders were very widely respected as nationalist leaders. As a result, many people became Christians. Today, about 30 percent of the South Korean population, more than fifteen million people, are Christians. Many of the largest churches in the world are in that country.

Apart from the popular and political advantages accrued by Christian leaders over time, the beginning success occurred because Christian leaders adapted their message to the culture. The use of the name Hananim proved to be providential and culturally correct. The evangelists used the Bible carefully to pour Christian truths into the meaning of that name. Even today, with numerous prayer mountains, large churches, and believers highly committed to spreading the Gospel, honor is brought to God's name in numerous ways. The Korean Christians around the world have proven to be an inspiration to other parts of the Body of Christ.

The second thing the cross-cultural evangelists among the Koreans did was to agree on a strategy plan. They sometimes disagreed among themselves, but they followed good principles and stayed with the plan. The principles they agreed upon (often called the Nevius Plan—see chapter three) were the beginning of what we call autochthonous principles today. The resulting churches which God has raised up among the Koreans have many times amazed the world. It is not uncommon for them to number into the tens of thousands and even the hundreds of thousands each! South Korea has many thousands of churches now. Koreans have dispersed to many parts of the world and planted churches there as well. Many Korean communities in the world are over 50 percent Christian.

With the help of the Holy Spirit and by using the principles found in this book, we can find strategies that are effective for evangelizing every people group in the world!

THE NATURE OF STRATEGY IMPLEMENTATION

Chapter eight reveals that the implementation of good strategies has already begun before cross-cultural evangelists enter the target culture. The implementation actually begins when the main goals are agreed upon and the evangelists are selected for training and fundraising responsibilities. But the key part of strategy implementation begins with the team entering the target culture on the field. It is very possible to have an excellent God-given strategy and still fail in the implementation of that strategy.

There are some key issues to remember concerning the nature of cross-cultural evangelism. First, our efforts succeed only insofar as we reveal Christ effectively to the target people. "His [God's] intent was that now, through the church, the manifold wisdom of God should be made known…according to his eternal purpose which he accomplished in Christ Jesus our Lord" (Eph. 3:10). However well-planned and God-given our strategies, we must reveal the reality of God's power in our lives before those to whom we minister in other cultures.

Paul understood this principle well. He knew the essence of what God was doing in his life. He wrote to the Galatians, "God, who…called me by his grace, was pleased to reveal his Son in me so that I might preach him among the Gentiles" (1:15–16). The way we live in a target culture must literally be a revelation of Jesus Christ. We are the only Jesus they will see in the beginning of our ministry among a target people. Yes, it is important to follow well-planned strategies in order to gain the maximum number of converts, and plant the maximum number of churches. Each soul counts to God! But we must never forget that our plans can only be as effective as the amount we live dedicated, sacrificial Christlike lives before the people we are called to love and reach for Him. While none of us will ever be perfect, we can humbly show His love and power through our commitment to Him and his purpose to evangelize our target people group. Pointing people to Him and His love and power will make up for any weakness of our own.

We must also recognize that we carry only part of the responsibility for our success in cross-cultural evangelism. Jesus said, "I will build my church" (Matt. 16:18). The Lord is far more interested in reaching souls and building His church than we could ever be. We should work as if everything depended upon us, and we should pray as if everything depended upon God. And whatever success results from our planning and work, we must humbly acknowledge that it is Christ building His church through us and He deserves the credit for building His church.

God's grace is the primary reason His judgment has not been poured out upon this sinful world already. It is the building of His Church and reaching all the peoples he wants reached that have forestalled his judgment upon this world. He still wants to redeem more people all around the world (2 Pet. 3:9) before the end comes (Matt. 24:14). And a proliferation of local churches is His chosen method for accomplishing that purpose. Whatever strategies God helps us establish, each goal and method must directly help to establish and build up local groups of believers who are committed to serving Christ as Lord. Each church is a lighthouse in a sin-darkened world. Each new body of believers is an invasion of the Kingdom of God into Satan-held territory. Each act of dedication and sacrifice by local groups of believers is the most eloquent testimony of the truth of the Gospel that people will ever see among the target peoples we evangelize.

The local church is both the goal and the means for evangelizing every people on earth. Our strategies and their implementation must focus on the well-being and effectiveness of local churches. As the number of believers and churches increase, their influence and the increase of their leadership must increase above our own. As churches are established in the target culture, we must increasingly channel our love and strength through those churches and leaders toward the unsaved in their culture. We succeed only as they succeed in their God-given callings. The planting of new churches must become a primary goal of the new believers, not just the evangelists. We must work to help the believers in the target cultures establish their own strategies and plans to reach their own people. Our success in reaching the goals of our strategies will be directly dependent upon how much the converts whom God gives us adopt similar goals as their own. That is why the principles of autochthonous church planting are so important. That is why planting reproducible churches is central to implementing our strategies. Our success in cross-cultural evangelism is totally wrapped up in the success of each local church and its ability to reproduce itself.

PRINCIPLES FOR IMPLEMENTING STRATEGY

Like there is no set strategy which will work among every people, there is no set formula for implementing strategies. We cannot prescribe a set of rules to follow for implementing strategies. But we can emphasize some principles to guide cross-cultural evangelists in making their strategies as fruitful as possible among any people group.

The better the strategy plan, the easier it is to implement. When good principles of setting goals and methods are followed, they serve as a guide to activity in the field among the target people. For instance, if an evangelist's goal is to reach level 3.5 on the checklist of speaking proficiency within two years (Appendix C), he knows he must follow all the principles of good language/culture learning contained in chapter five of this book. He will want to use the methods of the Life Language Learning System to guide his daily activities. He will want to use the checklist to measure and evaluate his progress. Implementing any strategy is similar to this illustration. The whole strategy is like the Life Language Learning System. The strategy helps us to see what methods and objectives are necessary in our daily activities. Evaluation of our progress is possible because we make our goals measurable and specific.

So the basic principle for implementing strategy is to let the strategy guide your daily activities. Use it to set your own objectives for each day. It takes discipline, but it is worth it! Use it to guide your evaluation progress. Your evaluations will help you make decisions about parts of the strategy which can be improved. Below are some more important principles for strategy implementation which can guide you in putting your strategy to work for God.

Group Dedication: When people are trained to enter combat, they are prepared in every possible way to face the enemy. They are steeled and hardened in body and mind. They are given the best fighting equipment possible. They are drilled and trained until they can push themselves to ever higher limits of endurance. This is done so they are prepared to advance into enemy territory, suffering whatever necessary to fulfill their assignments.

But all military leaders know that physical and mental preparation, plus the best military equipment in the world, cannot make a good soldier without one more important preparation. The soldier must have a spirit dedicated to his purpose and to those he works with to accomplish his mission. He must know what he is doing is worth fighting for and be committed to protecting the fellow soldiers in his unit. If he is going to face the battle with a willingness to lay down his life, he must be dedicated to his purpose and his team.

The same should be even more true of a cross-cultural evangelist. He is a soldier of the cross in the enemy's territory among unreached peoples. He too should be mentally and physically prepared to suffer, if necessary. He, too, must be dedicated to the higher purpose to which he has been called and to those with whom he is called to work. It will not do to be partially committed to the goals of the strategy. He must be willing to dedicate himself to those goals wholeheartedly. Just as combat soldiers depend on their comrades in arms for their own protection and safety, so too must he be committed to the well-being of the whole cross-cultural evangelism team.

Doing cross-cultural evangelism is not just an opportunity to travel or seek advancement to greater status. Neither is it an exercise to make big people out of little people, or good people into great people. It is an invasion of Satan's territory, pure and simple. It requires the dedication of every evangelist on the team to the goals of the strategy and to one another. Good spiritual, physical, and mental training of the evangelists is important, but it is not enough. They must also be willing to put the needs of the team and the target people above their own needs and ambitions.

The cross-cultural evangelism team must develop a good working relationship. Their interpersonal relationships must be based upon trust and mutual respect for one another. If they want to develop such relationships among the target people, they must focus on doing so among themselves first. Each team member must have room to develop the ministries for which he is responsible, but also be willing to help others in theirs as much as possible. Each should also respect the other member's domain of responsibility while remaining personally and emotionally dedicated to the success of each other team member. Competition about anything among team members—such as ministry roles, leadership positions, fundraising ability—will break down the effectiveness of the whole team.

English-speaking cultures tend to be individualistic and competitive. Because of that, some of these principles about group dedication to one another and mutual support among team members may seem a little idealistic and unrealistic to some people. But the task of cross-cultural evangelism requires just that kind of commitment and dedication toward others in order to be successful. Individualism and a competitive spirit are cultural luxuries of a Western value system. They have no place on a cross-cultural evangelism team. They also act against the Spirit's work in our lives (Gal. 5:16–26).

Instead of competitiveness and individualism, there must be a mutual flow of truth among the members of the cross-cultural evangelism team. Competitive people often do not offer suggestions to help others or help accomplish their mutual goals unless they are certain to get credit. Individualistic people are less likely to share their frustrations and plans with others for fear of failing in front of others, or appearing weak or incapable. These kinds of motivations have no place on successful cross-cultural evangelism teams. That is why members must be seasoned in ministry, be humble and vulnerable in spirit, and have a proven track record demonstrating their spiritual maturity.

Team members must be able to build up a great loyalty, trust, and respect toward one another. They need to know they are respected and trusted by other members of the team. That respect must be earned, and it must be given to others. Instead of feeling a need to try to hide their weaknesses or inabilities (everyone has some), team members need to know they can depend on the others to help them where they are weaker and help others to overcome their weaknesses as well. They must develop relationships with one another where they can openly and honestly share their true feelings with one another, including their anxieties. This will help them develop a common bond of trust and love. Team members must be firmly convinced that their success as a team depends upon the spiritual, emotional, physical, and mental strength of the team as a whole. And that must be built up and protected as if they were in combat. They are in spiritual combat without a doubt! They must be willing to put effort and energy into functioning as an effective unit—the only "Body of Christ" the target people will ever see (1 Cor. 12:12–31). Their success will be team success more than individual success. It will depend upon their commitment and dedication as a team to strategy goals. It will also depend upon their commitment and dedication to one another!

Organizing for Success: Any task must be organized in order to be successfully completed. If one person is doing the work, he must decide the necessary steps to accomplish the goal. If several people are responsible to complete a task, as is the case for a cross-cultural evangelism team, then the task must be divided among those responsible for its completion.

Division of Tasks: Each member of the cross-cultural evangelism team should always be aware of what responsibilities are his or hers, and which belong to others. The best way to divide responsibilities is to do so according to the goals and objectives of the evangelism strategy. Usually responsibilities are best divided at the objectives level (level 5) of the strategy plan. Each team member should be responsible for one or more such objectives until they are completed. He or she should be responsible for implementing the agreed-upon methods to reach those objectives. The objectives are small goals which define specific kinds of tasks. They are at the heart of meeting strategy goals. If experience or spiritual insight leads the one responsible to believe those objectives should be changed or modified, it is his or her responsibility to define what changes need to be made and why. Then the whole team should decide together if those changes are needed.

Many objectives will require more than one person to see them completed. Members of the team may be involved, and so will members of the target culture. When team members are helping to reach an objective, they should work under the leadership of the team member chosen to be responsible for that objective. They will also want other team members to work in cooperation with them to meet those objectives for which they are responsible.

When members of the target culture are also involved in completing an objective, as they almost always will be, good principles for autochthonous church planting should be followed. As will be discussed below, the goals and objectives of the strategy must find their counterpart in the goals and objectives of the local churches among the target people. Autochthonous principles require that the evangelist responsible to complete an objective in the team strategy must work to see them completed through the ministries of autochthonous local churches to the greatest degree possible. That means a team member will never want to assume authority or position over an objective which the local churches have adopted as their own. In those cases, the team member will simply manage the cross-cultural evangelist team's effort to help the local churches accomplish their goals which relate to the objective for which he or she is responsible.

This division of responsibility aids the team's work in a number of ways. First, it clearly defines areas of responsibilities for team members. Each team member will know his primary responsibilities. It also establishes the worth of each team member by placing them in charge of those objectives which best fit their abilities, burden, and vision for ministry. It also gives room for team members to grow spiritually and develop the gifts God has given to them. Yet it still allows them to retain the benefits of a team-member approach to ministry.

Leadership and Accountability: Every evangelism effort needs the help of direct leadership. If this is true in our own culture, it is even more true in other cultures at the outset of working for God. With the team approach, most of the direction comes through group decision-making. But there still needs to be at least one person who is given the general oversight of the whole team and its evangelism effort. He may be called the team chairman, the team leader, the field director, superintendent, or field pastor. The name chosen as a title is not as important as the work and functions he performs. Just as there needs to be leaders from the evangelism team who assume responsibility for different parts of the strategy, so there needs to be a leader who assumes responsibility for the whole effort before the churches on the field and the leaders back home. Such a leader must be a compassionate, understanding individual, but also must be fully committed to the strategy and accountable to leadership back home.

There must also be something we can call territorial flexibility. Every team member assigned to a particular geographical area to carry out his particular specialization of ministry must be completely free to carry out other forms of ministry in that geographical area without feeling hindered by any other team member who is the one primarily responsible for those kinds of ministry. Good communication and love goes a long way toward avoiding hurt feelings or the image of encroaching on the ministries of another person. We must communicate well, and we must rejoice in the effective ministries of other team members, even if they appear to be more effective than our own ministries.

Leaders who are effective gain respect from those they lead through love and service. Jesus' life is the model for good leaders. The team leader must have that same attitude and dedication in order to effectively build the team together as a group. He must never use his position as a weapon to dominate others (2 Pet. 5:3).

If the cross-cultural evangelism team has ten or more members, it may be wise to delegate some of their group decision-making responsibility to a smaller group of three to five people. Such a group can be called the field executive committee or the field leadership team or something similar. They should meet more often than the whole team, making operational decisions that do not require the presence of the whole team. The field leader takes responsibility for all field meetings.

The team leader must have a specific amount of authority that should be determined by the strategy planners, or those in charge of the evangelism effort at home. This should be established before the team leaves for the field. Every team member should understand how he is to work with and under that person's authority. He should know what he is responsible for as a team member and what kinds of decisions are to be made at each level of leadership. Each team member should be responsible directly to the team leader and members of his team, the leaders and supporters at home, and most of all, to the Lord himself. Integrity for the tasks, commitment to other team members and leaders, and commitment to the Lordship of Jesus must be the standard operating procedure for each team member.

The field team leader must be responsible to the home leaders who are in charge of the evangelism project's oversight for the home churches. He must represent the team's needs to those leaders, and he must represent the home leaders' authority to the team members. It is good to define these relationships of accountability as a part of the planning strategy. Teaching about these relationships must be part of the training for the team members. They should be written down in a policy manual so team members understand clearly the commitment they are making to become part of the team. The more clearly the lines of responsibility and authority and accountability are understood, the more smoothly the cross-cultural evangelism team will be able to function. There will be enough challenges in the work on the field. Interpersonal rivalry and dissension about field decisions must not be allowed to interfere with the important work of field ministry. Commitment to leadership and team decisions must be the priority of every team member.

New Unit Growth: Another important principle to underscore when implementing strategies is that growth occurs more quickly by multiplying growth units rather than by simply trying to make units grow larger and larger. A growth unit can be a local church or a group within a local church. A growth unit can be a Bible study group, an evangelism team, a prayer group, a community action group, or the whole group of believers who make up a local church. This principle acknowledges that churches should continue to grow as a part of their nature. But it also acknowledges that overall growth occurs fastest numerically and qualitatively by multiplying growth units. It is easy to demonstrate this principle by looking at two growing national churches, one in Brazil and the one in South Korea.

The Assemblies of God churches of Brazil have grown more rapidly than almost anywhere in the world. Existing churches "mother" new churches. They train by encouraging new leaders in local churches who are challenged to start preaching and teaching in "outstation churches." They are also encouraged to take extension courses in Bible and leadership principles from the Brazilian Extension School of Theology. As the church grows to a size large enough, the church planter is recognized as a credentialed pastor. He then trains other believers who show promise, challenging them to do the same thing he did, even as his church is growing. In this way, the Brazilian Assemblies of God has planted tens of thousands of churches and grown to tens of millions of believers.

The Full Gospel Central Church of Seoul, South Korea, which is described in chapter six, has fostered rapid church growth using similar methods. They use a system of reproducing cell-group leaders who start small group meetings all over the city of Seoul and surrounding areas. They train their cell-group leaders very carefully so they can conduct the meetings in homes, factories, apartment houses, or professional offices for one hour each week. They operate like a mini-church service with about eight to thirty people in each cell. They pray fervently, and God answers their prayers. Each cell group studies the Word together and discusses its meaning, using the notes from the pastor's sermon from the previous Sunday. In this way, the pastor preaches to all his people, since the members are too many to be at church each week. The cell groups do grow and multiply into other cell groups as leaders within the groups emerge and are trained. It is a constant process. There are many thousands of cell groups! But the Central Church is not allowed to grow any further. Instead, many thousands of new churches have been established all over that region and throughout the country by using this cell-group multiplication strategy. Those churches, in turn, operate their ministries in the same way as the central church in Seoul. Like many churches over time, there have been problems related to transitions in leadership, but the church has continued to multiply its ministry and its outreach. Millions have turned to the Lord in Korea as a result of this system of infinite church reproducibility!

This unit multiplication principle is based upon sociological fact and common sense. When there are more believer units of any size determined and dedicated to growing the Kingdom of God, the number of believers will grow much more rapidly than if there are a few units simply trying to grow larger. Church growth specialists also know that the faster a group of believers are growing numerically, the faster they will grow spiritually. The commitments and dedication necessary to foster and continue numerical growth are the same things necessary to foster spiritual growth, and vice versa.

In implementing planning strategy, the Principle of Reproducibility requires that we find the most effective ways to reproduce everything we do in the lives of other people. If we teach a new believer something, we need to teach it in such a way that he or she will be able to teach someone else to do the same thing (2 Tim. 2:2). Practicing the New Unit Growth Principle is essential for helping reproducibility and qualitative growth remain at the highest possible level.

Much of what we do with people in groups will reach a point where further growth within the group is more difficult. Growth will soon slow down or stop when the space to hold the people is full, or when the number of people becomes too large to effectively function well together in doing ministry. Such a slowdown can cause many to become less focused or discouraged. Often, people reason that they are not as spiritual or committed as much as they once were. Or they think that if they were better people in some other way, God would help their group keep growing like it did before. But they are not necessarily to blame. They may be even more spiritual than before, but still grow less. The reasons are sociological, not spiritual. While there can be many reasons for slowing the growth, there is a certain way to increase it. Simply perfect the method for multiplying new growth units and the leadership they require. An important way to do that is to be certain that the groups and their leaders are willing to split and multiply as their primary responsibility for Christian service. It is sociologically more comfortable to stay in familiar groups with people you know. People must be trained to overcome that desire in favor of winning other people to the Lord. They must become committed to multiplication above all else. Without that primary commitment within leaders and groups, they will not multiply effectively.

Goal Transfer: Transferring the ownership of goals from the cross-cultural evangelist to the believers is an extremely important objective of any good strategy. It is not enough that the evangelism team be committed to the goals of the strategy. The new believers in the target culture must come to value those goals also. They actually must become their own goals. This is more difficult to accomplish than simply showing the believers the strategy and expecting them to adopt it as their own. Experience shows that people will never fully value goals and work to achieve them unless they formulate the goals themselves. Since the new believers cannot be a part of the original strategy planning, it is impossible for those goals and methods to be completely owned by them. Later, they may help to modify the original strategy by showing the evangelists how the strategy can be improved. But initially, the believers must have an opportunity to hear from God in planning their own strategies to reach their own goals. Only then will they value those goals highly enough to dedicate their lives to reaching them. This does not mean the believers will automatically choose totally different goals than the evangelists have chosen. They will likely be very similar. But they will probably vary at least in the way they are selected and prioritized. They also may modify the way they are stated and understood.

The cross-cultural evangelism team must work together to help the believers formulate their own goals. Those goals may be formally stated and written down, or they may simply be agreed upon by consensus. But however they are formulated, the principles for their implementation must be adopted by local believers. The evangelists should do their best to teach good principles for making good goals. They should challenge the faith of the believers, but the believers must be very free to set their own goals without too much outside influence. They must be determined to please God, not just the evangelists. As the goals are set, the evangelists can skillfully help to make them specific and measurable as much as the culture will allow. He can ask questions to help the believers decide how they will evaluate their progress and how often to do so. Goals that are not written down need to be repeated in all their aspects very often.

If the believers' goals do not match the strategy of the cross-cultural evangelism team, the team must decide what to do. They can either wait, hoping the believers will eventually change their goals so they are closer to those of the strategy, or they can decide that the believers' goals are the best and most workable goals. They can change their own strategy to fit the goals of the local people. Either way, it will usually take a period of time for the goals of both groups to fit together harmoniously. The team members should avoid forcing or implying that the local leaders must fit into their goals. They should do the opposite, assuring local leaders that their goals will remain the most important for everyone to pursue. If the local goals are moving in the right direction, they should do their best to fit into them. Autochthonous principles require that the goals of local believers have local leaders to direct their completion. For the beginning, these local leaders should have as much freedom to pursue their goals as possible. The evangelists may train them, encourage them, and work with them. But they should never direct them. Those leaders are important to the work. They should be highly respected and built up in their faith and leadership potential. This will greatly increase the value placed upon local leadership and the growth goals and methods adopted by the local churches. The ability to select and pursue their own growth strategy is a key to growth among any target people.

Search for Cultural Keys: Many years ago, anthropologists believed that the worship of one God (monotheism) was a characteristic of developed societies. Believing in evolution, they theorized that the societies that worshipped many gods were simply younger in their evolutionary development. After they evolved long enough, they reasoned, they too would devise systems of monotheism. The anthropologists, therefore, set out to demonstrate that theory by investigating primitive polytheistic tribal societies. What they found greatly surprised them!

To the contrary of their theory, they discovered that people group after people group had some kind of concept of monotheism. The people might worship and appease lesser gods and spirits with which they were familiar. But they still kept at least a vague recollection of the greatest God somewhere in their worldview. Oftentimes, this greatest God would have abandoned their people for some reason. Or in some way the knowledge or relationship between this great God and the people would have been broken. The anthropologists discovered people after people who were thought to be polytheistic, but who had at least a trace of monotheistic belief in their worldview. This destroyed the anthropologists' theory, but it also opened an exciting door for those who do cross-cultural evangelism.

The apostle Paul found himself in a difficult communication problem when he was preaching in Athens. He was preaching to a people who lived among hundreds of statues of false gods. He was preaching Jesus to a people who thought they knew everything there was to know about the gods. Their response to his preaching was "What is this babbler trying to say?…He seems to be advocating foreign gods" (Acts 17:18). Their attitude was "We have enough gods of our own. We have tried them all. Why do we need to hear about another god who is foreign also? If there were a god greater than our gods, we would certainly know about him."

But six centuries earlier, a series of events occurred which provided a special cultural key to the hearts of the Athenians. The city was experiencing a plague with many people dying. The people appeased their gods to no avail. Finally, in desperation they sent for the famous Epimedes to come from Crete to advise them what to do. He told them to set loose a flock of black and white sheep on Mars Hill near Athens. If any of them rested instead of grazing on the grassy hill, then that would be a sign that an unknown god would accept the sheep as sacrifice and stop the plague. Some of the animals did lie down. They sacrificed the sheep to the unknown god, hoping he would stop the plague even though they did not know his name. The plague was lifted from the city. The people dedicated a memorial to this unknown god who was greater than all their own gods.[52] That altar was there to be a cultural link between the Gospel and the Athenians. The Athenians did not want to hear about another foreign god. But there was a historical curiosity about the unknown god whose memorial they had seen throughout their lives. The story of why the memorial was there was familiar to all of them. By divine inspiration, Paul declared that he was going to proclaim the knowledge of that unknown God. We can only imagine that the Spirit anointed him to preach about Jesus as the "Lamb of God" (John 1:29). He proclaimed the Gospel to them openly, declaring their need to repent and place their trust in this God who was finally being made known to them. Some of those hardened intellectual philosophers accepted Christ that very day! Others wanted to hear more later. The memorial to the unknown god became a perfect cultural key to Paul's preaching of the Gospel (Acts 17:21–34).

The experience of many cross-cultural evangelists seem to demonstrate that God has allowed cultural keys to be prepared in the history of many peoples in order to prepare them to receive the Gospel. Paul found the inscription to the unknown God and did not hesitate to use it. He found the closest symbol for God with which the people could identify. Then he poured historical biblical meaning

---

[52] Diogenes Laertius, *Lives of Eminent Philosophers*, trans. R. D. Hicks (London: Harvard University Press, 1925), 110.

into that symbol by teaching them about the true and living God. In that way, the Gospel came alive in the minds of the arrogant and hard-hearted Athenian intellectuals.

The same thing happened when the cross-cultural evangelists in Korea discovered the word *Hananim* as the best symbol for the true God. It also happened with the evangelist among the Motilone tribe of Colombia mentioned in chapter four. Remember that the tribe had a legend that God had disappeared through the root of the banana plant. According to their worldview, that great god left them because of their sinfulness. So the hundreds of Motilone who have become Christians found the true living God. To those who have become Christians, the true living God is called the God of the banana stalk. There are many other stories that illustrate this point. That is a good reason for doing good research into the worldview of each target people. It can provide just the kind of anthropologic and historical understanding which will become a key to presenting the Gospel to the target people. When backed by fervent prayer, such research can reveal the right cultural key to open the hearts of the people to the Gospel message. Such keys are powerful tools for evangelizing people groups. They are worth searching for!

Good strategies guide evangelists in the implementation of cultural keys. The goals and objectives of the strategy guide the activities of cross-cultural evangelism. But successful implementation of the strategy also depends upon the attitude of the evangelistic team toward the local believers. The evangelists must trust the Holy Spirit to speak to them and use them as they grow in witness and leadership. They cannot be directive in their approach. The strategy also must be implemented using principles and methods in harmony with autochthonous church planting. Group dedication, well-organized divisions of tasks, transferring goals to the local believers, searching for cultural keys—all these are good principles to follow for making the implementation of strategy fruitful and effective.

EVALUATE RESULTS

PRINCIPLES FOR EVALUATION

Figure 9.b: Strategy Planning Model

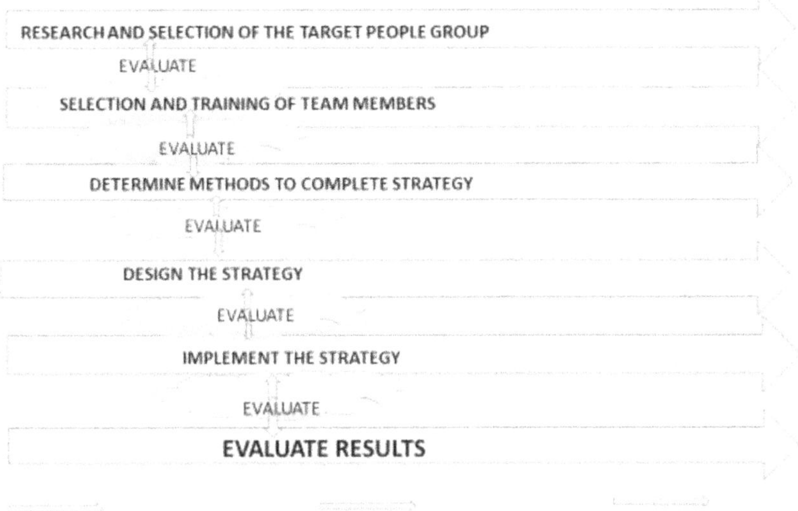

Strategy planning and implementation involves a constant process of evaluation. Evaluation occurs at each step of the planning process. Evaluation of needs leads to evaluation of personnel which leads to evaluation of goals and methods, and so forth through the planning of the strategy. But during the implementation of the strategy, there is also need for formal evaluation based upon the goals, methods, and objectives adopted. We need to check our progress against our strategy plans. In doing this, it is important to realize that everyone works as a team, evaluates as a team, and is accountable to God as a team. Evaluation is an opportunity to glorify God for the progress made, not to condemn anyone or even the whole team for failure to complete their goals. It is a tool to increase effectiveness and nothing else. The fact is that goals are almost never completed exactly as planned. But they are very valuable because they are clear indications of what goals to pursue, how to do it, and how to know when they are completed.

Evaluation is a key ingredient in a simple three-part cycle of activity. Whenever we want to accomplish anything of any size or importance, we must constantly be in the process of doing three basic things: make plans, implement plans, and evaluate (figure 9.c). Plans must be made and implemented, but rarely can an original plan be completely implemented without making adjustments. Evaluation provides opportunity for making adjustments to plans, goals, objectives, and methods. It provides an opportunity to make cyclical adjustments in their implementation. Our plans benefit greatly from these periodic adjustments as we carry them through toward completion.

Figure 9.c

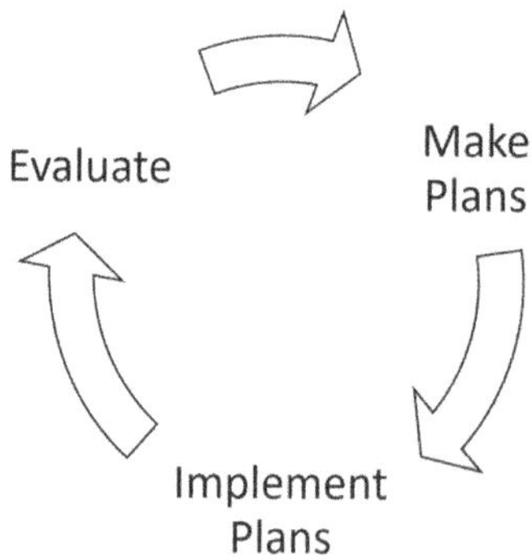

<u>Goals Are a Measuring Stick:</u> The specific and measurable goals of the planning strategy are the primary means to measure our progress in implementing strategies. When a goal or objective states that a specific task should be accomplished within a certain length of time, team members have a good guideline and even faith goals for planning their activities. For instance, if one objective is to translate the Gospel of John into a certain language within six months, it becomes necessary to schedule the amount of translation that must be completed within three months, one month, or one week. The translator divides his objectives into smaller parts, then checks his progress

against those time goals. The same process must apply to each goal and objective in the strategy.

There should be regularly scheduled times of evaluation for the whole strategy. It should be a time when the whole cross-cultural evangelism team can sit down together and evaluate the progress toward each goal and objective. It can happen every month, every three months, every six months, or every year, depending upon the level of goals being evaluated. Or, there can be a combination of scheduled times, with specific evaluation groups meeting more often than the whole team because they are concerned with goals or objectives that they alone are implementing.

Evaluation should be completed by regularly asking two questions: (1) Is the work effectively leading to the completion of specific objectives and goals? Does an honest evaluation say that present efforts will allow us to complete the work just like it was planned? (2) If the work continues as it is, will it allow us to meet the objective within the time limits which were planned?

If the answer to either of these questions is doubtful concerning any goal or objective, the team should decide exactly what needs to be changed. There may be need for more personnel or resources to help complete that goal on time. Or, it may become clear that the goal or objective itself should be changed or modified. Maybe the estimate of timing was not realistic. Maybe it is now clear that even with great faith and effort, it will take longer. Or maybe this goal needs to be completed later than we thought because of other goals which will also be completed later than anticipated. Or the reverse could be true. It may be that all the goals' timing will be completed faster. Many different conclusions and modifications can be made at strategy planning meetings. But they are just as important, and probably more so, than the original strategy planning sessions back home. These are the critical times when the strategy is adjusted to fit the new understandings, limitations, and opportunities which the team discovers on the field as they implement the strategy. The Holy Spirit can give insight to team members as they do their work. Strategy evaluation meetings should be the times when those insights and help from the Spirit can be incorporated into the work plans. Just be sure to stretch your faith and expectation for God's Spirit to do His work also.

Evaluating the Target People: An important part of the evaluation process includes the progress the target people are making toward accepting Christ. The best tool to use when evaluating the people group as a whole is the Conversion as a Process Chart (chapter six). At the early stages of strategy implementation, there may not be even one convert. But if an analysis of the people shows that a large percentage of the people have moved from -4 to -3 on the chart, then real progress is being made. The strategy may not need to be changed at all! If the people group continues to move closer to the point where they can make an informed decision to accept the Lord, many of them will eventually do so. If the attitudes, understandings, and level of belief of the target people continually move them toward the cross, there will be a great harvest of souls in the future. More important, they will be representative of the mainstream of that society, not a fringe group. Evaluating the growth toward Christ within the target people group is an important element of periodic strategy evaluation.

Evaluating Personnel and Resources: Strategy evaluation meetings should also examine the mix of people and resources which are dedicated to each goal and objective. If some goals are easily being completed with the amount of team members or finances available, it may be wise to shift some people/finances to help reach other goals which are not keeping up with the schedule. This flexibility on the part of the team members can greatly help maximize the results. It also enhances the team because people continue to be committed to doing what is needed more than just doing ministries they enjoy.

Evaluating Ministry Structures: Good evaluation practices include a close monitoring of the kinds of ministry in which local believers and the cross-cultural team are engaged. Answers to the following kinds of questions should be sought: (1) If the local church(es) continue to develop the kinds of ministries they are pursuing now, will they be able to reach the right objectives? (2) Are we teaching the local churches to establish the kinds of ministries which maintain a good balance between making disciples and teaching them? (3) Should the cross-cultural team change the emphasis of their own work to help build a more balanced work among the local churches? (4) What kinds of ministry structures should be established by the local churches to more effectively minister to the needs of their society? (5) What kinds of ministry structures need to be added to the local churches to help them better reach their goals in evangelism and building up the believers in their faith? Finding answers to questions like these should also be a part of the strategy evaluation sessions. It is also an opportunity for local and regional local church leaders to participate in the strategy sessions.

One of the greatest single causes of ineffective cross-cultural evangelism is the lack of effective management for reaching the desired goals. Evaluation is the key ingredient for managing the work. In oral communication, we pay close attention to the responses of other people while we are speaking. This feedback helps us to adjust our message according to the other person's responses. In the same way, evaluation provides a channel for evangelists, planners, and church planters to adjust their strategies according to the changing responses and effectiveness of those they are working to evangelize. Evaluation is not an afterthought. It is a key part of the process for being successful in God's work in other cultures.

TOOLS FOR EVALUATION

The Great Commission demands that the church grow in quality and in quantity. Making disciples is quantitative growth. If refers to the actual addition of numbers of new believers to Christ's body and to local churches. It honors God, and it honors and makes more effectual the sacrifice of Christ on the cross. Teaching them to obey Christ's commands is qualitative growth. If refers to the ways the church members are built up in their faith, and use that better quality of living to help others. When we evaluate strategies, we must measure growth in both quality and quantity.

Before people are converted, as we saw in chapter six, we can estimate the quality of their progress toward accepting Christ by measuring their understanding of the Gospel, their attitudes toward it, and how much they are learning about it. After they are believers, we can measure the quality of their growth by how well they reproduce themselves in ministry to believers and unbelievers as well. That is why the conversion as a process chart can be so helpful. It can be used as a guide to measure qualitative growth before and after conversion.

One way to measure both the quantity and quality of our growth is to simply measure how effectively churches are reproducing themselves numerically. People cannot grow in their faith and obedience to the Lord without consistently helping others. This means helping unbelievers find God as well as helping believers grow in faith. If the ministry of the churches is balanced as it should be, they will grow numerically. They will reproduce both inside their churches (they will have more people) and outside their churches (they will start new churches). So one method to evaluate strategies as a whole is to numerically measure the progress of growth goals.

Some people have a negative reaction to including numerical analysis in measuring spiritual activities. A common proof text to support this reaction is 2 Samuel 24:1–10 where God is displeased with King David for numbering the Israelites. But God had a specific purpose for his command in that instance. There are many times when God specifically commanded the Israelite leaders to take a census of their people (i.e., Num. 1:2–3). Luke, the writer of the book of Acts, was careful to keep a numerical record of the increases in the number of believers.

Statistical analysis by itself will not save anyone. But neither will an X-ray or a blood pressure gauge heal anyone. They are tools to help the doctor know how to provide a cure. A numerical understanding of the growth of churches does the same thing. Understanding the ways and the rates by which Christ's church grows will simply help us see what things help the churches grow faster, and what things cause their growth to slow or stop. If we emphasize those things that help the churches grow, and de-emphasize those things which keep it from growing, the effect will be to help more people come to Christ in a shorter period of time. That is the same purpose for which we use autochthonous church-planting principles. They maximize the growth of the Kingdom of God. Methods for understanding growth patterns are important evaluation tools to help us in strategy evaluation and planning. If used wisely, these tools can help us bring more people to Christ. This section discusses some important methods and tools for that kind of evaluation.

Measuring the Right Things: Using growth analysis tools requires the right kinds of information. We need to know what is important to measure, as well as how to measure it. Measuring growth requires keeping adequate records. Where we are measuring the growth of small groups, a single church, a group of churches, or all the churches in a country or region, we still need the same kinds of information. Figure 9.d shows an example of the types of information that is needed for good long-term growth analysis. You may decide you want to keep records on many different categories according the needs for information indicated by the goals of your strategy plan. Whatever categories you decide are best, be sure to help every leader keep adequate records. Make sure those responsible use the most accurate methods for getting the information, and that they follow them consistently. Once you decide which numbers averaged together are the best representation of your church's membership, add them together regularly (weekly, monthly, etc.). There must be a consistent way to know how many people attend your church meetings every week. That is your ***composite membership*** that can be used to evaluate and plan for the growth of your church or your group of churches. Just remember to try not to count the same people twice if they attend more than one kind of meeting.

Figure 9.d: DETERMINING COMPOSITE MEMBERSHIP

Evaluation	**DIAGNOSTIC PERIOD: ANNUAL**										Last Yr.
Category	20	20	20	20	20	20	20	20	20	20	20
Active Members											
Worship Attendance											
Life Group Attendance											
Organized Churches											
Preaching Points (PP)											
Ordained Pastors											
Evangelists											
Churches Planted											
CCEs Sent											

You may want to measure the growth from month to month, or even week to week. For doing long-term analysis, year-to-year measurements are best. Whatever time spans you choose, they should be filled in at the top of the column like on the chart, which is indicating yearly figures. In figure 9.d, the numbers written in should be end-of-the-year amounts. As a general rule, attendance at meetings should be averaged for the year, and figures which classify people should be expressed as the total number at the end of the year. Remember to keep records as an act of faith that God is helping you do what he called you to do. The records will help grow your faith and determination.

For whatever units of time you are measuring, it is important to get the figures for one extra unit in order to get a correct analysis. In figure 9.d, there are eleven years indicated because you need data from eleven years to measure growth for ten years. If you are measuring the growth for the last twelve months, you will need data for thirteen months. This chapter will help you evaluate growth consistently and accurately.

When you fill in your own charts, it is best to start with the last time period, then work backward. If you were using the example of figure 9.d, you would put in the figures for the end of last year first, then each year before that back to the beginning of the chart.

Using Graphs: After you have gathered all the needed information for the period of time you are measuring, and after you have filled in your charts with that information, you should use graphs to visually display the results. Figures 9.e and 9f show two different kinds of graphs.

Figure 9.e

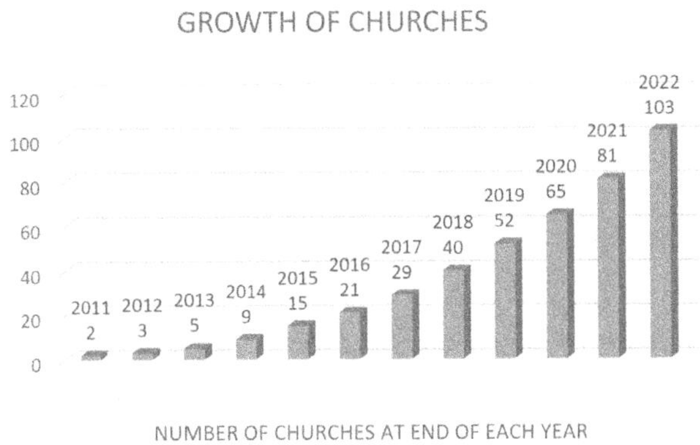

Figure 9.e is a simple bar graph showing the growth of a set of churches over a period of eleven years. Each team should have access to at least one computer to graph such information. Microsoft Excel is a good program to easily make such a graph. They are also available through other programs online. After selecting a program to use, label the vertical axis with the growth data from your chart you have already collected (figure 9.e). Label the horizontal axis with the data and the period of time you are covering—weeks, months or years. This will graphically show you the growth history for the time periods you are measuring. If there are periods when the numbers declined, the bar will show a shorter bar for that period of time. For periods when it increased, the bar will show a longer bar than the year before. Bar graphs are useful for showing amounts of growth, but not rates of growth, which is explained below.

Finding Membership Totals: Sometimes churches and denominations use different methods for deciding who is a member and who is not. Some cultures include people who were once baptized in the church, but no longer attend. Others have very strict rules about who can be a member and who cannot. Yet when both kinds of churches report their membership, they will likely be inaccurate. Therefore, we need a standard for comparing the growth of different churches—a way of measuring which overcomes these differences in counting membership. The simplest way to solve this problem is to simply measure the attendance at weekly worship services (see figure 9.d).

Types of Growth and Decline: It is very helpful for strategy planners to know the types of people who make up the growth figures for a local church or a group of churches. For instance, they may want to know how many people are joining the church as a result of conversion. There are three basic ways to classify the growth or decline figures for any church:

Conversion Growth: This is the portion of the growth which is due to people accepting Christ and joining the church. It is a direct result of the "making disciples" function of the church's ministry.

Transfer Growth: This is the growth that occurs not as a result of conversion, but at a result of the people transferring their church loyalty from another church. These people are already Christians (this should be confirmed), but are just changing from one church to another.

Biological Growth: This is growth which results from population growth within the church body. It occurs when local believers have children. This kind of growth can be figured by simply counting the newborn babies of church members.

Reversion Decline: This refers to those people who backslide and leave the church to return to their old life of sin.

Transfer Decline: This refers to people who transfer from the church being studied to another church. This is common when people move into cities from rural areas.

Biological Decline: This results from the deaths of believers in the church. And it needs to be included in the numbers used for church membership.

Figure 9.f: YEARLY GAINS AND LOSSES

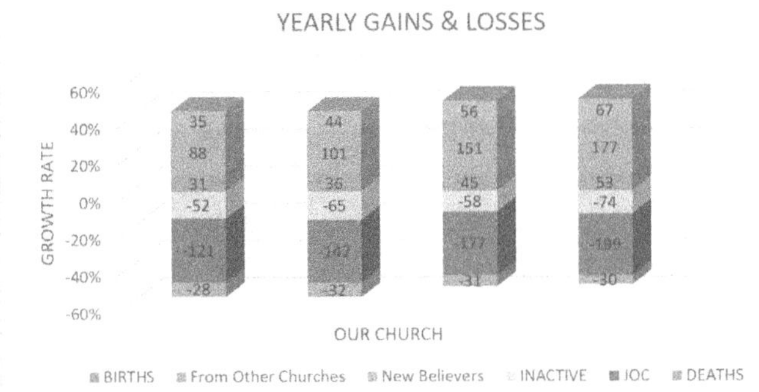

Let's show the importance of these types of growth and decline by taking an actual example from a church in a reached people group (name withheld). Figure 9.f gives an example of the figures for growth and decline displayed on a column graph. Those above the middle line (0) represent growth figures. Those below the line represent decline figures. Notice how all the figures in the three categories of growth and three categories of decline are added together, or stacked on top of one another to make the column graph.

The kind of information this further analysis of growth statistics provides can obviously be very helpful. It helps us see exactly the kinds of growth or decline a church or group of churches is experiencing. Some churches take great pride in the fact that they are growing rapidly. But an analysis of the types of growth like in figure 9.f may reveal that most of the growth is transfer growth from other churches. While such growth is good for a church, it certainly does not fulfill Jesus' commitment to make disciples. It may indicate that believers in a growing church are becoming worldly and not paying attention to that mandate to grow from the commands of Jesus. Yet new people are coming in, and believers think they are growing very fast.

Notice that figure 9.f shows a church which saw a decline in numbers over a four-year period. By adding the values of the bar graph, we can see that a total of 884 people joined the church, but a total of 1,019 left the church. That is a four-year loss of 125 people.

During all years, losses exceeded gains. It is also important to notice that there was a consistent number of losses by those who quit going to church, which was greater than new gains by conversion.

A graph like this automatically makes you want to ask questions about why. Why were more people turning away from following Christ than were turning to following Christ? Why were more people consistently transferring to other churches faster than those coming from other churches? Why were there so few conversions taking place?

Those questions are the fruit of good growth analysis, and it is easy to see how important they are. It helps leaders ask themselves the right questions. By finding their answers, leaders can increase those goals, methods, and ministries which enhance growth and avoid those which decrease growth. Since the nature of Christ's work on earth demands growing churches, we must make the best possible use of growth analysis tools to find answers to questions about growth.

Measuring Growth Rates: With the help of some fairly simple tools, planners can effectively measure the growth of any church or group of churches. This can be done by using the information and methods discussed above. It only requires that accurate records be kept. Even if accurate records are not available, close approximations can often be made which will still yield valuable information and insight into causes for growth or decline.

It is very useful not only to know the figures for the growth of a church or a group of churches, but it is also helpful to know the **rates of growth**. Knowing the rates of growth gives us a more accurate understanding of the health and vitality of a church's ministries. They lead us to ask even further questions about how we can improve the qualitative and quantitative growth of the church. In cross-cultural evangelism, the answers to these questions can be very important for planning and implementing strategies which help the churches grow faster and increase the quality of their spiritual life.

Annual Growth Rate: It is helpful to know how much a church grew from one month or year to the next. We can see that partially by simply comparing the membership totals over a period of time. But that does not tell us all that we need to know. Since all believers in the church should be doing "the work of the ministry" (Eph. 4:12), churches should grow faster in number as more people join the church. Since believers should reproduce by winning more people to Christ, the **rate** of growth should not decline and may even increase. But even in rapidly growing churches, this is often not the case.

For example, figures 9.g and 9.h show two different categories of growth of a single church on two graphs. The columns of figure 9.g show that the church is growing by one hundred people every year. But it also demonstrates that the growth is going down every year as indicated by the percentages shown at the top of each column. Figure 9.h shows the same percentage of growth information for the same church, but it emphasis the RATE of growth rather than the AMOUNT of growth

Figure 9.g

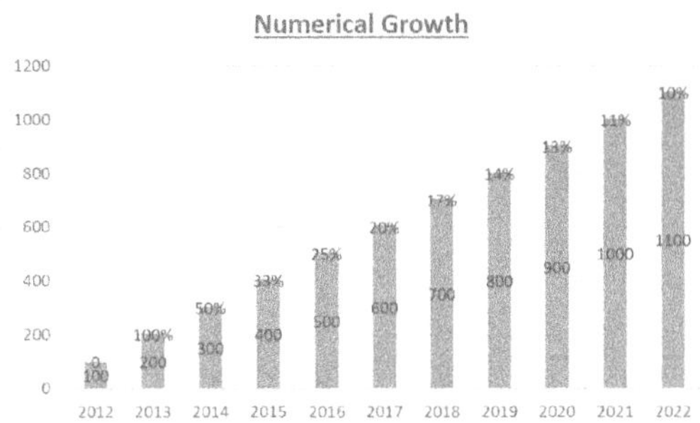

Figure 9.h

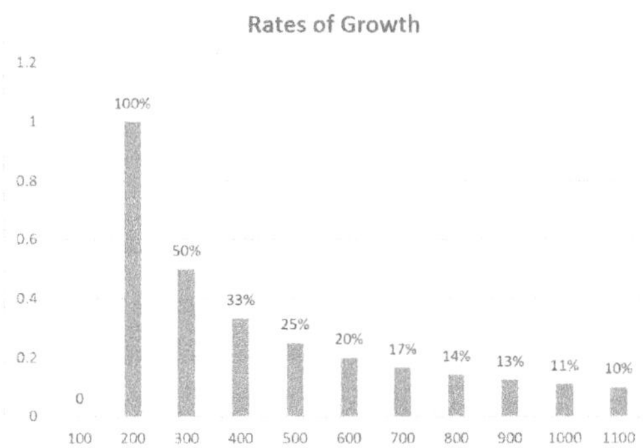

The numbers below demonstrate how these percentages are calculated. We will use the same numbers as on the graphs in figure 9.g and 9.h. Let's find the growth rate for the year 2014. This is the amount of growth for that year above the end of the previous year. Here is the formula:

Step One: Subtract the first year-end membership from the second year-end membership:

300
<u>-200</u>
100

Step Two: Divide the answer to step one by the **earlier** year's membership figure:

100/200 = 0.50

Step Three: Multiply your answer by 100 to show percentage of increase:

0.50 x 100 = 50%

Using this formula, it is easy to see that the <u>**rates**</u> of growth actually declined, even though the number of new members increased by the same amount each year. Here are the rates of growth for each succeeding year:

2014: 50%	2017: 20%	2020: 12.5%
2015: 33.3%	2018: 16.7%	2021: 11.1%
2016: 25%	2019: 14.3%	2022: 10%

Let's remember that each believer is responsible to do his part to win others to Christ. The charts and figures for the church in figures 9.g and 9.h (which is not a real church) show that fewer and fewer people are getting involved in helping to win other people to Christ each succeeding year. Reproducibility is declining every year. This demonstrates the importance of knowing growth rates, not just the increase in the numbers of believers. Knowing growth rates will help you predict your progress toward reaching your goals for both quantitative and qualitative growth in a strategy plan. Both types of growth are dependent upon each other.

Decadal Growth Rates (DGR): Knowing growth rates is helpful, but knowing decadal growth rates will give a clearer picture of how much a church has grown or will grow over a longer period of time. The decadal growth rate (DGR) measures growth over a ten-year period. This information can be used to help correct past mistakes or help us make projections for future growth to measure against our goals. Seeing past growth or decline over a longer period of time helps us see where we have been or where we are headed, then make corrections to help us reach our growth goals.

DGR: Standard (Simple) Calculation: If you have the membership figures for ten years, it is easy to calculate the decadal growth rate. The formula is given below. To illustrate the formula, let's use a church which has 250 members at the end of 2012 and 750 members at the end of 2022.

Step One: Subtract the number of members at the end of the tenth year from the number of members at the end of the first year. In this case:

750
-250
500

Step Two: Divide your answer by the number of members from the first year:

500/250 = 2.0

Step Three: Multiply your step two answer by 100 to yield the DGR expressed as percentage growth:

2.0 x 100 = 200% Decadal Growth Rate

Nonstandard DGR Calculation: It will often occur that you do not have the membership totals for the full ten years. Therefore, you will not be able to calculate the DGR using the simple formula above. In that case, there is a simplified system for solving that problem contained in the appendix section of this book. If you have an electronic calculator like engineers use, you can solve the problem by using the formula in Appendix D. But many people do not have such a calculator, and they do not know advanced mathematics. That is why appendices F, H, and I are included in the back of this book. They can be used to find the DGR without complicated mathematics.

Let's assume the figures in figure 9.f as an example to learn how to use these tools. Let's say we only know the membership figures of the church in figure 9.g (as an example) from 2016 through 2021 (five years). By finding the DGR for those years, we can project how many members should be in the church for any year in the future if the growth rate remains the same. Using the church in figure 9.g as an example, here is the formula for finding the DGR when using figures for other than a ten-year period.

<u>Step One:</u> Divide the last year figure by the beginning year figure (L/B in Appendix E):

1,000/500 = 2.0

<u>Step Two:</u> Find the result under the column marker L/B in Appendix E. (If the exact number is not there, find the one closest to your number.)

<u>Step Three:</u> Moving across the chart on the same line, locate the percentage figure which most closely represents the Average Annual Growth Rate (AAGR) under the column which shows the correct number of years between the last year and the beginning year. In our example, the AAGR is 14.87%. This is found by subtracting 2016

from 2021 (5 years), then looking for the AAGR under the column labeled "5."

Step Four: Go to Appendix E, which shows AAGR and DGR. Looking under the AAGR columns, find the answer to step three (14.87% in our example).

Step Five: On the same chart (Appendix E), find the DGR on the same line and under the next column to your right. This will be right next to where you located your AAGR in step four. That figure is your Decadal Growth Rate. For our example, that column shows the DGR is 300%.

The DGR can be used to make future projections. For instance, we can use our example to find out how many members the church will have by the end of 2027 if growth continues at the same rate. We simply multiply the membership for 2016 times the DGR we found in step five above (500 x 300% = 1,500) We can say that the church will reach a membership of 1,500 at the end of 2026 if it continues to grow at the same rate. We can do the same thing through 2031 by multiplying the figure for 2021 times 300%. That process yields a membership of 3,000 by 2031. This kind of information and calculations are extremely valuable when we are implementing our cross-cultural evangelism strategies and evaluating our progress along the way.

Average Annual Growth Rate: Notice that we mentioned Average Annual Growth Rate (AAGR) in step three above. This is the year-by-year average of growth for a church, or group of churches, when figures are known for a period covering more than one year. Knowing this figure helps us in two ways. First, as is demonstrated above, it leads us to the Decadal Growth Rate. You must find the AAGR before you can get the DGR when using Appendixes H and I. The first three steps out of the five listed above are the method for finding the AAGR.

The second way the AAGR helps us is to tell us how much we must grow each year in order to reach a long-term growth goal. For example, let's say there are a group of churches which want to grow at a decadal growth rate of 450%. By looking at Appendix E, under the DGR column at 450%, they can look one column to the left to see that the churches will have to average growing at a rate of 18.59% over those ten years. This will help those churches to set yearly growth goals effectively. For example, if a church has 450 members at the end of one year, they will need to add 74 new people to their membership by the end of the next year. The AAGR helps us to break our long-range goals down into shorter-range goals and track our progress. This is important for planning, evaluating, and adjusting our growth strategies.[53]

USING TOOLS FOR STRATEGY EVALUATION

Becoming familiar with the use of evaluation tools described above will help us in strategy planning, and in strategy evaluation. When making plans, some people feel hesitant to make them specific and measurable. One reason for this hesitancy is that people feel threatened by such goals because they are not sure how to measure their progress. These strategy evaluation tools help us to easily check our progress, and give us a greater understanding of how to project our goals into the future. Let's use some of these tools a little more together in order to become familiar with their use.

Let's use the strategy example we described in the last part of chapter eight. The primary purpose was to evangelize 20 percent of the Sasak people group on the island of Lombok, Indonesia, within 20 years. Now, let's say we are part of the cross-cultural evangelism team, and we have been on the island of Lombok for three years. Though we continue to polish our language ability, our two-year period of intensive language/culture learning is past. We have been

---

[53] The tools described and used in this book related to analyzing growth are derived from and used by permission of the authors Bob Waymire and C. Peter Wagner and their *Church Growth Survey Handbook* (revised third edition), published by OC International in 1988. Wagner was the author's doctoral mentor, and Waymire was a collaborator with the author at One Challenge International (formerly OC International). It is now out of print and very expensive on Amazon, but can still be purchased online at https://www.churchgrowthnetwork.com/resource-store/church-growth-survey-handbook. It is highly recommended that each field team obtain a copy of the handbook for use in their on-the-field planning.

working successfully to establish trust relationships with the Waktu Lima in the middle- and lower-middle class of the society. During our third year on the island, we have managed to start 3 churches and 11 house churches with a total membership of 545 people. The 3 churches are located in the 3 largest cities on the island, and at least one cross-cultural evangelism team member is living in each of those cities.

At the end of our third year on the island, it is time for our yearly strategy and evaluation planning meeting. In order to help us in the meetings, a list of obstacles which need to be overcome and a list of successes for which we can praise God have been prepared. Here are some of the things on the lists.

Successes to Encourage our Faith

1. The growth of the churches have mostly come through kinship patterns of relationships. People related to one another by family are sharing the work of the Lord in their lives, and that has been the vehicle by which most of the people in all three cities are finding the Lord as Savior.
2. Each of the churches have been established by having meetings in people's home compounds, that is, several homes on the same plot of land or several apartments in the same area. There are now a total of fourteen of these houses of prayer meeting regularly, but only three have their own rented facilities.
3. A total of thirty believers are taking leadership training in Bible courses three nights per week in the three different cities. These include all the pastors of the churches and the leaders of home meetings.
4. As was decided at last year's strategy and evaluation planning meeting, the believers are doing well at keeping their witness on a low profile. They are not attracting attention to their meetings, and they are sharing the Gospel only as the Lord directs them in developing strong relationships on an individual basis. Personal evangelism is the priority

focus. Each leader and group of believers approve invitations to the meetings before anyone is invited to join and only after strong faith and interest of the right kind is expressed by the outsider.

5. The leaders are proving very wise at using local cultural forms and behavior patterns to express their faith and attract the interest of others. Some leaders are becoming skilled at producing Bible stories using the Wajang Kulit puppet shows. It is the primary means of first attracting outsiders.

Obstacles to Overcome

1. There is a strong need and a strong desire for the believers in each city to meet together all at once. So far, they have only been meeting in home meetings, except for the three rented locations. Also, since many of the believers have family in other parts of the cities, they are enthused by the idea of having larger meetings so they can invite their families to join them. They want to have larger meetings and are excited about having more people come even before they have accepted Christ.
2. At first, the house of prayer meetings were considered by outsiders to simply be groups of spiritually devout Muslims who meet together regularly for prayer. Now there is a growing curiosity and suspicion in the communities about the meetings. Curiosity is high, and the believers are being very wise in what they share. Though the word *Christian* has never been used by agreement, the believers are coming to be known as followers of Isa (Isa means Jesus). This is sure to cause concern among Muslim leaders if it has not already.
3. While only a relatively small percentage of Muslim Waktu Lima goes to the mosque, some of the new believers have come from this more devout section of the Muslim society. While this is good for the growth of the churches and home

> meetings, the absence of these people from the prayers and meetings at the mosque is being noticed. So far, this has caused only a little concern, but it will undoubtedly cause problems with Muslim leaders when more people accept Christ.

The strategy evaluation and planning meeting opened with great praise and thanksgiving to God for an abundant harvest of souls during the previous year. There was great praise that so many people had accepted Isa (Christ), and that there were regular Bible (called Isa stories and teachings—word *Bible* not used) training programs for leaders and believers already underway. An infinitely reproducible system for training leaders and multiplying house of prayer meetings were being established. The local leaders of the groups had been wise in their choices of which cultural forms to keep, and which ones to discard in their worship of the Lord. Each believer was very enthusiastic about being forgiven, assured about their salvation, and were growing in their understanding and experiences concerning how much God loves them and is helping them. Nobody is called a Christian. They are privately known as Prophet Isa followers.

Each team member had already been given a list of the successes and obstacles before the meeting. So there was a lot of discussion about how to find places in each city where the whole group could meet together. There was also a heated discussion about how often to meet. There was much concern already about the rising visibility of the three churches (houses of prayer) meeting in rented buildings. Everyone agreed that there would come a time when the true nature of the groups would become known. A time of persecution would likely follow.

The team leader cautioned the group not to let the short-term dangers they face obstruct their vision for the long-term goals. Everyone knew they would need to be prepared for possible persecution in the future. "The report of the successes and obstacles is an accurate description of our progress to this point," stated the leader. "We are doing well starting groups and keeping a low profile, but we must prepare for the day when we are large enough and regarded well enough to openly declare our faith. How we do that will be critical. At the same time, we must also constantly check our progress on reaching our future strategy goals before making any planning decisions for the months and years ahead. Let's not let the obstacles we see coming dim our faith to reach those goals for the sake of all our people who need to hear the Gospel. God has helped us so far. He will surely help us make our strategy plans even better, if we ask Him. I do not believe God wants us to lower our goals, but to make them even stronger if necessary. I am sure God can turn these obstacles we see coming into opportunities for greater success—if we plan well and believe God for His help. We are doing what he wants us to do for now. Let's keep doing what we are doing the way we are doing it. If persecution comes, then let's become so big that this movement toward following Isa cannot be stopped and persecution will be dampened by our positive witness. Let's keep following the patterns we are using. They are being successful. Let's not worry about getting together all at once. That can come later."

At that point in the meeting, it was decided to do an evaluation of the amount of growth needed to meet the future goals of the strategy plan. They decided that the first information they needed was to find out how fast they needed to keep growing in order to reach their Secondary Goal Three. That goal states that they should have a total of at least 6,000 believers in 20 churches and 100 houses of prayer (HOP) groups by the end of 4 more years (ninth year of the project and seventh year of fieldwork).

By using the charts in Appendix E and F, they quickly calculated the Average Annual Growth Rate (AAGR) to reach that goal as follows:

Step One: Last year's believers divided by this year's number of believers.

6,000/545 = 11.0

Step Two: Find 11.0 under the L/B column of Table A (Appendix D).

Step Three: Moving to the right on the 11.0 line, find the AAGR under the "4" (for four years) column on Appendix D.

AAGR = 82.12%

Conclusion: an average annual growth rate of 82.12% per year for the next four years will enable us to reach our goal. This means we should have the following totals at the end of each of the next four years:

First year: 545 + 448 = 993
Second year: 993 + 816 = 1,809
Third year: 1,809 + 1,486 = 3,295
Fourth year: 3,295 + 2,706 = 6,001

After doing the calculations, there was some rejoicing because the figures showed that they had already grown in the first year more than was required in the second year to meet their goal. But they also realized that growth would be harder to sustain as more and more people found the Lord. This would especially be true if any serious persecution from the community put pressure on the House of Prayer group meetings. They decided that the key was to find ways to be positive examples in the community so people would admire their changed way of life. Any efforts at persecution would become opportunities to love others instead of shrinking back in fear. They studied the book of Acts again and asked God for greater courage no matter what may come.

During the discussion, one of the pastors of an established house of prayer said, "I praise God that we are growing fast, and I can see how we might be able to grow at an 82% rate over the next 4 years. We have already been growing faster. But I don't see how we will be able to grow from 6,000 to 180,000 within the next 6 years after that. That would be a phenomenal rate of growth!" Some of the other leaders nodded in agreement. That did sound like an impossible goal. "Maybe it ought to be changed to something more realistic," they said.

But the team leader said, "Before we jump to any conclusions, maybe we should find out exactly how fast we would have to grow during those six years. We can make any needed changes after we find out what we will need as an AAGR during those six years. Then we can make any changes if we need to. God has given us tremendous growth this year. By faith, we should aim for the highest level of growth possible. The more people we have, the safer we will also be during this period of time."

Some of the team seemed a little reluctant, but they agreed to go ahead with the growth evaluation for the seventh through the thirteenth year to see the rate of growth needed.

Their calculations looked like this:

Step One: L/B = 180,000 divided by 6,000 = 30

Step Two: The number 30 does not appear on Table A (Appendix E), so they used 31, which is the closest number. But using the method for extrapolation at the bottom of Appendix E, they noticed that 30 is 80% of the difference between 26 and 31, both of which appear on the appendix chart.

Step Three: Moving across the chart on the 31 line, they find 77.24 under the "6" (year) column. The figure for the 26 line under column 6 is 72.12. They know the rate for 30 is 80% of the difference between those two figures. So they calculate the AAGR as follows:

77.24 – 72.12 = 5.12 x 0.80 = 4.1
72.12 + 4.1 = 76.24 (AAGR)

The results of these calculations were both amazing and encouraging to almost everyone. Those who had been a part of the original strategy planning committee back home already knew what the figures would be. They had already worked through them in their strategy sessions. But those who had joined the leadership team from among the Waktu Lima had not been a part of those planning sessions, and this really encouraged them.

"Wow, I did not realize we could grow that much so fast if we just work hard to keep growing as fast as we are growing now," said the one who had expressed his doubts before. "The growth rates we need to sustain from the seventh through the thirteenth year are lower than the ones we need for the next four years! Let's see if we can continue to grow at our present rate, and we will be even bigger than that at the end of the thirteenth year."

Feeling encouraged, the team members decided to keep their secondary goals as they were. They also began to make plans for the next year with greater hope and faith. They began to realize by the AAGR calculations how very important it will be to keep all their efforts reproducible in the lives of all the believers. That means all believers will have to remain engaged in "the work of the ministry" (Eph. 4:12). And inside their hearts, they knew that the faster they could grow, the better they would be able to withstand whatever obstacles or persecution that may come their way in the future.

The next step the cross-cultural evangelism team decided was important was to make sure all the leaders within their fellowship could gather for a secret joint planning session in one place. When they did, the leaders shared the thoughts, calculations, and feelings which had been expressed in their earlier meeting with everyone there. The Waktu Lima house of prayer leaders and the cross-cultural evangelism team began to make and refine longer-term plans together for the first time. Everyone agreed to share their plans for growth only among believers who were committed not to tell outsiders about them. Among the goals, methods, and objectives they adopted for the next year were the following:

1. Keep meeting in house of prayer (HOP) meetings in homes and continue to develop further Bible training for leaders and believers. Keep the level of training low enough and local enough to make it easily reproducible by the local Waktu Lima leaders themselves as they learned.
2. Do not hold combined meetings for all the believers in one city until at least 2,500 believers join the fellowship in that city and are willing to meet together to celebrate their faith. When that number and commitment is reached, be sure a strong community reputation for believers has already been

established through community-oriented help by believers. Hold the large meeting only after it is agreed that the timing is correct, and that the response of the community as a whole will be one of positive interest.

3. Immediately begin to encourage the local HOPs to make specific plans and goals to help the believers start taking leading roles in community service and improvement efforts. This will be done in order to help the communities, and show the people that the believers strongly identify with their culture and the needs of their people. The believers do not need to carry out their community service in the name of their HOP identity, but only as followers of Isa. They simply need to glorify God and use opportunities for personal witness.
4. When the number of believers in each city reaches 2,500, the believers from the other cities will be invited to join them for a "Celebration of Isa" rally. The soccer stadium will be rented for the event. For the first time, the believers will collectively celebrate and worship together. A message in the Waktu Lima language and in Bahasa will accompany several nights of meetings. A special effort will be made to find personal evangelism opportunities among the higher classes as well as the common person. Selected public personal testimonies will be highlighted showing the change that comes from following God and accepting Isa as Savior. A full public confession of faith by prominent believers in the community and invitation for others to learn more about how to join this movement will be offered to outsiders.
5. At that point, it is expected that some public confusion will follow. Religious leaders will begin to emerge against the meetings. But with the size of the groups of believers, they should be able to withstand the persecution. History shows that persecution under these kinds of circumstances can bring great interest to the Gospel. The believers must be prepared to withstand the persecution that comes, while

humbly and personally testifying to the peace and love they have found in following Isa (Jesus). This will bring more rapid growth.

CONCLUSION

There is great value in learning to evaluate our work for God on a regular basis. This is true of our work among our own people, as well as among peoples of other cultures. The evaluation tools and principles in this chapter can help leaders and planners in many kinds of ministries. It is very important to use these principles and tools in cross-cultural evangelism. They will not only help us to check our progress as we implement our plans, but also, they will increase our faith by giving us clear insights into the nature and power of using good strategy plans.

Good strategy planning is very important for effective cross-cultural evangelism, or any evangelism for that matter. The Father himself made a good long-range strategy to bring redemption to mankind. "When the fullness of time was come, God sent forth his Son" (Gal. 4:4). Jesus was born at the right moment in history. He ministered to the right people the right way. He taught them to multiply the good news of salvation, just as the Father had instructed him to do. But he did not do anything according to his own plan. He followed the plan the Father had made from the beginning (John 5:19). The greatest strategy ever planned was the one planned by God himself! That strategy, according to Jesus Himself, will overcome the strategy of the Gates of Hell! (Matt. 16:18).

An important part of God's strategy is cross-cultural evangelism. It is the most important part. It was the last thing on Jesus' mind when He left this earth (Acts 1:8). We are living at a key point in history. The "fullness of time" has come for God's Church to march forward to evangelize every unreached people. It can be done. God delights in helping us to plan strategies to do it. When we do our best to plan and implement effective cross-cultural evangelism strategies, we are entering into partnership with the heartbeat of God!

QUESTIONS FOR UNDERSTANDING

1. Explain why there aren't any specific rules or methods for implementing a strategy, but there are principles. Explain how those principles can help the cross-cultural evangelists as they implement their strategies.
2. Describe the attitude that must be adopted by the cross-cultural evangelism team in order to be effective in another culture. What attitudes must be avoided?
3. Why is it important to assign specific parts of the strategy plan to be implemented by individual parts of the cross-cultural evangelism team? Using what is explained in this chapter, explain why this is important.
4. Explain in your own words the principle of New Unit Growth. Does the principle mean churches can grow too large? At what point could a church become too large? Why? What is the relationship between this principle and the Principle of Reproducibility?
5. Describe how we should help cross-cultural evangelists to work to adopt objectives with local church leaders that best fit the methods of the long-term strategy plan? Why don't we simply give them the methods of the plan and expect them to use them?
6. In your own words, describe the value of discovering "cultural keys" in a target culture. How did Paul the apostle discover a cultural key in Athens that helped him preach the Gospel?
7. Explain why cyclical evaluation and analysis is important throughout the planning process and during the completion of a strategy to evangelize a people group. Explain the parts of the evaluation cycle and how they are used.
8. Explain how the "conversion as a process" chart can be used to assess the status of an unreached people group. Explain how to use the chart over a period of years. What insights can be gained by using the chart?
9. Why should we continually evaluate local churches in terms of their balance between "making disciples" and "teaching them to obey" Christ's commands? Why is this balance so important?

How should it help the structures and direction of a church's ministries?

10. Explain how an analysis of quantitative growth can also become an analysis of qualitative growth of churches. How can numerical evaluation of growth serve as a valuable tool for planning strategies?
11. Explain how to calculate total composite membership. Let's say your church has the following figures for the week of October 2–9: (a) outstation evangelistic meetings / home churches: 230; community elementary education school: 480; a total of 560 people attending worship services at the central church. What would be the best way to calculate the *composite* membership for that week?
12. Explain conversion, transfer, and biological growth. List their opposites—three kinds of decline in growth. Explain their meaning also. Using a single graph, draw a sample chart comparing the three kinds of growth and the three kinds of decline.
13. What does DGR mean? Why is it important? How can it be used? If a church had a composite membership of 345 at the end of 2018, and a composite membership of 725 at the end of 2022, what is its DGR for that period?
14. What does AAGR mean? How can it be useful? Let's say you are a growth strategist for a group of churches with 2,038 members at the end of 2020. Your strategy plan calls for your churches to grow to 10,500 by the end of 2026. What AAGR would be necessary for your churches to reach their goal?
15. Your church has a goal of growing at a DGR of 550 percent over the next ten-year period. Your church has 1,100 members now. If the church grows at that rate, how many will it have in ten years? What is the AAGR needed to reach that goal? Use appendices H (Table A) and I (Table B). If this AAGR continues throughout the ten years, how many total members will there be after four years?

QUESTIONS FOR DISCUSSION

1. Describe what you consider to be the typical church leader in your country and culture. What kind of changes in attitude would be necessary to make such a person an excellent cross-cultural evangelist?
2. Discuss some principles for finding a good translation for the word "God" in an unreached people group. Should you always use the word for God which other Christians have been using in the area where the people you are evangelizing live? Why? Do you know where your own word for God came from? If you can, do some research online or in a library to find the answer.
3. How do you feel about using statistics and numerical analysis in evaluating spiritual work? Have you ever thought of doing that much? Do you think it provides helpful tools? Can you think of a time in the Bible when God himself ordered Israel to do a statistical analysis? Are the people in your culture accustomed to using numerical analysis for spiritual purposes? Do you think God is pleased with such analyses? Why
4. Discuss the concept of finding cultural keys to communicate to the hearts of a target people. How would an investigation of a people's worldview help you find such keys?
5. How do you feel about the system for planning and implementing strategies for cross-cultural evangelism presented in this book? Do you think you would try to use it, if you were to answer a call to cross-cultural evangelism? How do you think it might be improved? How could this system be used to help the churches in your own culture grow numerically and qualitatively?

CHAPTER TEN

Effective Organization For Cross-Cultural Evangelism

KEY POINTS IN THIS CHAPTER

1. Good organization is necessary for effective cross-cultural evangelism. Poor organizations discourage the people who are trying to work through them. Good organization increases the effectiveness of cross-cultural evangelism.
2. The relationship between the cross-cultural evangelism team and the churches among the target people will change according to the level of organization of the churches.
3. When churches establish organizations to oversee cross-cultural evangelism, they should give those organizations much freedom to plan and implement their strategies.
4. Organization cannot be effective unless it is based upon mutual trust and agreement by all the people involved.
5. It is important to respect autochthonous principles when establishing and operating new organizations in cross-cultural evangelism.
6. Cross-cultural evangelism organizations should not be established in such a way that they control or dominate other organizations with which they work. They should be formed according to the principles of partnership.

7. Cross-cultural evangelism strategies should include plans to help the target churches train and send their own cross-cultural evangelists.
8. The task of evangelizing unreached people groups is the responsibility of every church among every people where the Church has been established.
9. Every person who names Christ as Lord and Savior has a personal responsibility to do something specific to help evangelize unreached peoples.
10. Establishing autochthonous, infinitely reproducible churches is the best hope of fulfilling the Great Commission of Jesus Christ.

This final chapter focuses on organizing cross-cultural evangelism effectively and why it is important. Then it switches to the personal side of why this book is important. For those who really love the Lord Jesus Christ and want to follow his teachings, it is not possible to ignore the challenges this book presents.

The three previous chapters on planning strategies show how necessary it is to organize the task of cross-cultural evangelism. Haphazard planning leads to ineffective evangelism. The same principle is true of the organizational structures which emerge to accomplish cross-cultural evangelism. Whenever human beings agree to pursue the same goals together, their tasks must be organized. Experience shows that poor organization can be a strong hindrance to effective evangelism—especially evangelism across cultural barriers. On the other hand, good organization encourages good evangelism and rapid reproduction of new churches.

Some people have had such frustrating experiences in trying to work through different kinds of organizations that they have come to believe that any kind of organization is bad. But it is not organization itself which is to blame. It is very often the use of ineffective forms, or structures of organization. We can have good people working through bad forms of organization, and still see bad results. If we want to see the greatest fruitfulness, we must apply good basic principles for establishing effective organizations in cross-cultural evangelism.

Modern communications technologies increase individualism. People can easily ignore developing strong relationships with those they work with. They have the option to go online and bond with people who think just like they do, know only what they know about, and pursue only the interests common to those in their circle of friendship—even if they live across the world from one another. This kind of individualism easily increases myopic thinking about reality, what is important, and even about how we can best serve God. It also increases the tendency to develop churches that are more concerned with ministries in their own culture than ministries to the unreached cultures of the world. Such churches usually do not develop the kinds of organizational structure for accomplishing the Great Commission that are very effective. If they send cross-cultural evangelists, they tend to focus on the needs of the one who goes rather than the ones who hear the message. Yet organizing effectively for cross-cultural work is not trivial. It is so important that it can easily spell the difference between moderate success and enormous success in winning the lost.

When we refer to organizational structures, we are speaking about types or categories of organizations. This is to be distinguished from specific organizations themselves. For instance, we can say the Assemblies of God of South India is a specific organization. But it would fit into an organizational structure called denomination or national church. In this chapter, there are four basic organizational structures to which we will refer often:

SENDING CHURCH (SC): This refers to a church or group of churches which assume the responsibility for sending cross-cultural evangelists to evangelize other people groups. It also specifically refers to the organization which governs that church or group of churches. For instance, if the Southern Baptist Convention of India sends cross-cultural evangelists to other people groups (inside or outside their own country), they would be a Sending Church.

SENDING AGENCY (SA): This refers to a specific organization which is established to organize and administrate the work of cross-cultural evangelism. This agency is responsible to the organization(s) which established it—usually one or more Sending Churches (SC). It carries out the administrative tasks of planning strategies, organizing teams of cross-cultural evangelists, raising funds, and administering their use. It is very common for an SA to be established as a part of the organizational framework of an SC, but it is also common that an SA can be interdenominational or nondenominational and/or international.

RECEIVING CHURCH (RC): This refers to the churches which are started in other cultures as a result of cross-cultural evangelism efforts. It specifically refers to the organizational structure which leads those churches. This structure usually does not exist until the cross-cultural evangelism team becomes successful in starting a number of churches. Some people have referred to this structure as the national church. But often national churches really only represent one or more of the people groups in a certain nation. In this chapter, we will refer to them as Receiving Churches because they are the structures through which cross-cultural evangelists do much of their work. In that sense, they "receive" the evangelists into their fellowship to work together for God.

DAUGHTER SENDING AGENCY (DSA): This refers to an organization established by the Receiving Church to send cross-cultural evangelists from their own people to other cultures. These organizations are started by the churches of other cultures which have been established through the work of Sending Agencies. In that sense, these new Sending Agencies are Daughter Sending Agencies. DSAs may send cross-cultural evangelists to other people groups within their own country. This is sometimes called home missions. DSAs should also send cross-cultural evangelists to people groups outside their own region and country whenever possible. Sometimes this is called foreign missions.

There are some important principles for establishing the basic organizational structures listed above. Since those structures emerge in different cultures, it is not possible to give a set of rules which show exactly what those structures should be. They should be autochthonous, and therefore, they should follow different organizational patterns according the cultures in which they emerge. But it is possible to set forth some principles which will serve to guide leaders in organizing such structures. This chapter does that by showing the different ways these basic structures can relate to one another most effectively.

The key element in relationships between different structures is the concept of partnership:

> Just as each of us has one body with many members, and these members do not all have the same function, so in Christ, we who are many form one body, and each member belongs to all the others. (Rom. 12:4–5)

That is a perfect biblical description of partnership. Each organizational structure is like an arm or leg of the Body of Christ. They may have differing abilities, functions, and purposes. But each "belongs to" or is a vital part of the purpose and work of the other. Two partners have different functions, but work together because they have the same purpose. The basis of true partnership in cross-cultural ministry is a common desire to obey the commands of Christ in a bond of mutual trust, love, and purpose.

SENDING CHURCH—SENDING AGENCY PARTNERSHIP

When a church or group of churches begins to recognize their responsibility to send workers to evangelize other peoples, they also begin to recognize the need to form an organizational structure to help accomplish that purpose. Sending Agencies (SAs) can be organized at the level of the local church, a regional group of churches, the national level, or an international level. There are advantages and disadvantages at each level. Whatever level they are organized at, there are some important principles to guide the relationships between SCs and SAs.

Levels of Sending Agency Organization

The Local Church as Sending Agency: There are some advantages to sending cross-cultural evangelists from local churches. Those who are sent are known personally by those who send them. They usually emerge out of the Sending Church. They pray for them more regularly, and they support them more sacrificially. The evangelists feel part of their home church even while they are in the field. Organizing SAs in local churches is not as complicated and expensive as it is for a large group of churches. It is easier to keep control of the work, and keep in contact with the evangelists personally.

When sending cross-cultural evangelists to work among other people groups in their own country, it may not be necessary to support the evangelist's family with regular monthly contributions. It may only be necessary to pay the expenses necessary for them to relocate and establish a ministry. If there is another language to learn, there may also be some need of subsidy until the family can make their living among the target people. In this kind of situation, sending evangelists cross-culturally from a single local church can be very effective. Down through history, there has been much effective cross-cultural ministry using this model.

On the other hand, today's world makes the formation of SAs at the local church level impractical most of the time. This is especially true if the evangelist and his family must travel long distances to reach the target people. Travel expenses can be significant. Government regulations may require legal guarantees before they can issue visas. Living expenses in other countries can be more than in the evangelist's country. Such large expenses are usually too much for one local church to cover. The legal requirements for sending people to other countries can also be too complicated and time-consuming for volunteers from local churches. For these and other similar reasons, churches which want to send cross-cultural evangelists usually join together with other churches to form SAs at a regional, national, or international level. Joining others to send such evangelists also proves more effective in actually evangelizing an unreached people group. If they are serious about effective ministry among those who hear the Gospel in other cultures, most churches find a way to work with other churches to send cross-cultural evangelists or teams of such evangelists.

Regional Sending Agencies: One effective way to overcome some of the problems associated with forming SAs at the local church level is to combine the efforts of a number of churches within one geographical region, district, or state. With more churches participating, more cross-cultural evangelists can be sent. There is room for the churches to assume part of the support for an evangelist, even though they could not support him or her by themselves. This allows smaller churches to fulfill their responsibilities without waiting until they could fully support an evangelist by themselves. It also provides more stable support for the evangelist while on the field. If he is supported by only one church, it is possible for that church to undergo financial problems which would force them to cut off some or all of his support. With the evangelist unable to earn money on the field (which is usually the case in foreign countries), and without money to support his family and ministry, or maybe even to come home, such a cut in support would be extremely cruel and tragic. That is why sharing the support of evangelists among different churches is a common practice among SCs.

More solid financial support is not the only reason for forming regional SAs. It is usually easier to provide good cross-cultural training for the team members when several churches or more are supporting the effort. Also, regional SAs make better sense in some kinds of situations due to the structure of the SCs. If the strongest organization within the SCs occurs at regional or district levels, that may be the best level for forming SAs. For instance, there may be a loosely organized national structure composed of regional organizations of different people groups or regions of the sending country. In such a case, there would normally be strong organization at the regional level, with each people group forming their own organization. They would cooperate at a national level with the organizational structures of other people groups. This strong identity of the churches with their own regional structures would make it possible to develop good and effective regional SAs.

In spite of all these advantages, some of the same disadvantages which apply to local church SAs can also apply to regional SAs. Regional SAs may not have enough churches to effectively and consistently support a whole team of cross-cultural evangelists. If good strategy requires sending four families, but the regional SA can only send two, there must be some kind of cooperation with other regional SAs. This is usually less workable than organizing SAs at the national level. This means only larger regional structures will be able to form effective SAs. It is difficult for smaller regional structures to do much more than reach people in their own country or region. This can discourage smaller regional SAs. There needs to be organizational structures in place which can provide opportunities for even the smallest and newest churches and regions to participate heavily and effectively in world evangelism.

Another disadvantage of regional SAs is that it is often more difficult to handle the business aspects of relating to foreign governments and even the agency's own government. With the economic and national policies of different countries becoming more and more restrictive toward foreigners, regional SAs often do not have the expertise and manpower, finances, and influence for handling the business or official aspects of doing cross-cultural evangelism.

The training of cross-cultural evangelists also requires a large amount of resources, facilities, and personnel in order to be effective. Candidates for cross-cultural evangelism need the best possible training available. It is much more difficult to provide such training on many regional levels than it is on a national level. The candidates also need exposure to other cultures as they are training for their work. Regional training provides less opportunities for such exposure.

Regional SAs also tend to duplicate much of the same work that can be handled at a higher level when conducted on a national or international level. Each needs its own leaders, personnel leaders, financial system, training division, etc. It is often too costly and impractical to provide such administrative organizations at the regional level.

There are cross-cultural training systems that are open to candidates from many denominations or local churches. They are the best solution for independent churches and regional organizations that are not large enough to supply quality training on their own. But they cannot solve the problem of carrying out planning and administrative functions for those missionaries unless they are independent interdenominational Sending Agencies themselves. That presents other issues that local and regional groups of churches often do not agree to follow, as we shall see below.

Sending Agencies at the National Denominational Level: It is very often the best procedure to organize SAs by combining the resources and leadership of all the churches of one denomination or people group within a single country. The SCs can combine the work on a denominational basis. Though this might require a stronger commitment to partnership by regional and national organizations, it may be necessary due to the limitations of regional SAs described above.

National SAs within a single denomination are very common all over the world. If you are thinking about working for the Lord cross-culturally, and are part of a church denomination that is organized on a national basis, you can look online to find the mission Sending Agency that is part of your denomination. National SAs provide the greatest possible resources and leadership within a single country and denomination for developing, organizing, and administering cross-cultural evangelism, especially when the people groups being targeted are located outside the SA's own country. Though it may be useful to organize specific people group targeting on a local or regional level, it is usually most effective at the national level. Candidate training, administrative needs, liaison with the supporting churches, strategy planning, governmental relations—all of these essential functions are usually best accomplished at the national level. This requires a great spirit of love and partnership between the SA and the supporting churches. There must be consistent communication and participation in order to keep the churches inspired. With good communication and accountability, national SAs can be very effective structures for evangelizing unreached people groups of the world.

Interdenominational Sending Agencies: Sometimes more than one national church denomination forms an SA. They may do it because they are not large enough to organize and send cross-cultural evangelists by themselves. They may do it because they want the churches established on the field not to be so oriented toward becoming a denomination separate from other churches within the target people group. They may want to join with other national churches whose doctrines are enough like their own for the sake of Christian unity. Sometimes interdenominational SAs emerge through one group, but expand to include personnel and finances from other denominations also. Interdenominational groups are also very common throughout the world. Whatever part of the world you live in, you can search the World Wide Web (Internet) for "Interdenominational Missionary Sending Agencies" to find an organization that might fit your needs if you want to go or send cross-cultural ministers through an interdenominational SA.

Interdenominational SAs can often provide greater resources whereby smaller national churches can enter into partnerships with other groups to equip, train, send, and supervise cross-cultural evangelism efforts. Their advantage is mostly one of scale. Just as it is often better to form national SAs instead of regional SAs, so it can be beneficial to form interdenominational SAs in order to pool financial, administrative, and training resources. It can also be more conducive to establishing the autochthoneity of the churches which are established on the field. Such interdenominational SAs can also very easily incorporate cross-cultural evangelists from many countries at the same time. There are a significant number of such organizations who have grown to large numbers of participants from many parts of the world.

There can be some disadvantages to interdenominational SAs, however. The greatest single disadvantage is the fact that they may not see church planting as their primary ministry. If they send cross-cultural evangelists to start churches, what denominational or doctrinal affiliation would those churches have? If they give them a denominational name (Baptist, Methodist, Pentecostal, etc.), that may offend the supporters from other denominations back home.

Also, it may be difficult for the cross-cultural evangelism team members to agree on doctrines if they are sent by churches of different denominations through the same SA. This creates a pressure against church planting, and tends to focus ministries toward occupations, such as student ministries or relief efforts, instead of toward people groups and church planting. Since New Unit Growth and the planting of autochthonous churches is at the heart of effective cross-cultural evangelism, this is a major weakness of some interdenominational SAs. It becomes too easy to focus on the ministry success of the one who goes rather than the ministry success of the one who receives the Gospel. These issues can often be large enough to move interdenominational SAs away from church-planting efforts.

Since interdenominational SAs are often pressured not to plant churches themselves, they may be forced to work with existing churches in whatever cultures they are working. They can be a great help to such churches, if they use good strategies and principles. But that also may mean they will not be focused on reaching any of the thousands of unreached people groups where no churches have been established. Because of these kinds of pressures, interdenominational SAs tend to become service agencies focusing on human needs as much or more than spiritual needs. They may help existing churches grow and expand, which is important. But many such SAs are organized to provide physical aid such as medical services and emergency relief. These are valid and important Christian ministries, but they will never replace the need to start autochthonous churches among every unreached people. The best interdenominational SAs do meet physical needs and plant churches at the same time, AND they focus on unreached cultures as well. So if you are considering fulfilling your responsibility to help reach unreached peoples by working through an interdenominational SA, be sure to look carefully at their church-planting activities. Also look at the people groups where they are planting churches!

International Denominational Sending Agencies: It is increasingly common for denominations who have sister national churches in various parts of the world work together to send cross-cultural ministers. This has the advantage of making it less controversial to plant churches which are identified with the denominational name. Many denominations do this effectively, sharing resources and personnel from the various parts of the world where the denomination has churches. It makes targeting unreached people groups much more effective also. The Gospel does not masquerade as a Western religion when this kind of sending arrangement involves sending cross-cultural evangelists from several parts of the world to target individual people groups. It looks much more like a Gospel "TO EVERY PEOPLE FROM EVERY PEOPLE" in the minds of those who receive it. It is an attractive and focused strategy in that regard.

But it can also be laden with difficulties at the ground level. Such difficulties may arise from disagreements about everything from the methods for planting churches to the methods and amounts of funding for the cross-cultural ministry efforts. Evangelism personnel from one country may expect to be supported at a different level and in a different manner than those from another country. The principles for establishing and multiplying churches among a target people may not be agreed upon among the Sending Churches. The levels of authority and the international leadership of the joint projects undertaken may not be easily agreed upon. These are just a few of the difficulties related to international denominational SA efforts. For this form to be successful, the essential key element is to focus on the needs of the unreached people group and find a spirit of servant leadership throughout the cooperative effort. Participants must be willing to submit to one another and live on a similar standard for this type of SA structure to be successful. Nevertheless, it is highly needed and strategically valuable! If these kinds of structures do not emerge, then even efforts by the same denomination among the same people group can result in the establishment of many competing organizations in the field.

Autonomy for Sending Agencies

An event occurred that is recorded in the fifteenth chapter of the book of Acts which threatened to destroy the worldwide impact of Christianity. The church in Antioch, you will recall from chapter one, had already commissioned Paul and Barnabas to establish Gentile (non-Jewish) churches in southern Galatia (Acts 13:1–3). Word of the new Gentile churches reached Jerusalem, and groups of concerned believers, called Judaizers, went out from Jerusalem to convince Gentile believers to become circumcised and obey Mosaic law. When Paul and Barnabas returned to Antioch after their first missionary journey, they were confronted by some of those Judaizers who were demanding the circumcision of all the Gentile believers there. Paul and Barnabas argued against this teaching. The dispute was referred to the "apostles and elders" at Jerusalem (Acts 15:1–2).

The leaders at the Council of Jerusalem, as the meeting has come to be called, spent a lot of time debating the issue of whether the Gentile believers must follow the Jewish customs and Mosaic law (verse 7). But the testimony and arguments of Paul, Barnabas, and Peter convinced the council to write a letter to all the Gentile churches. The Gentiles were only required to follow four customs which were ordinarily required of Gentiles when they were in areas under Jewish control. They were to "abstain from food sacrificed to idols, from blood, from the meat of strangled animals, and from sexual immorality" (verse 29). These letters were delivered to the Gentile churches. They represented a great victory for Paul and his fellow cross-cultural workers among the Gentiles. The decision of the council meant that the Gentile churches would be free to grow and multiply without following the Jewish law and cultural norms. It was a great victory for the perpetuation of Christianity.

In every age, there is a natural tension which arises between the administrative structures of church leadership and the Sending Agency structures (SAs) organized by Sending Churches. There is a natural desire by church leaders to directly control the work of the SAs which have arisen down through history. The recognized administrators of the New Testament Church were the apostles and elders at Jerusalem. The first SA which was formed in that Church was the group of leaders in the Antioch church (Acts 13:1–3). They sent out Paul and Barnabas in response to the call of the Holy Spirit. They supported them with offerings for their journey. When they returned, the team gave a spiritual report to their sponsors in Antioch (Acts 14:26–27).

It is at this point that the authorities of the central church administration began to challenge the team's autonomy or right to decide how to do cross-cultural evangelism. If the decision of the Jerusalem Council had gone the other way, the autonomy of the cross-cultural evangelism team would have been severely curtailed. It would have forced the evangelists to do one of two things. They could break away from the Jerusalem Church, causing the beginning of many schisms or divisions in Christianity. Or, they could submit to the authority of the council, settling for culturally inappropriate and ineffectual evangelism. If they had done the first, Christianity would likely have failed to become a major force in the world. If they had done the second, Christianity would have likely been relegated to the ash heap of history as a minor Jewish sect! Either way, the dominance of the administrative structure over the Sending Agency structure would have dealt a powerful blow against the development of Christianity.

The organizational forces which threatened the Gentile outreach of the New Testament Church also threatens cross-cultural evangelism in each generation. There is not space enough here to detail the hundreds of cases throughout history where the same kind of structural dominance has repeated itself. But the general pattern can be described. Denominations usually organize at the national level before and at the same time that they form SAs. Sometimes denominations are formed even as a result of the biblical mandate and desire to form SAs. Leaders of the administrative structure usually see the SAs as a legitimate department of their national administrative structure. They naturally feel it should be under their direct control. Often they will insist on choosing the leaders of the SAs themselves. They may control the funds which are raised for cross-cultural evangelism. They also tend to approve or dictate the policies and strategies of the SAs.

While this at first seems to make logical sense in terms of administration, *it inevitably leads to the decline of the effectiveness of the Sending Agency*! This is because there are important differences in the nature of the two structures. When we say administrative structure, we are not referring to the leadership of local churches. We are referring to the leaders chosen to represent the churches at a regional or national level. The nature of these leadership structures is different than the nature of the Sending Agencies. Administrative structures:

1. Are primarily concerned with maintaining the vitality and growth of the churches they represent.
2. Seek a broad consensus among the churches in order to govern their advance among their own people group.
3. Are primarily concerned with nurturing the well-being of their own national churches.
4. Their daily administrative tasks force them to focus on the above issues, not the needs of other people groups.

On the other hand, Sending Agencies are dedicated to a specific task—evangelization of other people groups. From the newest cross-cultural evangelism team member to the highest agency leader, all are committed to world evangelization—not the conversion of their own people but that of other people groups. That is their main purpose. Their attention is not focused primarily upon the needs of their own people and churches, but on the needs of unreached peoples and the churches that emerge among them.

This requires a second decision after salvation and service in churches among a person's own people. Joining into the work of a Sending Agency requires a special commitment to an outward-looking task *<u>beyond</u>* one's own people group. That requires

1. special attention to the issues of cross-cultural ministry;
2. special training and preparation to go;
3. extraordinary means of financial support;
4. special strategies and ministry decisions; and
5. accountability to people experienced in cross-cultural ministry.

History shows that SAs are the most effective when they have enough autonomy to function in their task well, but enough control to be accountable to the churches which support them. They need freedom to plan their own strategies. They need personnel and control policies which relate to the strategies they devise. They need enough autonomy to raise and administer their own funds for the task. History shows that the more these elements of autonomy exist for an SA, the more effective they will be on the field.

History also shows that church administrative structures usually try to "swallow" SAs to make them a part of their own administrative structures and put them under their direct control. Sometimes SAs are organized under their direct control from the beginning. This diminishes their short- and long-term effectiveness. More often, SAs begin as more autonomous structures, responding to the desire of the churches to send cross-cultural evangelists. Eventually, however, the administrative structures of the Sending Churches increase control over their funding and activities in the field. When this happens, the natural tension between the purposes of the two structures quickly begins to lessen the effectiveness of the SA. More and more policy and financial decisions are made or approved by the administrative structure. Administrative leaders choose more and more of the leadership of the SAs themselves, and the Sending Churches themselves have less and less say about who will lead the SAs. Eventually, even the funding for the SA is channeled directly through the administrative structure offices, instead of going directly to the finance office of the SA. When this happens, the SA is subject to the administrative and budgeting authority of the administrative leaders. If those leaders have a great cross-cultural ministry vision, the SA may be somewhat effective for a period of time. But because of the difference in purpose and nature of the two structures, history shows the effectiveness of the SA will decline sooner or later when placed under direct control of the administrative structure. Just as it happened in the New Testament Church, it eventually threatens most SAs also.

This all sounds very theoretical and unimportant until you break it down into actual denominational examples, so let me give you one. The Assemblies of God in the USA was formed as a national church in 1914. Fortunately, it was formed largely as a result of the sending of cross-cultural evangelists. One of the early leaders was a man named Noel Perkin who had a strong vision to take the Gospel to the ends of the earth. He served on the Executive Presbytery (administrative structure) of the denomination for thirty-seven years. As a result, the cross-cultural ministry structure, or Division of Foreign Missions (DFM), was established and grew as a semiautonomous structure whose leaders were chosen by the General Presbytery—a larger group of leaders consisting of people chosen by churches to lead the denomination at regional levels. This served to provide both a greater responsiveness to the cross-cultural ministry vision of local churches and kept the decision-making for that vision in the hands of a Sending Agency (DFM) that was mostly independent of the administrative structure.

Partly as a result of this autonomous organizational structure for the Sending Agency, the results of the efforts of the Assemblies of God (AG) to plant churches in other cultures has been phenomenal. Scores of millions of people in cultures and countries around the world have become believers. Adherents in the churches of Brazil, for instance, number at least 14 million and is growing rapidly.[54] Over 70 million AG adherents worship in 144 countries. Obviously such growth is dependent upon many things, but the independence of the Sending Agencies of the Assemblies of God and the churches they establish is a big factor.

This example is mentioned for a reason. When studying in graduate training, the author wrote a fifty-page paper on the subject of the historical tensions between administrative structures and Sending Agencies. The paper traced the history of several denominations, including the Assemblies of God. In the paper, I showed how the Sending Agency structure in the Assemblies of God was kept independent of the administrative structure of the Assemblies of God in the USA and how that had been a source of its strength. I also predicted that if history was any teacher, that independence would soon come under attack. I outlined how that attack would

[54] https://rlp.hds.harvard.edu/faq/assembly-god.

likely take place. And I made a few suggestions on how to keep that from happening. Little did I know that after writing the paper, what I predicted began to happen in just a few months after I penned those words! The general superintendent of the Assemblies of God in the USA, Thomas F. Zimmerman, began a process that would greatly change and diminish the autonomy of the DFM and subsume it under his direct authority.

As this process was unfolding, I received a phone call from J. Phillip Hogan, the executive director of the DFM while I was teaching in Singapore. Someone had given him a copy of the paper I wrote. He wanted permission to send it to churches across the USA. I gave it to him. A few months later, three things happened. In their national convention, the church leaders first voted to keep the DFM autonomous. Second, the general superintendent (Zimmerman) was voted out of office. Third, the leader of the Department of Home Missions was elevated to become the Division of Home Missions (DHM), the same divisional level as the DFM, as was recommended in my paper. All this resulted in an even greater fruitfulness in the work of both the DFM and DHM of that denomination. And it is a counterpoint to all the denominations whose Sending Agencies were "swallowed" by their administrative structures. History shows that causes the decline of the denomination as a whole, not just its SA!

As a rule, SAs eventually lose their resources and their zeal for world evangelization when placed under strong control by administrative leadership. Their purposes are often made to be secondary to the needs of their own national churches. Funding for cross-cultural evangelism tends to become secondary to funding for other purposes in the home country. This leads to decline in resources, personnel, and vision in the Sending Agency.

It can also cause the Sending Churches to become selfish with the Gospel, consuming most of God's blessings upon themselves, without sharing its valuable message with other peoples around the world. That is very damaging to the balance of ministry functions in the Sending Churches. Because of the danger for SAs to come under direct control of the administrative structures, the following guidelines are valuable for organizing Sending Agencies:

1. SAs should be organized under the general and widespread authority of the Sending Churches, but not placed under the direct control of the denomination or church group's central administrators.
2. Key leadership for the SAs should be chosen by a wide representation of the Sending Churches, not by central denominational administrative officials.
3. SAs should be given autonomy to select, train, lead their own personnel; plan and implement their own strategies within general guidelines agreed to by all the churches; and raise, disburse, and manage the funds for these ministries autonomously.
4. The SAs should be able to communicate their plans and needs directly to the Sending Churches, and be primarily accountable to them.
5. Any policy-making boards or committees formed to govern the general policies of the operation of the SAs should be selected by a wide representation of the Sending Churches, not the top leaders of the administrative structure.

In the light of the history of the Church, these guidelines can help to establish strong, effective Sending Agencies. It will also help to encourage strong, effective local Sending Churches. SAs should never be completely independent of Sending Churches, but it is crucial that they not be "swallowed" by the administrative structures of those churches. They should be semiautonomous. They should be required to accurately report the results of their ministries and the use of their finances to the Sending Churches. Starting Sending Agencies on a strong semiautonomous foundation, free from dominance from above, will go a long way toward assuring there will be a healthy, vital cross-cultural outreach for years to come. It will also enliven the growth and effectiveness of the Sending Churches! These principles are true for any cross-cultural SA of any group of churches in the world!

SENDING AGENCY—RECEIVING CHURCH PARTNERSHIP

The relationships between cross-cultural evangelists and the churches they establish in another culture is very important, as we discussed in earlier chapters. The evangelists must assume the correct attitudes toward the target people and toward new converts. A spirit of personal sacrifice and loving service is the best foundation for building trust and respect among the people of the emerging churches.

The correct attitude will help cross-cultural evangelists to encourage the new believers to trust the purposes of the evangelists. The team members will also be representing the Sending Agency. Local believers will judge the SA by what they see in the cross-cultural evangelists' lives. Trust, mutual respect, a servant attitude, and a genuine love are the foundational pillars of building partnerships with organizations of the target culture. Team members must constantly work diligently to build up that foundation in relating personally to local believers and their leaders. When the local believers know they can trust the team members, and that there is a shared mutual respect, they will put forth the effort to solve problems and find solutions to reach common goals.

The organizational development of churches among target peoples can be described as a three-stage process. The **Formative Stage**, then **Organizational Stage**, and the **Sending Church Stage**. The attitude of the evangelism team toward the local believers should not change during these three stages of development. It should remain as described above. But the organizational relationships should change as the emerging churches grow stronger in their development. In this section, we will examine the first two stages and the relationship of the SA to the local churches at each stage. The last stage will be discussed in the next section.

Partnership in Formation

From the time the first convert accepts Christ among the target people, the cross-cultural evangelism team is called to partnership with the emerging church. The formative stage begins with the first converts, and continues until local churches have established a regional or national leadership organization (see figure 10.a). During the formative stage, the SA (here representing the cross-cultural evangelism team on the field) will take a leading role in the development of local churches. Their plans and strategies will include establishing strong local churches with good leadership and organization. The teaching and training they give to new converts must follow autochthonous principles. They must constantly seek to teach new believers to reproduce themselves. But they must be careful to use local cultural forms, local leadership patterns, and serve the emerging church with a servant attitude. Assuming a leading role during the formation stage of the development of the emerging churches does not mean the evangelistic team must assume a dominant role.

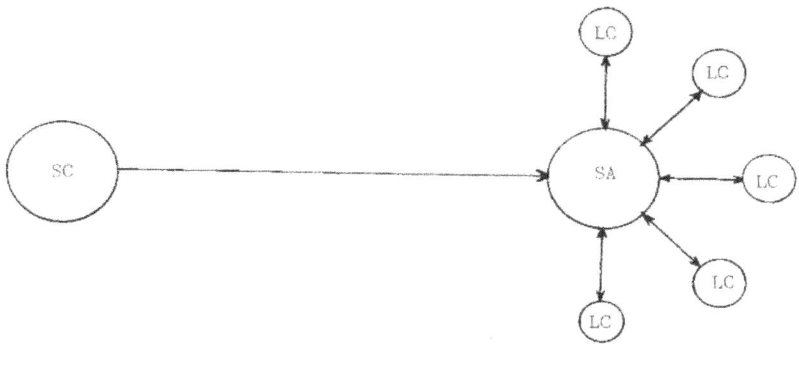

Figure 10.a

The SA evangelism team must be careful to follow good principles of nondirective leadership. As we discussed in earlier chapters, this involves teaching a lot of biblical principles and asking a lot of questions. As groups of believers emerge, the evangelists must be very careful not to insert their own mental picture of local churches (LC) into the minds of believers. They should simply show emerging local leaders the principles in Scripture for starting churches, and ask them to make decisions about how they think their churches should be organized.

The evangelism members, represented by "SA" in figure 10.a, should avoid assuming any official positions in the emerging churches no matter how much the local believers pressure them to do so. In the beginning, the evangelists will probably be asked to be pastors, elders, or financial officers by local churches. This is especially true if local believers are receiving or hope to get money for the work from the SA. The cross-cultural evangelists should graciously decline any position such as those mentioned here. They should work with the local leaders who are chosen and help them in their leadership decisions as needed. They should teach the principles of autochthoneity as their reason for refusal. It is important that local leaders learn as they participate in ministry. It will be very difficult for autochthonous leaders to emerge if they do not have good examples from among their own people from the very beginning.

Organizing Local Churches: There is no set pattern for governing and leading local churches which will work in every culture. Patterns of leadership, decision-making forms, organizational structure—all these things and many more vary from culture to culture. That is why it is so important to use autochthonous principles from the very beginning when starting churches in a target culture. The only ones who will be able to decide the best forms, structure, or leadership patterns are the local believers themselves.

That does not mean the new churches must lack good structure and organization. There are a number of categories where local leaders must make good decisions about the best way to organize their churches. Local believers must eventually reach agreement by studying Scripture and thinking about their own culture in each of the following areas.

Basic Tenets of Faith: A church is not ready to be organized until the believers have reached an agreement concerning the basic doctrines they all believe to be essential to their Christian faith. Basic doctrines about God, mankind, the person and work of Christ, the person and work of the Holy Spirit, man's separation from God through sin, eternal life, resurrection from the dead, heaven and hell, the return of Christ, etc.—all these areas of doctrine should be explored by local leaders in consultation and study with the cross-cultural evangelists. The evangelists should carefully steer the believers from error by showing them the Scriptures which deal with each important subject. But they should encourage the believers to state their beliefs in their own words. Even if these basic tenets require some modification later, it is better to have them stated and agreed upon by local believers as a result of searching the Scriptures together. Be sure to include all the doctrines the local believers feel are important, not just the ones the evangelists think are important. They will choose the doctrines which they think are most important for their people. Asking the right questions and listening to believer's questions should be the basis for exploring key doctrines in the Bible.

Standard of Membership: The local believers themselves should set standards of belief and behavior which are required for membership in their churches. They should form their own committees to examine candidates for membership, or discipline members who go astray, using their own understanding of Scriptures on those subjects. The rules and procedures must be their own. Team members can advise them if called upon to do so, but they should avoid making suggestions about solutions. Asking important questions is always better than suggesting rules. As a general rule, it is acceptable for a team member to serve on an examining committee if asked to do so. But he should never lead such a committee or allow himself to be used as the excuse for making an unpopular or controversial decision. More important, team members should not serve on discipline committees. Local leaders must carry that burden themselves.

Selection and Duties of Leaders: Leaders should be selected by local believers, not the cross-cultural evangelists. Though team members may work to train local believers to be leaders, the selection of who should serve in different leadership positions should be completely left up to the local church body. If possible, team members should ask the believers who should be selected for leadership training. They should also train the leaders in biblical principles for choosing leaders. The local believers will usually do a better job of selecting leaders than the evangelists, so long as they know the biblical standards for leadership. They know their people better. The categories of leadership should also be established as the local people study the New Testament leadership and autochthonous principles. They should agree upon the offices of leadership and the specific duties leaders should perform. They should also be sure to establish culturally appropriate mechanisms to make the leaders accountable for the work they do. It is not enough for them to be simply accountable to God. They must also be accountable in some meaningful way to the local believers with whom they serve God. As it is better not to have a stoplight on a roadway if a stop sign is sufficient, so leaders should be chosen only as the local people see their positions are needed.

Operational Rules: The local believers must also be encouraged to agree on the rules and policies for carrying out the ministry functions of their churches. There must be procedures for collecting, accounting for, and disbursing offerings to the Lord's work. There should be agreement concerning baptism and the Lord's Supper. Rules for participating in the different ministries of the churches should be agreed upon and understood. Even if the local culture requires that most of the decisions concerning operational rules should be made mostly by the leaders only, there should be good ways for the leaders to explain them to the whole group of believers before they are implemented. Operational rules should be functional and changeable as it becomes apparent it is needed. Everyone should understand them and commit to following them.

Constitutional Agreement: It has become common among most people groups to establish a written constitution which clearly describes the tenets of faith, standards of membership, primary doctrines, standards of membership, selection and duties of leaders, and operational rules of the local church organization. Such a constitution, or a similar standard set of agreements, can be useful for groups of church or even local churches. Constitutions can be very important tools to help churches grow and reproduce among a target people. It provides a means for having written standards on many important subjects. It does not have to be called a constitution. It can be called what local believers want to call it—"Rules that Our Churches Follow" or "Biblical Patterns for Church Leadership" or anything similar. But it is only valuable if it is produced and agreed upon by local believers and followed carefully without favoritism. Well-written constitutions can stop leaders from abusing their power so long as all leaders are held accountable to the responsibilities they assume. They also help keep strong standards of Christian service and love alive in the hearts of the people. Mutual trust among local believers is the fruit of such a document or set of agreements.

Before suggesting that local church leaders develop their own constitution, it is wise to first look at the other institutions that exist within that culture. Do the people follow the constitutions of those institutions, or are they a foreign construct imposed upon them? How do the people feel about organizational constitutions? Do constitutions have such a bad name and foreign smell that another form of leadership codification would be more effective? Should it even be called a constitution? The form and even the name a constitution assumes is not as important as the function it performs within a culture. Rules and accountability are important for churches just as they are in any organization. But they may be modified or even called something other than a constitution in order to be effective organizational tools in a given culture.

When local groups of believers have reached the size and maturity where they have made the above kinds of agreements, and have their own local leaders leading them in effective autochthonous work for the Lord, then they are ready to be officially recognized as organized local churches. This is a great event worth celebrating! And there should be some kind of event marking that achievement celebrated by the local church alongside other organized local churches. Whatever official recognition ceremony or celebration is used to signify that a local church is fully organized, it is best for the leader of the evangelism team to officiate in such celebrations only once. He should do so only for the first church that is organized. Though he may participate in future ceremonies, he should encourage the pastor or pastors of previously organized churches to officiate in future celebrations. That is important in order to be sure that each church member feels it is their church and feel a strong commitment to its future ministries.

Partnership in Organization

As local churches grow and multiply within the target people, it will become apparent to local leaders that they can do more effective work for the Lord if they work together in some areas. They may want to work together to start new churches in other parts of their city or in other areas of their country. They may want to produce literature or establish broadcasting or online ministries. They may want to establish an advanced Bible training system at a regional or national level. All these types of larger projects require some kind of larger organization to oversee their development and operation. After the Receiving Churches organize at the regional or national level, the SA should relate to local churches through the larger organization pictured in figure 10.b.

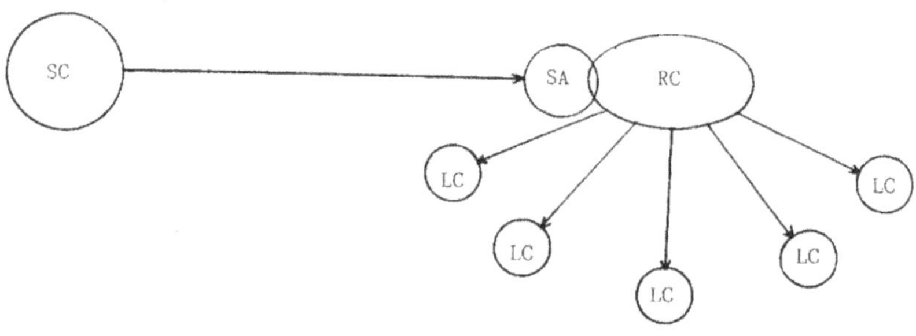

Figure 10.b

It is important to realize that regional or national church organizations can be started too soon. Organizations should never be started just because that is the pattern among other people groups. Larger church organizations should be established only as local churches recognize their need. Therefore, the evangelism team (SA) should not push the matter of regional or national organization. They should focus on reproducing churches. Regional or national organization should be suggested by local leaders themselves. Even after agreeing to establish such organizations, all efforts should be made by all leaders to establish such organization and leaders for them, not as a position of prestige but for service. Cooperative effort on the part of all leaders will be required to establish such organizations. When there are enough local churches that a regional organization and leadership is seen as important by local leaders, it will also be seen as important enough to be supported by local leaders.

The attitude of churches which organize at higher levels is very important. There may be many people groups within one country. Whenever a group of churches organize at a larger regional or national level, they must avoid attitudes of superiority toward other people groups. Hopefully they will help to evangelize those other groups with their own outreach and cross-cultural ministries. As churches arise and multiply within other people groups, they should be given opportunity to join the regional or national churches as equal partners in the Lord's work. But each people group in a region or country should be encouraged to develop their own regional or national organizations focusing on the evangelization of their own people group. That is of extreme importance. If they can come together for fellowship and celebration at a national level with other people groups, that is a great witness and a source of strength to develop even broader and more effective ministries on a national scale. Just as cross-cultural evangelists should not dominate the churches they establish, so those churches should not dominate the churches they establish among other people groups.

So when we speak of national churches, we may be speaking about the larger organization of a specific people group, or we may be speaking about the larger organization of a number of people groups who work together in unified purpose at the regional or national levels within the same country. The principles for organizing at this higher level are the same.

Organizing National Churches: The basic principles which apply to organizing local churches also apply to organizing at the national level. They key concepts are servant leadership plus agreement and cooperation in doing God's work. In addition to the standards and agreements at the local church level, there are a number of additional agreements that should be reached for national church organization.

Constitutional Agreement: At the national level, it is very necessary to have some kind of standardized agreement which governs the principles and methods for all the churches to work together at the regional or national level. A written constitution or code of agreement is the most widely used method for establishing this cooperation among all the participating churches and cultures. Whatever form of government and agreement is used, it must provide for the right kinds of leadership and rules of engagement in the tasks agreed upon at the national level. It must also provide a clear set of rules making leaders accountable to the churches and local leaders whom they serve.

Membership Agreement: As with local churches, there must be agreement on membership at the national level. Churches and groups of churches are included as members at the national level. They must agree on the purposes of national membership, and they must have representatives of their own as a part of the national leadership decision making organization. The standards for meeting membership requirements in the national organization must be agreed upon. The standards for biblical authority and doctrine must be agreed upon. The organization may be based upon a denomination, or it may be nondenominational. Proven leaders, not just the wealthy or elderly, are usually selected to be representatives of the churches at the national level. Each local church or group of local churches will normally choose leaders to represent them at this national level organization. There may be different classifications of membership at the national level, such as pastors, elders, business leaders, cross-cultural evangelists, church planters, etc. But clear rules for membership, responsibilities, etc., must be agreed upon and written down in a formal manner.

Levels of Leadership: There must be a clearly defined plan for establishing a hierarchy of leadership and responsibility levels within the national organization. From top-level administrative leaders to local evangelists and church planters, there should be an orderly pattern of leadership structure that is agreed upon by all the churches. The officers and their duties in the national organization should also be approved and agreed upon by the local churches which are a part of the organization. This standard of leadership structure is very helpful to the effectiveness of the work the churches do together. It helps establish lines of authority and accountability. It also helps define growth in leadership responsibility. Leadership must be based on a long record of exemplary service to the Gospel and nothing else. Rules for the selection of leaders and their discipline or dismissal must be clear.

Financial Agreement: There must be means for supporting the national organization and its work. The local churches must devise and agree upon a method to finance the work of the national organization. This includes finding an appropriate way to pay the expenses of the national offices. Under no circumstances should national offices' operating expenses be paid from outside the country. If there are full-time leaders, provision must be made to provide the necessary funds for operations. In some countries, Christian business leaders voluntarily pay for much of the operations budget. In others, the local churches give regular offerings or a percentage of the giving to operate the national offices. Sometimes there is a combination of sources used to fund the national office operations. It is very important that local churches see enough value in the national office and what is accomplished through the leaders there that they give at least some of the support for their operations. There may be areas where the SA can also contribute funds to the national organization to help without damaging the autochthoneity of local churches. An example would be for establishing an advanced school for training leaders at a higher level. The SA could also contribute to literature programs, broadcasting ministries, and Internet-based training systems without hindering autochthoneity, so long as the local churches are contributing and covering the normal operating expenses of the higher offices themselves. As a hard-and-fast general rule, the SA should never support a work of the national church completely. They should be partners in funding those ministries and programs the national church is willing to invest in also. This is discussed further below.

Organizational Structure: The pattern for organizing the different ministries and offices at the national level should also be initiated and agreed upon by the local churches and leaders. The need for such structures must be initiated by local church leaders because they see the need to do so, not by SAs. There should be good mechanisms or rules for changing those structures as needed, including the people who lead them. Structural organizational patterns should be autochthonous, with those patterns being seen as obviously needed by church leaders. Leaders should constantly be on guard not to establish any organization primarily in order to provide an opportunity for leaders to gain position or prestige. There is nothing more destructive to the health of a Christian organization than the lack of humility and servant heart on the part of its leaders. The needs for such organizations should be obvious even to common church members. It is undesirable to follow foreign structural patterns, even if other churches in their country have done so. SA team members should be very careful not to tell local leaders "how we do it at home." They should be encouraged to establish their own structures according to the needs they see.

Patterns of Partnership: When churches organize at the national level, there is much more room for partnership between the SA and the Receiving Church (RC). National level programs for evangelizing the rest of the target people group can be organized and put into operation. The SA and RC have opportunities to plan and implement strategies jointly. Funding for their plans can also be provided jointly, as long as the funds from the SA do not rob the RC from its sense of responsibility and sacrificial investment to reach its own people. The amounts and percentage of RC investment in new church planting may vary over time, eventually growing to the point SA investment in starting new churches or ministries is no longer necessary. There should be agreement between the SA and RC on how such a program will best function to reproduce new churches as rapidly and effectively as possible. Whenever there are programs of church planting jointly funded, there should be some kind of appropriate partnership structure to implement the programs smoothly. Above all, the needs of the unreached must remain paramount.

When the RC meets to plan programs which they fund and implement themselves, they should feel no obligation to include members of the cross-cultural evangelism team in the leadership of those programs. Departments of national ministry, such as youth ministries, women's ministries, online ministries, and evangelism programs would be examples of such activities which are led and administered entirely by the RC. In a similar manner, the SA team members will need to have business, planning, and evaluation meetings of their own work which need not have RC leaders present.

There will be need for many joint meetings to plan and implement projects which are jointly led and funded by the SA and RC together. Whenever the SA joins the RC in a project, a joint project structure is needed. The goals and interests of both partners should be protected. Whenever there is disagreement, "let's take our money and run" is not a solution. Leaders must work out disagreements and come to a compromise solution time and time again. This requires a development of humility, love, and cooperation that must be nurtured and protected. Figure 10.c shows the best structure for such joint administration. Both the RC and the SA evangelism teams select some of their group to serve on a joint committee which is given responsibility to plan and implement the joint projects. The committee should make all decisions jointly, hopefully by consensus, but at least by majority vote. This partnership committee should carry out their work in a manner that makes them accountable to the RC and the SA. The SA should not try to unnecessarily bring projects of the RC under the control of this committee just so they can control their administration. Neither should the RC try to put projects under control of the committee just so they can obtain more funding from the SA. Both partners must agree what projects should be administered through this partnership structure and how it should change over time.

Figure 10.c

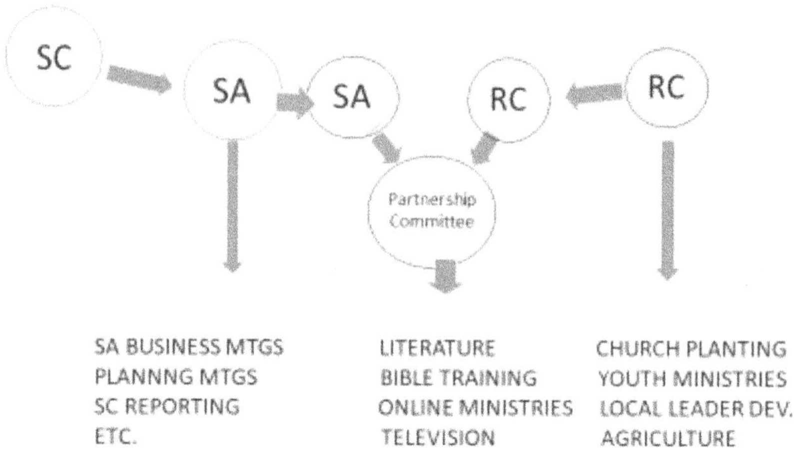

The key to joint projects is consensus. It may not be best to follow a strict democratic procedure in partnership meetings by giving each member a vote. Instead, it is usually best to give one vote to the SA and one vote to the RC when making decisions, and it should not matter how much funding comes from either organization. This will increase the desire for consensus, but there also must be a means to decide if both sides disagree. This is where it is difficult. It is also where the side with the most funding cannot dictate the result. The SA team, for example, must remain humble and sometimes agree to decisions they do not think is best even when they provide the most funding. The RC, after all, has more to gain or lose than the SA if a project fails. This mutual agreement provides the basis for strong commitments to the partnership projects. It also helps provide the unity necessary to carry out joint projects.

When decisions in partnership meetings are made, they must satisfy the needs of both partners. For instance, when joint funding is involved, the SA may have different requirements for financial accounting than the RC. They may also have different ideas about which kinds of projects can be funded. There should be some mutually agreed-upon principles for funding before decisions are made and those principles should be followed almost without exception.

There must be enough mutual respect by both partners to plan and implement the projects in a way which will satisfy the administrative needs of both.

One very valuable possibility for partnership meetings is the nonlegislative partnership meeting. The purpose of these kinds of meetings is to have a platform to discuss plans which are not governed by the joint committee, but which should still be communicated to leaders of the other group. People naturally are suspicious about things happening in meetings to which they are not invited. People will forgive anything except a lack of communication. Such a meeting does not take official action on anything. It is simply a time for discussion, for receiving communication and offering suggestions. Good communication between people is a key to maintaining trust and mutual respect. There should be time reserved within and apart from partnership meetings, formally or informally, that encourages this mutual sharing of information and even advice when warranted. Though no official action may be taken concerning areas that are controlled by only one partner, the flow of communication and building of trust is very necessary. As the RC structures become larger and more complex, this can prove to be a great blessing to everyone.

Whenever it is mutually agreed that a project can be funded and administered sufficiently by the RC, the partnership committee should place that program under the direct control of the RC. The pattern should be that there are increasingly fewer projects requiring joint leadership as the RC becomes larger and more capable. For instance, let's say there is a mutually recognized need to start a set of online ministries that have both evangelistic and community development purposes. This brings about a partnership committee. The RC leaders want all the help with technology and funding they can get from the SA. This is new territory for them, but they have some young people becoming adept at using these mediums of communication. In the beginning, most of the funding and some of the expertise comes through the SA. But as time goes by, more and more of the funding is returned through the online ministries themselves. As with all joint projects, planning should include projections toward the time when the online ministries become completely self-sustaining financially. As that time approaches, the partnership committee will want to decide when to transfer the complete control and administration of the program directly to the RC. SA team members may serve as advisers if asked, but total control of the online ministries should go to the RC. Joint projects may be under the partnership committee for a few months or for several years, depending upon the project and the need. Perhaps the only kinds of ministry that remain under the partnership committee long-term might be the effort to plant new churches, train leaders at the highest level, and work jointly to carry the Gospel to unreached people!

SENDING AGENCY—SENDING AGENCY PARTNERSHIP

There is another level of partnership in cross-cultural evangelism which is extremely important. It is a level which is gaining more attention as SAs arise in country after country around the world. It is not enough to simply form Sending Agencies from our own churches. We must also encourage the Gospel to go ***TO EVERY PEOPLE FROM EVERY PEOPLE***. That means we need to encourage partnerships with other SAs from any country to evangelize specific people groups. Many groups are ready to hear the Gospel and receive it if it is presented correctly. Many more are exposed to the Gospel through international media networks, but they need "boots on the ground" opportunities to hear the Gospel and see it in action. That means there will never be a time when cross-cultural person-to-person evangelism will not be needed. Those who are ready to hear need to feel the impact which is possible when many cross-cultural evangelism teams enter their culture with a unified cooperative strategy and Christian spirit. Though it is not possible to enter into partnership with every kind of Sending Agency, at least we should learn to enter into partnerships with groups of "like precious faith."

This section discusses three models of partnership at the SA-to-SA level. The first model demonstrates how to enter into partnership with the churches we start among target peoples. The second describes partnerships with other Sending Agencies which are formed to reach a specific people group. Finally, a model is presented which shows how interchurch partnerships are formed to provide structures to evangelize many people groups.

SA-DSA Partnerships

When planting churches among target peoples, part of the strategy should be to include plans to help the churches form their own Sending Agency. The needs of world evangelism should be taught to the believers from the very beginning. The SA team should be determined to model the behavior the target churches should follow as they learn to reach across cultural barriers themselves! Their vision to evangelize their own people should be a natural base for growing their faith and vision to reach the world. After churches among a target people grow and multiply sufficiently, they will want to participate in the cross-cultural evangelism task. And it should not require seventeen years to gain that vision like it did the ethnocentric New Testament Church (see Acts 11:20–21). Part of the training of leadership should help put this vision in the hearts of the leadership. When the churches feel they are ready, they should be encouraged to evangelize another people group. Their target people could be within their own country, or outside its boundaries. They should decide which. When they are at this stage, they should become thoroughly acquainted with the principles found in this book. They should be encouraged to start their own Sending Agency.

In many parts of the world, the daughter-church principle is well-known. Mother churches send workers to an area to start home groups, street evangelistic meetings, or other outreach meetings that become the beginnings of a new church. In some countries, such groups meet in secret. This is often called a daughter church (why not a son church, I do not know). Similarly, when an SA starts churches cross-culturally, and those churches form their own SA, we can call this new structure a Daughter Sending Agency, or DSA. Though it is formed by its own Sending Church, it is a Daughter Sending Agency in relation to the SA which started its churches.

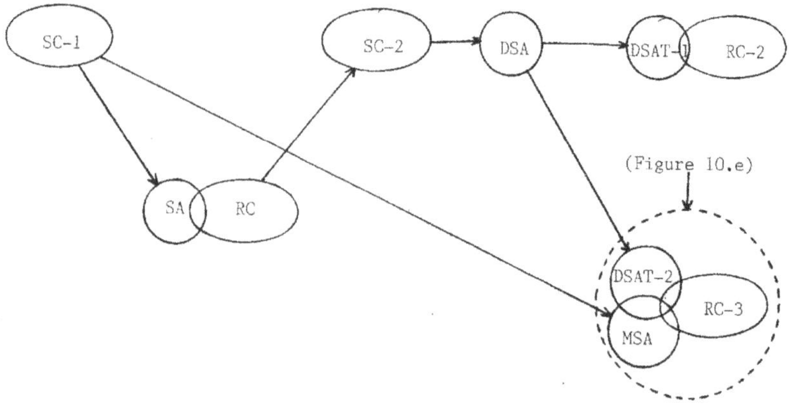

Figure 10.d

Figure 10.d shows how DSAs can be formed and how they can start churches in other cultures. Looking at the diagram, let's say Sending Church one (SC-1) is our own churches. We form our own SA which successfully starts churches (RC) among another people group. Eventually those churches send their own people to evangelize two other people groups (RC-2 and RC-3) through their own Sending Agency. We are calling that agency a Daughter Sending Agency (DSA).

One of RC's target people groups is in their own country. They plan a strategy, recruit and train team members, and support this team without any outside help. This team is the Daughter Sending Agency Team One (DSAT-1). The target people they are working to reach is labeled RC-2 in figure 10.d.

But the DSA decides they should also evangelize another target people, RC-3, who are located in another country. Their cultures and history are very similar, and they believe they can be effective within that target people (see figure 10.e). Since they have never evangelized outside their own country, they ask their mother Sending Agency (ours, MSA) to help. The MSA and the DSAT-2 form a partnership to evangelize the target people RC-3.

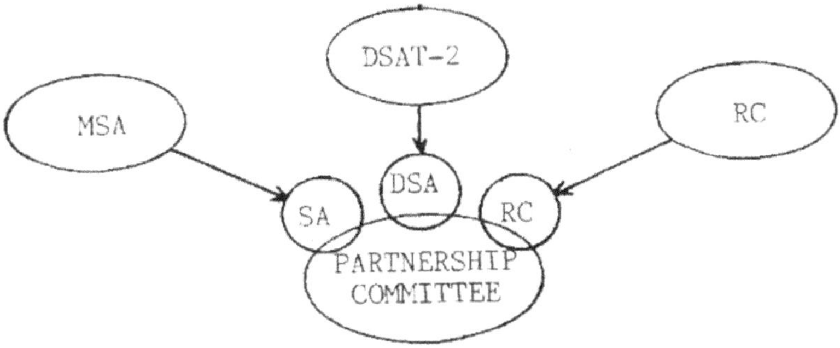

Figure 10.e

Notice in figure 10.e that there are partnership meetings required that are similar to what is described in the section above. At first, the partnership is formed between the MSA, RC, and DSAT-2 in order to plan a strategy to reach the target people who will form a Receiving Church (RC). As the RC begins to mature, the MSA, DSAT-2, and the RC will all have their own meetings to take care of issues that only concern them. But the major portion of the strategy will be implemented through the partnership structure. Each of the three structures will have leaders serving as representatives at the partnership meetings. As before, the time will eventually come when more and more of the leadership responsibility for the items under the authority of the partnership meeting will be transferred to the Receiving Churches (RC and RC-3).

Finances: It is important to mention finances when discussing SA-SA partnerships. Sometimes Receiving Churches are reluctant to form their own Sending Agencies because they are hard-pressed to find enough finances to operate the ministries to reach their own people group. Leaders of such groups may be tempted to think they should wait until they have enough finances to meet their own perceived needs before spending funds to reach other people groups. But Jesus gave us biblical principles which show that is not scriptural thinking. He said, "Freely you have received, freely give" (Matt. 10:8). He also said, "Give and it will be given unto you. A good measure, pressed down, shaken together and running over, will be poured into your lap" (Luke 6:38). As church leaders, we expect individual members to give to the local churches for God's work. We cannot expect less of local churches and national churches anywhere in the world under almost any financial circumstances! The scriptural principle is to give what we have received, expecting God to multiply the effect of what we give to meet other's needs and our own as well. If they are to follow the commands of Christ (Acts 1:8), then the churches themselves must also quickly gain a vision to give money and help to evangelize the lost of other people groups. If the early church had not reached out to evangelize other people groups, we ourselves would not know Jesus today! *If we consume all of God's blessings upon our own people, we will fail in God's purposes just as surely as did ancient Israel.* We must all be ready to sacrifice to evangelize other peoples, whether out of poverty or out of plenty. Reaching our neighbor across the world is no less important than reaching our neighbor who lives next to us!

In order to help Receiving Churches become Sending Churches sooner, many times the MSA will aid them in the financing of their cross-cultural evangelism efforts. This can happen at three different levels: (1) Cross-cultural training expenses, since SA members have already taken training and have experience themselves, they can help the DSA set up their own training program for cross-cultural workers. They may want to finance all or part of the training expenses in order to channel more DSA funds toward monthly support of their cross-cultural evangelists. (2) Logistical support, this refers to expenses which are of a one-time nature. They may include the initial team travel expenses to the field of service. They may also include other types of one-time expenses such as vehicles to use on the field, if necessary. But the regular monthly expenses, including that for equipment, should be borne by the DSA. (3) Project expenses, when it becomes clear to everyone that a special project the DSAT needs to complete in order to more rapidly expand its work, the SA team may decide to help with that project, if funding is available, at least in the initial stages. It needs to be sacrificial and faith-building for all groups involved.

It is dangerous to give the DSA help to cover regular monthly expenses. Those need to be borne by the Sending Churches. To do otherwise violates the Principle of Reproducibility and autochthonous principles in general. It would serve to stunt the development of the DSA and make it a project of the SA, not the DSA. Great care must be taken to make good decisions on this subject. When there is a need to expand the size of the DSA team, there can be a temptation for the SA to want to help support those new members in order to make the work more successful quickly. That would be a mistake. Most SAs do not have such excess money anyway. It really is possible to give too much and rob the DSA of its own determination and commitment to the purposes of God. Faith grows by being exercised sacrificially!

If the MSA wants to help and encourage the DSA, it is best to limit the financial help mostly to the three levels described above. It the MSA can pay some of the one-time only expenses for establishing different parts of the DSA's ministry, it will not usually harm the sense of responsibility for the ongoing work. Such help can also be a great encouragement to them and speed the evangelists to the field. Helping to train their members will serve to avoid many mistakes that would discourage them and the Sending Churches. It is important that the DSA continue to develop, refine, and support their own training system over time. Eventually, they will have their own experienced cross-cultural evangelists training their own new team members. The MSA can provide much very valuable assistance and encouragement to the DSA, especially in the beginning of its development. But it is very important not to give so much support and leadership that it robs the newly emerging DSA of the strength to grow and multiply its efforts by itself.

SA-SA-SA PARTNERSHIPS

It will often occur that Sending Churches will receive a call from the Lord to evangelize a target people where other Sending Agencies are already working. What should be their attitude toward those other SAs? How should they relate to the Receiving Churches which are already established when they arrive? These questions will become increasingly more important as more and more national churches become SCs.

There was a city in Latin America where five different evangelists from the same (foreign) country and type of church are located, but not working together. In that same city, there were two other evangelists from two other countries who also do not work together with any of the other cross-cultural evangelists. Yet all these people are from the same type of churches. They are trying to evangelize the same target people, and they believe the same Gospel and doctrine. The basic reason they don't work together is that they are mostly trying to start churches like the ones "back home." Each is trying to use cultural forms that fit the churches which sent them, not the cultural forms appropriate for the target people.

What should all these evangelists do? First, they should study principles like those found in this book so they can learn to leave the "cultural baggage" of their own forms at home. Then with their understanding enlightened, they should meet together to form a partnership structure which they use to plan a strategy for reaching the target people together. The resulting churches would not be like any of their churches back home. It should follow the local leadership patterns and cultural forms that are biblical yet appropriate for the target people. If all those evangelists were to follow good principles for doing cross-cultural evangelism, but work alone, the resulting churches would still look more like one another than their churches back home. So there is no reason why they cannot learn to work in partnership with one another, even as they work in partnership with God!

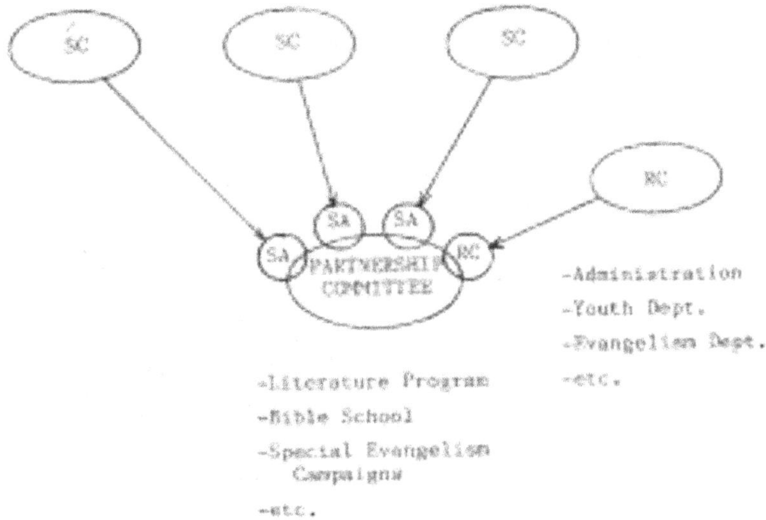

Figure 10.f

Figure 10.f

Figure 10.f diagrams how SA-SA-SA partnerships should function. It is very similar to what has already been described. But in this kind of partnership, representatives from each of the SAs meet together with representatives of the RC to form a partnership structure. The partnership meeting should function just like what has already been described. Those ministries which belong under the complete control of the RC should not be subject to the partnership meeting. But those ministries which require finance and leadership greater than the resources of the RC should be placed under the control of the partnership meeting. This meeting should be a policy-making body as well as a strategy development team. Relationships should be based upon mutual trust. Participants must be willing to trust one another, and they must trust the Holy Spirit's ability to guide and use one another. As before, no action or major decisions should be taken until there is consensus. They must also avoid competition between Sending Agencies. They must share the credit openly with supporters back home.

SA-SA-SA partnerships are perhaps the most needed types of structures in the world of cross-cultural evangelism today. They are a tool which allows a great amount of personnel and resources to be concentrated toward reaching specific unreached people groups. Forming these kind of partnership requires a strong desire to do what is best for the target people. And it takes visionary leadership who will go to the extra effort needed to form them. Like the building of all other relationships, building multiple SA partnerships requires hard work and commitment to the needs of other Sending Agencies as well as other people groups. To do nothing about forming partnerships of this type means we face many cities and areas of the world where cross-cultural evangelists are following the pattern of the Latin American city mentioned above. To do nothing about partnership means we are doomed to see the formation of many churches which believe the same doctrine, and even call themselves by the same kinds of names, but never learn to work together with greater strength for the glory of God (John 17:21). The resulting competition can be very destructive to the purposes of God and the glory He deserves as new churches are reproduced. The unity and message of the Body of Christ can suffer greatly as a result. Without partnership, it is too easy to find ourselves working to build our own kingdom, instead of the Kingdom of God.

By working to join our resources and love for God together through partnership, we can much more effectively evangelize unreached people groups. Whether in the shade of jungle banyan trees, or the air-conditioned offices of skyscrapers, we must form hundreds of interagency and interchurch partnerships if we seriously hope to bring a valid witness to the unreached peoples of the world.

Interchurch Sending Agencies

There is one more model for interagency cooperation which we should discuss. It is actually the structural opposite of the model given above. Instead of forming interagency partnerships to reach one people group, Sending Churches can also form partnerships among themselves to establish an international agency for reaching many people groups. That is what is pictured in figure 10.g.

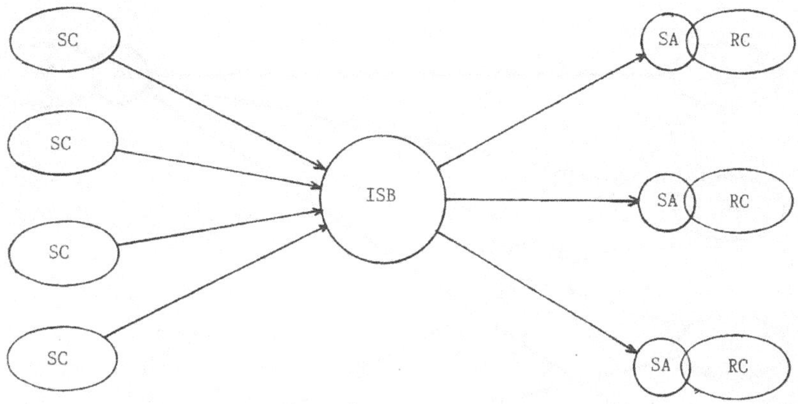

Figure 10.g

Sometimes it is easier to send cross-cultural workers when several national churches join together in partnership for that purpose. Representatives from several Sending Churches meet to form an agreement for jointly sponsoring evangelism efforts in target areas or among specific target peoples. Cross-cultural evangelism team members are recruited, trained, and sent out under the authority and directives of this interchurch sending board (ISB). This kind of partnership delegates a major portion of the responsibility for planning strategies, sending evangelists, and supervising their work to the jointly sponsored ISB.

This board can be sponsored by national churches of the same denomination representing different countries. That is one way to form such an ISB. Or, it can be sponsored by national churches of different denominations from the same country or from different countries.

Another more common variation of interagency partnership is pictured in figure 10.h. A group of churches who are sending, or want to send, cross-cultural evangelists join together in a regional association, or **interchurch associative partnership (IAP)**. The Sending Churches keep their own Sending Agencies, but they work in association with other SAs from other churches. Each SA sponsors and sends its own team members, but the associational partnership provides different kinds of help to coordinate and plan the cooperative work. IAPs can operate on a national basis or an international basis. On a national basis, it may involve SAs from several different people groups joining together to send missionaries internationally. On an international basis, it may involve the same kind of churches in different countries working together in partnership.

An excellent example is the World Assemblies of God Fellowship (WAGF). It is a loose affiliation of the Assemblies of God national church bodies around the world. These national churches together make up the fourth largest Protestant church group on a global basis, consisting of over 70 million believers in 144 countries. WAGF was formed (1988) so the national churches can work together for a number of reasons, but primarily to reach unreached peoples. Though each national church is autonomous and directs its own missionary work, it is done in cooperation and coordination with the Sending Agencies of other countries.

The amount of help given in partnership to the cross-cultural evangelism teams varies according to the way the partnership was formed. The IAP may only provide cooperative planning and logistical support. If so, the IAP would act more as a coordinating office to provide joint strategy planning to evangelize specific people groups or geographical areas with a number of people groups. The office might also coordinate funding transfers to the fields from one country to another country. At a deeper level of cooperation, the IAP may set qualification standards all participants agree upon for cross-cultural evangelists to meet. Rather than establishing cross-cultural ministry training schools in every region or country, regional schools might be established in cooperation with other countries. All members agree at this level on the standards and curriculum for such training. They may logically also assign oversight to the training system to the IAP.

This helps to provide top-quality training for much less overall cost, freeing more funds for cross-cultural evangelism teams.

There are literally hundreds of IAP structures working with local, regional, and national churches to send missionaries around the world. There are many kinds of missionary projects they undertake, from relief ministries to church planting. One only needs to look on the search engines online to find such agencies and what they do. We have already enumerated some of the strengths and weaknesses of the interdenominational versions of such agencies. If the reader is interested to learn more about them, he is invited to search the Internet fully. He or she and their leaders should think carefully about the principles found in this book before selecting such an agency to work with.

Regional partnerships of the IAP and ISB type are an encouraging sign on the horizon of cross-cultural evangelism. In forming such cooperative agencies, there are two extremes to avoid. First, the organization should not be so loosely organized, and be given so little authority and power, that it cannot effectively meet the felt needs of the partner agencies and their cross-cultural teams. It should not be an organization for organization's sake! It should be formed to meet specific kinds of needs which are common to member SAs. It should be more than just an excuse to meet together. It should be organized to provide services which are difficult or impossible for the member agencies to provide for themselves. Above all, it should be focused upon evangelizing whole people groups, not just sending workers into the cross-cultural harvest fields of the world.

The second extreme to avoid is organizing too much. Partnerships should not rob member SAs of their sense of responsibility for the work of cross-cultural evangelism. If the partnership structure is given too much authority and control over the work of individual member SAs, there will be a tendency to view the partnership as the only legitimate or "first rate" cross-cultural evangelism structure. This can cause the partnership structure to replace the SA structures of the member organizations. This kind of centralization can quickly rob the member churches of their vision and sense of responsibility, causing a decline in the overall cross-cultural evangelism efforts. Interchurch Sending Agencies should strengthen the efforts of member Sending Agencies, not lessen their influence and strength. Putting too much power in the hands of the partnership agency should be avoided.

CONCLUSION

Let's get personal for a moment. If you are like me, you realize just how short life really is. What is done for our own benefit does not last. What is done for Christ does. Win one person who wins others; plant one church that reproduces itself. That is how to produce lasting fruit in service to the Lord.

It was 1986 when I was in Argentina going every day to a new state to speak to leaders about their responsibility to take the Gospel to every people group. It was a grueling schedule, speaking several times a day and traveling by bus at night. On the last day, I got on a plane at midnight. I flew from Buenos Aires to Rio de Janeiro to New York City to Tokyo and finally to Singapore. It took forty-four hours to travel. I was unable to sleep sitting in a coach seat in the plane. I was unbelievably tired when I arrived in Singapore. Unfortunately, my assistant had scheduled the meeting and had forgotten that I would lose a day when I crossed the International Date Line over the Pacific Ocean. So within three hours of arrival in Singapore, I had to start training leaders from all over Asia about how to multiply churches among unreached peoples. God helped the adrenaline in my body to flow for several hours until I was finished, though I could hardly remember what I had said.

It was twelve years later when I was in the lobby of a church in California. An Asian man who looked familiar (but I could not remember why) started shouting across the lobby, saying, "Dr. Pate! Dr. Pate! Is that you?" And he rushed over to greet me. Then he began to recite in great detail everything I had said in those Singapore training sessions. He then proudly announced that since that time he had planted fourteen new churches! When we speak or train others, we often don't see the fruit of our labors. I was grateful to meet that leader from the Philippines that day. It was a good lesson for me.

If I had cancelled that trip or speaking engagement because of my exhaustion, a lot of people might not be in the Kingdom of God today. It has inspired me many times reflecting back on that event.

As I reflect on the many things I have seen and places I have worked for the Lord in sixty-nine countries around the world, I have come to realize also just how true is the central tenet of the Westminster Confession: "A Man's (or woman's) chief end is to love God and enjoy Him forever." When I was young and too full of my own importance, I confess that I thought that confession was not enough of a reason to live for God. I was determined to make my life worthwhile by serving God's purpose to reach every unreached people I could with the Gospel. I still am. And I expended my energies for that purpose with gratifying results. But now I realize that my purpose is not just to show God what I am willing to do for Him. It is to reach the unreached peoples of the world with a heart full of gratitude and joy—as a tribute of praise to Him and the love he has demonstrated toward me in Jesus Christ. That is what brings everlasting joy! It is not about me. It is about Him!

TO EVERY PEOPLE FROM EVERY PEOPLE

The task of world evangelization cannot depend upon one group of Christians. When Christ told us to make disciples among every ethnos or people group in the world, He added nothing about waiting until we have a strong economy like the "developed" countries. The churches of Latin America, Africa, Asia, and Oceania are rising to the challenge of cross-cultural evangelism. From those three continents alone, there are now more cross-cultural ministers being sent than in all the Western countries of the world put together. The author documented this trend in a previous book, *From Every People*, as has been stated before. There are now well over two hundred thousand Bible believing people preaching around the world where they have crossed cultural barriers with the Gospel. And they are sent from churches speaking many languages and located on every continent. This demonstrates that the power of God and resources he provides are available to help believers fulfill their responsibility to do cross-cultural evangelism. It is not limited to the richer countries of the world.

The harvest field among unreached peoples is still very plentiful (Matt. 9:37). There are currently about three billion people living in about seven thousand people groups separated from an adequate chance to hear and receive the Gospel! They are isolated by their cultures where the church of Jesus Christ still remains to be planted in the mainstream of their societies. Without question, the greatest single need in the Christian world today is this: we must believe God to raise up many more cross-cultural evangelists from every people where the Gospel has been planted to go make disciples among every people where the Gospel still needs to be planted! For every Bible-believing church among every people on earth, the evangelistic purpose must be the same. We must resolve to make disciples among our own people and among every other people as well. Cross-cultural evangelism is not an option. It is an integral part of the Gospel and is the central agenda of the Holy Spirit Himself as demonstrated in the book of Acts!

No church or group of churches is truly the church that Jesus came to build until it is fully participating in the evangelization of the peoples of other cultures near and far! There is no greater responsibility, nothing less selfish, and nothing less central to the purpose of the Church of Jesus Christ!

Quoting from the prophet Isaiah (52:7), the apostle Paul wrote, "How beautiful are the feet of those who bring good news" (see Rom. 10:15). In biblical times, much as it is in many parts of the earth today, the feet were considered the most dishonorable part of the body. Most traveling was done in sandaled feet. In everyday life, feet were always dirty—the most undesirable part of the body to look at. Yet the prophet, speaking with God's perspective, proclaimed that even the feet of those who proclaim the Gospel are beautiful in God's eyes.

Today, the feet of those spreading the Gospel of Jesus Christ are changing color! They are no longer just white feet. They are brown, black, yellow, and red also. That is beautiful in God's sight.

The Gospel no longer masquerades as an imperialistic white Western religion!

Let us gain a greater vision about those who proclaim the Gospel for the future. Let us catch a vision of a great and beautiful army of cross-cultural evangelists carrying the Gospel across every racial, linguistic, cultural, and geographical boundary on earth to penetrate the mainstream of every people group. No longer let the world view the Gospel banner as the religion of rich nations. As that army marches forward, let there be streams of beautiful brown, black, yellow, red, and also white feet joining in from every side! Let us see those feet marching—every one of them marching to the cadence of the Master—from every people where the Gospel has been planted to join this great and beautiful army. Let us see the unreached become the reached. Let us see the Gospel banner unfurled in the mainstream of every people group on earth! May God help us to do our part to see the good news go **TO EVERY PEOPLE FROM EVERY PEOPLE**!

QUESTIONS FOR UNDERSTANDING

1. List three types of sending structures, and explain their meaning. How are they related to one another?
2. List some advantages of forming a Sending Agency in a single local church? List the disadvantages.
3. List the advantages of organizing Sending Agencies at the national church level.
4. List the advantages and disadvantages of interdenominational SAs. What is the greatest disadvantage? Why is it important?
5. Explain why SAs should be semiautonomous, not being controlled by the administrative leaders of the Sending Church. What are the differences between the nature of the SA and SC administrative structures? From the Scriptures, give an example of the natural tension between the two structures.
6. List and describe the three-stage process of the organizational development of the churches of a target people.

7. List and explain five categories of agreement necessary to organize a local church within a target people group. Who should officiate at the ceremonies recognizing the formation of local churches? Why?
8. Who should decide when local churches among a target people group should be organized into a regional or national church? Why? How will the relationship between an SA and the local churches change after the regional or national church has been officially organized?
9. List and describe five types of agreement necessary to organize a group of local churches into a regional or national church structure.
10. Describe a partnership structure between an SA and the RC. What is the structure of the partnership committee? How does it function?
11. What is a DSA? How does it demonstrate the Principle of Reproducibility? How can DSAs enter into a partnership with MSAs?
12. Describe three levels of financial aid which MSAs might safely give to DSAs. What level of aid should be avoided, if at all possible? Why?
13. What is the purpose of SA-SA-SA partnerships? Describe how they operate. Why are many more structures of this kind needed in cross-cultural evangelism?
14. Describe two different kinds of interchurch Sending Agencies. How do they differ from each other? Which kind do you think is the most common in Western countries, Latin America, Africa, and Asia?
15. Explain two extremes which should be avoided in organizing and operating interchurch Sending Agencies.

QUESTIONS FOR DISCUSSION

1. Discuss the need for SAs to have a large degree of autonomy in performing their work. Discuss historical cases you know about which demonstrate this principle. Can you see any examples of

this principle operating between different kinds of secular business organizations that are the most successful?

2. Can you think of any churches or national church organizations which have formed their own cross-cultural ministry Sending Agencies? Discuss what categories those agencies would fall into, according to what you have learned in this chapter.
3. Discuss the strengths and weaknesses of interdenominational Sending Agencies. What kinds of work can they do well? Can you think of any SAs of this type with which you are familiar? What is their potential greatest weakness? Point out why partnerships are important to such agencies.
4. Discuss the concept of partnership in cross-cultural evangelism. Why shouldn't the SA be allowed to dominate the RC? Why shouldn't the RC be able to direct the work of the SA?
5. If you were planning to go as a cross-cultural evangelist to evangelize another people group, discuss what kind of SA you would like to have helping you. How would you organize such an SA among the churches of your own people?

ACKNOWLEDGMENTS

The author is strongly indebted to many authors and scholars who have developed more than a few of the principles contained in this book. A significant portion of the value and principles contained in it are derived from experienced scholars and practitioners who have gone before me. Primary among them are six people who all served as professors at Fuller Seminary, School of Intercultural Studies for a number of years: Dr. C. Peter Wagner, Dr. Charles "Chuck" Kraft, Dr. Donald C. Mc Gavran, Paul G. Hiebert, and Drs. E. Thomas and Elizabeth Brewster. Also prominent in providing seminal ideas and principles contained in this book are Dr. David J. Hesselgrave of the School of World Mission at Trinity Evangelical Divinity School and Marvin K Mayers, who taught extensively at the Summer Institute of Linguistics (Dallas), Wheaton College, and Biola University.

Equally important are the many leaders of the rapid surge in churches, denominations, and organizations that are arising from Latin America, Africa, Asia, and (lately) Eastern European churches who are increasingly engaging in cross-cultural ministry. Much of the practical knowledge and some of the theoretical knowledge contained in this book have been honed in discussion and interaction with such leaders around the world. These leaders represent a great hope and promise for completing the task of world evangelism. Those often unsung heroes of the faith provided a great deal of inspiration for the completion of this book. It is with a prayer that it will provide a useful and productive tool for their efforts as well as for those in the Western countries of the world.

I would be remiss also if I did not mention the personal help of my friend, Mr. Jimbo Hammock, of Corpus Christi, Texas. He has spent many hours on the manuscript helping me to correct everything from typos to content that was not clear. While I am sure he will receive his reward from the "Lord of the Harvest" for all his efforts, I want to express my profound appreciation for his labors on this project.

Last, but not least, my wife, Kathryn, deserves a lot of credit for covering all the bases at home that were necessary in order to free me up to keep working on this project. She deserves a lot more praise than she ever receives for who she is as well as what she does.

APPENDIX A

Principles And Perspectives

THAT SUCCESSFUL LANGUAGE LEARNERS UNDERSTAND AND IMPLEMENT

* Language acquisition is a social, not an academic activity.
* The ultimate purpose is not just learning the language, but getting to know the people.
* Learn a little and use it a lot!
* They develop a solid nucleus (core) around which explosive growth coheres.
* A language is learned rather than taught.
* Learners behave in child-like ways (to do so is not being childish).
* They learn language tools that, when used in the community, give them generative capacity -- the power to learn more.
* They structure their socio-cultural context in ways that enable them to get all the help and practice they need.
* They utilize the fact that people help people who are in need.
* They listen first (listen a tremendous amount), then mimic, then produce.
* They learn by discovery — hypothesis formulation and testing, which leads to confirmation of the hypothesis, or to refining or rejecting it.
* They learn from their mistakes.
* They are willing to be vulnerable.
* They are belongers, with an insider's name.
* Their resources are people, rather than just books.
* They follow a Learning Cycle
* They have fun!
* Their motivation is a commitment to the people of the language.
* They remember, rather than memorize.

(source: Brewster & Brewster, 1981; by permission)

THAT SUCCESSFUL LANGUAGE LEARNERS UNDERSTAND AND IMPLEMENT

- Language acquisition is a social, not academic activity.
- The ultimate purpose is not just learning the language, but getting to know the people.
- Learn a little and use it a lot!
- They develop a solid nucleus (core) around which explosive growth coheres.
- A language is learned rather than taught.
- Learners behave in child-like ways (to do so is not being children).
- They learn language tools that, when used in the community, give them generative capacity—the power to learn more.
- They structure their social-cultural context in ways that enable them to get all the help and practice they need.
- They utilize the fact that people help people who are in need.
- They listen first (listen a tremendous amount), then mimic, then produce.
- They learn by discovery—hypothesis formulation and testing, which leads to confirmation of the hypothesis, or to refining or rejecting it. They are active, not passive in their learning.
- They learn from their mistakes.
- They are willing to be vulnerable.
- They are belongers with an insider's name.
- Their resources are people, rather than just books.
- They follow a Learning Cycle.
- They have fun!
- Their motivation is a commitment to the people of the language.
- They remember from experience, not just memorization.

APPENDIX B

Language ____________________ Name ______________________

Date: ____________

LEARNING CYCLE EVALUATION GUIDE

GET

Phrases of Text One should give power to: Meet people, express desire to learn, express limitations, thanks, and a leave-taking. Text Card #___

LEARN

Names of Fluency Mimicry Activities I practiced with Helper: __________

____

To do these procedures more effectively/efficiently I could: __________

____

Phrases taped on 5-second loop tape: (y/n)______. Whole text taped on 30-second loop tape: (y/n)_____. Whole text taped on regular tape:____

Fluency Mimicry Activities taped: ______________________________

____

To make tapes more efficiently I might: ____________________

____

USE

Number of people communicated with today:______.

Number of hours spent in community:______.

Talking time (vs walking time) might be increased by: ______________

____

EVALUATE/ENVISION

Reflections on today: ______________________________

____

Name of text topic for day after tomorrow: ____________________

____

Text topic for tomorrow: ____________________________

Plan to improve tomorrow's Learning Cycle: ____________________

____

An Experience: ______________________________

____

____

What I've learned about myself: ______________________________

____

____

Observations about the community and culture: ____________________

____

____

Ideas for implementing my bonding goal: ____________________

____

(source: Brewster & Brewster, 1976; by permission)

Language_____________________________ Name:___________
Date:____________

LEARNING CYCLE EVALUATION GUIDE

GET: Phrases of TEXT ONE should give power to: 1) Meet people; 2) Express desire to learn; 3) Express limitations, thanks and a leave-taking Text Card #:

____

LEARN: Names of Fluency Mimicry Activities I practiced with Helper: ______________________________

____

____

To do these procedures more effectively/efficiently I could:____

____

____

Phrases recorded on repeating audio device? (Y/No) _____; Whole text recorded on repeating audio? (Y/No) ______ Fluency mimicry activities recorded:__________________________________

____

To make recordings more efficient, I might:

____

____

____

USE: Number of people communicated with today: ________.

Number of hours spent in the community: ________.

Talking time (vs. walking time) might be increased by:____

____

____

EVALUATE/ENVISION:

Reflections on today: ______________________

____

____

Name of text topic for day after tomorrow:

____

____

____

Text Topic for tomorrow:__________________

____

____

Ways to improve tomorrow's Learning Cycle:

____

____

____

An Experience: _________________________

____

____

What I've learned about myself:

____

____

____

Observations about the community and culture:

____

____

____

Ideas for implementing my bonding goal:

____

____

____

(Appendix A and Appendix B are adapted and used by permission from Brewster and Brewster, 1976.)

APPENDIX C

Language Learning Evaluation Guide Self-Rating Checklist Of Speaking Proficiency

Level Zero Plus

- ○ I can use more than 50 words of my new language in appropriate contexts

LEVEL ONE

- ○ (You are at Level One when you can confidently check each of the following Level One language activities.)
- ○ I can initiate conversations and use appropriate leave-takings to close conversations.
- ○ I can make a selection from a menu and order a simple meal.
- ○ I can ask and tell the time of day, the day of the week and the date.
- ○ I can go to the market or butcher and ask for vegetables, fruit, milk, bread and meat, and I can bargain when appropriate.
- ○ I can tell someone how to get from here to the post office, a restaurant, or a hotel.
- ○ I can negotiate for a taxi ride or a hotel room and get a fair price.

- ○ I can make a social introduction of someone else and also give a brief speech to introduce myself.
- ○ I can understand and correctly respond to questions about my marital status, nationality, occupation, age and place of birth.
- ○ I can get the bus or train I want, buy a ticket, and get off where I intended to.
- ○ I know how to find the meaning of a word or phrase that I don't understand on my phone or computer. I have practiced repeating spoken words or phrases from my phone or computer using the Life Language Learning System of repetition.
- ○ I can use the language well enough to assist a newcomer in all of the above Level One situations.

Level One Plus

- ○ I have One Plus proficiency because I can do all of the Level One activities and at least three of the following Level Two activities.

Level Two

- ○ (You are at Level Two proficiency when you can confidently check each of the following Level Two activities.)
- ○ I can take and give simple messages over the telephone
- ○ I can give a brief autobiography and also talk about my plans and hopes.
- ○ I can describe my most recent job or activity in some detail and also describe my present role as a language learner.
- ○ I can describe the basic structure of the government in both my home and host countries.
- ○ I can describe the geography of my home and host countries.
- ○ I can describe the purpose and function of the organization or group I represent.
- ○ I could use my new language to hire an employee or helper and agree on qualifications, pay, hours and special duties.
- ○ I feel confident that my pronunciation is always intelligible and I am rarely asked to repeat myself.

- ○ I feel confident that people understand me when I speak in the new language at least 80% of the time. I am also confident that I understand what native speakers tell me on the topics like those of Level Two.
- ○ I understand the language well enough to assist a newcomer on any of the Level Two situations, (assuming I also understand the newcomer's language).

Level Two Plus

- ○ I have a Two Plus proficiency because I can meet at least three of the following Level Three requirements.

Level Three

- ○ (You are at Level Three when you can confidently check each of the following Level Three items.)
- ○ I do not try to avoid any of the grammatical features of the language.
- ○ I now have sufficient vocabulary and grasp of grammatical structure to correctly complete any sentence that I begin.
- ○ I can speak at a normal rate of speech with only rare hesitations.
- ○ I can confidently follow and contribute to a conversation between native speakers when they try to include me.
- ○ I am able to correctly understand information given to me over a telephone.
- ○ I can listen to a speech or discussion on a topic of interest to me and take accurate notes.
- ○ I can speak to a group of native speakers on a professional subject and have confidence that I am communicating what I want.
- ○ I can understand opposing points of view and can politely describe and defend an organizational position or objective to an antagonist.
- ○ I could cope with a social blunder, an undeserved traffic ticket, or a plumbing emergency.

- ○ I can understand two native speakers talking with each other about a current event or issue.
- ○ I could serve as an interpreter for a newcomer in any of the Level Three situations.
- ○ I feel that I can carry out the professional responsibilities of my work in my new language.

Level Three Plus

- ○ (You are at Level Three Plus proficiency because you can meet at least three of the Level Four requirements.)

Level Four

- ○ (You are at Level Four when you can confidently check each of the following Level Four characteristics.)
- ○ I practically never make grammatical mistakes.
- ○ I can always understand native speakers when they talk with each other.
- ○ I can understand humor and language puns, and I can actively participate in fun and humorous situations.
- ○ My vocabulary is always extensive and precise enough for me to convey exact meaning in professional discussions.
- ○ I feel I have a comprehensive grasp of the local "knowledge bank."
- ○ I can appropriately alter my speech style for a public lecture, or a conversation with a professor, an employee, or a close friend.
- ○ I could serve as an interpreter for a "bigwig" at a professional or social function.
- ○ I feel I could carry out any job assignment as effectively in my second language as in English

Level Four Plus

- ○ My vocabulary and cultural understanding are always extensive enough to enable me to communicate any precise meaning.

- People feel that I share their knowledge bank well enough to talk about and defend any of their beliefs with me.

Level Five

- Native speakers react to me just as they do to each other—I am usually considered an "insider."
- I sometimes feel more at home in my second language than in English. My dreams are usually filled with positive experiences and are often experienced completely in the native language.
- I can do mental arithmetic in the native language without slowing down.
- I consider myself to be completely bilingual and bicultural, with equivalent ability in English and in my second language.
- I consider myself a native speaker of the language.

(Adapted with permission from Brewster and Brewster, 1976.)

Note: We are deeply indebted to the United States Foreign Services Institute and the National Defense Language School (Monterrey, California) for the concept of the Zero to Five proficiency rating scale and for the concept of the self-rating checklist.

APPENDIX D

Sample Graph

Note: Appendixes D through I are adapted or copied from THE CHURCH GROWTH SURVEY HANDBOOK; by Bob Waymire and C. Peter Wagner; published by The Global Church Growth Bulletin, Sanat Clara, Ca. They are used by permision.

APPENDIX D: SAMPLE GRAPH

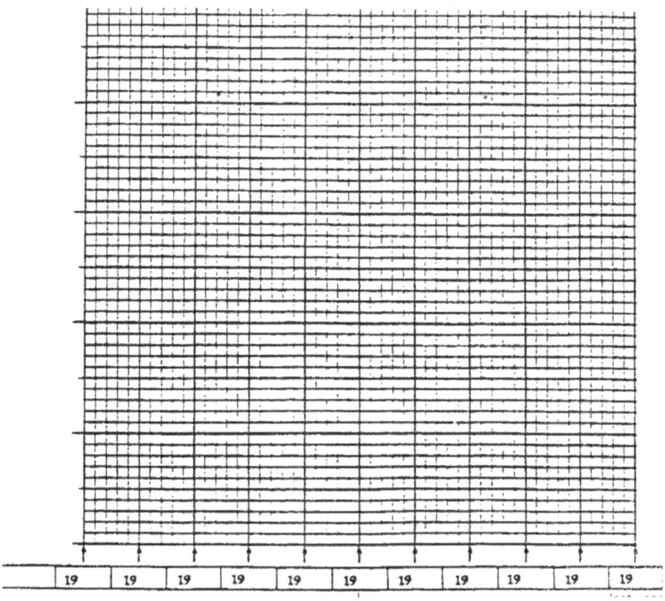

APPENDIX E

AVERAGE ANNUAL GROWTH RATE (AAGR)

(see Instructions below)

L/B	%INCR	Years: 1	2	3	4	5	6	7	8	9	10	15	20	25	50	75
1.01	1%	1.00%	0.50%	0.33%	0.25%	0.20%	0.17%	0.14%	0.12%	0.11%	0.10%	0.07%	0.05%	0.04%	0.02%	0.01%
1.02	2%	2.00%	1.00%	0.66%	0.50%	0.40%	0.33%	0.28%	0.25%	0.22%	0.20%	0.13%	0.10%	0.08%	0.04%	0.03%
1.04	4%	4.00%	1.98%	1.32%	0.99%	0.79%	0.66%	0.56%	0.49%	0.44%	0.39%	0.26%	0.20%	0.16%	0.08%	0.05%
1.05	5%	5.00%	2.47%	1.64%	1.23%	0.98%	0.82%	0.70%	0.61%	0.54%	0.49%	0.33%	0.24%	0.20%	0.10%	0.07%
1.06	6%	6.00%	2.96%	1.96%	1.47%	1.17%	0.98%	0.84%	0.73%	0.65%	0.58%	0.39%	0.29%	0.23%	0.12%	0.08%
1.08	8%	8.00%	3.92%	2.60%	1.94%	1.55%	1.29%	1.11%	0.97%	0.86%	0.77%	0.51%	0.39%	0.31%	0.15%	0.10%
1.10	10%	10.00%	4.88%	3.23%	2.41%	1.92%	1.60%	1.37%	1.20%	1.06%	0.96%	0.64%	0.48%	0.38%	0.19%	0.13%
1.12	12%	12.00%	5.83%	3.85%	2.87%	2.29%	1.91%	1.63%	1.43%	1.27%	1.14%	0.76%	0.57%	0.45%	0.23%	0.15%
1.14	14%	14.00%	6.77%	4.46%	3.33%	2.66%	2.21%	1.89%	1.65%	1.47%	1.32%	0.88%	0.66%	0.53%	0.26%	0.17%
1.16	16%	16.00%	7.70%	5.07%	3.78%	3.01%	2.50%	2.14%	1.87%	1.66%	1.50%	0.99%	0.74%	0.60%	0.30%	0.20%
1.18	18%	18.00%	8.63%	5.67%	4.22%	3.37%	2.80%	2.39%	2.09%	1.86%	1.67%	1.11%	0.83%	0.66%	0.33%	0.22%
1.20	20%	20.00%	9.54%	6.27%	4.66%	3.71%	3.09%	2.64%	2.31%	2.05%	1.84%	1.22%	0.92%	0.73%	0.37%	0.24%
1.25	25%	25.00%	11.80%	7.72%	5.74%	4.56%	3.79%	3.24%	2.83%	2.51%	2.26%	1.50%	1.12%	0.90%	0.45%	0.30%
1.30	30%	30.00%	14.02%	9.14%	6.78%	5.39%	4.47%	3.82%	3.33%	2.96%	2.66%	1.76%	1.32%	1.05%	0.53%	0.35%
1.35	35%	35.00%	16.19%	10.52%	7.79%	6.19%	5.13%	4.38%	3.82%	3.39%	3.05%	2.02%	1.51%	1.21%	0.60%	0.40%
1.40	40%	40.00%	18.32%	11.87%	8.78%	6.96%	5.77%	4.92%	4.30%	3.81%	3.42%	2.27%	1.70%	1.35%	0.68%	0.45%
1.45	45%	45.00%	20.42%	13.19%	9.73%	7.71%	6.39%	5.45%	4.75%	4.21%	3.79%	2.51%	1.88%	1.50%	0.75%	0.50%
1.50	50%	50.00%	22.47%	14.47%	10.67%	8.45%	6.99%	5.96%	5.20%	4.61%	4.14%	2.74%	2.05%	1.64%	0.81%	0.54%
1.55	55%	55.00%	24.50%	15.73%	11.58%	9.16%	7.58%	6.46%	5.63%	4.99%	4.48%	2.96%	2.22%	1.77%	0.88%	0.59%
1.60	60%	60.00%	26.49%	16.96%	12.47%	9.86%	8.15%	6.94%	6.05%	5.36%	4.81%	3.18%	2.38%	1.90%	0.94%	0.63%
1.65	65%	65.00%	28.45%	18.17%	13.33%	10.53%	8.70%	7.42%	6.46%	5.72%	5.14%	3.39%	2.54%	2.02%	1.01%	0.67%
1.70	70%	70.00%	30.38%	19.35%	14.19%	11.20%	9.25%	7.88%	6.86%	6.07%	5.45%	3.60%	2.69%	2.15%	1.07%	0.71%
1.75	75%	75.00%	32.29%	20.51%	15.02%	11.84%	9.78%	8.32%	7.25%	6.42%	5.76%	3.80%	2.84%	2.26%	1.13%	0.75%
1.80	80%	80.00%	34.16%	21.64%	15.83%	12.47%	10.29%	8.76%	7.62%	6.75%	6.05%	4.00%	2.98%	2.38%	1.18%	0.79%
1.85	85%	85.00%	36.01%	22.76%	16.63%	13.09%	10.80%	9.19%	8.00%	7.07%	6.35%	4.19%	3.12%	2.49%	1.24%	0.82%
1.90	90%	90.00%	37.84%	23.86%	17.41%	13.70%	11.29%	9.60%	8.35%	7.39%	6.63%	4.37%	3.26%	2.60%	1.29%	0.86%
1.95	95%	95.00%	39.64%	24.93%	18.17%	14.29%	11.77%	10.01%	8.71%	7.70%	6.91%	4.55%	3.40%	2.71%	1.34%	0.89%
2.00	100%	100.00%	41.42%	25.99%	18.92%	14.87%	12.25%	10.41%	9.05%	8.01%	7.18%	4.73%	3.53%	2.81%	1.40%	0.93%
2.05	105%	105.00%	43.18%	27.03%	19.66%	15.44%	12.71%	10.80%	9.39%	8.30%	7.44%	4.90%	3.65%	2.91%	1.45%	0.96%
2.10	110%	110.00%	44.91%	28.06%	20.38%	16.00%	13.16%	11.18%	9.72%	8.59%	7.70%	5.07%	3.78%	3.01%	1.49%	0.99%
2.15	115%	115.00%	46.63%	29.07%	21.09%	16.54%	13.61%	11.56%	10.04%	8.88%	7.96%	5.24%	3.90%	3.11%	1.54%	1.03%
2.20	120%	120.00%	48.32%	30.06%	21.79%	17.08%	14.04%	11.92%	10.36%	9.16%	8.20%	5.40%	4.02%	3.20%	1.59%	1.06%
2.25	125%	125.00%	50.00%	31.04%	22.47%	17.61%	14.47%	12.28%	10.67%	9.43%	8.45%	5.56%	4.14%	3.30%	1.64%	1.09%
2.30	130%	130.00%	51.66%	32.00%	23.15%	18.13%	14.89%	12.64%	10.97%	9.70%	8.69%	5.71%	4.25%	3.39%	1.68%	1.12%
2.35	135%	135.00%	53.30%	32.95%	23.81%	18.64%	15.30%	12.98%	11.27%	9.96%	8.92%	5.86%	4.36%	3.48%	1.72%	1.15%
2.40	140%	140.00%	54.92%	33.89%	24.47%	19.14%	15.71%	13.32%	11.56%	10.22%	9.15%	6.01%	4.47%	3.56%	1.77%	1.17%
2.45	145%	145.00%	56.52%	34.81%	25.11%	19.63%	16.11%	13.66%	11.85%	10.47%	9.37%	6.16%	4.58%	3.65%	1.81%	1.20%
2.50	150%	150.00%	58.11%	35.72%	25.74%	20.11%	16.50%	13.99%	12.14%	10.72%	9.60%	6.30%	4.69%	3.73%	1.85%	1.23%
2.55	155%	155.00%	59.69%	36.62%	26.37%	20.59%	16.88%	14.31%	12.41%	10.96%	9.81%	6.44%	4.79%	3.82%	1.89%	1.26%
2.60	160%	160.00%	61.25%	37.51%	26.98%	21.06%	17.26%	14.63%	12.69%	11.20%	10.03%	6.58%	4.89%	3.90%	1.93%	1.28%
2.65	165%	165.00%	62.79%	38.38%	27.59%	21.52%	17.64%	14.94%	12.96%	11.44%	10.24%	6.71%	4.99%	3.98%	1.97%	1.31%
2.70	170%	170.00%	64.32%	39.23%	28.19%	21.98%	18.00%	15.25%	13.22%	11.67%	10.44%	6.85%	5.09%	4.05%	2.01%	1.33%
2.75	175%	175.00%	65.83%	40.10%	28.78%	22.42%	18.36%	15.55%	13.48%	11.90%	10.65%	6.98%	5.17%	4.13%	2.04%	1.36%
2.80	180%	180.00%	67.33%	40.95%	29.36%	22.87%	18.72%	15.85%	13.74%	12.12%	10.84%	7.11%	5.28%	4.20%	2.08%	1.38%
2.85	185%	185.00%	68.82%	41.78%	29.93%	23.30%	19.07%	16.14%	13.99%	12.34%	11.04%	7.23%	5.38%	4.28%	2.12%	1.41%
2.90	190%	190.00%	70.29%	42.60%	30.50%	23.73%	19.42%	16.43%	14.24%	12.56%	11.23%	7.36%	5.47%	4.35%	2.15%	1.43%
2.95	195%	195.00%	71.76%	43.42%	31.06%	24.16%	19.76%	16.71%	14.48%	12.77%	11.42%	7.48%	5.56%	4.42%	2.19%	1.45%
3.00	200%	200.00%	73.21%	44.22%	31.61%	24.57%	20.09%	16.99%	14.72%	12.98%	11.61%	7.60%	5.65%	4.49%	2.22%	1.48%
3.20	220%	220.00%	78.89%	47.36%	33.75%	26.19%	21.39%	18.08%	15.65%	13.80%	12.33%	8.06%	5.99%	4.75%	2.35%	1.56%
3.40	240%	240.00%	84.39%	50.37%	35.79%	27.73%	22.63%	19.10%	16.53%	14.57%	13.02%	8.50%	6.31%	5.02%	2.43%	1.65%
3.60	260%	260.00%	89.74%	53.26%	37.74%	29.20%	23.80%	20.08%	17.36%	15.30%	13.67%	8.91%	6.61%	5.26%	2.59%	1.72%
3.80	280%	280.00%	94.94%	56.05%	39.62%	30.60%	24.92%	21.01%	18.16%	15.99%	14.28%	9.31%	6.90%	5.49%	2.71%	1.80%
4.00	300%	300.00%	100.00%	58.74%	41.42%	31.95%	25.99%	21.90%	18.92%	16.65%	14.87%	9.68%	7.18%	5.70%	2.81%	1.87%
4.20	320%	320.00%	104.94%	61.34%	43.16%	33.24%	27.02%	22.75%	19.65%	17.29%	15.43%	10.04%	7.44%	5.91%	2.91%	1.93%
4.40	340%	340.00%	109.76%	63.86%	44.83%	34.49%	28.01%	23.57%	20.35%	17.89%	15.97%	10.38%	7.69%	6.11%	3.01%	2.00%
4.60	360%	360.00%	114.48%	66.31%	46.45%	35.69%	28.96%	24.36%	21.02%	18.48%	16.49%	10.71%	7.93%	6.29%	3.10%	2.06%
4.80	380%	380.00%	119.09%	68.69%	48.02%	36.85%	29.88%	25.12%	21.66%	19.04%	16.98%	11.02%	8.16%	6.48%	3.19%	2.11%
5.00	400%	400.00%	123.61%	71.00%	49.53%	37.97%	30.77%	25.85%	22.28%	19.58%	17.46%	11.33%	8.38%	6.65%	3.27%	2.17%
5.50	450%	450.00%	134.52%	76.52%	53.14%	40.63%	32.86%	27.58%	23.75%	20.85%	18.59%	12.04%	8.90%	7.06%	3.47%	2.30%
6.00	500%	500.00%	144.95%	81.71%	56.51%	43.10%	34.80%	29.17%	25.10%	22.03%	19.62%	12.69%	9.37%	7.43%	3.65%	2.42%
7.00	600%	600.00%	164.58%	91.29%	62.66%	47.58%	38.31%	32.05%	27.54%	24.14%	21.48%	13.85%	10.22%	8.09%	3.97%	2.63%
8.00	700%	700.00%	182.84%	100.00%	68.18%	51.57%	41.42%	34.59%	29.68%	25.99%	23.11%	14.87%	10.96%	8.67%	4.25%	2.81%
9.00	800%	800.00%	200.00%	108.01%	73.21%	55.18%	44.22%	36.87%	31.61%	27.65%	24.57%	15.78%	11.61%	9.19%	4.49%	2.97%
10.00	900%	900.00%	216.23%	115.44%	77.83%	58.49%	46.78%	38.95%	33.35%	29.15%	25.89%	16.59%	12.20%	9.65%	4.71%	3.12%
11.00	1000%	1000.00%	231.66%	122.40%	82.12%	61.54%	49.13%	40.85%	34.95%	30.53%	27.10%	17.33%	12.74%	10.07%	4.91%	3.25%
16.00	1500%	1500.00%	300.00%	151.98%	100.00%	74.11%	58.74%	48.60%	41.42%	36.08%	31.95%	20.30%	14.87%	11.73%	5.70%	3.77%
21.00	2000%	2000.00%	358.26%	175.89%	114.07%	83.84%	66.10%	54.49%	46.31%	40.25%	35.59%	22.50%	16.44%	12.95%	6.23%	4.14%
26.00	2500%	2500.00%	409.90%	196.25%	125.81%	91.86%	72.12%	59.27%	50.27%	43.62%	38.52%	24.26%	17.69%	13.92%	6.73%	4.44%
31.00	3000%	3000.00%	456.78%	214.14%	135.96%	98.73%	77.74%	63.32%	53.61%	46.46%	40.97%	25.73%	18.73%	14.72%	7.11%	4.69%
36.00	3500%	3500.00%	500.00%	230.19%	144.95%	104.77%	81.71%	66.85%	56.51%	48.91%	43.10%	26.99%	19.62%	15.41%	7.43%	4.89%
41.00	4000%	4000.00%	540.31%	244.82%	153.04%	110.16%	85.69%	69.98%	59.07%	51.08%	44.97%	28.09%	20.40%	16.01%	7.71%	5.08%
46.00	4500%	4500.00%	578.23%	258.30%	160.43%	115.06%	89.29%	72.80%	61.38%	53.02%	46.65%	29.08%	21.10%	16.55%	7.96%	5.24%
51.00	5000%	5000.00%	614.14%	270.84%	167.23%	119.54%	92.57%	75.36%	63.47%	54.79%	48.17%	29.97%	21.72%	17.03%	8.13%	5.38%
61.00	6000%	6000.00%	681.02%	293.65%	179.47%	127.54%	98.41%	79.91%	67.17%	57.90%	50.85%	31.53%	22.82%	17.87%	8.57%	5.63%
71.00	7000%	7000.00%	742.61%	314.08%	190.28%	134.56%	103.49%	83.85%	70.38%	60.58%	53.15%	32.87%	23.76%	18.59%	8.90%	5.85%
81.00	8000%	8000.00%	800.00%	332.67%	200.00%	140.82%	108.01%	87.34%	73.21%	62.95%	55.18%	34.04%	24.57%	19.22%	9.19%	6.03%
91.00	9000%	9000.00%	853.94%	349.79%	208.86%	146.50%	112.08%	90.49%	75.74%	65.07%	57.00%	35.08%	25.30%	19.77%	9.44%	6.20%
101.00	10000%	******%	904.99%	365.70%	217.02%	151.69%	115.80%	93.34%	78.05%	66.99%	58.63%	36.03%	25.96%	20.27%	9.67%	6.35%

FINDING THE AAGR AND DGR

Step 1 Find AAGR by dividing members (or churches) for "latest" year by "beginning" year members (L/B). In "L/B" column locate the number closest to your answer, then locate the AAGR in the appropriate year column.

Step 2 Convert AAGR to DGR by going to the 10 year column and locate the number you have for AAGR per Step 1 above (or the closest number to it). Once you've located the number, move horizontally across to the left to the "%INCR" column and read the DGR.

Note If the exact number doesn't appear in the 10 year column, turn to Table B which is an expanded 10 year column. If the exact number is there, read the corresponding DGR. If not, and you want to get the exact number, follow the steps outlined below Table B.

APPENDIX F

DECADAL GROWTH RATE (DGR)

EXPANDED 10 YEAR AAGR TABLE

(see instructions below)

L/B	AAGR	DGR	L/B	AAGR	DGR	L/B	AAGR	DGR	L/B	AAGR	DGR	L/B	AAGR	DGR	L/B	AAGR	DGR
1.01	.10%	1%	1.96	6.96%	96%	3.00	11.61%	200%	4.04	14.98%	304%	5.08	17.65%	408%	6.60	20.77%	560%
1.02	.20%	2%	1.98	7.07%	98%	3.02	11.69%	202%	4.06	15.04%	306%	5.10	17.69%	410%	6.70	20.95%	570%
1.03	.30%	3%	2.00	7.18%	100%	3.04	11.76%	204%	4.08	15.10%	308%	5.12	17.74%	412%	6.80	21.13%	580%
1.04	.39%	4%	2.02	7.28%	102%	3.06	11.83%	206%	4.10	15.15%	310%	5.14	17.79%	414%	6.90	21.31%	590%
1.05	.49%	5%	2.04	7.39%	104%	3.08	11.91%	208%	4.12	15.21%	312%	5.16	17.83%	416%	7.00	21.48%	600%
1.06	.58%	6%	2.06	7.49%	106%	3.10	11.98%	210%	4.14	15.27%	314%	5.18	17.88%	418%	7.20	21.82%	620%
1.07	.68%	7%	2.08	7.60%	108%	3.12	12.05%	212%	4.16	15.32%	316%	5.20	17.92%	420%	7.40	22.16%	640%
1.08	.77%	8%	2.10	7.70%	110%	3.14	12.12%	214%	4.18	15.38%	318%	5.22	17.97%	422%	7.60	22.48%	660%
1.09	.87%	9%	2.12	7.80%	112%	3.16	12.19%	216%	4.20	15.43%	320%	5.24	18.01%	424%	7.80	22.80%	680%
1.10	.96%	10%	2.14	7.90%	114%	3.18	12.26%	218%	4.22	15.49%	322%	5.26	18.06%	426%	8.00	23.11	700%
1.12	1.14%	12%	2.16	8.01%	116%	3.20	12.33%	220%	4.24	15.54%	324%	5.28	18.10%	428%	8.20	23.42%	720%
1.14	1.32%	14%	2.18	8.10%	118%	3.22	12.40%	222%	4.26	15.60%	326%	5.30	18.15%	430%	8.40	23.72%	740%
1.16	1.50%	16%	2.20	8.20%	120%	3.24	12.47%	224%	4.28	15.65%	328%	5.32	18.19%	432%	8.60	24.01%	760%
1.18	1.67%	18%	2.22	8.30%	122%	3.26	12.54%	226%	4.30	15.70%	330%	5.34	18.24%	434%	8.80	24.29%	780%
1.20	1.84%	20%	2.24	8.39%	124%	3.28	12.61%	228%	4.32	15.76%	332%	5.36	18.28%	436%	9.00	24.57%	800%
1.22	2.01%	22%	2.26	8.50%	126%	3.30	12.68%	230%	4.34	15.81%	334%	5.38	18.33%	438%	9.20	24.85%	820%
1.24	2.17%	24%	2.28	8.60%	128%	3.32	12.75%	232%	4.36	15.86%	336%	5.40	18.37%	440%	9.40	25.12%	840%
1.26	2.34%	26%	2.30	8.68%	130%	3.34	12.82%	234%	4.38	15.92%	338%	5.42	18.41%	442%	9.60	25.38%	860%
1.28	2.50%	28%	2.32	8.78%	132%	3.36	12.88%	236%	4.40	15.97%	340%	5.44	18.46%	444%	9.80	25.64%	880%
1.30	2.66%	30%	2.34	8.87%	134%	3.38	12.95%	238%	4.42	16.02%	342%	5.46	18.50%	446%	10.00	25.89%	900%
1.32	2.82%	32%	2.36	8.97%	136%	3.40	13.02%	240%	4.44	16.07%	344%	5.48	18.54%	448%	10.20	26.14%	920%
1.34	2.97%	34%	2.38	9.06%	138%	3.42	13.08%	242%	4.46	16.13%	346%	5.50	18.59%	450%	10.40	26.39%	940%
1.36	3.12%	36%	2.40	9.15%	140%	3.44	13.15%	244%	4.48	16.18%	348%	5.52	18.63%	452%	10.60	26.63%	960%
1.38	3.27%	38%	2.42	9.24%	142%	3.46	13.22%	246%	4.50	16.23%	350%	5.54	18.67%	454%	10.80	26.87%	980%
1.40	3.42%	40%	2.44	9.33%	144%	3.48	13.28%	248%	4.52	16.28%	352%	5.56	18.72%	456%	11.00	27.10%	1000%
1.42	3.57%	42%	2.46	9.42%	146%	3.50	13.35%	250%	4.54	16.33%	354%	5.58	18.76%	458%	12.00	28.21%	1100%
1.44	3.71%	44%	2.48	9.51%	148%	3.52	13.41%	252%	4.56	16.38%	356%	5.60	18.80%	460%	13.00	29.24%	1200%
1.46	3.86%	46%	2.50	9.60%	150%	3.54	13.48%	254%	4.58	16.44%	358%	5.62	18.84%	462%	14.00	30.20%	1300%
1.48	4.00%	48%	2.52	9.68%	152%	3.56	13.54%	256%	4.60	16.49%	360%	5.64	18.89%	464%	15.00	31.10%	1400%
1.50	4.14%	50%	2.54	9.77%	154%	3.58	13.60%	258%	4.62	16.54%	362%	5.66	18.93%	466%	16.00	31.95%	1500%
1.52	4.28%	52%	2.56	9.86%	156%	3.60	13.67%	260%	4.64	16.59%	364%	5.68	19.97%	468%	17.00	32.75%	1600%
1.54	4.41%	54%	2.58	9.94%	158%	3.62	13.73%	262%	4.66	16.64%	366%	5.70	19.01%	470%	18.00	33.51%	1700%
1.56	4.55%	56%	2.60	10.03%	160%	3.64	13.79%	264%	4.68	16.69%	368%	5.72	19.05%	472%	19.00	34.24%	1800%
1.58	4.68%	58%	2.62	10.11%	162%	3.66	13.85%	266%	4.70	16.74%	370%	5.74	19.09%	474%	20.00	34.93%	1900%
1.60	4.81%	60%	2.64	10.19%	164%	3.68	13.92%	268%	4.72	16.79%	372%	5.76	19.14%	476%	21.00	35.59%	2000%
1.62	4.94%	62%	2.66	10.28%	166%	3.70	13.98%	270%	4.74	16.84%	374%	5.78	19.18%	478%	22.00	36.22%	2100%
1.64	5.07%	64%	2.68	10.36%	168%	3.72	14.04%	272%	4.76	16.89%	376%	5.80	19.22%	480%	23.00	36.83%	2200%
1.66	5.20%	66%	2.70	10.44%	170%	3.74	14.10%	274%	4.78	16.93%	378%	5.82	19.26%	482%	24.00	37.41%	2300%
1.68	5.32%	68%	2.72	10.52%	172%	3.76	14.16%	276%	4.80	16.98%	380%	5.84	19.30%	484%	25.00	37.97%	2400%
1.70	5.45%	70%	2.74	10.61%	174%	3.78	14.22%	278%	4.82	17.03%	382%	5.86	19.34%	486%	26.00	38.52%	2500%
1.72	5.57%	72%	2.76	10.69%	176%	3.80	14.28%	280%	4.84	17.08%	384%	5.88	19.38%	488%	27.00	39.04%	2600%
1.74	5.70%	74%	2.78	10.77%	178%	3.82	14.34%	282%	4.86	17.13%	386%	5.90	19.42%	490%	28.00	39.55%	2700%
1.76	5.82%	76%	2.80	10.84%	180%	3.84	14.40%	284%	4.88	17.18%	388%	5.92	19.46%	492%	29.00	40.04%	2800%
1.78	5.94%	78%	2.82	10.92%	182%	3.86	14.46%	286%	4.90	17.22%	390%	5.94	19.50%	494%	30.00	40.51%	2900%
1.80	6.05%	80%	2.84	11.00%	184%	3.88	14.52%	288%	4.92	17.27%	392%	5.96	19.54%	496%	31.00	40.97%	3000%
1.82	6.17%	82%	2.86	11.08%	186%	3.90	14.58%	290%	4.94	17.32%	394%	5.98	19.58%	498%	36.00	43.10%	3500%
1.84	6.29%	84%	2.88	11.16%	188%	3.92	14.64%	292%	4.96	17.37%	396%	6.00	19.62%	500%	41.00	44.97%	4000%
1.86	6.40%	86%	2.90	11.23%	190%	3.94	14.70%	294%	4.98	17.41%	398%	6.10	19.82%	510%	46.00	46.65%	4500%
1.88	6.52%	88%	2.92	11.31%	192%	3.96	14.75%	296%	5.00	17.46%	400%	6.20	20.02%	520%	51.00	48.17%	5000%
1.90	6.63%	90%	2.94	11.39%	194%	3.98	14.81%	298%	5.02	17.51%	402%	6.30	20.21%	530%	61.00	50.85%	6000%
1.92	6.74%	92%	2.96	11.46%	196%	4.00	14.87%	300%	5.04	17.56%	404%	6.40	20.40%	540%	71.00	53.15%	7000%
1.94	6.85%	94%	2.98	11.54%	198%	4.02	14.93%	302%	5.06	17.60%	406%	6.50	20.58%	550%	81.00	55.18%	8000%
															91.00	57.00%	9000%
															101.00	58.65%	10000%

INSTRUCTIONS FOR FINDING DGR

A. 10 year period: Divide "latest" members by "beginning". Locate the number closest to your answer in column L/B. Read both AAGR and DGR.

B. Other than 10 year period:

- Step 1: Locate AAGR using Table A
- Step 2: On Table B, in AAGR column locate AAGR from Table A
- Step 3: Read corresponding DGR

(see example on page 10)

Note: If exact AAGR number does not appear on Table B, by choosing the closest number you will still be within one percent (1%) of the exact DGR (up through DGR of 500%). However, if you want to calculate a more precise DGR, you can make the following calculation (interpolation).

Finding DGR to the nearest 1%

A. Up to 500% DGR, increments on Table B are every 2% DGR. The following example shows you how to obtain DGR to the nearest 1%.

Example (say your AAGR is 11.88%)

Step 1

From Table B:

	AAGR	DGR
A	11.83%	206%
B	11.87% *	207%
C	11.91%	208%

Step 2: 11.87% is nearest your AAGR of 11.88% for a DGR of 207%.

* Note: To find B, subtract A from C, divide answer by 2 and add this answer to A: $\frac{C-A}{2} + A = B$

B. Above 500%, DGR increments on Table B are 10% or more. A similar process can be used to determine a more precise DGR. You may need to repeat the above formula 2 or 3 times to narrow the answer down to the nearest 1%.

BIBLIOGRAPHY

Arn, Win, Ed. *The Pastor's Church Growth Handbook Volume II* (Pasadena: Institute for Church Growth, 1982).

Beals, Alan R. *Culture in Process*, 3rd edition (New York: Holt, Rinehart, and Winston, 1979).

Cameron, J. E. M., ed. *The Lausanne Legacy: Landmarks in Global Mission* (Peabody: Hendrickson Publishers Marketing LLC., 2016).

Conn, Harvey M. *Reaching the Unreached: The Old New Challenge* (Phillipsburg: Prebyterian and Reformed Publishing Company, 1984).

Conn, Harvey M. and Samuel F. Rowen. *Missions & Theological Education* (Farmington: Associates of Urbanus, 1984).

Dayton, Edward R. and Fraser, David A. *Planning Strategies for World Evangelization* (Grand Rapids: William B. Eerdmans Publishing Company, 1980).

Don M. McCurry, ed. *The Gospel and Islam: A 1978 Compendium* (Monrovia: Missions Advanced Research and Communications Center, 1979).

Douglas, J. D. Ed. 1990. *Proclaim Christ Until He Comes* (Minneapolis: Worldwide Publications).

Engel, James F. and Wilbert Norton. *What's Gone Wrong with the Harvest? A Communication Strategy for the Church and World Evangelism* (Grand Rapids: Zondervan, 1975).

Engel, James F. *How Can I Get Them to Listen? A Handbook of Communication Strategy and Research* (Grand Rapids: Zondervan Publishing House, 1977).

Gbade, Niyi, ed. *The Final Harvest Mobilizing Indigenous Missions: A Compendium of International Consultation on Missions, Nigeria 1985* (Challenge Press, 1988).

Glasser, Arthur F. et. al. *Crucial Dimensions in World Evangelism* (Pasadena: William Carey Library 1976).

Hesselgrave, David J. 1991. *Communicating Christ Cross-Culturally*, 2nd edition (Grand Rapids: Zondervan Publishing House, 1980).

———. *Planting Churches Cross-Culturally: A Guide for Foreign Missions* (Grand Rapids: Baker Book House, 1980).

Hesselgrave, David J. and Rommen, Edward. *Contextualization—Meanings, Methods, and Models* (Grand Rapids: Baker Book House, 1989).

Hodges, Melvin L. *The Indigenous Church* (Springfield: Gospel Publishing House, 1976).

Kraft, Charles H. *Communication Theory for Christian Witness* (Maryknoll: Orbis Books, 1991).

———. *Christianity with Power* (Ann Arbor: Servant Publications, 1989).

Kraft, Charles H. and Wisley, Tom N. *Readings in Dynamic Indigeneity* (Pasadena: William Carey Library, 1979).

Larson, Donald N. and Smalley, William A. *Becoming Bilingual a Guide to Language Learning* (New York: University Press of America, 1984).

Loewen, Jacob A. *Culture and Human Values: Christian Intervention in Anthropological Perspective* (Pasadena: William Carey Library, 1977).

Luzbetak, Louis J. *The Church and Cultures* (Pasadena: William Carey Library, 1977).

Mayer, Marvin K. *Christianity Confronts Culture a Strategy for Cross-Cultural Evangelism* (Grand Rapids: Zondervan Publishing House, 1974).

Mortenson, C. David. *Basic Readings in Communication Theory*, 2nd edition (New York: Harper and Row Publishers, 1979).

McGavran, Donald A. *Understanding Church Growth* (Grand Rapids: William B. Eerdmans Publishing Company, 1970).

———. *Effective Evangelism: A Theological Mandate* (Phillipsburg: Presbyterian and Reformed Publishing Company, 1988).
Miles, Delos. *Church Growth a Mighty River* (Nashville: Broadman Press, 1979).
Mortenson, C. David. *Basic Readings in Communication Theory* (New York: Harper & Row, 1979).
Nida, Eugene A. *Customs and Cultures—Anthropology for Christian Missions* (Pasadena: William Carey Library, 1979).
Read, William R. *New Patterns of Church Growth in Brazil* (Grand Rapids: William B. Eerdmans Publishing Company, 1968).
Richardson, Don. *Peace Child* (Glendale: Regal Books Division, G. L. Publications, 1974).
Roberts, W. Dayton. *Strachan of Costa Rica: Missionary Insights and Strategies* (Grand Rapids: William B. Eerdmans, 1971).
Schrek, Harley and David Barrett. *Unreached Peoples: Clarifying the Task* (Monrovia: MARC and Lausanne Committee on World Evangelism, 1987).
Stock, Frederick and Margaret. *People Movements in the Punjab* (South Pasadena: William Carey Library, 1975).
Stott, John and Robert T. Coote. *Gospel & Culture* (Pasadena: William Carey Library, 1979).
Sweazy, George E. *The Church as Evangelist* (San Francisco: Harper and Row Publishers, 1978).
Tey, David Hock. *Chinese Culture and the Bible* (Singapore: Here's Life Books, 1988).
Wagner, C. Peter. *Strategies for Church Growth* (Ventura: Regal Books, 1987).
———. *Your Spiritual Gifts Can Help Your Church Grow* (Ventura: Regal Books a Division of Gospel Light, 1994).
Whiteman, Darrell. *Melanesians and Missionaries* (Pasadena: William Carey Library, 1983).

Peoples Mission International

Evangelizing unreached peoples in partnership with Two-Thirds World Missions.

ABOUT THE AUTHOR

Dr. Larry Pate is a specialist in developing non-Western missionary activities. He has served as a missionary to Bangladesh, an international consultant, leadership trainer, and strategist serving missionary organizations from Latin America, Africa, and Asia who send workers cross-culturally. He has also served on the Missions Commission of the World Evangelical Fellowship. He published a newsletter in five languages called "Bridging Peoples" for the benefit of non-Western missionary leaders.

Dr. Pate is well-known outside the United States for his writings focusing on the needs of the non-Western missionary movement. His book, *From Every People*, documents the growth and development of the missionary movement emanating from the churches of the non-Western countries. According to Pate's global research, there are now more missionaries from non-Western countries than from Western countries. This demonstrates that Christianity has come full circle. Those countries traditionally thought to be receivers of missionaries currently are sending more cross-cultural missionaries than they are receiving.

Pate also wrote the best-selling missionary training textbook in Latin America, Missionologia, Nuestro Cometido Transcultural. The book has been instrumental in the growth of missionary-sending throughout Latin America and is published in Spanish and Portuguese. Pate consults and works with the leaders of non-Western missionary Sending Churches and agencies to assist them in training, planning, and implementing their missionary work.

Dr. Pate has worked in sixty-nine countries of the world, working with church, business, and political leaders to build strategies for innovation and dynamic spiritual growth. He has even written planning strategies for the heads of state in several countries. He states, "The gospel no longer masquerades as a white, Western imperialistic religion. It is increasingly spreading 'To Every People From Every People'. The church in the whole world must work together to finish the remaining task of carrying the gospel from every place and people where it lives to every place and people where it does not. PMI works to assist those missions from other parts of the world to multiply churches where they do not exist among people groups who will not hear unless that task is completed."

Larry Pate has earned BS, MA, MA, MBA, MDiv, and DMiss degrees from five universities and graduate schools, including Denver University and Fuller Theological Seminary. He has worked both in ministry and business in sixty-nine countries of the world. For twenty-six years, he has founded businesses in Africa and the USA, using all the proceeds to fund his ministry around the world. He has taught in several universities full- and part-time in a number of countries while focusing primarily on assisting in the development of cross-cultural ministry movements on six continents. He has authored two other books in English: From Every People, Missions Advanced Research center, a division of World Vision, Monrovia, California, USA; Starting New Churches, Global University, Springfield, Missouri, USA (published in seven languages). Dr. Pate has also served on the Missions Commission of the World Evangelical Fellowship. He resides in Arlington, Texas, and can be reached at www.peoplesmissioninternational.com.

CPSIA information can be obtained
at www.ICGtesting.com
Printed in the USA
LVHW112140080422
715402LV00007B/17

9 781638 149477